A Note From The Publisher

The Educational Book Division of Prentice-Hall, Inc. is committed to the publication of outstanding textbooks. One important measure of a book's excellence is how well it communicates with its readers. To assure a highly readable book, the content for this text was selected, organized, and written at a level appropriate for the intended audience. The Dale-Chall readability formula was used to control readability level. An inviting and meaningful design was created to enhance the book's visual appeal as well as to facilitate the reading process. The authors, editors, and designers are confident that the students for whom this book is intended will read it, comprehend it, and learn from it.

The following paragraphs describe additional features that should prove useful to both students and teachers. A page reference is given to provide an example of each feature.

- STUDY AIDS: Each chapter begins with a list of *objectives* constructed to guide a student's study of the chapter (page 14). *Important terms* are printed in boldface type and defined within the text (page 68). They are also listed at the end of each chapter for review purposes and defined in the glossary at the end of the book for general reference. *Charts, diagrams,* and *photographs* (most in full color) are used to illustrate important points throughout the text (pages 140, 166, and 343). A *summary* follows the text of each chapter (page 174). *Review* and *discussion questions* also appear at the end of each chapter to help students review and retain the material covered (page 144).

- APPLICATIONS: Two *Applications* appear within each chapter to help students build skills in various aspects of speech communication (page 151). End of chapter material includes two sets of *Activities,* one set for students to undertake outside of class and one set to be done in class (page 221). A practical, *"how-to" approach* throughout the text allows students to apply what they learn through their reading (page 136). This approach is highlighted by a *checklist* in each chapter for students to judge their own progress in developing particular skills (page 118).

- SPEECHES: Examples from actual *student and professional speeches* are used throughout to illustrate important points within the text (pages 234 and 235). An *appendix* contains the complete texts of speeches given by well-known people and student speakers (page 408).

- A FOCUS ON THE FUTURE: Each chapter features a *Communicator Close-up,* based on an interview with someone actually involved in a particular communication situation (page 270). Capsule descriptions of a variety of *careers* that depend greatly on speech-communication skills appear at the end of each chapter (page 101).

SPEECH

Exploring Communication

SPEECH
Exploring Communication

J. Regis O'Connor

Professor and Chairman of the Speech
and Theatre Department

Western Kentucky University

Bowling Green, Kentucky

Prentice-Hall, Inc., Englewood Cliffs, New Jersey

SPEECH: Exploring Communication

J. Regis O'Connor (Ph.D. Indiana University) is Chairman of the Speech and Theatre Department of Western Kentucky University. He has taught at both the high school and college levels and has been a supervisor of student teachers in speech, drama, and broadcasting. He is the author of numerous articles and publications and is a member of both the Speech Commmunication Association and the Southern Speech Communication Association. Dr. O'Connor is listed in *Who's Who in Education* and *Dictionary of International Biography*.

Special acknowledgment:

Jill K. Peterson, Assistant Professor of Theatre at the University of Portland, Portland, Oregon, for writing Chapter 15, Drama.

Supplementary material:

Teacher's Guide with Tests

Text and photo acknowledgments appear on page 431.

ISBN 0-13-827253-0

10 9 8 7 6 5 4

PRENTICE-HALL INTERNATIONAL INC., London
PRENTICE-HALL OF AUSTRALIA, PTY. LTD., Sydney
PRENTICE-HALL OF CANADA, LTD., Toronto
PRENTICE-HALL OF INDIA PRIVATE LTD., New Delhi
PRENTICE-HALL OF JAPAN, INC., Tokyo
PRENTICE-HALL OF SOUTHEAST ASIA PTE. LTD., Singapore
WHITEHALL BOOKS LIMITED, Wellington, New Zealand

Critic readers

Morgia Belcher
Franklin Pierce High School
Tacoma, Washington

Mary Anne Ellis
Chesapeake High School
Passadena, Maryland

Carol W. Foster
Jefferson County Schools
Lakewood, Colorado

Joseph P. Haley
Manchester High School West
Manchester, New Hampshire

Carol Haugeland
Arcadia High School
Phoenix, Arizona

Albert J. Higgins
Emporia High School
Emporia, Kansas

Frank Latimer, Jr.
Lufkin High School
Lufkin, Texas

Sister Maria Martin, IHM
Villa Maria Academy
Malvern, Pennsylvania

Robert K. Mott
Elgin High School
Elgin, Illinois

Phyllis C. Nardy
Lake Brantley High School
Altamonte Springs, Florida

Gregory Parker
Shawnee Mission Northwest High School
Shawnee Mission, Kansas

Charles Ringle
Wayne Valley High School
Wayne, New Jersey

Sally W. Smisson
Needham Broughton High School
Raleigh, North Carolina

Eloise W. Smith
John Adams High School
South Bend, Indiana

Jared R. Towler
Glastonbury High School
Glastonbury, Connecticut

Kathryn Wagers
Cupertino High School
Cupertino, California

Larry James Winn
Western Kentucky University
Bowling Green, Kentucky

Marc Zicari
R L Thomas High School
Webster, New York

CONTENTS

unit four   Debate and parliamentary procedure   274

Charts, Lists, and Diagrams

Checklists for

Communicator close-ups

To the student

This text has a single purpose—to help you develop the skills of effective communication. Unit One offers an introduction to the many speech situations you will explore during this course as well as a discussion of the physical processes involved in speech communication. In Unit One you will also learn ways to become a more effective listener. Unit Two will help you develop the skills needed for more effective one-to-one and group communication. Unit Three will prepare you for public speaking. Unit Four will help you meet the challenge of competitive speaking. It will also help you become familiar with the rules for conducting meetings. Unit Five presents an introduction to the performing arts. This final unit should help you increase your enjoyment of the performing arts and may lead you to take an active part in them as well.

Many aids and features have been included in this book to help you develop the skills involved in effective communication.

Objectives. At the beginning of each chapter you will find a list of objectives to guide you in your study.

Important terms. Within each chapter, you will find that each new vocabulary term is printed in boldface type and clearly defined. These new terms are also listed at the end of each chapter and included in the Glossary at the end of the book.

Illustrations. Charts, diagrams, and photographs are used throughout the book to help you grasp the most important points.

"How-to" approach. The practical "how-to" approach that is found in every chapter of the book will help you apply what you are learning as you read.

Checklists. Each chapter includes a list of important points that you can use to check your progress in developing new skills.

Applications. Each chapter also includes two special activities within the body of the chapter so that you can immediately apply the skills you are acquiring.

Communicator close-ups. Near the end of each chapter, you will find a short feature about a real person who uses, on a daily basis, the skills you are studying.

Chapter summaries. Each chapter ends with a concise summary, which you can use either for *previewing* what you will read or for *reviewing* what you have read.

End-of-chapter activities. End-of-chapter activities include *questions* for checking your understanding of the chapter and *activities* for applying what you have learned.

Careers. Following end-of-chapter activities there are brief descriptions of interesting careers requiring good communication skills.

Model speeches. Excerpts of speeches given by well-known people and by students are used throughout the book to illustrate important concepts. You will also find the complete texts of some of these speeches in the Appendix.

Glossary and Index. The Glossary and Index found at the end of the book will help you find specific information quickly.　J. Regis O'Connor

1

HOW COMMUNICATION AFFECTS YOUR LIFE

When you have completed this chapter you should be able to

Define the term *speech communication.*

Recognize the importance of speech communication in your own life.

List and give examples of the four different types of speech communication.

List four ways in which effective speech communication can be of use to you now and in the future.

Describe seven characteristics of an effective speech communicator.

Give at least two specific reasons why you think you will benefit from a course in speech.

The German author Thomas Mann once defined communication, or more specifically speech, as "civilization itself." Mann believed that "the word, even the most contradictory word, preserves contact—it is silence which isolates."

Imagine yourself in a world without communication. You would be able to see and smell and taste and feel. But you would not be able to get your ideas across to others. You would also be unable to take in ideas that other people wished to express to you. In a very real sense, you would be isolated in a silence even more profound than that felt by a person who was deaf or mute.

Communication is a complex process, but one that is full of rewards. This chapter will begin with a few basic definitions and then move quickly to explore the rewards—the ways in which you can improve your own speech communication.

What is communication?

Communication is the process of sending and receiving messages to achieve understanding. You have undoubtedly heard the expression "Say what you mean and mean what you say." Saying what you mean is precisely what communication is all about. Anytime you speak a sentence, make a gesture, or merely grunt, you are "saying" you have some idea in your mind that you wish to transfer to another person.

How do people communicate?

Human beings use various means of communication. You can show that you agree with someone just by nodding your head. You can walk in such a way as to indicate something about your personality or the

What kind of feeling are these people expressing? The hand-over-heart salute to the flag is a gesture which communicates without a word being spoken.

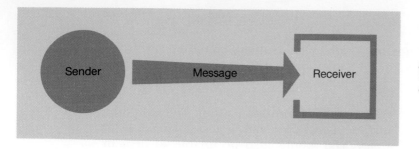

The communication process involves a sender transmitting a message to a receiver.

way you feel. You can also communicate something about yourself to almost everyone you meet by what you wear. These are all examples of **nonverbal** communication.

Human beings, however, communicate best through speaking and writing. These are **verbal** forms of communication. By using words to stand for, or to symbolize, the ideas they have in their minds, people can transfer the meaning of those ideas to other people. That is what communication between people is all about—getting the meaning of thoughts one person has in his or her mind into the mind of another as clearly and accurately as possible. When people do this by transmitting words with their voices, it is called **speech communication**.

How is speech communication used in everyday life?

You have probably heard and used the word communication many times, but have you ever thought about the many different ways people communicate through speech every day? Take time now to follow a typical high-school student through one day's activities.

6:45 a.m.   Awakes to a radio-alarm clock; listens to news, weather report, two commercials, and two musical recordings while getting ready for school.

7:15 a.m.   Eats breakfast; makes plans for baby-sitting that evening with younger sister while parents attend League of Women Voters' meeting to hear speeches by mayoral candidates.

7:30 a.m.   Leaves for school; meets new classmate on corner and describes school to him.

7:50 a.m.   Arrives at school; introduces friends to new classmate before directing him to his homeroom.

8:00 a.m.   School starts; listens to announcements over the public-address system; attends class where English teacher explains homonyms; watches a movie about the presidency of Theodore Roosevelt; takes a Spanish grammar test.

12:00 noon   Eats lunch in cafeteria with friends.

12:30 p.m.   Attends gym class and listens to instruction on the rules of volley ball; has conference with guidance counselor about next year's schedule; receives advice from art teacher on how to improve posters being made by class to advertise school play; conducts an experiment that demonstrates osmosis in science class.

3:00 p.m.   Attends school newspaper staff meeting to plan layout of next edition.

4:30 p.m.   Walks home with friend; stops to buy record heard on radio that morning.

5:30 p.m.   Arrives home; calls classmate to plan oral report on the causes of lead poisoning; calls family doctor to make appointment to interview her on number of cases of lead poisoning she has treated over the years.

6:00 p.m.   Walks dog, eats dinner, takes out trash.

7:30 p.m.   Listens to parents give instructions on when sister should be put to bed and where they can be reached in an emergency.

8:00 p.m.   Reads sister a story about astronauts before putting her to bed.

8:30 p.m.   Does homework.

9:30 p.m.   Watches television before getting ready for bed.

Communication played a large part in this student's day. Your life is also filled with communication situations. Actually, communication is so constant and widespread, you cannot escape its influence. Whenever you are awake and in the presence of others, you are communicating. Even though you may not be speaking to others, your appearance, eyes, and movements all represent communication. You even communicate when alone, through a kind of inward talking to yourself called **intra-personal communication**.

What types of speech communication are there?

The events in the life of the typical student given in the last section are all examples of **interpersonal communication.** Though many other forms of communication are possible, (talking to oneself, talking to an animal,

Casual conversation between friends is one of the most common types of one-to-one communication.

talking to a computer), this book is specifically about interpersonal communication—talk between two or more human beings. You will find many different types of interpersonal communication exist.

One-to-one communication

One-to-one communication involves talking with one other person. Included here are face-to-face conversations, telephone conversations, and interviews. Usually the sender and receiver switch roles often during one-to-one communication. The student whose day was described in the previous section was engaging in this type of communication when telling a new classmate about the school and when conferring with the guidance counselor. If you study the list of events, you will undoubtedly find many other examples of one-to-one communication in the student's day. Chapter 4 explores this very important type of communication in more detail.

Group discussion

Group discussion is a second type of interpersonal communication. It involves three or more people with a common purpose. The purpose may be to solve a common problem, to make a decision, or to answer a question that interests all the members of the group. Each member of a group generally has an opportunity to communicate.

Group communication includes such things as committee meetings, conferences, and workshops. Most group discussions take place in fairly small groups of less than fifteen members. The student you read about took part in a group discussion when plans were made for baby-sitting. A review of the student's day will uncover a number of other

Groups may join together to resolve problems, to make decisions, or to answer questions.

examples of group discussion. Group discussion is widely used because it offers one of the most effective ways of reaching decisions. Chapter 5 will explore this type of communication in depth. Later on Chapters 12 and 13 will discuss **debate** and **parliamentary procedure**.

Public communication

Public communication is a type of interpersonal communication in which one or more people communicate with an audience. A typical example of public communication is **public speaking**. For centuries public speakers have wielded powerful influence over society. Teachers, attorneys, preachers, politicians, and many others have used this form of interpersonal communication to reach large numbers of people through

Gesturing dramatically, a public speaker is holding the audience in rapt attention.

In the performance of a musical play, costumes and stage props are combined with the performers' movements and words to communicate a particular period of history to the audience.

the spoken word. Often those who have developed their skill at public speaking have found they have become better all-around communicators. Thus, this book devotes Chapters 6 through 11 to helping you acquire the ability to use this important form of public communication.

Two other forms of public communication are **oral interpretation of literature** and **drama**. Oral interpretation of literature is a performing art form in which literature is read aloud to an audience. Reading a story to a young child is perhaps the simplest example of oral interpretation of literature. Drama is a performing art that uses both language and action to present a picture of human life to an audience. The number of actors can vary from one to as many as the stage will hold. Chapters 14 and 15 will deal with these forms of public communication.

Mass communication

In **mass communication** one person or perhaps several senders communicate with a large number of listeners. Usually these listeners are not physically present when the sending takes place. Newspapers and magazines are examples of mass communication. Because this book deals with speech communication, however, the types discussed here will be those of radio and television rather than written communication. This kind of mass communication differs from the other types of communication in that the receiver can "turn off" the sender at will, usually by the simple flick of a switch. As you know, this is seldom

Inside a television studio, the camera is focused on participants in a morning talk show. Unseen and offstage, thousands of viewers may be listening to and watching the discussion on home television sets.

possible in face-to-face communication. Several examples of mass communication, such as television and radio, are found in the student's list of daily events given at the beginning of this chapter. Chapter 16 will consider radio and television in depth.

Application: Exploring your own use of speech communication

Write a list of all the communication situations in which you took part yesterday. Discuss your lists with your classmates. Try to find as many examples of different types of speech communication as possible.

What are the goals of speech communication?

You've undoubtedly heard the expression "So-and-so just speaks to hear himself talk." Though there may be some tendency for everyone to do this at times, people usually use speech as a tool to achieve very important goals. What are some of these goals?

You learn by communicating

One reason people use speech is to learn. Almost from the moment children learn to speak, they are asking questions. Teachers could not teach if they were not allowed to speak, and students could not learn if they were not allowed to listen and ask questions. If you give directions to someone about how to build a bookcase, that is teaching for you and learning for the other person. Both teaching and learning require speech-communication skills.

Decisions are made by communicating

Speech is important in helping people make decisions. Though many daily decisions may be labeled as "personal," arriving at a great number of them depends on speaking with others. You may make a "personal decision" to play basketball on the school team, but that decision might partly depend on a discussion with the coach. You may be trying to make up your own mind about whether to ask a certain person for a date, but you might first wish to get advice from a friend. Many of your daily decisions demand tact and skill as a speaker.

Group decisions make even greater demands on a person's ability to use speech communication. Representatives of labor and management are called upon to display their finest skills in speaking around a bargaining table. Members of juries must often use speech to convince one another of the guilt or innocence of the accused. If you are asked to plan a school talent show or to work on the yearbook staff, your speaking skills and those of the rest of your group may largely determine the success or failure of that talent show or yearbook.

Decisions in government also involve communication. A city council, like Congress, holds debates and committee meetings on issues. The President has discussions with Cabinet members and other advisors to decide what policies to adopt. Officials of city, state, and national government make speeches to keep people informed. Citizens, informed about problems, then speak freely about them in order to affect the actions of their elected officials. The First Amendment of the Constitution of the United States guarantees such freedom of speech. With freedom, however, comes the responsibility to exercise it wisely. The freedom to say what you think does not give you the right to distort the truth or to harm others by your words. It does, however, give you the chance to try to persuade others to share your views and to reach the decisions you favor.

People find pleasure in communicating

Another important use of speech is for pleasure. Human beings enjoy good conversation and the company of others. Psychological studies have shown that people need to interact with others to remain healthy and happy. The wider your experiences are and the better your skill at relating them, the more enjoyable you can be as a conversationalist. Whether face-to-face or over the telephone, good conversation can be one of life's most enjoyable pastimes.

Graduation from school is not graduation from learning. It is just the beginning of a lifelong information-acquiring process—a process which depends heavily on an ability to communicate with others.

Your future depends on communicating

Speech communication skills are vital to your future. Learning is likely to continue throughout your life. Though you may not "learn something new every day," you probably will average that much during your lifetime. In learning, both in and out of school, communication is the key tool. You are bound to spend a major portion of your adult working life communicating with others. You may not become involved in all forms of speech communication, but you will certainly be engaged in some of them. How well you succeed in communicating may have a great deal to do with how happy and successful you are in your future career.

Accurate directions, instructions, and information must often be communicated through the spoken word. Directions explaining how to perform a task or instructions about new methods and equipment require the giving and receiving of correct information by word of mouth.

In some jobs, speech communication is required to convince others. Sales people must be persuasive in promoting their product or service. Managers must be capable of verbally motivating their workers. Elected officials must constantly convince the people they represent that they are adequately doing their job.

Studies conducted by the Menninger Clinic discovered that seventy percent of the workers who lose their jobs do so because they fail to communicate clearly, not because they do not have the technical knowledge to perform their work. In another study over a thousand people were asked to evaluate the importance of training in speech communication for themselves. Included in the group were accountants, homemakers, unskilled laborers, sales clerks, and professional people. Seventy-five percent of the group responded that skill in speaking was important or essential to their work. Ninety percent of the executives interviewed said speech training was particulary important to them. Business and industry are realizing more every day the importance of having employees who are skilled communicators. Most professional people such as attorneys, clergy, doctors, and teachers must use speech extensively in their work. Unless you, too, develop skill in speaking, your success in life may be severely limited.

In each chapter of this book you will find a Communicator Close-up. Each was prepared by interviewing a person involved in some type of communication. Notice, as you read them, the great number of careers that are connected by the common tool of speech communication. At the end of each chapter you will find a Careers section. There, some of the other possibilities for jobs using speech communication are described.

Application: Discussing speech goals

Discuss the goals of speech communication with your classmates. Which of the goals mentioned do you consider most important? Which least important? Can you think of other goals that could be accomplished through the spoken word which have not been mentioned?

What makes an effective speech communicator?

Throughout history the people who have had the greatest impact on other people's lives have been those skilled in speaking. In the United States, Thomas Jefferson, Abraham Lincoln, Susan B. Anthony, Franklin D. Roosevelt, Martin Luther King, Jr., and Margaret Mead were all effective communicators, able to speak with power and persuasiveness. As you have read, developing skill in speech communication is also important in your own life. What are the skills that make someone an effective communicator?

FIRST, effective speech communicators must be sincere. That is, they must themselves believe in what they say. Other people must believe they mean what they say in order for communication to be successful in the long run.

SECOND, effective speech communicators must speak knowledgeably. Whether talking in a small group meeting, giving a public speech to a large crowd, or in one-to-one conversation, speakers should know enough about the subject to make it worthwhile for people to listen. At times this requires much research and preparation on a speaker's part. At other times, little advance preparation is needed. In any case, to be an effective speaker you must be able to speak with confidence and knowledge about your subject.

THIRD, effective speech communicators must be well organized. Some speakers are like the man who jumped on a horse and rode off first in one direction then in another. The rider wound up going nowhere and it definitely confused the horse! A clear message begins with a definite purpose and proceeds in a single direction to the end.

FOURTH, effective speech communicators must know how and when to listen. At least half of the oral communication process consists of listening. Occasionally you may talk to yourself, but most often you expect someone to be listening when you speak. Effective communicators know they may learn more during their listening time than when they are speaking. Good listening is often neglected, but a good speaker will remember this important "flip side" of the speaking process.

FIFTH, effective speech communicators must use language carefully. A speaker's choice of words can make the difference in whether or not the message is received and understood as the speaker intends it to be. Learning to choose the best words to suit a particular audience and occasion is one of the most difficult tasks for a speaker. It is also what separates great speakers from the rest.

SIXTH, effective speech communicators must make good use of nonverbal communication. Speakers "say" a great deal with the tone of their voice, their body movements, and their eyes. Even clothes and grooming communicate to others. Good communicators are aware of what they are communicating nonverbally as well as verbally.

SEVENTH, effective speech communicators will generally be able to reach certain goals. When an effective speaker presents information

People in many different jobs need to be effective speech communicators. Anthropologist Margaret Mead's ability to communicate the excitement and importance of her research to others is what brought her public recognition. A pilot, explaining how an airplane flies to young children, chooses words his listeners will be able to understand so later they can talk about the airplane themselves.

about a topic, the receivers will almost always know more about the topic after listening than they did before. If a skilled speaker tries to convince an audience to accept his or her solution to a problem, the listeners will generally be partially or fully convinced. The goal will not always be reached immediately. A salesperson attempting to sell a stereo may make an effective sales presentation, but the customer may wish to compare prices for the same model in other stores before making the purchase. Most of the time, however, an effective speech communicator will be able to achieve the desired response regularly.

In each chapter you will find a checklist highlighting some important points for improving your speech communication. The first one is general in nature, dealing with the basic characteristics of effective speech. Those in later chapters will deal with particular aspects of speech communication.

 Checklist for effective speakers

1. Am I sincere in whatever I say?

2. Am I well prepared to speak about whatever topics I have chosen?

3. Am I well organized?

4. Am I a good listener as well as a good speaker?

5. Am I careful in my choice of words?

6. Am I aware of what I am "saying" nonverbally?

7. Am I generally able to get the results I wish from my listeners?

Why study speech communication?

The value of good speech communication is clear. It can help you learn, make decisions, enjoy yourself, and succeed in your chosen career. The basic skills needed to become an effective speaker are also clear. They are listed in the checklist above. With these factors in mind, you may ask why take a course to practice something you have been doing every day for years? Why not just continue speaking, keeping these seven factors in mind? The answer is that speech communication is not that simple. Many people have problems communicating with others in various situations.

- *Do you sometimes have trouble choosing the best words to express your ideas?*

- *Have you ever spoken without preparing your remarks carefully?*

- *Do you ever have difficulty paying attention when others speak?*

- *Do people ever ask you to repeat something because they could not hear or understand what you said the first time?*

- *Have you ever been asked to give a speech or be in a play and refused out of timidity?*

- *Have some of your in-class reports over the years fallen a bit flat because of the way you presented them?*

- *Do you sometimes feel that your friends do not listen to what you say?*

- *Can you argue effectively and logically with someone?*

- *Do you have difficulty remembering a speaker's main points several hours after hearing a speech?*

If you answered "Yes" to any of the questions listed, a speech course can help you. Perhaps you can think of other reasons for studying speech communication, as well. Even if you are already an effective speaker, improvement is always possible.

This course will provide you with opportunities to practice oral communication in a variety of speaking situations. Some of them may be new to you. Interviewing, group discussion, public speaking, debating, oral interpretation of literature, and drama are among the types of situations included.

As you progress through the course, you will learn to identify your assets and your liabilities as a speech communicator. Listen carefully to your teacher's and classmates' comments. Do not assume your ways of speaking are necessarily the only ways or the best ways. Some of your methods may prove to be best. It will be reassuring to hear people say so. Other methods that you now use may not be best. This is where you

Jack Nelson speaks rapidly, firing off sentences with all the speed of an electric typewriter going full tilt. But his voice is softened by the lyrical phrasing of southern speech, evidence of a youth spent in Alabama. His is a pleasant voice to listen to. This is fortunate because Nelson spends a large amount of time talking to people, and, what is more, trying to persuade people to talk to him. He is a reporter, presently Bureau Chief for the *Los Angeles Times* in Washington, D.C. Speech communication is a major part of his business.

Nelson's job is to gather news, information about what is happening in Washington that *Times* readers on the West Coast will want to read about. His chief means for gathering news is the interview, since news is not so much a concrete occurrence (a flood or a Senate vote) as it is a reporting of what people have to say about different incidents. If, for instance, Nelson were to get word that a major hotel had burned down during the night, he would dispatch a photographer to the scene while he himself would pick up the telephone to make a series of calls. In interviews with the local fire chief, a firefighter who had fought the blaze, a spokesperson for the owner of the hotel, and perhaps a guest who was injured while escaping from the blaze, Nelson would get the information he needed to write the story.

Later, Nelson might leave his office to interview other people face to face. "If it's a story that involves some kind of wrong doing, I'd much prefer to look the person I'm interviewing in the eye," he says. "The reaction of the person you're talking to is important, and you can't always get the complete reaction if you can't see the person."

But interviewing is not the only form of speech communication Nelson uses in his job. At breakfast and lunch meetings, he picks up other bits of information, talking conversationally and asking questions as part of a group of journalists selected to discuss news events. At press conferences he listens while a spokesperson relays information about happenings inside institutions or large companies, or while a politician holds forth on a controversial issue. In casual conversations, a chance meeting in a restaurant or a hall, Nelson receives other news items, which may lead him to investigate still other news sources, until "the pieces of the story sort of fall together."

Meanwhile, Nelson talks constantly to other *Los Angeles Times* reporters, coordinating his news gathering efforts with theirs. During an important investigation, six to eight *Times* reporters may be assigned to cover different angles of the same story. This group will meet frequently to discuss and weave together the story's diverse strands, and to make plans for future newsgathering forays. In addition, Nelson is in contact with West Coast *Times* editors, who must be kept abreast of breaking stories, of why the news contained in the stories is important and worth printing.

Operating, as he does, a central switchboard for news in the nation's capital, Nelson has naturally become an authority on the news of the day. As a result, he is called upon frequently to speak about news happenings. He is also active as one of a pool of knowledgeable journalists on a weekly television show called "Washington Week in Review," which analyzes news events in Washington.

Without speech communication, reporters such as Jack Nelson would be hard put to gather and transmit our daily news. Then again, without speech communication there would be little news to gather.

can gain the most from a speech course. Make a determined effort to rid your speech of those habits that make you a less effective communicator. Being able to speak and being skilled at speaking are two very different things. This course can help you develop the skills you need to become a better speech communicator.

Summary

Without communication people would truly be isolated, unable to give and receive ideas. Civilization itself would be impossible.

WHAT IS COMMUNICATION? Communication is the process of sending and receiving messages to achieve understanding. When this process takes place orally, it is called speech communication. People may also communicate in writing and in nonverbal ways through gestures, movement, and dress. All aspects of your life are likely to involve communication of one form or another. Even "talking" silently to yourself is a form of communication, called intrapersonal communication.

WHAT TYPES OF SPEECH COMMUNICATION ARE THERE? Interpersonal communication (communication involving more than one person) can be divided into four different categories. One-to-one communication involves give and take between two people. Group discussion involves three or more people, again with an exchange of ideas. Public communication takes place when one or more speakers address a larger audience. Mass communication calls for one or more speakers and a very large audience, usually at a distance from the speaker. Television and radio fall into this last category. Though you will not be continually involved in all of these forms of communication, you are certain to be involved in some of them every day.

WHAT ARE THE GOALS OF SPEECH COMMUNICATION? Communication is a very necessary part of learning and decision-making. It also adds enjoyment to people's lives and can play an important role in helping a person achieve success in almost any career.

WHAT MAKES AN EFFECTIVE SPEECH COMMUNICATOR? Effective speech communicators must have several important skills. They must be sincere and thoroughly knowledgeable about what they are saying. They must be well organized, know how and when to listen, and be able to use language effectively. In addition, they must also be able to make good use of nonverbal communication and achieve the desired results from their audience.

WHY STUDY SPEECH COMMUNICATION? A course in speech communication will give you a chance to practice the skills needed to become an effective speaker under the careful guidance of your teacher. A determined effort on your part will rid you of any poor speech habits you may have acquired and sharpen those positive ones you already possess.

Vocabulary

communication	debate
nonverbal	parliamentary procedure
verbal	public communication
speech communication	public speaking
intrapersonal communication	oral interpretation of literature
interpersonal communication	drama
one-to-one communication	mass communication
group discussion	

Review questions

1. What is communication?

2. What other forms of communication do people use besides speech communication?

3. What are four general kinds of interpersonal communication?

4. Describe two major differences between what was described as public communication and mass communication.

5. What are the four important goals that people can achieve through the use of speech communication?

6. How does speech communication relate to learning?

7. Give three reasons why speech communication is important in government and courts of law.

8. What are some ways in which people can use speech communication for pleasure?

9. Name six careers in which skill in speaking is an essential part of the profession.

10. List seven characteristics of an effective speech communicator.

Discussion questions

1. Give examples from your own life to show the truth of the statement "Whenever you are awake and in the presence of others, you are communicating."

2. Discuss ways in which you use the four general types of speech communication in your school life.

3. Explain how speech communication plays a vital role in the survival of a democratic society.

4. Compare the uses to which you can put skill in speaking while in school to the purposes for which you can use it after graduation. Which seem more significant, and why?

5. Show how taking a course in speech communication can help you now and in the future, even though you have been speaking for years and you may not plan a career involving public speaking.

At-home activities

1. Write a brief essay, describing how your life would be different if you were unable to communicate with anyone else. Come prepared to read your essay aloud in class or to turn it in.

2. List four forms of speech communication mentioned in the chapter. Then place an X beside the two you engage in the most. How do you suppose your use of these various forms of speech communication will change in the next ten years? Which will increase in usage? Which will decrease? Ask your teacher and parents how the usage of some forms of speech communication has changed in the last ten years.

3. List the seven characteristics of an effective speech communicator discussed in the chapter. Then name two current public figures whom you consider the best examples of effective speech communicators. Does each person fulfill all seven characteristics? Are there other characteristics they seem to share?

In-class activities

1. Take part in a class discussion of the importance of communication in daily life. Include examples of people who have become successful or well known, particularly due to their skill as speech communicators.

2. If you have attended a courtroom trial, a session of the U.S. Congress, a meeting of your state legislature, the U.N., or any similar bodies, report briefly to the class about your visit. What forms of speech communication were used? How effective did the various speakers appear?

3. There are a number of differences between conversation, group discussion, and basic public speaking, on the one hand, and oral interpretation and drama, on the other. What are some of these differences? Discuss in class.

4. Take part in a class discussion on the topic "How will this speech class be different from most of my other classes?" Give consideration to the role of your teacher as well as your own role in this class. Will each of you behave differently than in most other classes?

Careers

SURVEY WORKERS (INTERVIEWERS) interview people to gain information for statisticians and market analysts. No special educational requirements are needed, but survey workers should be outgoing and pleasant and must communicate clearly and graciously. Positions of this type are usually found in large urban areas where research agencies are located.

DIRECTORY-ASSISTANCE OPERATORS provide telephone information to callers by referring to a variety of directories arranged either alphabetically or geographically to answer questions.

High school courses should include English and speech. Directory-assistance operators should be courteous, have pleasant voices, good hearing, finger dexterity, and the ability to adjust to routine work.

SALES MANAGERS are in charge of selling goods and services. They supervise all sales activities and those engaged in them. Sales managers usually begin as sales representatives. High school courses in psychology, English, speech, and business are helpful. A college degree is necessary for advancement.

2

THE PROCESS OF COMMUNICATION

When you have completed this chapter you should be able to

Describe the functions of memory and thinking in the communication process.

Tell what factors may affect your decisions to communicate.

Describe symbols used in communication, and know the major differences in the operation of verbal and nonverbal symbols.

Define the various types of nonverbal communication.

Describe the process of vocalization, showing the functions of the various parts of the body involved.

List and describe the basic steps involved in the process of communication.

Think for a moment about a recent conversation you have had with someone. It may have been with a classmate, a friend, a teacher, or one of your parents. No matter who the other person was, or what the topic, both of you talked automatically. You concentrated on the meanings being exchanged and probably never gave a thought to the process you were using. However, if you had some way of recalling how you felt when you first learned to talk at about age two, you would be much more aware of how difficult and complex the communication process really is. In fact, it is so complex, it's amazing that humans communicate with one another at all.

As you read this chapter you will explore the process of communication. You might ask "Why should I analyze something I do so naturally? If I concentrate too hard on my speech, I might wind up not being able to speak at all!" There is not much danger of this happening, and a great deal can be gained from looking closely at the communication process. Even though you communicate naturally and automatically, examining each part of the process can help you see how your personal communication skills can be improved.

Getting ideas

Communication begins in a person's head. When you think of communication, you may first think of moving mouths, but that is only one step in the communication process. Before a person's mouth can move with meaning, the person's brain must have decided what ideas the mouth should express. You may have heard the expression "Be certain your brain is in gear before putting your mouth in motion." Actually humans *must* have their brains in gear before they can even begin to speak. Thus, the first step in communicating with another consists of having ideas in your head.

Storing information in your memory

Where do people get ideas? From infancy you begin collecting bits of information through your senses—sight, hearing, touch, smell, and taste. Human brains are like computers in many respects. As bits of information are received by the brain through the senses, they are put into the **memory,** which serves as the brain's storage bin, for later use in communicating.

But a person's memory differs from a computer's memory. For one thing, a computer can only store items in its memory that are intentionally put there. A human's memory will store items of information picked up both consciously and subconsciously. Have you ever done something or said something that later puzzled you? You could not figure out why or how you could have done or said that particular thing?

"And yet, all this is less complex than the brain of a chicken."

Undoubtedly, at that moment, information or experience from your past, which had been stored in your memory, influenced what you did or said.

A second major difference between computer and human memories is that a computer can recall any information entered into its memory, no matter how much material has been entered or how long ago. A human, on the other hand, can often experience what is called "loss of memory." Actually, what people experience is a loss of recall ability rather than a loss of memory. Have you ever *known* there was a joke you wanted to insert in a conversation but couldn't remember how it started or how the punch line went? That joke was stored in your memory, but you simply could not recall it at that moment. Later, when the pressure to recall the joke was gone, you probably remembered it with ease. Knowing that everyone experiences this difficulty at times can make you more tolerant of yourself and others who experience this problem during communication.

In addition to storing information and experiences, your brain also stores the words needed to express these ideas. Words are symbols that stand for ideas or experiences. Sometime during your early childhood, you adopted language as your primary means of thinking and communicating. Now, when you have an idea you wish to communicate, your brain scans its store of available words (your vocabulary) for the symbol that best identifies that idea. Although this process takes place in fractions of a second, it is quite complex. During this short period, you must decide on a word (a symbol) that best identifies your idea not only for yourself but for your receiver as well.

While these young people are talking, each must also think of new ideas to express and of the words that will best express them.

Reasoning

Your brain has another function besides storing ideas and the words that represent them in your memory. That function is **thinking,** or **reasoning.** Animals have memories, but humans have a highly developed ability to put two or more ideas together and produce a new idea. This ability to reason gives humans a tremendous advantage over other forms of life. Thus, you have two major advantages over other living beings. You can put ideas together by thinking, and you can label your ideas with words.

The process by which you obtain, store, reject, and combine ideas constitutes intrapersonal communication—a kind of subconscious talking you carry on continually within yourself. Having ideas is the beginning of interpersonal communication—communicating with others.

Deciding to communicate

Having ideas in your mind is the starting point for interpersonal communication. You usually make a specific decision to communicate with another, although such a decision takes place so rapidly and automatically that sometimes you are not aware you are making it.

The need to communicate

Reasons for deciding to communicate with another vary greatly. For many people the mere presence of others is often sufficient reason to begin a conversation. People are social creatures by nature and feel a need for a certain amount of communication. If you are the type who starts a conversation with a stranger in a dentist's office, you may have a strong need to interact with others. People who have an above-average urge to communicate will strike up more conversations with strangers than persons without such a strong need. Sometimes people who seem to lack such a need to communicate may, instead, have a fear of being rejected by others. People having this fear seldom start a conversation with a stranger unless some other stronger need drives them to do so.

Research has indicated that the angle at which chairs are arranged can help people overcome fear of rejection and begin communicating. Seats which face one another on a 45-degree angle encourage conversation more than side-by-side seats, facing the same direction. Having some unusual object in the room, such as an abstract art print, can also make conversation between two strangers more likely, even if both are highly sensitive to rejection. The object appears to serve as an ice breaker, providing an excuse to talk about something impersonal.

The importance of common interests

Having common interests is one of the most frequent reasons for deciding to communicate. Did you ever notice how quickly the time slips by when you are having a phone conversation with one of your friends? Or what brief phone conversations you usually have with someone who doesn't share any of your interests?

Sometimes your common interests with others can last a long time. Generally, family members and friends share common interests

The students here are more likely to converse with each other because their chairs face each other and a table makes a common ground between them.

during their entire lifetimes. Even after long separations they find it easy to communicate with each other on many subjects.

With other people, however, you may find common interests for only a short period of time. You find it easy to talk with a classmate about a school play in which you are both performing. But when the play is over, you may decide that you do not have any other common interests. Carrying on a conversation with a salesperson is interesting to you both only until your business is completed. Then you may never have an occasion to communicate with that person again. Whether short-lived or enduring, common interests are an important reason for deciding to communicate.

Application: Analyzing a decision to communicate

Analyze a recent occasion on which you began a conversation with another person. Try to recall the mental process you went through just prior to opening the conversation. Can you identify the point at which you decided to open the conversation? Describe your mental sequence to the class.

Choosing symbols

Once you have decided to communicate with someone, the next step is to use symbols to **encode** your ideas. It might be nice if there were some method of simply pouring the ideas from your head into someone else's, but there isn't. You must transfer ideas into a symbol system, or **code,** known to both you and your receiver, and then hope that the receiver will **decode** the symbols correctly. Of course, if the symbols are unknown to your receiver, you will fail to communicate. Imagine yourself conversing with someone who understands English but who knows nothing about roller coasters. If you suggest riding on a roller coaster, the person will have no idea what you are talking about.

A **symbol** can be a word, a gesture, eye contact, dress—anything that stands for an idea and is used to communicate. Since words are the symbols most often used, they will be explored in more detail first.

Language symbols

Words are language symbols. They are also called **verbal symbols.** In certain respects language is like money. Language is a medium of exchange for ideas as money is a medium of exchange for goods and services. Putting a price on a new car is a way of making money represent that type of car. You've heard people make remarks such as "Oh, yes, she just bought a $10,000 station wagon." In somewhat the same

The verbal symbol justice *may suggest different images to different people.*

way, language represents, or symbolizes, the ideas people have in their minds. Notice that the phrase *$10,000 station wagon* is not the same thing as the actual *station wagon*. It is merely one way of representing a type of automobile. Words are not the ideas they represent. They are only a way of symbolizing those ideas.

People often think that a word will represent the identical idea in a receiver's mind that it represents in their own. Unfortunately, this seldom is the case. Have you ever found yourself talking to a friend about a person named Tom, only to discover that your receiver had a different Tom in mind during the first few moments of the conversation? Or consider the different images evoked by a word like *justice*. One person may picture the traditional symbol of a blindfolded lady holding a scale. Another may see a courtroom scene. A third might envision a criminal in prison. Some of these impressions are positive, others negative. Some are practical, others theoretical. Some are general, others specific. It is important to remember that words are symbols that can evoke different meanings in different minds. This realization will prevent much miscommunication.

Actually most words do have a basic meaning. This meaning is known as a **denotation.** The denotative meaning of the word *home*, for example, is a place where a person or family lives. Differences in meaning represented by the same word are largely due to **connotation.** Connotation refers to meanings people attach to words that are beyond the dictionary meaning. They are meanings that come to different people because of their different past associations with an idea. For example, when someone uses the word *home* in front of an audience, each member of the audience may attach his or her own meaning to that idea. For someone who had a miserable home life while growing up, the connotation may be quite negative. For another, whose home provided comfort, warmth, and love, the impression may be much more agreeable. Someone who grew up in an orphanage may think of an institution when hearing the word *home*. Even though all the listeners share the same basic meaning, their strong associations with the word can often be more important than the basic meaning.

Thus, if you wish to communicate clearly, you must be careful in choosing the words to encode your ideas. You must remember that some of the people you speak to will not know the meaning of a word that comes to your mind. Even if they do know the meaning of the word, they may attach a different connotative meaning to it. In most cases, however, your meaning will be clear if you use simple words, and adjust your vocabulary for the listener or listeners you are addressing on each occasion.

Nonverbal symbols

Nonverbal symbols include all of the ways you encode your ideas without words. You may smile or nod to show you agree with someone. Tapping your foot may indicate that you are impatient. People who study nonverbal communication claim that well over half of the meaning exchanged in face-to-face communication comes from nonverbal symbols rather than from words.

Nonverbal symbols communicate a bit differently than verbal symbols. First, it is often more difficult to attach a definite meaning to a nonverbal symbol than to a word. Suppose you are talking with a friend, and your friend frowns at something you say. You will probably get a negative impression from the frown, but you may not be able to decide whether the frown means lack of understanding, disagreement, or something else. If your friend yawns while you are talking, it may mean boredom with what you are saying, or it may simply mean your friend is sleepy. Second, we receive feelings more than ideas from nonverbal symbols. If you ask someone for a date, and the person responds

Body motion is helping this student communicate.

with "I'd really like to go with you, but. . . ." while trying to avoid looking you straight in the eye, you will probably get the *feeling* that the person really doesn't want a date with you. The words say the idea "I'd really like to go with you" but the eyes express the feeling "I don't want to go with you."

KINESICS. What are some of the most common nonverbal symbols? One category is body motions. The study of the use of body motions to communicate is called **kinesics.** Rolling one's eyes, frowning, staring, laughing, gesturing, crossing one's legs, or any similar body movements fall into this category. Unless you stop and think about it, you may not realize how much people depend on body motion to help them communicate. People in business often hold initial job interviews over the phone, but they will seldom decide to hire a person until that person has been interviewed face-to-face. They want to see how a job candidate "moves" as well as hear the person speak before making a decision. People express a great deal with their movements. They can communicate nervousness or calmness, intensity or relaxation, even sincerity or hypocrisy. In some cultures parents can often tell if little children are lying simply by whether or not the children are willing to look them in the eye. In other cultures children indicate respect for their elders by deliberately not looking directly into their eyes.

PROXEMICS. A second category of nonverbal symbols involves the use of space to communicate. The study of spatial communication is called **proxemics.** People (usually without realizing it) arrange the distance between themselves and those with whom they are talking in such a way that the degree of closeness communicates in itself. When people are good friends, they usually express this by standing or sitting closer to each other than they would with strangers or new acquaintances. Closeness can also be a signal that a person wants to discuss personal matters. Greater distances indicate that the discussion is to be on an

DISTANCE	TYPICAL SITUATION
Touching to 18 inches (0 to 46 cm)	Giving comfort or aid, whispering, conversing with close friends or family.
18 inches to 4 feet (46 to 120 cm)	Talking with friends or business associates, instructing in a sport.
4 feet to 12 feet (1.2 to 3.6 meters)	Discussing impersonal or business matters with someone in authority, taking part in a small group discussion.
12 feet to 25 feet or more (3.6 to 7.6 meters or more)	Public speaking, teaching a class, leading a pep rally.

The business executive in the top picture occupies an office by himself in which furniture has been arranged to give the impression of spaciousness. The size and elegance of the office tells visitors "This person is important." The desks in the communal office in the bottom picture are positioned close together, an indication that these office workers occupy jobs of less importance than the executive with an individual office.

impersonal level. The table on page 40 shows approximate distances most Americans use for typical communication situations.

The way in which space is arranged in homes, offices, schools, and at other public places can communicate certain ideas. The Gateway Arch on the riverfront in St. Louis, Missouri, symbolizes the gateway to the West. The Astrodome in Houston, Texas, indicates the existence of big-time sports. The size and shape of your school's classrooms tells you something about the present or past philosophy of education in your school system. The furnishings in your home give visitors an idea of your lifestyle.

Arrangements of furniture within a room or space allotments within a building also communicate. Have you noticed that top executives generally have larger and more splendid offices than other employees? This is arranged to say to a visitor or a client: "This person has high status in this company. This person is important." People in their homes try to arrange their furniture to create the most inviting atmosphere for conversation and relaxation. Notice how space is used constantly to communicate in many different ways.

PARALANGUAGE. A third category of symbols that many researchers include as part of nonverbal communication is called paralanguage.

Paralanguage consists of the ways in which you say words. It includes volume, pitch, speaking rate, and voice quality. **Volume** indicates how loudly or softly you are speaking. **Pitch** is how high or low the sounds of your voice are. **Speaking rate** is how fast or slowly you are speaking. **Voice quality** is what makes people able to recognize you by your voice alone. Volume, pitch, and speaking rate change according to the particular speaking situation. Your voice quality, however, usually remains the same whatever the situation.

Volume and pitch work together to create **stress**—the amount of emphasis you place on different words in a sentence. By changing the words that are stressed in a sentence, you can change the meaning of the sentence. Consider the different ideas expressed in the following statements:

"*I* like him very much."

"I like *him* very much."

"I like him *very* much."

Using the same words, but changing the patterns of volume and pitch can make the words carry three quite different meanings.

Changes in the speaking rate can also change the meaning of your message. If you wished to be assured that a friend felt certain about a matter, which speaking rate would give you more confidence?

"I feel sure about that."

"I . . . feel . . . sure about . . . that."

The first sentence, spoken more rapidly, would cause most listeners to have greater confidence in their friend's "sureness."

In addition, paralanguage includes a number of specific sounds people make (coughing, grunting, saying "uh" or "er") as well as the silent pauses between words or sounds. Yawning, sighing, hissing, or snoring are also forms of paralanguage.

Unintentional communication

Not all communication is intentional. At times you send a message (often through nonverbal means) that you do not mean to send, or that you are not even aware of sending. Edward T. Hall, a noted researcher in cross-cultural communication, tells the story of a United States diplomat in a foreign country who set up an appointment to meet with representatives of the local government. In the United States, the accepted method for keeping such an appointment is to arrive either slightly ahead of the stated time or no more than three or four minutes after it. Arriving any later than that demands an apology in our culture. The United States diplomat, however, was in a country where it was expected that a person might be as late as forty-five minutes without a word of apology or explanation. When the local residents arrived nearly an hour late and made no apology, the United States diplomat took it as an insult. But they had not intended to insult him or the United States and were probably not even aware that anything was wrong! This is an example of unintentional communication, using *time* as the channel of expression.

Similarly, mix-ups can occur if space, body movements, clothing, touching, eye contact, or language is used without full realization of the effect it may have on the receiver. In some parts of the world people stand very close and often touch one another when discussing business or other impersonal matters. Americans usually do not. They generally consider touching or standing too close violations of their space. Use the checklist below to see if you are unintentionally communicating unfavorable images or ideas about yourself.

 Checklist for good communication habits

1. Do I look into people's eyes often enough when listening to them converse? Do I sound genuinely enthusiastic, sympathetic, interested—in a manner appropriate to the situation?

2. Do I take pride in my appearance? Am I neat and clean or do I look like a sack of potatoes run over by a truck?

3. Do I communicate respect and interest for others by being on time for appointments?

4. Do I avoid standing too close and crowding others when conversing with them?

5. Do I sit alertly in my chair when participating in a class or meeting?

6. Do I give others a chance to speak when part of a group?

7. Do I speak up enough in a group so others are aware of my ideas?

Vocalizing

Once you have chosen the ideas you wish to communicate and the word symbols through which to express those ideas, it is time to set your vocal mechanism in action. Have you ever laid a wide blade of grass between your thumbs and blown against it to produce a shrill, vibrating sound? If you have, you know something about how speech sounds are made. Your lungs provide a flow of air as you exhale which can be forced through your vocal cords causing them to vibrate. This produces sound which in turn passes through your throat and past your tongue, lower jaw, and lips, where it is molded into vowel and consonant sounds to produce speech. Let's look at each part of the speech mechanism step by step.

Getting enough air

Your lungs are like an air compressor that is always running. At the base of your rib cage you have a thick muscle called the **diaphragm.** As you inhale, the diaphragm lowers creating a larger chest cavity and a partial vacuum. Air rushes in. When you exhale, the center of your diaphragm rises, making the diaphragm again dome shaped, and forcing air out the **trachea,** or windpipe. This happens naturally, and usually without your being aware of it, when you are breathing. To produce speech, however, you need an extra large supply of air, particularly when you speak to a large group. So you must concentrate more on your breathing process to "pump up the air pressure" in your lungs. Becoming aware of how quickly and completely the diaphragm can fill the lungs with air can aid you in producing a forceful voice at a moment's notice.

The larger the group you are addressing, the more conscious you need to be of your breathing. When giving a public speech to a large audience without a microphone, you should remember two things about breathing. First, you should inhale through your nose rather than through your mouth, using your diaphragm to fill your lungs with air. Second, as you speak, you should pace your exhalation so that you will have enough air to complete longer thoughts without having to steal a breath at awkward moments.

Application: Practicing breathing

To practice breathing for public speaking, stand up and place your hands at the base of your rib cage. Inhale deeply through your nose. You should feel your hands rise as you inhale, indicating that you are filling your lungs with air. Now say a loud, continuous "ooh" for as long as you can. Notice how your hands gradually sink in as you lose your supply of air. You may also be able to feel your diaphragm and rib muscles tightening near the end of your "ooh." For speaking you must be able to regulate the flow of outgoing air so as not to run out at an awkward moment.

Treating your vocal cords with care

Vocal cords vibrate to produce sound. As you begin to speak, these two folds of membrane located in your voice box, or **larynx,** tighten and move closer together, creating a narrow slit. When exhaled air is forced through this slit, the cords vibrate and produce sound, in much the same way that blowing air between your thumb and a blade of grass produces sound. Since women's vocal cords are usually a bit shorter

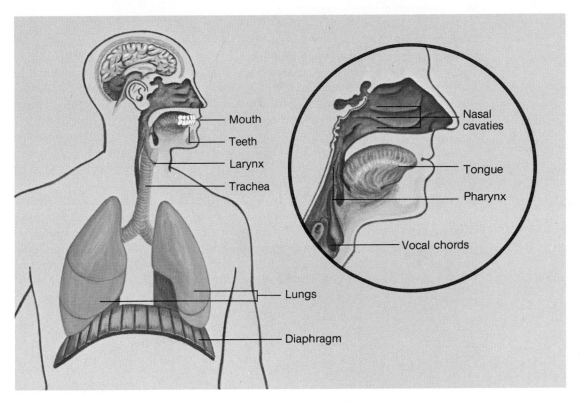

Mouth
Teeth
Larynx
Trachea
Lungs
Diaphragm

Nasal cavaties
Tongue
Pharynx
Vocal chords

Many parts of the body are involved in the process of vocalizing.

and thinner than men's, women's voices ordinarily produce a slightly higher pitched sound. It is important not to strain your vocal cords by prolonged yelling or by constantly trying to make yourself heard above loud noises.

Making use of resonators

The sound produced by your vocal cords is weak and thin. Before the sound waves leave your mouth, however, they pass through several resonating chambers. These **resonators** are your **pharynx** (the back part of the throat), your **nasal cavities,** and your mouth. Each acts much like a hollow chamber does to amplify or increase sound. If you have ever spoken inside a stairwell or tunnel, you know how much a chamber can increase the sound of your voice. Fortunately, your built-in resonating chambers are always handy to boost the level of your vocal sounds.

Articulating clearly

You are probably beginning to notice that the production of vocal sounds occurs in a kind of assembly-line fashion. The process begins with breath in the lungs and ends with the emergence of words from your mouth. The final step on this assembly line is the forming of sounds produced into recognizable symbols—words. This is the job of the articulators. The **articulators** are the tongue, teeth, lower jaw, and soft palate. By the movement of these organs into various positions, sound waves are molded into the vowels and consonants that form words. Sometimes speakers allow their **articulation** to become lazy. By not moving their articulators vigorously enough, they begin to produce "goin" for "going," "pacific" for "specific" and "wen" for "when." When they use their articulators correctly, however, speakers are able to produce clear, crisp sounds that are easily heard.

Once you begin to study it, you realize that the process of vocalizing—the producing of vocal sounds—is a very complicated one. Because it happens so rapidly in actual communication, you are rarely conscious of the individual steps. When you consider that vocalization is just one part of the total communication process, you realize how amazing human beings are. Look at the illustration on page 45 and notice how many different parts of the body are involved in vocalizing.

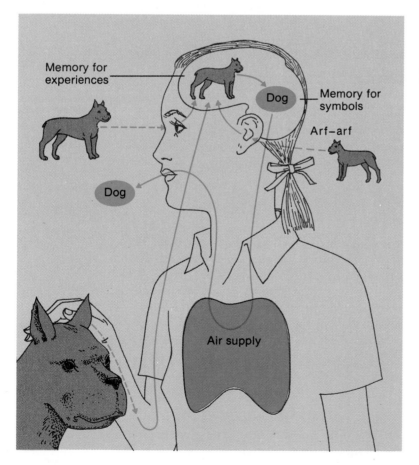

The communication process is extremely complicated.

Now that you have looked at each part of the sending side of the communication process, let's put it all together in the form of a model. The one shown on page 46 is simply a way of picturing what occurs when a person begins to communicate.

Reception

Perhaps when defining sound in your science class, your teacher asked you the question "If a tree falls in a remote forest and no person or animal is close enough to hear it, is there any sound?" The answer depends, of course, on how you define *sound*. But if you are talking about interpersonal communication and ask "If no one hears or sees a person sending symbols, is communication occurring?" the answer is "No!" Communication is a two-way process. When someone is sending, but no one is receiving, the only thing that is occurring is *sending*, not communication. Interpersonal communication is the process of using symbols to evoke a meaning in someone else's mind, similar to a meaning you have in your own.

So far this chapter has only dealt with the sending half of the communication process. **Reception** is a kind of mirror image of this first half. When senders select certain ideas from their memory bins and change them into sound or sights, the resulting messages go out across space to receivers' ears or eyes. The receivers then attempt to connect the symbols they receive with experiences in their own minds. This process is called decoding. To the extent that the senders and receivers have similar backgrounds and experiences, they will probably achieve shared meanings. If the receivers have no experience of something the senders are describing or are not familiar with the symbols the senders use, communication will fail. If someone speaks to you in a language you do not understand, communication is difficult, at times impossible. The problem, of course, is primarily that you and the sender do not share enough verbal symbols for things. If you were looking at pictures, you might both understand the same basic idea—that of someone serving food, for example. But while you would use the English language symbol *waiter* to represent this concept, a person from France would use the symbol *garçon* (pronounced *gar sown*). Unless you speak French, the word symbol used wouldn't mean anything to you.

Many people think that when communication fails it is always the fault of the sender. Actually, the receiver shares part of the responsibility for incomplete communication. Placing all the blame for poor communication on the sender is a bit like having a broken TV set and blaming your local channel because you can't see your favorite program. Besides an effective sender, communication involves a receiver who has sufficient knowledge, experience, and vocabulary to be able to tune in on different kinds of messages. It also involves good listening habits on the part of the receiver, a topic that will be considered in the next chapter.

When Vivian Belmont raises an eyebrow, paragraphs are spoken. Her yawn produces an essay on sleepiness. She can tell you where she's going and why by the way she walks—fast or slow, silly or sad—all without saying a single word.

Miss Belmont is a professional mime, a performer who speaks with her body rather than her voice. She can express ideas with a precision equal to the most carefully worded sentence. So skilled is she at body communication that she is able to create walls, chairs, or tables where there are none, dress herself in imaginary costumes, or carry on animated conversations between two or three people, all by herself.

Miss Belmont is an articulate woman who certainly has nothing against the spoken word. But she is fascinated by the vocabulary of movement. Movement can create whole worlds of sound and color, space and motion. The vocabulary is one many people are aware of only subconsciously. Part of the fun of seeing Miss Belmont perform is recognizing in her motions the movements which everyone makes daily. Watching her makes one realize that there is a lot of communication going on every day which is not necessarily through words.

Miss Belmont calls mime "a wonderful kind of theater." It is different from other body-movement arts, such as dance. "Dance is more for the beauty of the movement," she says. "Mime is much more for the sake of the idea. If dancers want to express the idea of talking on the telephone, they might each do three pirouettes and end with a beautiful arabesque. A mime takes the action as it appears in everyday life and stylizes it slightly. Mime is the art of essence, one movement for each thought."

When Miss Belmont, who has performed on stages throughout the country, teaches mime classes at The Hudson Street Studio in New York City near her home, she teaches the use of specific movement for specific kinds of communication. Just as children learn to speak by first learning individual words, so beginning mimes are taught the basic words of movement. "Before you can speak with your whole body you have to learn how to control the parts of your body individually," Miss Belmont said.

Her students experiment with the way one arm can show feelings of sadness or boredom, or the way a hand can show the flight of a bird. They learn to use and control rhythms of movement in the same way speakers learn to control rhythm in their voices. They learn to create the illusion of weight through body angles and to make space where there is none. They learn the art of looking as if they are walking somewhere when they are really moving in place.

The techniques of mime, used together, produce a body monologue which can tell a story, create a personality, or display subtle shades of emotion.

"Very often, as a mime, I want to express an idea which would probably be better expressed with words," Miss Belmont said. "And yet there are other ideas which are better expressed with mime." Emotions are an example, she said. "You might have to sit and listen to someone for half an hour to find out why they were sad. But you would know why I was sad after fifteen seconds by watching my movements."

Mime is a theatrical art, not a means of daily expression. Still, by separating body language from the spoken word, it shows how movement plays an important role in the way all people communicate.

Feedback

Feedback consists of ways the receivers react to messages they receive. It can consist of words, nonverbal symbols, or both. Feedback makes it possible for speakers to judge how well they are communicating. Whenever anyone sends a message to another person, some sort of feedback takes place. Sometimes it is easy for the speaker to detect: The listener has gone to sleep. The audience begins to walk out during a public speech. The interviewer leans forward and says "Good, tell me more!" At other times feedback is less obvious. TV news commentators, unable to see their listeners, must rely on mail or phone surveys to discover how the audience responds to their broadcasts. A person talking on the telephone must frequently rely on an occasional "uh-huh" to know the listener is still there. But no matter how difficult some feedback is to detect, it is always present whenever communication occurs. Short of leaving the presence of a sender, it is impossible for a receiver *not* to provide feedback. Even when a receiver sits perfectly still, says nothing, and keeps a deadpan expression on her or his face, the sender can read this as a lack of interest. The receiver has supplied feedback.

In face-to-face conversation, interviews, and small group discussion, a good balance of verbal and nonverbal feedback is possible. A good receiver will maintain a sufficient level of both forms of feedback to inform senders constantly about how effectively they are getting their ideas across.

When talking on the telephone, however, the sender cannot see the receiver, so the feedback is primarily verbal. The word *primarily* is necessary because nonverbal feedback, in the form of paralanguage, may be used at times as feedback over the phone. A change in the tone of voice or in the speaking rate, silence, and sounds that are not words are available to the listener as forms of feedback.

In public speaking, the usual form of feedback is nonverbal. This is because, if a large number of audience members began responding

Feedback always occurs during the communication process.

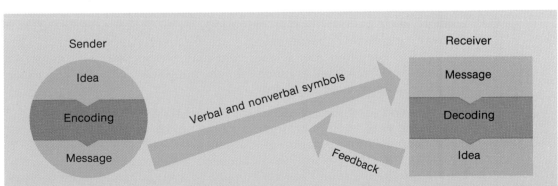

aloud, it would soon be impossible to hear the speaker. So most audiences confine their feedback to kinesic symbols—smiles, frowns, and nods of their heads. Some paralanguage, consisting of yawns, occasional boos or hisses, and clapping, may also be used as feedback.

Performers on radio or television sometimes receive feedback from a studio audience. Feedback from the audience at home will often be in the form of telephone calls or letters. This type of feedback usually reaches the sender after the performance. It cannot help the speaker adapt the message to the receivers during the performance.

Summary

People usually take the process of human communication for granted. It is actually so complex, however, that a close look at its various stages can show numerous reasons for frequent communication breakdowns. Studying communication in detail can also uncover opportunities for people to sharpen their communication skills.

GETTING IDEAS. Communication begins in your brain with a kind of talking to yourself called *intrapersonal communication*. This consists of acquiring, sorting, storing, and recalling information. Your brain also enables you to reason. Your memory stores words with which you can label ideas for use in *interpersonal communication*—talking with others.

DECIDING TO COMMUNICATE. People occasionally decide to communicate with others subconsciously, but generally a conscious decision is made to do so. Some people require a greater push than others to cause them to initiate communication. Sometimes a simple matter such as the arrangement of furniture can help start conversation. One of the best reasons to communicate is having common interests with another.

CHOOSING SYMBOLS. Once you have decided to communicate, you must encode your ideas in order to exchange them. Code systems consist of verbal and nonverbal symbols. In order for communication to succeed, the symbols you choose must evoke a meaning in your receiver's mind similar to the meaning these symbols have for you. Language is the symbol code used most frequently. However, nonverbal symbols, such as body motions (kinesics), use of space (proxemics), and the way of speaking (paralanguage) are frequently used together with language to communicate. Though you may pick up a great amount of meaning from nonverbal symbols, the meaning will not be as precise or specific as that evoked by words.

VOCALIZING. Since people most frequently use language as a symbol system, vocalizing is an important part of the communication process. It begins with the diaphragm forcing air through the trachea during exhalation. As this air is forced between your vocal cords, the cords vibrate, producing sound waves. The pharynx, mouth, and nasal cavities act as resonating chambers amplifying the sound. Finally, as the sound passes the lower palate, tongue, lower jaw, teeth, and lips it is formed into recognizable vowels and consonants which make up words. Vocalization is just one step in the complex process of communicating.

RECEPTION. Reception is the second half of the communication process. Once the message leaves the sender, it is picked up first by the receiver's ears or eyes (only occasionally by the nose or sense of touch). The message is decoded into ideas in the receiver's mind. Reception is clearest when the experiences and vocabulary of sender and receiver closely match. If there are great differences in the ideas or symbol systems, communication is difficult and sometimes impossible.

FEEDBACK. Communication is never complete without feedback. Feedback is the total of all types of receivers' reactions, the responses that allow senders to know how effectively they are "getting through." In some communication situations feedback is primarily verbal. At other times feedback may consist mainly of nonverbal reactions. Sometimes a balanced mixture of the two works best. In any case, feedback must always be present before communication is complete.

Vocabulary

memory	nonverbal symbols	trachea
thinking	kinesics	vocal cords
reasoning	proxemics	larynx
encode	paralanguage	resonators
code	volume	pharynx
decode	pitch	nasal cavities
symbol	speaking rate	articulators
verbal symbols	voice quality	articulation
denotation	stress	reception
connotation	diaphragm	feedback

Review questions

1. Where does communication originate?

2. Which functions of the brain are most important to communication?

3. What does "loss of memory" mean in everyday situations?

4. What three factors influence the decision to communicate?

5. What are considered the basic symbols of communication?

6. What is denotation?

7. What is connotation?

8. What are three kinds of nonverbal communication people use? Give several examples.

9. What parts of the body are involved in the vocalization process? What is the function of each one?

10. What is feedback?

Discussion questions

1. What is the earliest event you can remember in your life? Give all the specific details you can remember about that event. Discuss the event, details, and surrounding circumstances with your classmates to see if you can determine why you remember this event more clearly than others.

2. Discuss with your classmates the people with whom you find it easiest to communicate about personal feelings; about objective information. (Try to include some of your teachers, parents, friends, brothers and sisters, etc.) Are you equally comfortable communicating in both ways with the same people? Try to understand the reasons why you are or are not comfortable in each situation.

3. Develop a list of connotative terms for each of the following denotative terms. Discuss which one(s) have the strongest connotations. Which one(s) have positive connotations and which one(s) have negative? Do you and your classmates agree on the connotative meanings of the terms you listed?

    person
    government
    flower

4. Discuss the ways in which the following elements of nonverbal communication function among your classmates. What are acceptable and unacceptable standards for each? Are there different standards for different kinds of situations?

    dress
    posture
    promptness
    spatial relationship

5. Choose a popular song or a poem you like and work either alone or with a classmate to present its message in pantomime. After the performance discuss with your classmates the message they received and the one you intended. Are they the same or different? See if you can understand why you did or did not communicate clearly.

At-home activities

1. If you know a foreign language, speak a phrase or sentence to a friend who does not know that language. What causes your friend's puzzled looks? Is any form of communication occuring between you as you speak?

2. Analyze your own need to communicate with others. How can you make yourself less fearful of communicating with others? Make a written list, and try to put it into practice.

3. Turn the sound completely off on your home television set, so that you pick up only the picture. Watch for three minutes, seeing how much you can understand. Then turn the sound up and close your eyes so you only hear the words. Can you understand more of what is being communicated during this three-minute period? Report your impressions in class. Did the type of program make a difference in how much you understood each time? What types of verbal and nonverbal communication did you miss when you only watched the picture? What types of nonverbal communication did you miss when only listening to the sound?

4. An old saying claims that the best way to learn something is to teach it to others. After rereading the part of this chapter dealing with vocalization, explain in your own words to someone else how humans produce words. Keep at it until you are certain the person understands.

5. Attend a play or public speech. Position yourself so you can see and hear audience feedback easily. Write a brief report on the various forms of feedback you observed, and come prepared to read your report to the class.

6. Without saying what you will be observing, speak for one minute about any topic to a friend. Afterwards list all the types of feedback you noticed.

7. As a way of reviewing the major steps in the process of human communication, rearrange the steps in the following list into the order in which they occur. Write a definition in your own words for each term.

> vocalizing
> feedback
> getting ideas
> choosing symbols
> reception

In-class activities

1. Take part in the following nonverbal experiment. The class should be divided into four small groups. The teacher will have prepared four large squares of construction paper—one for each group. The squares should be cut into a number of shapes to form a simple jigsaw puzzle. All of the puzzles should be identical. Each player is given several pieces of his or her group's puzzle. See which group can put its puzzle together first, *using only nonverbal communication* (no words). What does this experiment tell you about the nature of nonverbal communication?

2. Enter a contest to determine which class member can sustain his or her breath best while speaking. Each member should stand in front of the class and read as much of a textbook selection as possible while using a single breath. Each speaker must speak loudly enough to be easily heard by your teacher in the back of the room.

3. Check your powers of articulation by saying any of the following sentences aloud three times in succession, rapidly. Let your classmates judge how well you succeed:

> My mother makes muddy mudpies maddeningly.
> The thickest thicket's sickening thistles thwarted Theobold.
> Buddy Badder badly battered Bobby's badger.
> Does Benny Denny pay a penny to Penny Denny?

Careers

AUCTIONEERS sell property or merchandise to the public by taking bids from interested buyers and accepting the highest offer. This position requires no specific educational background, but auctioneers must learn as much as possible about the type of property they will be selling. A thorough background in English, speech, and drama is the best preparation. Auctioneers are either self-employed or work for companies.

SPEECH PATHOLOGISTS specialize in the diagnosis and treatment of speech and language problems. They provide guidance to speech- and language-handicapped individuals. High school subjects such as biology, physics, English, math, speech, and psychology are helpful. Usually a master's degree is required. Speech pathologists work in schools, hospitals, and medical offices.

3

LISTENING

When you have completed this chapter you should be able to

Explain the difference between hearing and listening.

List four reasons for improving your listening skills.

List five barriers to effective listening and tell how you can overcome them.

Describe three major responsibilities of an active listener.

Recognize the central ideas in the messages you hear.

Recognize a number of different types of faulty reasoning.

Explain the importance of nonverbal communication in effective listening.

Explain how providing feedback can prevent the misinterpretation of a message.

If you are like most people, you probably think a good communicator is someone who can speak well. Speaking, however, is just part of the total process of communication. In order for speakers to get their messages across, someone must also be listening.

Listening is not an easy task. "Doesn't everyone know how to listen?" you might ask. The answer is "No." Effective listening involves more than just **hearing**, or the reception of sound. To be a good listener you must also understand and interpret sound in a meaningful way. Hearing and listening are often confused. People think that if they can hear automatically, they can listen automatically. But this is simply not true. A good deal of thinking must go on in effective listening.

When messages are misunderstood, it is easy to blame the speaker. The listener, however, must share the responsibility for effective communication. It takes a lot of concentration and effort to be a good listener. Statistics show, in fact, that most people are poor listeners. The average person misses about 75 percent of what he or she hears.

The encouraging fact is that no one has to remain a poor listener. Listening, like speaking, reading, or writing, is a skill that can be learned. Learning to listen does, however, take a lot of self-motivation and practice.

This chapter will give you some important reasons for learning to be a better listener, describe the most common barriers to good listening, and give you a few basic steps to follow in becoming a better or more active listener. You will also receive hints on how to remember what you hear, how to analyze the speaker's logic, and how to interpret nonverbal messages.

Reasons for learning to listen effectively

Why learn to listen? There are many good reasons. As you read through the ones discussed here, think carefully about how each applies to you. The more reasons you can find to improve your listening behavior, the easier it will be to learn and practice good listening skills.

To avoid misunderstandings

Has one of your teachers ever asked for a homework assignment that you didn't realize was due? Have you ever been introduced to someone and then a few minutes later called them by the wrong name? Misunderstandings such as these are easy to avoid when you become an active listener.

You will also be able to do things right the first time when you learn to listen effectively. If friends give you directions or tell you where and when to meet them, you won't have to ask for a recap or phone later with questions if you know how to listen well. You will be able, if

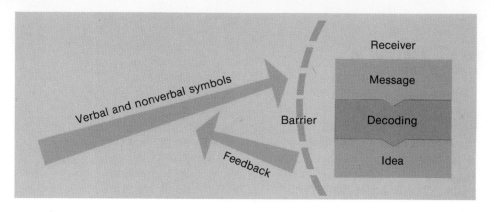

The receiver is as important to the communication process as the sender is.

you listen actively, to spend your energy on productive activities. You won't have to worry about how you are going to solve the problems created by poor listening.

In addition, practicing good listening skills may help you become more confident. You will know that you can understand and interpret correctly what other people say to you. People will learn to depend upon you.

To learn more about the world

You probably spend a lot more of your time speaking and listening than reading and writing. Therefore, most of what you know comes from what people tell you. Television and radio as well as conversations with friends, parents, and teachers, all contribute to your understanding of your immediate environment and the world in general. The more knowledge you gain, the more you will be able to enjoy and appreciate the things around you.

It is difficult to carry on a conversation with another person if your knowledge is limited. Active listening will help you acquire a storehouse of helpful and interesting information, and it will enable you to relate better to people with a variety of interests.

To get along better with others

No one likes to talk to someone who doesn't listen. Think about the people you know. Which of them do you enjoy talking to? You probably most enjoy talking to those who seem honestly interested in what you have to say.

Listening attentively to your friends shows that you sincerely care about them, too. It is a very high compliment when you listen to another person. Just by listening you can give a speaker a feeling of confidence and self worth.

To be more successful in school and on the job

Listening skills are very important in school. Grades and interest in school activities usually improve when students make an effort to develop their ability to listen.

Good listening skills can also favorably affect your future. Regardless of what your career plans are, you have a better chance of getting the job you want and being successful at it if you know how to listen. One salesperson analyzed a typical work day and discovered that one third of the salary received was for listening.

Think for a minute about all the jobs that require good listening skills. Telephone operators, nurses, auto mechanics, teachers, and lawyers must all be able to listen carefully in order to do a good job. What would happen if a telephone operator kept giving callers the wrong number, or if a nurse didn't follow a doctor's instructions and wrote down the wrong medication? Consider a lawyer or judge who didn't pay attention to most of what went on in the courtroom. It is difficult to think of any job where good listening would not be an asset.

Recognizing barriers to listening

At one time or another, you have probably had the nerve-wracking experience of trying to carry on a conversation with someone in a noisy room. The sounds of traffic, machinery, or even a dance band can produce such a racket that it is often impossible to hear what the other person is saying. Or perhaps you have tried to call someone long distance on the telephone and could hardly hear them over the static on the line. Noises such as these can cut off communication entirely.

This lawyer is giving advice to a client, but half the burden of the communication process must be borne by the client. While the lawyer talks, the client must listen effectively. Similarly, when the client speaks to explain a problem, the lawyer must listen carefully in order to understand what kind of advice is needed.

Noise, however, is only one possible barrier to communication. Anything that blocks or distorts the message that a speaker is trying to get across to a listener is a barrier to the communication process. Barriers can come from problems caused by the environment, the speaker, or the listener. Whatever the original source of the problem, a good listener should make every effort to overcome it.

Being able to recognize barriers is the first step toward overcoming them. In the next few pages, you will look at five different types of barriers as well as ideas for combating them.

Distractions

There are almost always **distractions** when people communicate. Some distractions are environmental. Perhaps there are people talking close by. A radio may be playing or a television may be on. Even the temperature of the room or the time of day may influence your ability to keep your mind on the speaker's message.

Another type of distraction can come from the speaker. Have you ever heard someone remark after listening to a public speech, "I'm not sure what was said, but the speaker spoke beautifully"? Actually, this is not a compliment. If the *way* the speaker delivered the message is all the receiver can remember, something is wrong.

Good listeners must learn to keep their minds on the basic message, not on the speaker's delivery. Whenever you find yourself concentrating on how relaxed a speaker looks, how smooth a speaker's gestures seem, or how pleasant someone's voice sounds, force your mind back to the content. Effective listening means concentrating on *what* the speaker says rather than on *how* it is said.

Whenever you feel yourself being distracted, whether it be by the conversations of other people, the temperature of the room, or the speaker, you should mentally remind yourself to listen. It helps if, as you enter the room for a meeting, speech, or play, you remind yourself that you aren't going to let anything distract your attention from the message you came to hear. Of course, this is easier to decide than to carry out. With real determination, however, you will gradually become better at overcoming distractions of all types.

Application: Listening for distractions in the classroom

As a class, sit quietly with your eyes closed and listen. Make a mental note of all the sounds you hear. After a few minutes compile a list on the board. Which sounds were most distracting? Does your classroom present a good environment for listening? Are there any ways you could improve it?

Daydreaming

Another very common barrier to listening is daydreaming. Daydreaming is really a form of internal distraction. Your mind wanders off and you miss much of what the speaker is saying. One of the reasons this happens is that people can think much more rapidly than they can speak.

The average public speaker articulates at the rate of about 150 words per minutes. Research has shown, however, that listeners can understand the message just as well when the rate is as fast as 380 words per minute—more than double that of normal speech! Just think, if your teachers could learn to speak at the rate of 380 words per minute, you could learn about as much as you do now and be out of school before noon each day! Unfortunately, speakers cannot articulate at such a high rate of speed.

This big difference between comprehension speed and speaking rate makes it easy for people to acquire bad listening habits. Since listeners can often complete a sentence mentally before a speaker can complete it verbally, they may get bored and begin to think about something else. Instead of daydreaming, however, good listeners learn to use this extra time to concentrate on what they are hearing. Rather than letting yourself daydream about tomorrow's football game or the history exam you have next period, use your bonus time to summarize to yourself the main points the speaker is making. Think about the topic being discussed and keep asking yourself questions that will keep your mind on the subject.

Close-mindedness

Try to recall some of the most recent arguments you have had. What were they about? Did you go into the discussions prepared to fight immediately to support your side, or did you really make an attempt to listen first to what the other person had to say? Were you prepared in any way to let the other person convince you that she or he was right?

When people disagree, they often become so involved with defending their own positions that they forget to listen to the facts that the other person presents. Responsible listeners, however, keep an open mind until they have heard all of the information. They listen to and weigh the merits of someone else's opinion, no matter how strong their own opinions may be.

People who refuse to expose themselves to ideas that are different from their own are basically **close-minded.** Such a person may not even be willing to attend a speech by a candidate from another political party or to read a newspaper article that supports a position with which they disagree.

An **open-minded** person, on the other hand, does more listening than speaking. An open-minded person has the attitude, "I hold a

The student in this picture is listening carefully with an open mind to what his friend is saying.

certain opinion which I believe is true, but I am willing to listen carefully to the ideas and opinions of others before I make my final decision."

As a good listener, you should try to be open-minded and suspend judgment until you have heard all of the facts. Carefully consider all the information that is presented. Seek out situations in which you will hear views that are different from your own so that you will have a chance to practice careful listening. Certainly, when you get an opportunity to speak you will want the same kind of consideration and genuine listening from those who do not agree with you.

Overemphasizing the source

If you heard a speech calling for more lenient treatment of juvenile offenders in our courts, would you be more convinced if it was presented by (1) a juvenile court judge, (2) a criminal, or (3) an ordinary citizen? When an experiment was conducted using this exact situation, the researchers found that those listeners who thought a judge was presenting the information were much more favorable in their attitude toward juvenile criminals than those who were told that the speech was being given by a criminal or an ordinary citizen. Those who thought the speaker was a criminal accepted the message least.

What does this experiment tell you about listening? For one thing, it tells you that people seem to accept a message more favorably from a person they respect than from a person whose reputation they question. However, it also points out the danger of paying too much attention to the source of a message and too little to the message itself.

Although you will naturally be influenced by your feelings about the speaker or your knowledge about the speaker's reputation, as a responsible listener you must be careful to evaluate what is being said apart from who is saying it. A message should not be judged entirely on the basis of how you feel about the speaker.

The next time you attend a public speaking event, you might take some time before the speech begins to analyze your feelings about the speaker as a message source. Do you like the speaker? Do you think the speaker is reliable? What do you know about the speaker's background? If the score is very low or high—if you have a most unfavorable or very high opinion of the speaker—you will know that you must be very careful in making judgments about what the speaker has to say.

Listening only to what is easy to understand

Another common barrier to good listening is listening only to what is easy to understand. If you become accustomed to "turning off" whenever you become confused, it won't be long before this behavior becomes a habit. If you avoid material that is difficult and only expose yourself to things that are already easy for you, you will never have the opportunity to improve your listening ability.

If you have studied a foreign language, you know that the first time you listen to someone speaking in that language it sounds very confusing. It is easy to become frustrated and give up because you get lost very quickly. As you practice and become more familiar with the foreign sounds, however, you soon begin to actually *enjoy* listening to someone speaking that language.

The more often you challenge yourself by listening to difficult material, the better you will become at following and understanding what you hear.

Becoming an active listener

To become a good listener you should be ready to do some hard work. Remember that as a listener you have certain responsibilities both to yourself and to the speaker. Not only must you avoid the barriers to listening that were just discussed, but you must also actively do your part to insure that you get the most out of each listening experience.

Prepare to listen

In order to hear and understand everything a speaker has to say, be ready to listen from the very beginning. This means arriving early enough to get a good seat at a play or getting to a meeting on time. If you go into a class after the teacher has already begun the day's work, you not only interrupt your classmates but you create a difficult situation for yourself. You have to then try to make sense out of what is being discussed without having heard the introductory remarks.

If you know that you will be doing a lot of listening, a good idea is to get sufficient rest beforehand. If you are tired, hungry, or upset, it is much harder to focus on the message than if you listen when you are alert and rested.

Finding out as much as you can beforehand about a speaker's topic, the plot of a play, or the agenda of a meeting are other ways you can prepare yourself to listen. If you have thought about some of the ideas you will be hearing in advance, you can better understand what the speaker is talking about. You become like a runner who has used warm-up exercises before jogging. The runner can perform better because he or she has made a smooth transition from a relaxed to an active state. Sometimes, of course, it is not possible to discover information about a topic ahead of time. But do not overlook opportunities to prepare yourself to listen more effectively.

Apply the message to yourself

As an active listener, you must also apply the speaker's message to yourself as you listen. Search your mind for circumstances under which you could use the information you are hearing. Find something in what is being said that arouses your interest.

When you have freely chosen to get involved in some listening situation, you should have no difficulty in applying the message to yourself. If you like surfing, you should find it easy to relate to a speech

The expressions on the faces of this audience tell you all you need to know about the effectiveness of the speaker. He is giving a good speech, one which may get better as he notices, and responds to, the excitement he has inspired.

on Big Sur. Many times, however, you will find yourself in a situation where the subject is not of great interest to you. Your tendency then, as an unwilling participant, may be to escape from listening.

Deciding not to listen in any situation is like betting the speaker will have nothing helpful to say to you. Either way you lose. Why spend your time and not get any personal benefits? Practice searching for ideas that can apply to you and your interests, regardless of the topic. You may be surprised at how many ways you will be able to relate what the speaker is saying to your own needs. Constantly ask yourself questions such as:

■ *Do I believe what this speaker is saying?*

■ *How can I put this information to use?*

■ *Do I feel differently about this subject than the speaker does?*

Provide feedback

Good listeners encourage the speaker by providing feedback—by actively responding to what they hear. Signs of attention and interest help a speaker present the message in the most effective way possible. Most public speakers, for instance, even prefer frowns and the shaking of heads to blank stares or drowsy eyelids. At least the frowns let a public speaker know the listeners are following what is being said. If the audience makes no response, speakers have no way of judging if they are speaking successfully.

It is just as important and much easier to give feedback when the communication situation is less formal. Feedback is extremely valuable in meetings, group discussions, or one-to-one conversations. Remember that when you ask a question, nod your head, or laugh, you are helping the speaker get the message across. Unless speakers know what your reaction is to their words, they cannot tell whether or not they are accomplishing their purposes.

Whenever you listen to any speaker, think about what types of feedback are appropriate. The following list suggests some of the more common ways in which listeners can let the speaker know that they are following the message.

Look the speaker directly in the eyes much of the time.

Nod your head slightly to indicate understanding or agreement.

Frown or shake your head to show lack of understanding or disagreement.

Smile or laugh at humorous remarks the speaker makes.

In informal communications, occasionally interject a word of encouragement such as "Yes," or "I see."

If seated, maintain an upright, alert posture. Don't slouch in your chair.

In informal communications, lean forward to show interest in what the speaker is saying.

It is also important that your feedback be clear enough so that the speaker can easily interpret it. In many instances, the feedback you provide as a listener will be nonverbal. Nonverbal signs are very easy to misread. Thus, you must take extra care to insure that you are sending the message you intend through your facial expression, body posture, and eye contact.

Understanding the message

One of the main reasons for learning to become a better listener is to acquire new information and ideas that you can use at a later time. Therefore, it becomes very important for you to understand and remember what you hear. If you begin to practice some of the following skills, you are likely to improve your comprehension and retention.

"Some sort of in-joke, I presume."

Pick out the central ideas

Many people, untrained in listening, become fascinated by stories, examples, and statistics and lose sight of the **central idea** a speaker is trying to communicate. Good listeners, on the other hand, who have learned to pick out the key ideas, have less difficulty in understanding what they hear because they know that they should not waste time trying to remember *all* the less important details.

Most well-organized public speeches contain very few main ideas, often no more than two or three. A play usually contains one main plot and perhaps a few subplots. The same is true of literary selections that are read aloud. Therefore, if you begin to look for these main ideas you will have a better understanding of the speaker's primary message. Other facts and details presented by the speaker, instead of confusing the issue, can be used to clarify these central points.

Learning to identify main ideas takes practice. A speaker often mentions main ideas near the beginning and end of her or his remarks. The rest of the speech may develop these central ideas by giving reasons for them. If you hear the same idea mentioned several times, you can be quite sure the speaker considers it an important point. Listen carefully for words and phrases such as "first," "second," "most important," "to summarize," and "remember." These verbal cues usually indicate an important point is coming next.

One good way to identify main ideas in formal speaking situations is to take notes in outline form. Most speakers organize their message in some way. If you make an effort, you are likely to become very good at recognizing different organizational styles and picking out main points. Outlining will also help you identify the relationships between ideas.

The organization of ideas in conversations tends to be somewhat less logical, mainly because ideas are generally not organized in advance. Locating the speaker's main ideas in informal communication situations is therefore more difficult. But this problem can be offset by the increased opportunity you have to give feedback to the speaker and to participate in the communication.

When you listen to another person in an informal setting such as a one-to-one conversation, a group discussion, or a meeting, practice restating in your mind what you feel were the main ideas expressed. Then ask the speaker if you are correct. This is particularly helpful when you are discussing a controversial topic with another person, since it is even more difficult to listen well to someone with whom you disagree. In one-to-one and small group situations it is important to use this opportunity to ask questions during the conversation to insure that you understand the main points being made.

Almost all speakers will appreciate a listener who focuses on the main message they are trying to present rather than on the small details used to illustrate their points. Learning to pick out a speaker's main ideas is one of the most useful listening skills you can acquire.

Application: Finding main ideas

Practice finding main ideas in a speech by having someone read the speech on page 410 aloud. As the speech is read, pick out the main ideas and outline the speech. Compare your outline with those of your classmates and discuss the different methods you used to locate the main ideas.

Expand your vocabulary

One aid which will help you to understand better and benefit more from what you hear is the development of a good vocabulary. Words are symbols that a speaker uses to convey ideas. In order for the ideas to reach their destination, however, the listener must also be familiar with the words the speaker has chosen. You can think of good listeners as being similar to good carpenters—the more tools they know how to use, the better the job they can do. The more words listeners have at their command, the more effective they can be. If your listening vocabulary is limited, so is your ability to learn new and useful things.

Can you define *epitome*? *regurgitate*? *calcify*? If you don't know the meaning of words such as these, you might consider spending some time each day expanding your vocabulary. Whenever you hear a word or phrase that is unfamiliar, find out its meaning right away. Then, search for opportunities to use the new word in your conversations during the next several days. Using the unfamiliar word yourself will implant it firmly in your memory so that its meaning will be easily recognized the next time you hear it used.

Remember what you hear

If one of the main reasons for learning to be a better listener is to acquire new information, it is important that you be able to remember what you hear.

You receive so many messages each day that you probably have a hard time sorting them out and deciding which ones should be remembered. Think for a moment about how many people spoke to you yesterday. Now, how many of their messages can you remember in detail? Unless you have an exceptional memory, probably not as many as you would like. It takes a conscious effort to remember what you hear, but it is worthwhile because that is the only way the information you receive will be useful to you.

One of the surest ways to remember something is to have a strong reason to remember it. Did you ever notice how attentive everyone in a class becomes when a teacher says, "This will be on the exam"? Of course it's easier to listen closely when you are strongly motivated. When the conversation is boring or the meeting is dull, a good listener must rise to the challenge. There are many occasions when you have to *find* good reasons to remember.

Another way to remember something is to connect new information you are hearing with something you already know. This is called the **process of association.** An example of this process of association would be if a speaker claims that a certain part of the ocean is 15,000 feet (4600 meters) deep. You want to remember that number. If you already know that Mt. Whitney is approximately 15,000 feet (4600 meters) in altitude, you can associate the ocean depth with the height of the mountain. Later, you will likely remember the ocean depth by recalling, "Oh yes, that was about the same as the height of Mt. Whitney."

Interpreting the message

Although picking out main ideas, knowing the definitions of the words being used, and making good use of your memory are important, there is a great deal more you must do to be an effective listener. A good listener must also be able to interpret the sender's message. This can be done by considering factors such as motives, reasoning, and nonverbal communication. The active listener must be a critical listener. **A critical listener** is one who analyzes and interprets messages carefully. Your ability to analyze and interpret a message correctly depends upon how carefully you listen for what is "behind" the speaker's words.

You might remember that in *Alice in Wonderland* "things weren't always what they seemed." The same is often true in real life. It is up to you as a good listener to consider all factors involved in a particular message so that you are in a position to decide on the value and meaning of what you hear.

Listen for faulty reasoning

Part of your responsibility as a listener is to analyze what you hear. Listeners who believe everything they are told can get into a lot of trouble. Be especially alert when listening to messages that are meant to persuade you. Be prepared to catch the speaker who has not constructed an argument using sound reasoning but depends, instead, on misleading you.

Thus, in order to make intelligent decisions about the information that comes to you, you need to analyze the speaker's methods. Clever speakers will often seem to be giving you the facts when really they are misleading you with deceptive reasoning. It is important to be alert for false methods of reasoning, which are called **logical fallacies.** Descriptions of a few of the most common fallacies follow.

Name calling is the term used for the faulty reasoning involved when a speaker gives a person or idea a bad label without providing any evidence to prove what is said. When you hear a speaker call someone a criminal, a cheater, or a liar, don't be misled. Make sure the speaker gives good reasons for using such labels.

Card stacking is a method whereby the speaker, instead of presenting all of the important evidence, tells the audience only those facts that support the point she or he is trying to make. The speaker leaves out the bad aspects of the idea and neglects to point out the benefits any alternatives may have.

The **bandwagon technique** gets its name from the fact that the speaker asks the listeners to "jump on the bandwagon," to become part of a supposedly overwhelming group in favor of some person, product, or idea. The speaker tries to convince you that because everyone else is doing something—using a certain shampoo or voting for a particular candidate, for example—you should do it too or you will regret being left out. Television commercials use this approach often. Watch for it!

A **glittering generality** is a word or phrase that is so vague that everyone can agree on its value but no one is really sure exactly what it means. Politicians may say they are in favor of "freedom of speech" or "equal rights." Later, however, you may discover that what they meant by these terms is different from your own interpretation of the words.

A **testimonial** is the opinion of some well-known person on a particular subject. However, the person, although famous, may not be an expert on that subject. Is a movie star really more knowledgeable about dish detergent than anyone else? Whenever you hear a testimonial, make sure that you ask yourself, "Is this person in a position to really know the facts?"

In the fallacy called **begging the question**, speakers never really prove the points they are trying to make. They take it for granted (and sometimes may want you to, also) that their ideas are true without providing proof. Suppose a speaker says, "Juana is the best president our student council ever had. We should reelect her." If no reasons are given for believing Juana to be the best council president ever, the speaker would be guilty of begging the question.

The term **non sequitur** is a Latin phrase meaning "It does not follow." A speaker guilty of a *non sequitur* may provide evidence to back up a statement, but if you examine the evidence you will find that it does not really prove the point. Suppose you were to campaign for class president by stating that you were the best candidate and then emphasizing how well you played tennis or how good you were at Chinese cooking; you would be guilty of this kind of faulty reasoning.

A **hasty generalization** occurs when the speaker does not really have enough evidence to support the broad conclusion drawn. Suppose during a recent visit to Denver, Colorado, friends of yours ate at three restaurants. When you ask them about the trip, they tell you Denver restaurants are terrible. Drawing the conclusion that all restaurants in

Denver are bad just because the three they ate in were unsatisfactory is not good reasoning. Hasty generalizations are a very common type of faulty reasoning.

The fallacies of begging the question, non sequitur, and hasty generalization often occur not because speakers are attempting to deceive their audiences but because they have not given enough thought to their arguments. Good listeners, though, will insist on sound reasoning in the messages they hear. It is up to you, as a listener, to detect these common faults.

Recognize nonverbal cues

In order to arrive at an accurate interpretation of a message, it is important to focus not only on a speaker's verbal message but also on the speaker's nonverbal communication. Analyzing nonverbal communication can give you important information about the speaker's attitude, emotional state, and motives. You will discover that the nonverbal portion of a message carries considerable impact in projecting the overall meaning.

A good speaker strives to use gestures, facial expressions, and a tone of voice that support and reinforce the verbal message. Sometimes, however, a speaker's verbal and nonverbal messages contradict. A good listener will recognize this and interpret the speaker's meaning by considering both the words and the nonverbal cues. Think for a moment of a parent scolding a small child. Along with a stern look and a serious voice, the child hears, "Johnny, we don't use crayons on the wall!" The

"I'm lost. Can you tell me how to get to . . . ?" Even if he doesn't know all the street names, the boy in this picture will get the girl where she's going with a few descriptive hand gestures.

Most Wednesday nights Bob Waltz works harder for an hour and a half just listening than he works all day at his job. Waltz is a Factory Planning Engineer at a telephone manufacturing plant located in Indianapolis, Indiana. On Wednesday evenings after work he drives over to the Pendleton Reformatory, located northeast of Indianapolis, for a special talk session with inmates.

Waltz is one of a number of PACE (Public Action in Correctional Effort) volunteers active throughout Indiana in correctional institutions. The idea behind the program is to give inmates a chance to communicate directly with people outside prison walls. The prisoners can talk about themselves and their problems—practical problems such as where to find a job after leaving prison or private problems such as how to handle an inmate's feeling of isolation.

"The point of the meetings is for us to be receptive listeners," Waltz said. "I try to let the inmate direct the conversation and not to force him in any direction. It's hard work. I've got to concentrate—to say to myself, 'I've got to listen.' For a while when I started

visiting the reformatory I wasn't listening well enough. Then one day I thought, Hey, I don't even know the inmates' names. You have to work with yourself to give them all your attention."

Learning to be a good listener has helped Waltz communicate more completely with the inmates. They open up to him, as to a friend, because he shows a real interest in their lives. When he does speak to offer advice or support, they feel he has understood what they were telling him.

"The English language is so difficult," Waltz said. "When you're getting to know somebody you often miss what they mean at first, and that happens everywhere, in play as in work." Words mean different things to different people. One person's joke may be taken as a serious statement by someone else.

Eye contact is important to Waltz. "If you are sincere—really listening—you've got to have eye contact. If it's not there, you're not communicating." He also has become adept at recognizing inmates' feelings by watching their body movements as they talk. Occasionally an inmate, not believing Waltz is sincere, tests him by telling exaggerated stories or showing false emotion. It doesn't work for long. Waltz, who has been visiting the reformatory for more than ten years, has learned to tell the difference between "a good line" and the truth.

The years of listening at the reformatory have helped Waltz relate better to people in other areas of his life too. When his 20-year-old son drops by to see him, the two share deeper insights than they did in the past. "He and I have a better understanding of each other now because I listen to him instead of just talking. Toward the end of a visit, he really opens up. Not because of anything I've said really, just because I've listened."

words are important, but Johnny may cry as much because of the vocal tones and facial expressions as because of what is said.

Every communication situation combines nonverbal elements with verbal. Even a telephone conversation incudes vocal tones, volume, speaking rate, pausing, laughing, and other forms of paralanguage. In Chapter 2 you learned that paralanguage is the *way* something is said rather than the words themselves. Thus it is considered a form of nonverbal communication. If you pay close attention while listening you will discover that the stress a person uses to say different words can make a big difference in the meaning you receive. Imagine having a telephone conversation with a classmate about your school's principal. Your friend makes the statement, "I think Mrs. Jones is a fair person." If you had received these words in written form, you would not know whether your friend means that, in her opinion, Mrs. Jones is only an "average" person, or whether she means Mrs. Jones treats everyone equally. However, your friend's vocal stress on *fair* makes the meaning immediately obvious. Tone of voice is also important. Through tone a speaker can indicate sarcasm, disgust, anger, or other feelings that cannot be conveyed through words alone.

While paying close attention to the speaker's words, the careful listener must also be alert to the importance of all forms of nonverbal communication. The following list includes some of the elements you should take into account:

movements
gestures
eye contact
paralanguage (stress, voice tone, speaking rate, pauses, etc.)
proxemics (how close the speaker is to the listener or listeners)
body posture

By keeping all the senses tuned in, an active listener will pick up much more than those listeners who attend only to the speaker's words.

Use feedback to check your interpretation

Have you ever had a good friend ask you "What's the matter?" even though you had not said anything was wrong? Paying attention to nonverbal cues, as you know, is essential in order to fully understand a communicator's message. It is, however, very easy to misinterpret nonverbal communication. In the preceding example, your somber expression and slow movements, which your friend interpreted as an indication that you were unhappy, may have simply been the result of not getting enough sleep. Your friend, expecting to see your usual smiling face and fast walk, may easily have misread the nonverbal signs you were sending.

Although verbal messages create less of a problem, they too can be misinterpreted. If your teacher says, "The exam will be coming up soon," you may not worry because you assume you have another weekend in which to study. When your teacher announces later that day that the exam will be tomorrow, you may be upset. Such problems in communication happen all the time.

In order to avoid these breakdowns in communication it is important to check your understanding and interpretation of the messages you receive. Ask the speaker questions. Restate what you think the speaker has said so that you know whether or not your interpretation is correct. If your sister says, "I'll be back in a little while," you might ask, "Do you expect to be back before noon?" to be sure you understand what she means.

Many problems and misunderstandings can be avoided if you remember your responsibility as an active listener and do not expect the speaker to do all of the work. Remember that listening is an active process and requires that you do your part to improve the communication process.

 Checklist for developing good listening skills

☐ 1. Do I try to adjust to distractions when I listen?

☐ 2. Do I avoid daydreaming and concentrate on the message instead?

☐ 3. Am I open-minded?

☐ 4. Am I judging what I hear on its own merits, rather than simply relying on my feelings toward the speaker?

☐ 5. Am I willing to listen carefully to material that seems difficult?

☐ 6. Am I prepared when I listen? Am I rested? Have I found out all I can about the speaker and the topic beforehand?

☐ 7. Do I apply the message to myself?

☐ 8. Do I encourage the speaker by providing feedback?

☐ 9. Do I listen for main ideas?

☐ 10. Do I make an effort to expand my listening vocabulary?

☐ 11. Do I try to remember what I hear?

☐ 12. Am I a critical listener?

☐ 13. Do I pay attention to nonverbal cues?

☐ 14. Do I use feedback to check my interpretation of what I hear?

Summary

Listening to speech involves much more than simply hearing. Listening is a learned process that requires a search for understanding and a careful interpretation of the speaker's words. People often fail to recognize the importance of listening, even though it is just as essential to communication as speaking.

REASONS FOR LEARNING TO LISTEN EFFECTIVELY. There are many important reasons why you should improve your listening skills. A good listener avoids misunderstandings and is therefore more dependable than someone who is constantly getting confused. A good listener also learns many interesting and useful things. Other people enjoy talking to someone who listens to what they have to say. People who have good listening skills are also more successful in their jobs because they can follow directions and relate easily to other people.

RECOGNIZING BARRIERS TO LISTENING. It is essential that you recognize and overcome a number of common barriers to listening. You can learn to overcome distractions and avoid the temptation to daydream by concentrating on the speaker's ideas. You will also find your listening improved if you practice suspending your judgments and keeping an open mind until you have heard all of the facts. Finally, you should avoid placing too much emphasis on the source of a message and listening only to what is easy to understand. All of these barriers can be overcome if you recognize that they exist and make an effort to combat them.

BECOMING AN ACTIVE LISTENER. An active listener does everything possible to assure that communication will be effective. Learning as much as possible about the subject beforehand and also arriving on time, well-rested, and ready to listen, the good listener is well prepared to carry out the important job of active listening. Listening becomes easier and more meaningful if the listener relates the speaker's subject to his or her own interests and needs. Finally, the active listener provides feedback in order to let the speaker know that the message is being received.

UNDERSTANDING THE MESSAGE. Unless you understand and remember what you hear, the information a speaker presents is of little value to you. Learning to pick out the speaker's main ideas and expanding your vocabulary are two good ways to improve your listening comprehension. In order to remember the message, you can think about how it applies to you and associate it with other ideas with which you are already familiar.

INTERPRETING THE MESSAGE. An active listener must also listen critically and analyze the speaker's verbal techniques and logic. Name calling, bandwagon technique, card stacking, and testimonials are just a few of the logical fallacies a clever speaker may use to try to convince you to believe a particular idea. A good listener also knows that the meaning of a message is conveyed by more than words alone. Attending to nonverbal communication is a very important part of the listening process. Likewise, the effective listener provides verbal and nonverbal feedback to the speaker in order to make sure that the message is being interpreted correctly.

Vocabulary

listening

hearing

distractions

close-minded

open-minded

central idea

process of association

critical listener

logical fallacies

name calling

card stacking

bandwagon technique

glittering generality

testimonial

begging the question

non sequitur

hasty generalization

Review questions

1. What is hearing?

2. What two elements must be added to hearing in order to achieve active listening?

3. What are four things you can accomplish through active listening?

4. What are five barriers that may interfere with effective listening?

5. What can you do to overcome each of the barriers you listed in Question 4?

6. What are three techniques you can use to become a better listener?

7. What are three skills you can use to understand a speaker's message more easily?

8. What four things must you consider in interpreting a speaker's message?

9. What are five common logical fallacies?

10. What nonverbal elements should you consider in interpreting a speaker's message?

Discussion questions

1. Discuss ways in which better listening in everyday situations would improve your overall communication with your family and with your classmates during after-school activities.

2. Talk about ways in which a speaker can set up barriers to an audience's ability to listen. Which are verbal and which nonverbal?

3. Discuss TV talk shows you have seen. How well did the host and the guests listen? Discuss signs that active listening was going on.

4. Discuss jobs in which listening is essential to performing the job well. Distinguish between jobs in which listening is central to day-to-day performance and those in which it is important only in a secondary way.

5. Advertising is often guilty of using the logical fallacies listed in this chapter. Discuss with your classmates which fallacies appear in advertisements. What were the copywriters trying to accomplish?

At-home activities

1. Practice using the following technique to remember the first names of the next five people to whom you are introduced: As you meet each one, concentrate on the person's name by repeating it to yourself immediately after hearing it. Several moments later and again at the end of your conversation intentionally use the name aloud in your conversation with the person.

2. The next time you plan to attend a speech, play, or oral reading, practice the following techniques for preparing to listen. Discover as much as you can about the speech topic, play, or piece of literature beforehand. Find out what you can about the speaker, actors, or readers. Arrive early and pick a good seat. Bring with you a strong determination not to be distracted.

3. The next time you have a discussion with one or both of your parents, try using a greater degree of positive feedback than you normally would while your mother or father is speaking. Look them in the eye frequently, maintain an alert posture, nod or shake your head at appropriate points, and show a genuine interest in what they are saying. Do you notice any change in their speaking as a result of your positive feedback? If so, what kind of change?

4. Like everyone else, you probably have a favorite kind of music. Chances are you can hum the tune or sing the lyrics of a favorite song because you have listened carefully to it a number of times. Now try this exercise to expand your listening powers: Get a recording of some instrumental music of a kind that is new to you—perhaps jazz or a classical symphony. Concentrate on listening to it carefully. How many replayings does it take before you can hum or whistle the melody? What factors aided or impeded your ability to memorize the music?

In-class activities

1. Check your ability to pick out the main ideas in a message by outlining one of the next in-class speeches. Write down the speaker's main ideas in outline form as you listen. After the speech, compare your listening outline with the speaker's outline. How well did you pick out the main ideas?

2. Pick one of your classes (other than your speech class) and concentrate on providing positive feedback to the teacher for a week. Look at the teacher consistently during this class, nod your head occasionally when you understand, frown slightly or raise your hand when you do not understand, sit upright in your seat, and be willing to answer the teacher's questions. At the end of the week, report on whether these forms of active listening improved your participation and understanding.

3. Following a classroom speech, make a list of every type of listening barrier you were conscious of during the speech. Include distractions caused by the environment or the speaker as well as internal distractions such as daydreaming. Discuss your list with other students and notice how frequently these barriers can interfere with clear listening.

Careers

AUDIOLOGISTS specialize in the evaluation of hearing, prevention and rehabilitative services for auditory problems, and research related to hearing disorders. High school subjects such as biology, physics, sociology, English, and speech should be helpful. A master's degree is required. Audiologists work in schools, clinics, speech and hearing centers, hospitals, government agencies, and in private industry.

SOCIAL WORKERS work closely with people to aid them in solving problems caused by poverty, broken homes, and physical, mental, and emotional handicaps. High school courses such as history, government, sociology, psychology, English, and speech are helpful. A master's degree is required for areas of specialization. Many social workers are employed by federal, state, county, and city agencies.

Interpersonal communication   unit two

4

ONE-TO-ONE COMMUNICATION

When you have completed this chapter you should be able to

List three common types of one-to-one communication.

Discuss different factors involved in becoming an effective conversationalist.

Discuss several of the nonverbal aspects of one-to-one communication.

Describe effective use of the telephone in social and business situations.

List a number of factors that must be considered when you are being interviewed for a job.

Prepare for, conduct, and follow up an interview seeking information.

In Chapter 1 you were asked to list all the various kinds of communication events in which you participated during a single day. Chances are good that your list was fairly lengthy and included many different kinds of communication situations. Which events from that list occupied most of your communication time? If you're like most people, the forms of one-to-one communication accounted for the majority of your time that day and most other days as well.

One-to-one communication plays a very important part in almost everyone's life. It occurs most often in face-to-face conversations, and frequently in telephone calls and interviews. Speaking with just one other person demands certain speech skills that differ from those needed for other types of communication. These special skills are the subject of this chapter.

The verbal aspects of conversation

Face-to-face conversation, as you have already discovered, is the most common form of one-to-one communication. **Conversation** consists of talk about various matters of common interest to both of the people involved. There is often no single goal or topic. Conversations, unlike many other types of communication, are usually not planned or rehearsed beforehand. But good conversation requires adherence to a few rules, which you should be aware of if you wish to be an interesting person to talk with.

Send and receive messages accurately

As in all types of communication, the most important aspect of conversation is accuracy—the accurate sending and receiving of messages. Careful thought in advance about what you will say and how you will say it is not possible with unplanned conversations. But, on the other hand, having only one receiver makes it possible for you to adapt your words and topics to that particular person as you speak.

Choose words you are sure your receiver will understand. Your choices should largely depend on who your listener is. Your listener's age and experience must be considered, as well as the particular communication situation. You would not use technical words in describing automobile engines to someone not familiar with them, for example. Rather, you would explain what you mean in simple words, adding definitions for any technical terms you found necessary to include.

Close attention to the feedback you receive can aid you in making sure the listener is understanding you. If your listener looks puzzled, unhappy, or displeased, perhaps you will need to clarify your meaning.

She understands, and shows it with a smile. Paying close attention to a listener's feedback will tell you when you can go on to make the next point, or when you should stop and rephrase an idea.

You can rephrase an idea in a different way if your listener doesn't seem to understand what you mean. Giving an example or story as an illustration of what you mean is another way to clarify your message. Merely repeating what you have already said seldom helps to make your meaning clear.

Sometimes a speaker presents ideas too rapidly for another person to follow. Don't assume that your listener will understand your reasoning. Present your ideas in a logical, step-by-step way so that the other person will see how you reached your conclusions.

Listen carefully during conversation. Listening helps assure your understanding of the speaker's ideas. Concentrate on the ideas you are hearing and learn as much as you can. Remember that listening makes up one half of the communication process.

Nothing is more difficult for a speaker during a two-person conversation than having to speak to someone who does not seem to be listening. Provide supportive feedback while listening. Look interested in what the other person is saying. Smile, frown, or nod at appropriate times. Ask questions to clarify points of which you are not sure. It is by your feedback that you show your interest and understanding.

Be courteous

Good conversation involves taking turns. Some of the most unsatisfactory conversations are those in which one party talks like a jackhammer and the other person simply sits there and takes a pounding. Of course, no one wants to have a conversation in which each person's speaking time is clocked with a stopwatch. But unless each speaker is willing to yield the floor regularly to the other, what starts out to be a conversation soon turns into a public speech with an audience of one.

Avoid interrupting to express an idea of your own while the other person is speaking. If what you have to say is valuable, it can wait until it is your turn to speak. Be careful, too, not to interrupt your listening to plan your next comment as long as the other person continues to speak. You may miss an important point he or she is making.

It is much easier for people to accept criticism about a situation than about themselves. When disagreeing with someone, avoid verbally attacking that person's character or motives. Unlike a letter that can be destroyed before it's mailed, words, once they have been spoken, cannot be unsaid. Try to explain how you feel about the issue calmly and logically without hurting the other person's feelings. Emotional outbursts of anger rarely lead to improved relationships between people.

Try to be open-minded. People often change their opinions after receiving new information. Even if you still disagree, after hearing different ideas, show respect for the other person's point of view. That person, in turn, will then be more likely to give your ideas a fair hearing since he or she has already been shown the same courtesy.

Be able to speak on a number of topics

Conversation deals with topics of interest to both people involved. In order to carry on stimulating conversations you should try to develop a variety of interests. More people will seek your company if you can converse on a wide range of topics intelligently. Sports, music, politics, current events, fashion, communication, hobbies, school, and energy conservation are all possibilities. If, on the other hand, you are viewed as "one-topic Tim" (all you ever talk about is your stamp collection), you will soon find yourself having fewer and fewer conversations.

When you change the subject during a conversation, use words or phrases to relate the new topic to the previous one. In this way your conversation will flow smoothly. Jumping from one unrelated topic to another without discussing any one of them thoroughly makes conversations less meaningful.

Of course, good conversation does not deal only with topics of interest to you. It deals with topics of interest to the other person as well. In conversations with friends, you should regularly attempt to bring up subjects you know the other person finds fascinating, even though these may not be your favorites. With new acquaintances, search for topics of common interest. When the other person brings up a subject that is new to you, listen carefully. Good conversation can be one of the most pleasant ways of learning about new ideas.

Learn to enjoy conversation

Good conversation is an art you can develop. During periods when you are the speaker, speak dynamically and enthusiastically. No one likes to listen to someone who converses in a flat, dull monotone with a deadpan face and no gestures of any kind. To develop the art of conversation, let your enthusiasm for your topic show in your voice and body movements.

Try to make the conversation interesting and pleasant for everyone involved. Avoid talking too much about yourself. Using pet phrases and exclamations too often also makes conversation less interesting. Choose good standard language forms that will make your message clear and lively. Illustrate your ideas with stories your listeners will find relevant and fascinating.

Finally, learn to enjoy face-to-face conversation. You will find that it can provide one of life's most pleasant means of both teaching and learning. In addition, friendships can be established and deepened through good conversation. For those who take the trouble to develop it as an art, it can provide an enjoyable form of recreation and relaxation.

 Checklist for effective conversations

☐ 1. Do I choose words my listener will understand?

☐ 2. Do I rephrase my ideas or give examples to clarify meaning when the listener indicates a lack of understanding?

☐ 3. Do I explain my ideas so that my reasoning is clear?

☐ 4. Do I listen carefully during one-to-one conversations?

☐ 5. Do I show interest and understanding by my feedback?

☐ 6. Do I take turns speaking and avoid interrupting?

☐ 7. Do I avoid personal attacks on people I disagree with?

☐ 8. Am I open-minded?

☐ 9. Can I converse intelligently on a variety of topics?

☐ 10. Are my conversations interesting and enjoyable to others?

The nonverbal aspects of conversation

Most forms of one-to-one communication rely heavily on the nonverbal means of communication. As you read in Chapter 2, researchers agree that in face-to-face communication over half of the meaning is carried by nonverbal signals. Even in telephone conversations, much of the message is transmitted through vocal tones, pauses, and sounds that are not words. Imagine how dull a face-to-face conversation with one of

The noise of the jet airplane is deafening. Words would never convey the message. At airports, ground crews rely on hand signals to direct aircraft to their proper positions.

your friends would be if your friend stood at attention while speaking, looked straight ahead, never moved a muscle, and spoke in the monotone voice of a robot. Nonverbal communication—body movement, timing, eye contact, and vocal variety—add feeling and life to the words in a message.

Although nonverbal forms of communication account for a large proportion of meaning, they cannot convey as specific a message as words do. If someone smiles at you, you are likely to react in a generally positive way, but you may not be certain whether the smile means friendliness, agreement, understanding, or respect.

While nonverbal communication is not as specific in meaning as verbal communication, it often makes a deeper and longer-lasting impression. Review in your mind the last five times you were introduced to new acquaintances. Your first impressions were probably based largely on such matters as the amount of enthusiasm shown, the facial expressions used, the ways in which the persons moved and gestured as they spoke, and the warmth of their smiles. If you are like most people, you have remembered those nonverbal signals better than what the people said.

Sometimes nonverbal communication acts as a substitute for language. This usually occurs in situations where words would be impractical or too time consuming. A jet pilot, for example, relies on the ground crew's hand signals to park a roaring plane.

More often, however, nonverbal communication occurs together with language as an aid to total communication. Nodding one's head while saying "Yes, I'll go with you" can strengthen that "Yes." The tone of your voice may deepen the impression that you're angry. Keeping these general principles about nonverbal communication in mind, look now at some specific types of nonverbal communication in one-to-one communication situations.

Using body motion

If you have ever seen a good pantomimist perform, you know how much can be communicated through body motion, or kinesics. Marcel Marceau or Red Skelton can create a mood or tell a story simply through body movement, gesture, and facial expression. Most people similarly pantomime a bit in their everyday conversation.

What kinds of kinesic communication do people regularly use? One of the most powerful tools of nonverbal communication is found in the eyes. Strong messages about your feelings and attitudes are conveyed by how you look at another when speaking, how frequently you look, and how long you gaze into another's eyes. In the American culture, such people as employers and parents seem to expect great amounts of eye contact from a listener. They appear to want the other person in face-to-face communication to look them in the eyes regularly. However, when speaking, the person in authority often does not provide steady or regular eye contact to the listener. There is one predictable moment, though, when both parties are likely to establish eye contact. This is when either is about to finish speaking and yield the floor to the other. Eye contact at this point appears to serve as the major signal that the person is about to finish speaking.

Words are unnecessary to express the feeling projected by Marcel Marceau. Something in his face says "I feel sad, and tired, and resigned to my fate."

What emotions do you think this student is expressing?

When conversing with another—even someone in authority—it is important to avoid the extremes of too much or too little eye contact. Not looking at the speaker frequently enough may be taken as a sign of lack of interest. Looking too much at the other party may distract the person. Research has shown that in two-person conversations, speakers gaze at their listeners an average of 38 to 41 percent of the total conversation time. Listeners look at speakers about 62 to 75 percent of the total time. An unwillingness to look an interviewer in the eyes, for example, will probably leave a very negative impression, even though the interviewee's answers may be excellent.

Your eyes may be a most effective means of body-motion communication, but they have their greatest impact when viewed as part of a larger tool of nonverbal expression—the face. Your facial muscles can be arranged in an almost infinite variety of postions to express a wide range of emotions. They can also show the degree of interest you have in a conversation, and even give certain information about your personality. Though your face is capable of displaying a blend of different

Safe! This arm-hand gesture is universally recognized. It signals an instant message to the baseball stadium crowd, a message they could not hear if the umpire simply yelled.

emotions, at any one time you are more likely to show single emotions such as anger, sadness, fear, surprise, happiness, or disgust with the greatest accuracy. It is important for you to be aware of your expressions and the messages they continually communicate to others.

Another widely used form of body-motion communication in two-person interaction consists of arm-hand movements. You can use your arms and hands to describe, locate, emphasize, and symbolize. Imagine how silly a traffic cop would appear trying to direct traffic in a straight-jacket. Or think about a baseball umpire relying only on vocal volume to signal "Safe." Of course, some people "talk" more with their hands and arms than others. You probably have seen any number of persons making arm-hand gestures when talking on the phone. Holding some people's arms would make it nearly impossible for them to speak.

As with any form of communication, however, extremes in using arm-hand movements should be avoided. The interviewee who sits perfectly still, hands in lap, and never moves a muscle during a half-hour interview is likely to be seen as lacking in dynamism and drive. On the other hand, the conversationalist whose arms are continually waving about with the velocity of a windmill may distract the listener's attention from the basic verbal message. Arm and hand movements should grow out of a natural urge to complete the total communication process. They should never be forced, but instead reflect the real communication goals of the person using them.

Using space

In Chapter 2 you read about how much closer two friends will sit when talking than two strangers will. This is just one way in which people use space to communicate nonverbally. The study of spatial communication, or proxemics, can tell you a great deal about a level of communication that is often carried on subconsciously in two-person communication. It seems that all people leave an invisible territory around them that they consider their own private domain. Whom you allow to invade your territory, how closely, and for how long, says much about your feelings and reactions towards others.

Family members or close friends generally allow close proximity when talking. Allowing another to sit close enough to touch you and being relaxed about it says to the other person "I like you, I trust you, I am willing to take you into my close confidence." On the other hand, sitting too close during a business interview or while talking with a new acquaintance may cause problems. Giving the other person too little breathing room may make that person feel uncomfortable. Americans like to reserve close distances for those they know well. Chapter 2 discussed basic distances, used in various communication situations.

You have probably met some people who regularly invade your space. A new acquaintance may stand so close while talking that your noses nearly touch. A student may take the seat right next to yours at the library study table when many other seats are available. These are usually unintentional instances of bothersome communication, but they can be annoying nevertheless. When such space invasion occurs, many people back away, turn their backs slightly to a seated invader, or lay their forearms on the table as a barrier to the intruder. Since moving in too closely often causes embarrassment, it usually hinders communication. Watch your use of space so you don't make others uncomfortable. If others invade your space, realize that it is probably unintentional.

Using time

Have you ever considered what an enormous impact time has on your life? You eat at certain times. You sleep for certain lengths of time. You often ask what time it is. You clock your life through birthdays and anniversaries. Time also has a great impact on communication.

Suppose one of your classmates says, "Did you hear? John just spent an hour and a half in the principal's office!" You know immediately John and the principal were not just chatting about the weather. The length of their conversation tells you their business must have been significant. Suppose one of your teachers announces "This test will only take five minutes." You can assume that the test you are about to take won't cover the entire book.

Executives frequently use time to tell visitors how highly they regard them and their visit. Those whose prestige is not great or whose business is not considered pressing may "cool their heels" in the outer office while the executive finishes up a few other matters. Allowing frequent interruptions such as telephone calls during a conversation may also make the other person feel less important.

People can communicate their attitudes and feelings towards others by their punctuality. You may make a special effort to be on time for a meeting with one of your teachers. You may not be as concerned about arriving exactly on time when meeting a friend. This difference communicates greater respect for the teacher and your perception of the teacher's higher status. Unfortunately, being late regularly for appointments with a friend also speaks clearly about the importance you attach to that friendship. Remember that the way you make use of time can sometimes say more than words.

Using appearance

Appearance also acts as a nonverbal form of communication in two-person communication. One of the chief reasons business people hold job interviews is their desire to see what kind of appearance a person makes before deciding to hire her or him. People are inclined to make snap judgements about others the first time they meet based largely on personal appearance. Hair style, clothing, height, weight, neatness—all communicate something about you, whether you like it or not. The visual image you present influences others' interpretation of your personality, your character, your intelligence, and your likeability. Sometimes these first impressions can be totally incorrect, but once made, they are very hard to erase.

You need not constantly go about looking as if you had just stepped out of a fashion magazine. Rather, the key ingredients for a favorable appearance are being neat and well-groomed. They are particularly essential for a good interview. If you are clean and carefully dressed, you will make a good first impression. At all times you will find these two things can have a marked influence on the opinions of others.

Using paralanguage

Paralanguage refers to forms of communication connected with vocal sounds. It concerns how words are produced vocally, but does not include the words themselves. Suppose, for example, you scream at someone with whom you are angry "I've told you not to do that!" Your voice volume, the high pitch (tone) of your voice, and your rapid rate of speaking are all part of your paralanguage. These vocal characteristics communicate anger more clearly than do the words themselves. On the other hand, suppose you calmly answer a simple question. Your vocal cues are quite different. You use a lower volume, a lower pitch, and a slower rate. Again your calm attitude is conveyed less by what you say than by how you say it.

A common problem for many people during one-to-one communication is the habit of frequently inserting vocalized pauses into their speech. A **vocalized pause** consists of filling the spaces between words with non-meaningful sounds, such as "uh," "er," "like," or "you know." A certain number of vocalized pauses are acceptable, since they occur naturally in nearly everyone's speech. If they occur regularly and frequently, however, they are likely to make a negative impression on the listener. They can lead the listener to perceive the speaker as insecure, unsure of the information, possibly deceitful, or even stupid. Vocalized pausing is usually just a bad habit. Once a speaker is aware of it, such pausing can be cured with patience and concentration.

As you can see, paralanguage can be very important in one-to-one communication. It enables a listener to reach conclusions such as "He's tired," or "She's angry," or "She's kidding." Paying close attention to the type of information paralanguage conveys can make the difference between successful or unsuccessful communication.

Application: Discussing aspects of conversation

Act out several face-to-face conversations in class. Before each demonstration you should decide on the setting in which the conversation is occurring. Settings might include a supermarket, a home, a bank, a classroom, or a bus. Vary the situations to include strangers, family members, close friends, and others. After each skit, discuss with your classmates the verbal and nonverbal techniques used.

Speaking on the telephone

The telephone is a marvelous aid to human communication. Until such time as picturephones or some other new form of visual technology comes into widespread use, however, people must continue to rely totally on their voices when communicating over the phone. This means that telephone conversations are often more difficult than face-to-face conversations. Thus, a special effort is called for in order to make telephone conversation efficient, courteous, and pleasant.

Follow conversational rules for social calls

The telephone is very useful for extending invitations, deepening friendships, correcting misunderstandings, or simply enjoying good conversation. The telephone is especially valuable when distance makes face-to-face conversation impractical. For these purposes efficiency is somewhat less important than courtesy and friendliness. Most of the rules for face-to-face conversations also apply to telephone conversations as well.

When you are the caller, you are disturbing the privacy of another person's home. Thus, you should make social calls at times when you are least likely to disturb the family or individual. Early in the morning, late at night, or at mealtimes are generally poor times to call.

Always identify yourself as soon as someone answers. Give your name first and then ask to speak to the person you are calling. When someone answers the phone, say, for example, "Hello. This is Joe Lincoln. May I please speak with Maria?"

When the person with whom you wish to talk reaches the phone, introduce yourself again. If the purpose of your call is to extend an invitation or correct a misunderstanding, you will want to make some brief opening comments before proceeding with your main purpose for calling. If you called simply to visit, use a more relaxed approach.

Avoid tying up the line for long periods of time. Others may be expecting a call or wish to make a call of their own. If you are the caller you are responsible for bringing the conversation to a close. Always be sensitive and avoid extending the conversation too long.

Follow more formal rules for business calls

Business calls are made for specific purposes. They may be made to give or receive information, to sell or buy a product or service, to make appointments, or to resolve problems. When making business calls, efficiency is of great importance. All businesses exist in order to make a profit. Wasting time on the telephone during business hours involves greater expense and less profit.

One way to increase efficiency is to be sure of the number you are calling. If you are not sure of the number, look it up. Another way to be efficient is to be prepared. Have any materials you intend to refer to or relay to your party at hand before placing your call. Also have writing materials ready to write down any information you may receive.

As soon as you reach the number, identify yourself, then ask for your party. Make a brief opening statement of courtesy, then relate your business immediately. Speak directly into the mouthpiece using a conversational volume. Don't forget that your vocal tones, rate, and articulation all play a part in conveying your message.

Taking part in an interview

There are many different kinds of interviews. When interviews are mentioned, most people are likely to think first of the face-to-face communication held when someone is seeking employment—the job interview. But workers are interviewed periodically after they have been

Business telephone calls mean business. Efficiency is of great importance. Time wasted on the telephone during business hours can cost a company money and interfere with job success.

on the job for awhile. People with problems are interviewed by psychological counselors. Government officials are interviewed by news reporters seeking information. Couples are interviewed by members of the clergy before getting married. Students are interviewed by guidance counselors, teachers, and sometimes principals about their schedules, grades, or behavior. People applying for admission to a vocational school or college are usually interviewed before they are accepted. At some time in your life you will certainly take part in a face-to-face interview of some kind.

Unlike conversation, an **interview** is a more formal kind of communication event with a particular and definite goal in mind. An interview may last a few minutes or may continue for several days, but it is ordinarily planned in advance and directed toward a definite outcome.

Being interviewed

Interviews are held with people seeking all kinds of jobs. These include positions in private industry, in government service, in schools, and in professional offices such as those of lawyers and doctors. Since many of the principles involved in job interviews are typical of other forms of interviewing, and since practically everyone engages in a job interview at least once in his or her life, emphasis here will be given to this type of interview.

PREPARE THOROUGHLY. If you are seeking employment, you are the **interviewee.** A good job interview demands three things of the interviewee: thorough preparation, active participation, and good follow-up.

Thorough preparation includes finding out all you can about the organization, the job, and the interviewer beforehand. It means preparing answers to the types of questions you can expect to be asked. It means readying questions of your own to ask the interviewer.

Some form of correspondence often takes place before a job interview. In this correspondence, ask for any brochures or other written information about the company. Read it carefully when it arrives. Educate yourself about the firm's history, its products or services, and its size. Try to discover who will conduct your interview and his or her name beforehand.

Though there are frequently unexpected questions during an interview, most job interviewers ask a number of similar questions. Here are some you should prepare answers to beforehand:

- *Why do you want to work for this company?*

- *What experience have you had that prepares you for this position?*

- *What kind of grades did you receive in school? (Or what grades have you earned thus far in school?)*

- *What would you expect as a starting salary?*

- *If you are hired for this job, how long would you expect to stay with this company?*

- *What are your long range career goals? (Or what do you expect to be doing five years from now?)*

- *What hobbies or outside interests do you have?*

- *How much do you know about this firm?*

- *What do you feel are your major strengths for this job?*

Most interviewers ask the same kind of questions when they conduct job interviews. An interviewee can make a more positive impression by preparing answers to these questions ahead of time.

Laws have been passed to insure equal treatment for all people applying for jobs. Because of these laws, you will probably not be asked any questions about your national origin, race, sex, religion, or marital status. Physical and mental handicaps usually are discussed only if they might relate to the performance of the duties of the job. Age can be discussed only if the interviewee is a minor or over seventy. If you should be asked questions you feel are improper, politely refuse to answer them.

A good interviewer will give you the opportunity to ask questions during an interview. Actually, your ability to ask intelligent questions will probably make a more positive impression on the interviewer than your answers to the interviewer's own questions. If it appears that the interviewer is about to close the interview without giving you such an opportunity, ask for it. Here are sample questions of the type you may wish to ask:

- *What would my specific duties be?*

- *Can you tell me a little bit about the people with whom I would be working directly, including my immediate superior?*

- *What kinds of fringe benefits accompany this position?*

- *At what salary would I start? (Ask this late in the interview if it has not already come up.)*

- *What is the likelihood I would be asked to move to another town to keep my job or get a promotion? Would the company pay moving expenses?*

Several of these questions apply mainly to an interview for a full-time position after graduation. However, even during brief interviews for summer employment, you will want to ask questions about duties, hours, fringe benefits, and wages. Don't be timid about such matters. You have a right to know about them before you accept a job.

BE AN ACTIVE PARTICIPANT. Your skill at verbal and nonverbal communication probably creates the single most important impression during an interview. The following suggestions will help to make that impression a favorable one.

Be on time for the interview. Several minutes early is perfectly acceptable. Five minutes late could spell disaster.

Be certain your appearance is neat, clean, and generally conservative. Good grooming applies to any job interview, even if the job itself requires work clothes and getting dirty. Sit in a relaxed manner, but do not slouch. You want to appear alert, but not overly tense. Do not fidget in your seat.

Answer the interviewer's questions completely, but do not ramble. Once you have answered a question fully, stop. At the other extreme, avoid single-word answers, such as "Yes" or "No." The interviewer

"Tell me, Mr. Wallberg—what in particular can you offer this firm with your so-called youth?"

wants to hear you talk. Do not try to bluff. If you do not understand a question, ask the interviewer to explain it. If you do not know the answer to a question, say so. If you are a "C" student, don't claim to be a "B" student.

Emphasize any of your past experiences that show you have been in a position of responsibility or leadership, no matter how insignificant they may seem. If you were class president in school, for example, mention it. If you have been a summer-camp counselor, mention that.

Speak in a voice that can be easily heard, but is not too loud for the size of the room. Speak clearly. Show enthusiasm through your voice by varying volume, pitch, and rate of speaking.

Listen carefully to everything the interviewer says. Be sure to maintain regular eye contact with the interviewer as you listen. Keep a pleasant, interested expression on your face during the interview. You will make the best impression if you seem to be enjoying the interview and its challenge.

FOLLOW UP. If you are not offered a job at the close of the interview, correct follow-up may determine whether you will get it later. This generally consists of mailing a business letter to the interviewer the next day. In the letter, thank the person for the opportunity of being interviewed and enclose your résumé if you have not previously presented it. A résumé is a neatly typed summary giving your name, address, education, and previous work experience. Close the letter by offering to send any additional information the interviewer may want about you. Emphasize that you hope to hear from the interviewer as soon as possible.

If you are offered the job during the interview, write a letter thanking the interviewer. Express your intention to do the job well.

Application: Practicing for a job interview

Take part in a series of mock job interviews in class. A few minutes will be needed to prepare and rehearse each interview beforehand. One member of each pair should take the role of interviewer and the other that of interviewee. The interview may be portrayed as an example of smooth and effective communication, or it may be done as a comical display of poor interviewing techniques. Each presentation should last about five minutes. Discuss each interview at its conclusion.

Conducting an interview

The interview is often a source of information. Business people, government officials, and news reporters use interviews to gather material. Students conduct interviews when preparing material for reports or speeches. Suppose you need information about accidents involving bicycles for a report you plan on bicycle safety. Interviewing a local police officer about bicycle accidents would be a possible source of information for that topic. Experts in many fields are generally available in every community.

There is one main difference between being an interviewee and being an interviewer. The interviewer must manage the interview.

PREPARE THOROUGHLY. After deciding what information you need, choose the person you wish to interview. Preferably, choose the best available expert on the subject. For example, if you need information about city government and the mayor is unavailable because of a busy schedule, try contacting a member of the city council or someone working for a city agency who might be able to help you. A person, long involved in city affairs as a concerned citizen, could also prove to be a good source of information.

Once you have located someone to consult, make an appointment for the interview. Be courteous. Tell the person why you wish an interview. Arrange a time and place convenient for the interviewee. Be sure

James Bond sells vacuum cleaners door to door. He likes his work because he likes meeting people and talking with them, and because he feels confident of his ability to communicate effectively face to face.

Bond, who works in Williamston, North Carolina, once received an award from his vacuum cleaner company for being their number two salesperson in the United States. The award, which was based on the number of dollars worth of vacuum-cleaning equipment sold in a year, was a significant one because the company employs hundreds of salespersons coast to coast. It was also significant because, although Bond didn't necessarily knock on more doors than other salespersons, he was able to sell more vacuum cleaners.

Obviously, Bond was more successful than the other salespersons at communicating the benefits of the vacuum cleaners. How did he do it?

There are two skills every good salesperson must have to work effectively, Bond says. One, of course, is an ability to talk convincingly about the product. Good salespersons know the facts, or "selling points," of their products and can speak about them authoritatively, marshaling their facts with order and precision, so that a customer will have no doubt that they know what they are talking about. Salespersons must also believe in the selling points of their products. They must speak with sincerity, look customers squarely in the eye, so they will believe the salespersons are good people selling good products.

The second skill is more subtle. While he is talking to a customer, Bond keeps alert for reactions. He watches like a hawk for facial expressions or body movements which tell him whether the customer is interested in his presentation, only vaguely curious, or downright bored. He listens, with the keenest of ears, to what the customer says. By staying alert to the moods of a potential customer, Bond is in a position to draw on the trump card of his profession, the ability to tailor his presentation to the response of each customer.

If a customer appears interested in vacuum cleaners, but shows signs of feeling pressed for time, Bond accommodates by speaking only briefly about the product. Then he suggests that he call on another day when the customer may find it more convenient for leisurely discussion. If the customer reacts eagerly, Bond knows he can bring a vacuum cleaner in for display and spend perhaps an hour detailing its points. Similarly, when Bond talks to someone who seems "down," or depressed by something, he makes a few jokes to cheer the person up. (Over the years, he has gotten a lot of joke mileage out of his name, which is identical to the James Bond of 007 fame.) Bond can tell in an instant when someone is not interested in the product he is selling. Then he leaves, politely and immediately.

Bond's mastery of one-to-one, face-to-face communication has developed over time, through his experience of meeting hundreds of people on his rounds. His recognition that monitoring customer reaction is as important as persuasive speaking goes a long way towards explaining his success as a salesperson.

to thank the person before concluding your conversation. Be polite even if the person refuses to grant you an interview.

Next you will need to study material available on your topic. An informed interviewer always does a better job. Also study any background information you can find about the person to be interviewed. Know all you can about the subject and the person with whom you will be speaking.

Finally, write down questions to ask. Remember your interviewee's time is valuable. Do not plan to ask questions that could easily be answered by consulting books, public records, or other sources. Avoid questions that can be answered with only a yes or no.

MANAGE THE INTERVIEW CAREFULLY. As the person conducting the interview, you are responsible for managing it well. Make sure your appearance will make a good impression. Arrive promptly. Greet your interviewee with a firm handshake and express your pleasure at being able to talk with him or her.

Start the interview by explaining its purpose. Try to make the interviewee relaxed and comfortable. People are more likely to speak freely if they feel at ease. Do not follow your list of questions too closely. Perhaps your interviewee will say something that will suggest questions you had not considered in advance. Go ahead and ask them. Without straying too far from the subject, encourage the interviewee to express his or her views fully. Perhaps the interviewee will want to ask you some questions. Constantly be aware of the nonverbal aspects of your interview. Maintain frequent eye contact. Smile frequently and show your interest. Give encouragement by nodding. Sit close enough to converse easily.

Making an appointment to interview someone is most often accomplished by telephone. Keeping a note of the time and place of the interview, after they have been decided, will help the interviewer arrive in the right place at the correct hour.

Using a tape recorder during the interview will assure that the information you gather will be accurate. Be sure, however, to ask permission of the interviewee before using a tape recorder. Once you have permission to use it, test the recorder to be sure it is working properly and place it so that the recording will be clear. If the interviewee refuses to allow you to use a tape recorder or is made uncomfortable by its presence, don't use it.

If you are unable to use a tape recorder, take notes of important points. Try to do this without interrupting the flow of conversation. You may wish to record several quotations to be included in your report. It would be a good idea to repeat these to the interviewee to be sure the quotation is exact.

End the interview when you have the information you need. If you notice that the other person is tired or anxious to get on with other matters, try to conclude quickly. Do not overstay your welcome. Conclude by expressing your thanks. Tell the interviewee how helpful he or she has been.

FOLLOW UP. People like to know they have helped others. Follow up by sharing the outcome of your interview with the interviewee. You may send the person a copy of your report or speech. Include a letter thanking the interviewee again for the help you were given.

Write a letter even if a copy of the material using the interview is not available. Perhaps you can explain how you used the interview in your presentation. You may include favorable reactions from your readers or listeners. Remember to express your thanks before concluding.

Summary

One-to-one communication accounts for much of our daily communication. Most of us spend more time engaged in face-to-face conversation than in the other forms of speaking. While we take one-to-one conversation pretty much for granted, it involves certain special characteristics and rules.

THE VERBAL ASPECTS OF CONVERSATION. Good conversation demands the sending and receiving of messages with accuracy, courtesy, and a genuine interest in a wide range of topics. You should also learn to enjoy the art of conversation. The checklist in this chapter can help you evaluate the effectiveness of your own conversational style.

THE NONVERBAL ASPECTS OF CONVERSATION. Most forms of one-to-one communication rely heavily on the nonverbal channels. More than half of the total communication in two-person situations is carried in this manner. Although these nonverbal messages are not as specific in their meaning as the verbal messages, they often make a deeper and longer lasting impression on the receiver. Sometimes nonverbal signals substitute for words. More often they occur together with spoken language to complement, emphasize, and sometimes contradict what is being said.

Body motion is very important in one-to-one communication. Eye contact can signal when a speaker is about to yield the floor to the listener. Too little eye contact can indicate a lack of interest. Too much can be distracting. People also use space during two-person conversations, moving closer to signal a liking for the other person or a greater feeling of intimacy. Other distances may be used for more businesslike or less personal situations. Time is another factor that can express much about your feelings. Being on time for meetings or interviews, giving sufficient time to conversations, and not allowing frequent interruptions during a discussion all speak clearly of your attitudes towards others. Appearance plays a major role in most interviews. For example, such matters as hair style, clothing, and neatness of appearance can often be the deciding factor in the outcome of a job interview. Finally, your speaking rate, voice pitch, volume, and vocalized pauses may sometimes make a greater impact than your words themselves. Paralanguage has an especially strong impact in telephone conversations.

SPEAKING ON THE TELEPHONE. Telephone conversation depends on the voice alone to convey the message. Whether using the telephone for social or business conversation, you must remember the importance of efficiency, courtesy, and friendliness.

TAKING PART IN AN INTERVIEW. Though there are many types of interviews, the job interview is the kind most commonly encountered. Being interviewed for a job demands careful preparation, active participation, and good follow-up. Conducting an interview also requires all of these things as well as careful management.

Vocabulary

one-to-one communication
conversation
vocalized pause

interview
interviewee

Review questions

1. What are three common examples of one-to-one communication?

2. What are the three "rules" to remember for good conversation?

3. What are three ways you can send messages accurately when conversing?

4. Besides face and body movements, name three other nonverbal aspects of conversation?

5. Why is a telephone conversation more difficult than face-to-face conversation?

6. Besides words, what are three other speech elements that carry your message in a telephone conversation?

7. What kinds of questions should you be prepared to answer at a job interview?

8. What kinds of questions should you be prepared to ask at a job interview?

9. What are some factors that may influence the impression you make on the interviewer during a job interview?

10. How should you follow up a job interview that you have had?

Discussion questions

1. Discuss the importance of eye contact in conversation. Analyze the way you use it in conversing with your family, friends, teachers, coaches, and so on. To what extent do you vary your eye contact in different conversations?

2. Newspaper and magazine reporters use interviews to gather much of the information they need. Analyze the Communicator Close-up in this chapter as if it were a story from your local newspaper. See if you can reconstruct the interview from the quotations. What questions might the interviewer have asked?

3. Analyze an interview on a TV news show. Discuss how effective the reporter was in asking questions that would elicit valuable information from the interviewee.

4. Watch a TV talk show and discuss the communication that took place. How good was the host at asking interesting questions? How completely did the guest answer the questions? How did the guest "dodge" any questions he or she did not want to answer?

5. Keep a log of your telephone use for one week. Record the main purpose of each call as social or business. Record also the length of each call. Record all incoming calls in the same way. Share your findings with your classmates. How do your uses differ?

At-home activities

1. Make a "nonverbal communication profile" of a television news commentator from each of the three major networks. Watch their facial expressions, eye behavior, and appearance. Listen for vocal tones, speaking rate, volume, and voice quality. Keep lists of your positive and negative impressions of each commentator for a period of two weeks. Report your impressions to the class.

2. The next time you find yourself in face-to-face conversation with a friend, notice your eye behavior and that of your friend. Who does more looking toward the other—the one speaking or the one listening? How does each of you use your eyes to regulate taking turns during your conversation?

3. Ask your parents to describe job interviews they have had. Tell them what this chapter suggests about being interviewed for a job and see if they agree.

4. Write a list of questions you might be asked during an interview for college or vocational school admission. Also describe the steps you would take in preparing for such an interview, using adaptions of the information given in this chapter on job interviews.

5. Interview your grandparents or several older friends about the changes they have seen in communication since their youth. Prepare a report about these changes. Include several quotations.

In-class activities

1. Participate in a series of mock telephone conversations in class. These may follow good telephone-conversation form, or be a comedy of intended errors. Your local phone company may be able to supply you with dummy phones for this demonstration. The class should discuss the strong and weak points of each conversation at its conclusion.

2. With the other students in your class, arrange a tour of the facilities of the nearest telephone company. During the tour, ask the telephone representatives what suggestions they have for proper use of the telephone. If a tour is not possible, perhaps a representative of the telephone company could visit the classroom. Prepare questions in advance.

3. Invite a person who conducts job interviews for a local business organization to visit your class. Ask what characteristics the interviewer especially looks for in a job applicant. What communication skills make a difference during a job interview?

Careers

EMPLOYMENT INTERVIEWERS talk with job applicants to find out if they have the necessary qualifications for jobs. They may also administer tests, check references, and consult with former employers. High school courses in subjects such as psychology, English, and speech are helpful. College training or a bachelor's degree is becoming increasingly important. Employment interviewers can be found in both private business and industry as well as government, social, and educational agencies.

NEWS REPORTERS conduct research and interviews to secure information and write stories about news events. High school courses such as English, speech, journalism, typing, and social studies are helpful. College graduates are preferred. News reporters can be found working for small or large newspapers, press services, and news magazines.

POLICE OFFICERS patrol assigned beats on foot, horseback, motorcycle, or in a patrol car to control traffic, prevent crime or disturbances of the peace, and arrest violators. They must become familiar with the people on their beats. They give first aid at accidents and file daily activity reports. High school courses in physical education, history, psychology, sociology, foreign languages, English, and speech are helpful. A high school diploma is required for this position, and college training is useful.

CLINICAL PSYCHOLOGISTS diagnose mental and emotional disorders and administer programs of treatment. They interview patients in clinics, hospitals, prisons, and other institutions and study medical and social case histories. Clinical psychologists also administer and interpret psychological tests. High school subjects such as psychology, biology, social studies, math, English, and speech should be helpful. A Ph.D. is usually the minimum educational requirement. Clinical psychologists work in hospitals, private practice, and in schools.

RECEPTIONISTS receive callers at establishments, answer questions, and sometimes perform other clerical duties. High school courses in English, speech, bookkeeping, business math, and typing are helpful. A high school diploma is usually required.

5

GROUP
DISCUSSION

When you have completed this chapter you should be able to

Give examples of the important role group communication plays in modern life.

Describe the various types and forms of group discussion.

Discuss factors that affect group discussion.

List three types of discussion questions.

Prepare a discussion outline for each of the three types of questions.

Describe the beginning, regulating, and concluding functions of group leadership and use each of these functions in a classroom discussion.

List the three major outcomes possible in any discussion, and name the most desirable.

Discuss the uses of brainstorming and the nominal technique.

Have you ever seen the play *Twelve Angry Men*? The entire play takes place in a jury room following a murder trial. On the first vote, all the jurors but one wish to condemn the accused. After an hour and a half of intense discussion, the jury unanimously votes to acquit. They return to the courtroom, exhausted after their deliberation. Not all group communication demands this much effort, but it always takes a certain amount of hard work.

Group discussion is rapidly becoming one of the most widely used forms of interpersonal communication in modern society. In the world of business, managers may spend up to fifty percent of their time in meetings. The average citizen may discuss upcoming elections with neighbors. Public meetings may be held to discuss the budget proposed by a school board or a city's new zoning laws. Students may be asked to carry out assignments in small groups.

People communicate in groups for several purposes. Sometimes three or more people come together in a group simply to enjoy social conversation. At other times groups meet in order to solve a problem or to reach a decision. Groups may also meet to share information. As in one-to-one conversation, there is often no single goal or topic and no planning of a group's social conversation beforehand. The rules for successful group conversation are similar to those presented for one-to-one

In the movie "Twelve Angry Men," twelve jurors struggled to reach a unanimous decision through tense and sometimes furious discussion.

conversation in Chapter 4. Therefore, in this chapter the focus will be on group discussion used to arrive at decisions and to share information, rather than on group conversation.

The nature of group discussion

Group discussion occurs any time three or more people meet to solve a common problem, arrive at a decision, or answer a question of mutual interest.

The idea of *cooperation* is basic to discussion. It means that the members of the group must share a desire to achieve a common goal. They may not all wish to achieve that goal in exactly the same way. But they must be willing to devote their energies to reaching a group solution, rather than to promoting their own individual solutions or opinions. This does not mean that there won't be differences of opinion in group discussion. Rather, it means that each member must enter the group with an open mind, genuinely prepared to listen as well as to argue.

Discussion groups are generally formed for a definite purpose, to achieve a particular and sometimes urgent goal. Ordinarily, such a goal can be reached only when the members are *prepared*. If a member has prepared actively to participate and achieve the group's goal, she or he can not only help the group reach a decision but can also have considerable influence in forming the group's decision.

Types of group discussion

Discussion groups can be classified by their *purpose* and their *audience*. Groups classified by purpose usually meet for one of two reasons: **decision-making** or **enlightenment.** A board of directors of a corporation generally meets to decide upon action for the future. A group of TV commentators discussing unemployment on a news broadcast, on the other hand, generally has the enlightenment of the listeners as its primary purpose. Determining whether a discussion group exists for the purpose of decision-making or for enlightenment is one of the basic ways of classifying different types of groups.

Groups can also be classified by their audience, that is whether they are engaged in closed-group or public discussion. If the members of the group are communicating only with each other, the discussion is a **closed-group discussion.** If they are also communicating with listeners outside the group, the discussion is a **public discussion.** It is a public discussion even if the audience is not physically present, as in the case of a TV or radio broadcast.

These types of discussion can, of course, occur in combination. When a group of students meets to study together before a big exam, it is a closed-group, enlightenment discussion. If those same students were

When a group of students meets to study together, it is a closed-group discussion and its purpose is enlightenment. The students here will not make a group decision, although they may agree that next week's exam will be a tough one.

gathered to plan a dance, the format would be a closed-group, decision-making one. When city council members discuss recreation facilities available in their city in front of an audience it is a public, enlightenment discussion. Suppose the council members were to discuss whether they should build a new city hall or repair the old one. If an audience was present, the discussion would be a public, decision-making one.

Forms of discussion groups

Probably the most common form for closed-group discussion is the committee. A **committee** is a small subgroup of a larger organization that has been given a specific task or set of tasks to perform. The committee is often used for decision making. Some committees have only the power to recommend action or policy to the larger body of which they are a part. Others can actually make a decision or carry out a task. A board of directors for a corporation is a special kind of elected committee. They have been given the authority to carry out decision-making tasks for the owners of the corporation.

Another common form of closed-group discussion is the **round-table discussion.** Perhaps you remember King Arthur's Round Table. It was, according to legend, a circular table around which King Arthur and his knights discussed their adventures. The circular shape of the table was to prevent arguments about each knight's relative importance

A round-table discussion offers the advantage of having everyone seated in positions of equal importance.

in the group. During a round-table discussion, a circular table is often used for the same reason. Although the term *round-table* is sometimes used to apply to almost any type of closed-group discussion, it most often means a closed-group session in which information-sharing or enlightenment of those taking part is the object. For example, a group of teachers would be using a round-table form if they met to discuss changes in the curriculum.

Public discussion often takes the form of a panel. A **panel** is a group that discusses a topic in front of an audience. The panel's purpose could be either enlightenment or decision-making. In either case they are discussing for the benefit of an audience as well as for themselves.

A similar form of public discussion is the symposium. In a **symposium**, one group member gives a short, uninterrupted speech, which is followed by a speech from the next member, and so on until all members have spoken. A symposium, then, is really a series of short public speeches generally given by experts, and is thus not a true group discussion. In a symposium, the free interaction of ideas that is so important in group discussion does not exist.

Either the panel or the symposium can be opened up to questions or comments from the audience. When this is done, the form is called either a **panel-forum** or a **symposium-forum.** This arrangement can be quite effective with live or radio and television audiences where listeners or viewers can call in questions or reactions by telephone.

Factors affecting group discussion

Several factors affect whether or not a group discussion is successful. Two of these are the size of the group and the physical environment in which the group meets. Seating arrangements and the time of the discussion, as well as various personal goals of the members, also affect discussion.

Size of the group

At least three people must be present in order to have a group discussion. Discussion groups seldom have more than fifteen members, however. Each member of a discussion group must have the opportunity to take part in the discussion. Too many members can cause verbal traffic jams, preventing the group from arriving at a decision. The group size which seems to work best for most situations is five or seven—not six! Suppose a group has an even number of members and half favor a proposal and half oppose it. A vote on the issue would result in a tie, and the discussion would be deadlocked. If, on the other hand, the group has an odd number of members voting, a tie could not occur.

Physical environment

The physical setting in which a group meets can affect its discussion. Members should try to avoid communication barriers caused by meeting in an unsuitable environment. For example, the temperature of the room should not be so high that members have trouble staying awake. On the other hand, the temperature should not be so low that people are uncomfortable.

Noise and visual distractions can prevent a successful discussion too. Doors or windows may have to be closed to keep outside noises or the activities of others from distracting group members. Conversations within the group which are not related to the discussion question should also be discouraged. The time for social conversation is before or after group discussion. A quiet, uncluttered room that offers privacy is the best environment for group discussion.

Seating arrangement

As you read in Chapter 2, it is important to consider proxemics, or the use of space, when communicating with others. In discussion, comfortable seating arrangements can sometimes mean the difference between whether or not a group reaches its goal. Chairs should be placed close enough to make discussion easy. On the other hand, group members should not be made uncomfortable by being so close that they feel their personal space has been invaded.

Good seating arrangements will make it possible for each group member to maintain eye contact with every other member. Being able to look at each other helps to keep members actively engaged in the discussion process.

Time for discussion

The best group discussions are held at times when members are most alert. Members should avoid scheduling a discussion just before lunch or at the end of a busy day. People who are hungry or tired are less able to reason well.

Groups should be sure there is enough time to share the information or to reach the decision called for by the discussion question. If the goal cannot be reached in one meeting, members should hold the next session as soon as possible. Members of the discussion group will remember better what was done at the first session if the second one follows shortly afterward. Summarizing what happened at the first meeting will also help members pick up where they left off.

If a discussion is expected to be lengthy, members may need a short break. After moving about and relaxing for a few minutes, a group is often able to resolve issues more successfully.

Personal goals of members

People take part in groups to achieve some kind of common goal. The goal may be to make a joint decision, to solve a mutual problem, or to share information. In addition, each member of a group, generally wishes to achieve certain personal goals. These may include a position of leadership, a feeling of comradeship, or a desire for security. Sometimes fulfilling personal goals helps to achieve group goals. At other times, personal goals may become barriers to group goals.

A personal goal involving leadership can have a strong effect on a group. Many people prefer to lead rather than follow. But it is difficult for several in a group to lead at the same time. In new groups, members sometimes spend so much of their discussion time in power plays for leadership, that the group has no energy left to solve a problem or reach a decision. When a group forms, there is often a period of time during which the group must either elect leaders or wait for leaders to emerge naturally. This is normal. It is only when the group allows personal matters to overshadow group goals that jockeying for leadership positions must be controlled. The controlling of power plays is never easy. It requires a willingness on the part of those members seeking leadership to recognize the needs of the entire group and to place those needs ahead of a personal goal.

A member's need for acceptance by the group is another personal goal that can affect group discussion. Sometimes, the desire to be liked and accepted will cause a member to give way to majority influence. Research has shown that a person will go along with what he or she thinks is a majority opinion, even when it is directly opposite to his or her own view of the situation. Occasionally, two or three very persuasive members of a group can cause their opinion to seem like the majority opinion, when actually it is not. If other members of the group then "tag along," what is a minority view can become the group's decision or policy. To avoid this each member of a group should be sure that his or her opinion is heard and understood. No member should ever agree with another's opinion unless convinced it is the best solution the group can produce.

A third personal goal that involves a group's cohesiveness can also affect discussion. **Cohesiveness** is a kind of group spirit. The cohesiveness of the Three Musketeers was indicated by their motto, "All for one and one for all." When a group has cohesiveness, each member is dedicated to the unity of the group. The attainment of this personal goal of dedication allows a person to draw strength from being a member of a productive group. When cohesiveness is low, members generally show poor effort in their discussions. Meetings may be carried on politely but are boring. They often end quickly. Important decisions are usually made hastily with practically no disagreement or weighing of evidence. With little cohesiveness, members do not really care about the group or its decisions, so they tend to make poor decisions. The only solution for this lack of cohesiveness is for members to become dedicated to the group and begin to be active and concerned about its goals. They must participate fully in the group's discussions and devote their energies to achieving quality solutions to group problems.

Preparing to participate in a group

Many opportunities for discussion in groups exist in school situations. Members of student government, clubs, and teams use discussion groups to share information and to solve problems. A classroom group discussing a bill pending in the state legislature may report its recommendation in a persuasive letter to lawmakers.

A successful discussion should be planned in advance. Sometimes a leader of the group or several of the group's members will make plans for the discussion. Another very good way to plan is for all members of the group to hold a prediscussion meeting. During the planning stage, members of the group can choose the topic they want to talk about. They can decide on the type of question they want to discuss and take time to word the question carefully. Finally, they can write an outline or list of questions about the topic. This outline or list can then serve as a guide during the discussion.

If all members are not present during the planning meeting, those that did not attend should be notified of the question to be discussed. They should also be given the outline to guide them in doing research on the topic.

Choose a topic

The first step in making a discussion a success is to choose a suitable topic. A topic for group discussion should be interesting, significant, and manageable.

A well-chosen topic must be of interest to at least several persons. If the discussion is to be a public one, the subject should already be of interest to the audience or be one about which they can become interested. The members of the group themselves will participate best when the topic is of interest to the group as a whole as well as to each individual member.

It is not enough, though, that the topic be interesting. It should also be significant. The topic should affect the lives of the group members and of the audience, if one is present at the time of the discussion. For example, it might be interesting, but not very significant, for a high-school group to discuss the question "How can sales managers develop better on-the-job relationships with their sales representatives?" Such a topic would lack a sense of immediacy for most or all of the students involved.

Finally, a well-chosen topic must be manageable. Discussion is a slow process at best. A group should not attempt, for example, to solve the world's economic problems in a one-hour discussion. Groups should choose a topic that can be discussed thoroughly in the time allotted. If the time for research is limited, the topic may need to be narrowed or the research responsibilities divided among the group members during the prediscussion meeting.

Application: Choosing topics for group discussion

Have a class discussion to decide which of the following topics would be interesting, significant, and manageable for a 45-minute group discussion involving seven members of your speech class:

The energy crisis in this state	The problems of aging
High school students and alcohol	The sport of ballooning
Capital punishment throughout history	Books and reading
Extracurricular activities in our school	Caring for house pets
Teenagers and their parents	Science versus art
The stock market today	

"How can a student job center provide the best service for students?" The question, being discussed here between students and a career guidance counselor, is a question of policy.

Decide what type of question to discuss

After an interesting, significant, and manageable topic has been chosen, it should be worded in the form of a question. Groups usually discuss one of three types of questions. These are questions of fact, questions of value, or questions of policy. **Questions of fact** deal with whether a situation exists, under what circumstances it exists, or how it may be defined. "Is there an energy crisis?" is basically a question of fact. Groups should not discuss questions of fact that could better be answered by research. A question such as "What is the current world record time for the 1500-meter run?" could be answered more efficiently by a single researcher than by a group.

Questions of value go a step beyond those of fact. While questions of fact deal with the existence of something, **questions of value** revolve around the worth of the object, person, or situation. A question of value emphasizes whether a thing is good or bad, desirable or undesirable, promising or hopeless. If a question requires judgments of worth, it is usually called a question of value. "Is the two-party system the best political system for the United States?" would be a question of value.

Questions of policy are usually the most complex type of discussion questions. Questions of policy are also those most commonly discussed. Questions such as "How much and what kind of support should our school give to its drama program?" and "What role should the federal government assume in the fight against industrial pollution of our waterways?" are **questions of policy.** These often include the word *should*.

Questions of policy are directed toward some course of physical or mental action. A group does not necessarily need to have the power to put their decision into action in order to discuss such a question. Many groups that can only recommend action have great influence.

Word the question carefully

As soon as a question is chosen, someone needs to narrow it down by wording it in clear, concise, and unbiased language. Many discussions become cloudy, and many more fail to achieve productive results, because no one has taken the time to state the question in a careful way. Precious minutes and sometimes even hours can be wasted in discussing a topic before someone in the group says, "But, wait a minute, I thought we were discussing only how we could *conserve* our oil and gas supplies. Now we're discussing ways to *increase* our supplies. Just what is the question?"

In wording a discussion question, the most important thing to remember is that it should *be worded as a question*, not as a statement. Furthermore, it should usually be worded so that it has three or more possible answers. A question such as "Should capital punishment be abolished?" allows only a "Yes" or "No" answer. This tends to turn the discussion into a debate, with two group factions, each arguing for its own opinion. A better way to phrase this question would be: "How should our criminal justice system handle people convicted of murder?" With the question phrased in this manner, capital punishment becomes just one of several possible solutions to be considered.

A well-worded question should also *be clear*. Avoid unclear questions such as "What about our school system?" It is not a question of fact, value, or policy. A group would not get very far if they tried to discuss such a vague question. The words within a discussion question must also be clear. Group members should agree on definitions for all the words used in each question. Suppose your group is to discuss the question "What should our representatives in Congress do about the energy crisis?" The word *crisis* should be defined before the discussion is started.

Conciseness is also important in a properly worded discussion question. Extremely long and involved wording can confuse, rather than clarify, a group session. Picture yourself trying to discuss the following question: "What kinds of required subjects, such as Math, English, and History, and what kinds of electives, such as Band, Debate, and Typing should high-school and junior-high students be made to take or be allowed to take at various grade levels?"

This exaggerated example could be discussed better with the wording: "Which subjects should be required and which should be elective in grades seven through twelve?" The rest of the ideas contained in the first example would be more properly included in the discussion outline than in the question.

Finally, if you are given the responsibility for wording a discussion question, be sure that your wording is *not* one-sided or *biased*. Suppose you were opposed to raising money for a class trip by having a bake sale. You would display your bias if you used wording such as "How can we earn money for the trip without selling anything?" On the other hand, "How can we earn money for the trip?" would be asking an unbiased question.

Application: Wording discussion questions

Using the topics you chose in the exercise *Application: Choosing topics for discussion*, write a carefully worded discussion question for each. Be able to tell whether your questions are ones of fact, value, or policy. Share the questions with your classmates.

Prepare the outline

If you were driving from New York to California for the first time, you would probably use a road map. You would plot the best route beforehand, and decide about how far you would drive each day. If you were planning a leisurely vacation, however, you might not adhere to a strict schedule. Whenever an interesting side trip presented itself, you might depart from your planned route. A discussion outline serves much the same purpose as a road map does on a vacation. It provides the necessary guidance to keep the group moving toward its goal. But it should never be followed so rigidly that it stifles creative thinking among the members. Just as leisurely vacation travelers readjust their plans, so a discussion group should feel free to depart slightly from its outline because of changing conditions.

Since questions of policy are most commonly discussed, the emphasis here will be on preparing an outline for such a question. A policy question generally demands an outline with three main divisions or phases:

1. Analysis of the background and causes of the problem or situation.

2. Consideration, evaluation, and comparison of alternatives or various possible solutions.

3. Agreement and disagreement about the best solution or action to take.

Most policy discussions will include each of these phases, usually outlined in the above order. The actual discussion, however, might sometimes move briefly into one of the latter phases before an earlier one is completed.

The discussion outline could easily be drawn up by the entire group in a prediscussion meeting. Outlines are general in nature. Questions rather than statements are used in main heads and subheads. Before the actual discussion, a leader may want to draw up a more specific outline consisting of questions within each phase which will be used to stimulate group members' thinking during the discussion. It is probably best if the leader's detailed outline is not distributed to the members in advance. Answers will then occur freely and naturally during the discussion. However, in some forms of public discussion, such as radio or television programs, it may be necessary to give the members of the group a preview of the kinds of questions that they will be asked to deal with.

Research the topic

All members of a group should prepare for discussion by doing research on the topic. The first step in doing research is to think carefully about the topic and the prepared basic outline. Remember any experience or knowledge you may already have that relates to the question to be discussed.

If you are discussing a question of fact, you will need information on the background and causes of the problem. Use newspapers, magazines, books, or interviews to gather the information you need.

When discussing a question of value, you will need to do more than collect information. You will have to analyze that information in order to compare and judge various possible solutions.

Discussing a policy question also requires the gathering of information and then the consideration of all alternatives, as well as ideas,

Preparing in advance for group discussions is important. It can mean the difference between being a well-informed member who can aid in making sound decisions and a participant who can offer only vague generalities.

before choosing a solution or course of action. You probably will have decided upon a solution you favor before taking part in the actual discussion. Be prepared to support your opinions with facts and sound reasoning. Remember to keep an open mind when listening to the opinions of others.

Leading a group

In most groups, certain members exercise greater degrees of influence than do others. Such influence is referred to as group leadership. Researchers used to feel that leadership ability was something that certain people had and others did not. If you had it, you turned out to be a group leader. If you didn't, you would only be a follower in practically any group in which you found yourself. The more recent view is not quite so simple. It holds that a given group possesses a kind of group personality, called **syntality.** Syntality is like an individual's personality. Whenever any group member says or does something that has a major influence upon group syntality, that person is exercising leadership in the group. A member's influence or leadership of the group can vary from day to day. If Maria makes a statement in the group meeting today that opens up an entirely new approach to the group's problem she is exercising leadership. Yesterday, under different circumstances, the group might have paid little or no attention to the comment. If so, Maria would not have been exercising leadership then.

Although many acts of leadership may occur almost by chance, there are certain standard leadership activities that must be carried out at any meeting. In this section, you will look first at these basic leadership roles and then at the ways these duties may be carried out by one or more members of a group.

Leadership roles

A discussion has three basic parts—a beginning, a middle, and an end. Whenever any group member fulfills one of the functions of beginning the discussion, regulating communication, or concluding it, he or she will be acting as a leader at that particular moment.

BEGINNING THE DISCUSSION. The introduction of group members to each other and to the audience, if the discussion is public, is of primary concern at the beginning of a discussion. Effective leadership and group cohesiveness depend on members being acquainted with each other. Any time two or more people you know come together, the question should pop into your mind "Do these people know each other?" If the answer is "No," your immediate task is one of making introductions.

The rules for properly introducing people taking part in group discussion are the same as those used on social occasions. They are based first on age, then sex, and then status. When introducing persons of different ages, begin by mentioning the older person's name first. "Mr. O'Rourke, I'd like you to meet Janice Schmidt, a reporter on our school newspaper." When introducing persons of opposite sex, mention the woman's or girl's name first. "Mimi Rivera, may I introduce my teammate, Greg Chiang." If there is a difference in the status of the two individuals, begin with the person of higher rank. "President Franklin, allow me to introduce Jesse Stoner, our newest member." Introduce members of a group to an audience in order from left to right so the audience can locate each person as he or she is introduced.

The second task when you begin a group discussion is to introduce the topic. The group will have already worded the topic for discussion as a question. The question should be repeated to the group and, if the discussion is public, introduced to the audience. Stating the question at the start of the discussion will prevent uncertainty about the subject to be discussed.

Finally, enough background information about the question should be given to show why the group has assembled to discuss it. Assume seven members of your class are about to begin an in-class panel discussion. The topic is "Energy." If you were chosen as leader, you could begin the discussion briefly and effectively by opening the discussion like this:

"For the remainder of the period today, our panel is going to discuss the question 'What sources of energy should this country utilize during the last two decades of this century?' As you know, we are all concerned about the suitability of nuclear power and the high cost of oil and gas as sources of energy for our nation. Today we will compare these sources with other energy sources such as the sun, wind, and coal to find the best possible combination to use for the next twenty years."

REGULATING COMMUNICATION. Several leadership tasks must be attended to during the central part of any discussion. All members should feel free to speak their minds fully and frankly. This means that the leader must not only invite but also encourage members to contribute to the discussion. The leader should promote the idea that each individual's ideas are valuable and need to be aired. Encouraging such participation is frequently done by means of a general statement early in the discussion. Then, if the need arises, the leader may use more specific urging at necessary points along the way.

Keeping participation balanced during discussion is another leadership task. In any group some members are going to talk more than others. This is all right as long as no one monopolizes the discussion, and no one sits back and says nothing. The leader must exercise tact when suppressing those who talk too much. An appropriate comment might be "Sam, that's a very interesting point you just made. I wonder what some of the rest of us think about that. Sarah, what is your opinion?" But the leader must be careful not to embarrass or put a

In this student council meeting, group leaders, seated in the middle, are keeping track of the flow of discussion. By recognizing when side issues begin to monopolize council time, the leaders can gently steer the discussion back to the main topics.

quiet member on the spot by suddenly asking "Mike, what do you think?" A better approach might be "This seems to be a critical point we are discussing. Why don't we get everyone's opinion on this?" Then, by starting on the opposite side of the circle from Mike, the leader gives the quiet member time to plan ideas and words.

A leader must also be prepared to step in when two or more members of the group begin to argue. Progress cannot be made in a discussion that becomes an argument. This is especially true if those who are arguing freeze everyone else out or begin to deal in personal attacks. Group morale and productivity will quickly decline. When this occurs, the leader must step in with a comment such as "David, Maureen, I think each of your positions is pretty clear to all of us. Perhaps we need to hear some other opinions on this matter. Leon, do you have an opinion about this you'd like to share with us?" By taking the floor away from those arguing, you can often stop an argument.

Leaders are expected to keep the discussion on the track. This means recognizing a major detour from the prepared outline as it develops and gently reminding the group that it is getting off onto a side issue. An excellent way for a leader to keep the discussion moving towards its goal is by inserting brief summaries for the group after they finish discussing each major part of the outline.

Sometimes a few group members may have excellent ideas, but they aren't very successful in expressing them clearly to the group. When this happens, it becomes the leader's job to save each worthwhile idea. A leader may say something like "I think that's a fine idea, Maxine! If I understand you correctly, you're saying. . . ." If you restate the idea in clearer terms, others will be able to understand it.

Finally, leaders are responsible for watching the time limit. This can be an especially important leadership function in public discussions, such as those produced for radio or television.

CONCLUDING THE DISCUSSION. There are two major concluding functions of leadership. First, when leaders feel the group has adequately covered the discussion question or a preset time limit has almost been reached, leaders should summarize the major ideas and outcomes of the discussion. At the same time they must be careful not to overload the summary with their own ideas. Second, leaders should save enough time for each group member to disagree with the summary or to insert a minority opinion if they wish.

Different forms of leadership

In some discussion groups all the leadership tasks are handled by a single group member. Jean may already be president of a club, so all the leadership functions of that group naturally fall to her. Mark may be elected by group members to serve as leader of a different group. Ricardo may be named leader of a committee by the principal. If all the leadership duties fall to a single individual, that person is called an **appointed leader.** An appointed leader is usually a very busy person during the discussion.

Some discussion experts suggest dividing the functions of the leader among several, or even among all, of the group members. One may begin the discussion. Another may keep participation balanced and the discussion moving toward its goal. A third may tone down arguments that arise. Another may watch the time limit and conclude the discussion with a summary. Whenever this shared form of leadership is arranged beforehand, it is also a form of *appointed leadership.*

Still other researchers have found it is best not to appoint or assign any particular duties to anyone. Ideally, all the group participants should understand what leadership functions are necessary. If they do, some group member will handle each function of leadership as the need for it arises during the discussion. This natural form of leadership is known as **emergent leadership.**

 Checklist for leading a group discussion

☐ 1. Am I prepared to introduce members to each other and to an audience?

☐ 2. Will I remember to state the discussion question so there will be no confusion about the subject of the discussion?

☐ 3. Am I prepared to give enough background information about the question so the reason for the discussion is evident?

☐ 4. Will I remember to encourage all members to contribute to the discussion?

☐ 5. Will I step in to break up arguments when they are harming group productivity?

☐ 6. Am I prepared to clarify ideas by restating them when necessary?

☐ 7. Am I prepared to keep track of any time limits?

☐ 8. Will I remember to summarize major ideas and outcomes of the discussion for the group?

Outcomes of discussion

If a group meets in an enlightenment discussion, it is considered successful when members have learned new information about the topic from each other. It is also successful if members have learned new ways of looking at a situation because of the ideas they have exchanged. In concluding an enlightenment discussion, it is often useful for each member to give a brief summary of the new ideas they have learned during the discussion.

A decision-making group, on the other hand, is successful when their problem is solved or a decision is reached. A group can do this in one of three ways. All of the members can agree on a solution or decision. This is called **consensus.** A decision can also be reached when the members agree to **compromise.** That is, each member or group of members gives up part of the solution or decision they want. In exchange each retains another part of the solution they favor. **A majority vote** is the third way of reaching a decision. The solution or decision favored by over half of the members becomes the solution or decision for the entire group.

Consensus is the most desirable of the three possible outcomes. When everyone genuinely agrees on a single solution, everyone is happier and more committed to helping carry out the group's decision. Unfortunately, consensus is not the most common outcome of group discussion. Compromise and majority votes are frequently necessary.

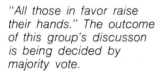

"All those in favor raise their hands." The outcome of this group's discusson is being decided by majority vote.

Some years ago, Barbara Diehl decided to run for a position on her town's school board because she was unhappy with the way the board was operating.

"It was a 4-3 board," she remembers. "But basically, it was a two-man board." Although seven members participated, decision-making power had become centered in the hands of two members who had acquired leadership status over the others. "There was a group of three board members who would always vote together, and a second group of four members who would always vote together," she explains. "All you had to do was check with the leader of each group before a vote and you would know how the vote would go."

Votes on school issues ranged from the buying of cookies for the school cafeteria to the buying and selling of buildings. The votes followed one of two patterns. Either the board voted unanimously, 7-0, to approve or defeat a measure, or it voted 4-3, in a split decision, Barbara Diehl said.

Mrs. Diehl, mother of two school-age children, ran for the board as an "independent." By refusing to side with either of the groups, she hoped to add a third voice to the board, and to break the stranglehold of the power groups so that the school district would be more fairly represented.

Mrs. Diehl won, and she also gained some first hand knowledge of how decision-making groups can defeat their own purpose when power plays made by individuals get out of hand. In recent years, the school board has become a more balanced committee, with members making up their own minds independently. "Now there's no way you can tell which way the vote is going to go," Mrs. Diehl says. "It makes discussion more interesting, and I think people in the district feel they are represented better."

At its best, group discussion is an important means of communication, she believes. She says, "There's a lot to be gained from group meetings. When just two or three people meet together, you don't get the ideas out. No one head can think of everything." On Mrs. Diehl's board, of which she is presently vice president, meetings are conducted with the idea that everyone must be allowed to voice his or her opinion. Anything that interferes with the freedom to speak out is seen as destructive of the board's purpose. It is up to the board's president, for instance, to see that no one member does all the talking or draws conversation off the track. The president must also discourage shouting matches.

Feelings run high at some meetings as board members find they disagree over important issues. Over the years, Mrs. Diehl has found that a board's effectiveness frequently depends on the control which individual members exercise over themselves. "We used to have people who would sit there and fume and then walk out of the meeting," she says. This upset the flow of group discussion considerably. "Right now," she continues, "we are a very polite board. Even when we get angry, we still act like polite, civilized people."

The result, she says, is that the board has become highly productive and can handle a multitude of problems speedily and intelligently.

However, compromise and majority votes, when they arise out of honest differences of opinion, are better than false consensus. **False consensus** occurs when several group members keep serious disagreement to themselves and "go along just to make it unanimous." False consensus is an outcome that usually does the group more harm than good.

Alternatives to group discussion

This chapter has dealt primarily with the form of group communication called group discussion. Group discussion is one of the most widely used forms of group communication in everyday life. However, group discussion can be a rather slow and difficult process, especially when the group is large. Let's look briefly at two alternative forms of group communication—brainstorming and the nominal technique. Each has certain advantages over group discussion in certain situations.

Brainstorming

Brainstorming is a technique sometimes used in business when it is desirable to produce a large number of creative ideas in a short period of time. Like group discussion, **brainstorming** usually involves three or more people who meet to solve a problem or to share information. A brainstorming session, however, consists of rapidly throwing ideas out on the table, without taking time to evaluate each idea as it is spoken. Since the purpose is only to generate ideas, criticism of any ideas presented is not allowed during a brainstorming session. Group members are encouraged to mention any idea about the topic that occurs to them, even if it seems unusual. The purpose is for each member's idea to spark additional ideas in other members. Brainstorming is only a first step in solving a problem or reaching a decision, however. The ideas are recorded, but not evaluated during the brainstorming session. Evaluating and sorting through the ideas occurs during a later group-discussion session. Sometimes the group discussion of ideas is conducted by the same members who participated in the brainstorming session. Sometimes a different group takes part.

The nominal technique

The nominal technique is an alternative form of group communication designed to reduce two problems that often arise in group discussion. One of these problems is the amount of time group discussion takes. The second is the fact that a few members may try to dominate a group discussion. Others may not get a word in edgewise.

A group using the **nominal technique** begins by asking each member to write down a list of possible solutions to the group's problem.

The group size should be no more than 7 to 9 members, and this first step should take only about 10 to 15 minutes. Each member is then asked to state one idea from her or his list. Each idea stated is listed so that all may see the entire list. The group may ask for a second or third idea from each member to list publicly, depending on the size of the group and the number of ideas desired. The third step consists of a brief discussion of the ideas on the board. This discussion is primarily to clarify, but may also involve some evaluation of the ideas. Next a secret vote is conducted with each member ranking the ideas in order of personal preference. Finally the rankings are tabulated, and the solution with the highest ranking becomes the group's solution.

The nominal techniques may reduce the amount of time needed to reach a decision and may prevent a few members from dominating the whole group. However, the nominal technique does not permit the in-depth discussion of a problem that often results in the wisest decision.

Summary

Group discussion is rapidly becoming one of the most widely used forms of interpersonal communication in modern society. Though there are several forms of group communication, this chapter has focused primarily on group discussion used to arrive at decisions and to share information.

THE NATURE OF GROUP DISCUSSION. In order to hold a group discussion, three or more people must meet to solve a common problem, arrive at a decision, or answer a question of mutual interest. Each member should come fully prepared to discuss the topic. Each member should also be open minded and prepared to listen as well as to speak.

Discussion may involve decision-making or enlightenment, depending on the basic purpose for which the group has been assembled. It may either be a public or a closed group, depending on whether the group members are interacting only with each other or with a listening audience. Common forms of a closed-group discussion are the committee and the round-table discussion. Public discussion often takes the form of a panel or a symposium.

FACTORS AFFECTING GROUP DISCUSSION. Among the many factors that affect group discussion are the size of the group, the physical environment, and the seating arrangement. The time of day when a group meets can also affect the discussion. Personal goals of members may sometimes become barriers to successful discussion.

PREPARING TO PARTICIPATE IN A GROUP. Effective group discussions demand a great deal of preparation beforehand. The topic must be one that is interesting, significant, and manageable within the time limits available to the group. The topic must be phrased in a well-worded question that is clear, concise, and unbiased. It may be a question of fact, of value, or of policy. An outline must be prepared that is detailed enough to assure that the group stays on the right track.

LEADING A GROUP. Group leadership today is viewed as all those instances of communication that exercise a major influence on the group's overall personality (called *syntality*). Standard leadership activities fall into three major categories. Those at the beginning of the discussion include introducing the group members, introducing the topic, and providing background information about the topic. Leadership activities during the discussion include encouraging full participation, keeping participation balanced, suppressing arguments, keeping the discussion on the track, and clarifying ideas. Concluding functions of leadership are watching the time limit, summarizing, and saving time for minority opinions following the summary. Any or all of these functions may be carried out by one or more appointed leaders or through emergent leadership.

OUTCOMES OF DISCUSSION. An enlightenment group is a success when the members know more about the topic after discussion than they did before. A decision-making group may reach a decision in one of three ways. A consensus involves basic agreement of all members. A compromise involves give and take. A majority vote favors the solution of over half the members. Although consensus is the most desirable outcome, compromise and majority vote are much better than false consensus.

ALTERNATIVES TO GROUP DISCUSSION. As a decision-making process, group discussion has many strengths. It also contains several weaknesses that make it inefficient in certain circumstances. It is often a slow process, and a few members may dominate the discussion. Two alternative forms of group communication, *brainstorming* and the *nominal technique* can sometimes ease these problems.

Vocabulary

group discussion	symposium	appointed leader
decision-making group	panel-forum	emergent leadership
enlightenment group	symposium-forum	consensus
closed-group discussion	cohesiveness	compromise
public discussion	question of fact	majority vote
committee	question of value	false consensus
round-table discussion	question of policy	brainstorming
panel	syntality	nominal technique

Review questions

1. What are the main purposes of any group discussion?

2. What are the two types of closed-group discussion?

3. What are the recommended size limitations for effective group discussion?

4. What are three personal goals that may interfere with a productive group discussion?

5. What are the three main types of discussion questions? Describe the differences to be found among the three types.

6. Why should discussion questions answerable by yes or no be avoided?

7. What kinds of activities should a leader perform at the beginning of a group discussion?

8. During the central part of a group discussion, under what circumstances should a leader intervene?

9. What are the two responsibilities of a leader in concluding a group discussion?

10. What are three possible ways in which a group may reach a decision?

Discussion questions

1. Discuss the ways in which physical factors such as room size, seating arrangement, and time affect group discussions.

2. Discuss situations in which personal goals may be in conflict with the goals of the group. How can the leader or other members of the group overcome this problem?

3. Discuss the advantages and disadvantages of the nominal technique. In what situations might this technique be more useful than a group discussion?

4. Watch one of the weekly TV panel discussion shows. Discuss how its format does or does not follow the guidelines in this chapter. If it departs from the guidelines, see if you can determine why it does.

5. Discuss the role and performance of the moderator of the panel show in light of the functions of a leader described in this chapter.

At-home activities

1. The next time you find yourself talking with two or more other people, ask yourself whether the group is having a conversation or a discussion. What factors must be present for a discussion? Be prepared to describe your example in class and defend your reasons for labeling it a conversation or a discussion.

2. Participate in preparing for a panel-forum on a topic of school interest at an upcoming school assembly. You and the other panel members may wish to present your discussion in class first in a rehearsal session. Your teacher

or a representative from your panel will need to make arrangements for the presentation of the panel-forum with the school principal.

3. In preparing to take part in a panel or committee discussion during class, research carefully to discover supporting evidence for statements you plan to make. The section "Organizing Your Thoughts" from Chapter 7 will show you the kinds of supporting evidence you are looking for and where to find them. These forms of evidence apply in a group discussion just as they do in a public speech.

4. Develop a list of five discussion questions you would like to hear discussed during class. Be certain each is worded properly. Turn these in to your teacher for consideration as in-class discussion topics.

5. Prepare an outline for a group to follow for a discussion on one of the following questions:

To what extent should the United States use nuclear energy in the future?

What are the advantages and disadvantages of the electoral college system?

In what ways does high school prepare a person for later life?

In-class activities

1. Join with other class members in attending a meeting of your local school board. Later discuss what elements of group discussion the board members used in their meeting. Were there any other forms of group communication being used, such as brainstorming or the nominal technique?

2. Take part in an in-class brainstorming session held to develop a list of topics for later class discussions. Remember that the topics suggested should be interesting, significant, and manageable within the time limits.

3. Use the nominal technique in class to consider a current topic. Then hold a group discussion on that topic. Later compare the two techniques. Did the nominal technique save time or assure greater balance in participation? What advantages did the group discussion have?

4. Participate in two in-class group discussions of the same topic. Each discussion should take the same length of time and have the same number of participants. In one group, elect one member leader for the entire discussion. In the other, allow the leadership to emerge as needed. Following the second discussion session, discuss the advantages and disadvantages of appointed versus emergent leadership.

Careers

LABOR RELATIONS MANAGERS manage the labor relations of business organizations. They analyze collective bargaining agreements and verify adherence to the terms of labor contracts. High school courses in economics, psychology, English, and speech are helpful. A bachelor's degree is required with a master's degree for advancement. Labor relations managers may be employed by government or private companies.

TRAINING REPRESENTATIVES are in charge of training programs for a company's workers. High school courses such as psychology, business, English, and speech are helpful. Educational requirements vary according to the company, but some college is desirable. Training representatives must have good communication skills, both written and oral, in order to develop on-going training programs.

6

BUILDING
CONFIDENCE

When you have completed this chapter you should be able to

List the causes of stage fright.

Explain why controlled stage fright can be helpful.

Tell why uncontrolled stage fright is harmful.

Control nervousness by preparing thoroughly and using various relaxation techniques.

Begin developing an attitude of concern for your audiences.

Make use of communicative body movements.

Recognize your own stage fright symptoms and know how to deal with them.

Begin to seek opportunities to gain public-speaking experience.

"The human brain is a wonderful thing. It starts working the moment you are born and never stops until you stand up to speak in public." This quote from well-known entertainer George Jessel illustrates what is probably the most common problem faced by those who give public speeches—the problem of **stage fright.**

Until now you have been learning about and participating in the "calmer" forms of speaking. As you begin your study of *public speaking* you probably feel less calm about standing alone in front of the class than you did about doing an interview or taking part in a small group meeting. That age-old scourge of public speakers, stage fright, may begin to bother you even before your teacher assigns your first speech.

Stage fright is a significant problem for most beginning speakers— an obstacle that can make the difference between success or failure in accomplishing your speech purpose. In this chapter you will face stage fright squarely. You will explore its causes, see what effects it can have (*good* as well as bad), and learn methods for controlling it. Once you can view stage fright as a normal part of a public speaking experience, you are ready to begin building the kind of confidence needed to be an effective speaker.

Understanding stage fright

Of course, you may be one of those people who do not experience stage fright. Some speakers feel as relaxed in front of a large audience as they do chatting with a few friends around the dinner table. If you really feel this way, be happy about it, but do not get overconfident. Being free of stage fright does not automatically make a person a better public speaker than one who suffers from it.

Most people experience stage fright

An old saying goes "misery loves company." If you have been feeling that you are the only one in your class who gets sweaty palms and a queasy stomach at the very thought of giving a speech, you couldn't be more wrong! As a matter of fact, you are part of the majority. Research figures show that over half of the beginning speakers surveyed reported stage fright, and very few experienced speakers were totally free of nervousness. If you were to poll the members of your speech class right now, probably 80 to 90 percent would report some form of nervousness about giving a public speech.

Although the term stage fright is often reserved for public speakers and actors, these same symptoms are also common among tennis and baseball players, concert pianists, and circus clowns—in other words, among most people who must give a public performance of any kind. Nor are these uneasy feelings reserved for inexperienced speakers and

Sir Winston Churchill learned to control his stage fright and delivered some of the most inspiring speeches of the twentieth century.

performers. Many famous persons, seasoned in appearing before the public, have reported stage fright. Even Sir Winston Churchill, considered one of the most influential speakers of this century, once confessed to a regular dose of stage fright when delivering his speeches. The major difference in the effect stage fright has on a beginner and on an experienced speaker comes from how each handles the nervousness once it occurs. Although there is no substitute for platform experience in learning to control stage fright, speakers can start to build confidence with their first speech if they begin correctly.

Why stage fright occurs

The first step in building speaker-confidence is understanding why you usually feel nervous when speaking in public (or even while *preparing* to speak in public). Stage fright affects most people in physical ways—sweaty palms, queasy stomach, dry mouth, excessive perspiration, increased heart rate, shortness of breath. But the beginnings of stage fright are mental, not physical. When you are preparing to give a public speech, a strong psychological **tension** can build up within you. This tension comes from two conflicting realizations: (1) I desperately want to perform well and make a good impression, and (2) I may not be very successful. Your realization that all eyes will be focused on you and that you will be the center of attention intensifies the desire for success and the fear of failure and embarrassment. Most students find it difficult, if not impossible, to take a nonchalant, "so what" attitude about the outcome of speeches they are about to give.

This mental tension carries over to your body, readying you physically as well as mentally to perform well. Just before the start of an

Will she hit a home run or be thrown out at first? The tension an athlete feels before an important athletic event is not unlike that experienced by a public speaker about to step to the podium.

important test or athletic event, you have probably experienced this same kind of mental conflict and physical tension. You wanted to succeed so badly you could almost taste it, but you also feared failure and defeat. Once the test or event got underway, however, what happened? Probably you were able to use that tension to think more clearly and perform better. To give you an idea of how necessary this tension is, some coaches of athletic teams check their players' palms before a big game to help them decide on the starting lineup. The players with sweaty palms have the right tension. They are "up" for the game.

Controlled stage fright is helpful

You can make good use of tension when you are preparing to deliver a speech. Such internal tension causes your muscles to tighten, your heart and breathing rates to increase, and more adrenalin and oxygen to pump throughout your body. The result is that your brain and body muscles become "supercharged." Your body is carrying out its natural function of preparing you to meet a special situation.

Good public speakers can take this result of stage fright and make it work for them by learning how to control it and channel it properly. Well-known speakers have reported that their most successful speeches have been those they were most nervous about beforehand. On other occasions when they were less concerned about making a good impression, or felt overconfident, their presentations fell flat. The simple realization that stage fright is natural before a speech—and actually an aid to sharper thinking—can itself be a means of controlling it. **Controlled stage fright** can then aid you in becoming a successful speaker.

Uncontrolled stage fright can be harmful

Inexperienced speakers, unused to feeling the symptoms of stage fright, often think that their dry throat or sweaty palms spell certain doom for their speech. The greater these feelings become the more intense the stage-fright symptoms become. This in turn leads to more worry, which leads to worse symptoms, and so on, and so on. The result is **runaway stage fright.** Its effects are quite different from controlled stage fright and may ruin a well-prepared speech.

Runaway stage fright takes one of two forms. The first form is born of **lack of confidence** and usually strikes before the speech begins. Many times the speaker who experiences this form is actually well-prepared for the speech, but has allowed the symptoms of stage fright to snowball. As a result, self-confidence is at a very low point by the time the speech begins, and this leads to runaway stage fright. The second form arises from poor preparation combined with **overconfidence** and ordinarily does not occur until after the speech has begun. Read in a quote from Mark Twain's famous story how Tom Sawyer suffered great embarrassment when he experienced this form of runaway stage fright.

> Tom Sawyer stepped forward with conceited confidence and soared into the unquenchable and indestructible 'Give me liberty or give me death' speech, with fine fury and frantic gesticulation, and broke down in the middle of it. A ghastly stage fright seized him, his legs quaked under him and he was like to choke.

As you have read this second form strikes suddenly and takes the speaker by surprise. Inadequate preparation does not always surface during introductory remarks, but it may become very obvious once a speaker has gotten into the body of the speech. At that point, a moment of forgetfulness is all that is necessary to trigger sudden stage fright.

Since both too little confidence and overconfidence can initiate stage fright, the wise speaker must aim for that critical degree of self-assurance that comes from thorough preparation, mixed with a realization of the unpredictable nature of a public speaking situation.

Stage fright feels worse than it looks

Stage fright is a problem that is much more noticeable to the speaker than to others. Beginning speakers sometimes experience the feelings caused by stage fright so intensely they fail to realize that their listeners aren't nearly so aware of their nervousness. The audience can't see or hear your tightening stomach muscles, nor will they ordinarily notice your sweaty palms or dry mouth. They might notice a slight tremor in your voice occasionally or a faster-than-normal breathing rate, but even these symptoms bother the speaker much more than the listeners. Realizing this fact can make a big difference for some stage-fright sufferers.

Chronic victims of stage fright are generally not content to worry only about their possible inability to speak clearly or remember ideas. They like to worry in big bundles, so they also get concerned about what kind of impression their stage-fright symptoms will make on the audience. For such giant-economy-size-worriers, it should be comforting to realize that stage fright always feels much worse than it appears to others. Unless speakers foolishly call specific attention to their stage fright by comments such as "I'm so nervous, I'm sure this speech isn't making much sense," the audience will often be unaware that the speakers are nervous.

Controlling your nervousness

Before you began reading this chapter you very likely imagined that the best way to deal with stage fright was to rid yourself of it. By now you know that a limited amount of stage fright can be helpful. The trick is to control that amount—not to get rid of it entirely. The next question, then, is "How do I go about controlling my stage fright?"

Prepare thoroughly

One effective method for controlling stage fright is to prepare thoroughly for each public speech. Since most stage fright comes from a fear of not succeeding in front of the audience, thorough preparation can guarantee that about 90 percent of your speech will go smoothly. When you are the speaker, you are the person with the greatest control over what occurs during the speech. Make sure you are well prepared.

1. Study your topic.

2. Analyze the needs of your audience.

3. Research and outline the ideas of your speech.

4. Rehearse your presentation sufficiently.

If you do all these things, you will have little reason to fear that something unplanned or unpleasant will happen. Thus you can begin your speech with confidence.

The possibility always exists that something unexpectedly disturbing will occur (a loud noise, a heckler, a fire drill), but such interruptions occur very infrequently. Just keeping in mind this possibility will keep you sufficiently alert, but not allow you to become overconfident.

Thorough preparation can not only give you the right level of confidence *before* your speech begins but also support you once you have

One way to control stage fright is to prepare thoroughly for a speech in advance. Confidence in your mastery of the subject matter will give you confidence to deliver the speech well.

started speaking. One of the greatest fears of most beginning speakers is the fear of forgetting part of their speech. Once you have gained some experience at giving speeches, you will realize this is not such a serious problem as it may first seem. For one thing, the audience ordinarily does not know in advance what you intend to say, so even if you leave out a large section of your planned speech, no one is the wiser. (Don't call attention to an omission by mentioning you have forgotten something or by appearing confused.) Second, most speakers have note cards available during their speech to help jog their memories if they forget a point. Finally, forgetting is seldom a problem if a speaker has rehearsed thoroughly and correctly. You will see in the next chapter that correct preparation does not mean word-for-word memorization of your speech. If you try to do this, you put a tremendous burden on your memory and are likely to forget.

Relax before you speak

Even when thoroughly prepared, many speakers experience physical tension shortly before they are to speak. Some can feel their neck muscles tightening. Others will experience tense stomach muscles.

Some may have problems with their facial muscles. Though these are symptoms rather than causes of stage fright, speakers quite frequently find it helpful to relax physically before beginning a speech. Relaxing one's body is a way of convincing oneself that matters aren't really so hopeless after all.

Listed here are several relaxation techniques that will help reduce the physical symptoms of stage fright. They should be done as close to the start of a speech as possible, without being noticeable to your audience. Most of these techniques can be done privately just before you join your listeners.

1. Force yourself to yawn widely several times. Fill your lungs with air each time by breathing deeply.

2. Let your head hang down as far as possible on your chest for several moments. Then slowly rotate it in a full circle, at the same time allowing your eyelids to droop lazily. Let your mouth and lower jaw hang open loosely. Repeat this rolling motion five or six times, very slowly.

3. Sit in a slumped position in a chair as if you were a rag doll. Allow your arms to dangle beside the chair, your head to slump on your chest, and your mouth to hang open. Then tighten all muscles one at a time, starting with your toes and working up your body to your neck. Next, gradually relax each set of muscles, starting at the top and working back down to your toes. Repeat this process several times.

Application: Practicing relaxation techniques

Practice the above relaxation techniques in class. Then discuss the effects they seemed to have had. Did you actually feel more relaxed after completing the series? Which technique did you find most relaxing? Can you think of similar exercises that will promote relaxation before a speech?

Realize audiences tend to be sympathetic

Audiences are usually sympathetic to the problem of stage fright. Most listeners realize that they could have the same feelings if they were the one at the podium, and they show by their sympathetic treatment of the speaker that they would expect the same charity in return. Audiences want to see speakers succeed, not fail. To the extent that listeners *do* notice symptoms of stage fright, they will usually react in a friendly and encouraging fashion.

Develop the right attitude

If you are like most speakers you are destined to feel some of the symptoms of stage fright before every speech. Since it is probably impossible to prevent these symptoms from occurring, the key to success lies in your mental attitude toward the feelings. Once the butterflies-in-the-stomach and the shaking knees begin, train yourself to think in the following sequence:

1. Since the time for my speech is getting near, what I'm feeling are symptoms of stage fright.
2. This is my body's way of preparing me to meet a special speech situation.
3. Once my speech begins, this tension will serve as a spring to sharpen my thinking and give vitality to my presentation.

If you look upon stage fright as something positive, you are less likely to experience the kind of runaway stage fright that befalls speakers who see it as totally negative experience. Controlled stage fright will then aid you in becoming a successful speaker.

Concentrate on your topic

Many beginning speakers lack confidence because they are thinking too much about themselves: "Will I do as well as that last speaker when my turn comes?" "Should I be making more gestures?" "My mouth feels dry." Instead, begin to develop a positive attitude. Say to yourself: "I have a topic that I really want to share with these listeners. I want to make certain they are informed (persuaded, entertained), and I will do everything in my power to assure that they are." Once you begin truly thinking in those terms, the worst symptoms of stage fright are likely to disappear.

How can you begin developing such an attitude? For one thing, choose your speech topics carefully. Select something you are genuinely interested in and let your speech be an opportunity to share your enthusiasm for that topic with your audience. Don't get up in front of your audience with the feeling "I *have* to give a speech today," but with the feeling "I have a speech to give today!"

Concentrate on your audience

While you are actually delivering your speech, search the faces of your audience to make certain they are following your ideas and to see whether the listeners agree with your ideas. If you perceive boredom growing among your listeners, change tactics and attempt to regain their attention and interest.

Of course, in any audience, some listeners will appear more interested than others. It is perfectly all right to give more of your attention while speaking to the interested listeners. Their obvious appreciation for your speech can be a great confidence-builder for you.

Some speakers make the mistake of attempting to interest the most bored or disgusted-looking member of the audience. Nearly every audience will have one or two such "sourpusses." If you change your tactics to suit them, you may be ruining what was a highly rewarding speech for 90 percent of your listeners. Only when a large portion of your audience shows boredom or disinterest should you begin changing your approach.

If you concentrate on looking for audience feedback and making an appropriate response to it, you will have little time to think about yourself. As you think less about yourself, your stage fright will be controlled and your confidence will increase.

Inject a little humor

Humor has long been used as a means of reducing tension between speaker and audience. Getting a laugh from an audience builds confidence rapidly; a speaker is assured that there is little to fear from the listeners. Once your speech has begun, injecting a bit of humor, particularly near the beginning, relaxes you more effectively than anything else. If not overdone, humor can actually relax your audience as well. When using humor, observe these precautions:

1. Prepare humor thoroughly beforehand, making certain it will be understood and appreciated by this particular audience. A joke that falls flat can destroy a speaker's confidence rather than build it.

2. Use humor mainly during the speech introduction, sprinkling lesser amounts throughout the remainder of the speech.

3. Do not overuse humor.

4. Avoid offensive jokes.

Move about, use gestures, and make eye contact

Believe it or not, moving while delivering a speech can help reduce nervous tension as well as the other symptoms of stage fright. Have you ever narrowly missed being in a car accident? If so, you probably noticed that right after your near miss you were trembling. Your body was getting rid of the tension that had built up suddenly when you saw the accident coming. In much the same way, movement of one's body while speaking helps dissipate some of the tension the speaker feels.

Any movements you make should be suited to the speech and the audience. All kinds of movement will reduce tension, but some forms look pretty ridiculous during a public speech. Beginning speakers, in a subconscious attempt to reduce stage fright, occasionally use movements that tend to distract the listeners from the message. Among these awkward movements several have become fairly common, and might be given names.

The Ping-Pong Pacers constantly pace to and fro in front of the audience until the listeners appear to be viewing a ping-pong tournament. The Lectern Leeches grab the sides of the lectern so tightly their knuckles turn white. The Hair-Tossers, whose hair may not really be in their eyes, regularly toss their heads to get it out of the way. The Pencil-Twirlers manage to draw all eyes to a pencil, paper clip, rubber band, or note card they are folding, spindling, or mutilating as they speak.

Movements that help communicate your message nonverbally are the only kind you should strive to make while speaking. Such movements release nervous tension just as effectively as the distracting ones but have the added advantage of helping you get your message across. The chapter on delivery will present communicative body movements in detail. For now, notice that they fall into three broad categories:

TOTAL BODY MOVEMENT. Except for very formal occasions, a speaker should occasionally change positions on the platform. Moving the entire body is called **platform movement.** Such movement looks best when it is made on a diagonal: not directly on a forward-backward

Moving about while delivering a speech can help reduce nervous tension. But remember that the movements should be suited to the speech and the audience.

While a speaker who gestures too much during a speech can distract the audience, the use of a few natural arm and hand movements will help to emphasize important points.

axis, nor completely on a side-to-side axis, but between the two. Total body movement is especially appropriate when a speaker is making a major transition in thought patterns or when it is desirable to get closer to one part of the audience where attention seems to be flagging. Movement can also be useful in simply providing variety after a speaker has been in one position for some time. Naturally any amount of total body movement that resembles the antics of a Ping-Pong Pacer is too much.

GESTURES. Although some people tend to "talk with their hands" more than others do, most beginning public speakers tend to be too "quiet" with their arms and hands. Practicing specific gestures for a particular point in a speech is not wise. Gestures during a live performance should not look practiced. Gestures should look natural and be natural. One way to achieve this is to use general arm and hand movements during rehearsal. This is likely to loosen you up and lead to similar natural arm and hand gestures during the speech.

Gestures also include movements of the head and face. While speaking, try to move your head frequently to look from one part of your audience to another. You should also vary your facial expression to correspond with the thought patterns of your speech. Again, your movements should be natural.

EYE CONTACT. Remember that your eyes may be your most effective means of body-motion communication. Many students ask, "Do I have to look right into the eyes of my listeners?" Eye contact is very desirable because of the feeling it gives each audience member that you are speaking to him or her personally. However, if you find in your first few speeches that you get less confused and nervous by simply looking at your audience as a whole and not directly into individuals' eyes, then do so. However, you should make it your goal eventually to look directly into the eyes of your listeners.

Handle specific symptoms of nervousness

Some symptoms of stage fright may bother you more than others. The following chart shows several of the more obvious ones with suggestions for handling each. Successfully handling symptoms that you find particularly annoying will help build your confidence.

SYMPTOMS	SOLUTIONS
Trembling hands and a rattling manuscript	Use 3 x 5 note cards. Place them on the lectern and slide each card to one side after it has been used.
Stumbling over words—getting "tongue twisted"	Deliberately slow down your speaking rate until the problem disappears.
The feeling that you cannot get enough breath	Speak slowly. Take longer pauses between sentences. Breathe from your diaphragm through your nose.
Unwillingness to look at the audience	In the beginning, do not look directly at individuals. Instead look just above their heads or slightly to one side of their faces. Later, pick the friendliest face in the audience and look first at that person.
Excessive perspiration	Ignore it. Do not call attention to it by wiping your hands or forehead.
Cold hands and feet	Make some platform movement and gestures.
Hoarse or squeaky voice	Before a speech, tape record your rehearsal sessions and concentrate on eliminating vocal problems. If this problem occurs during a speech, ignore it.
Dry mouth	Speak slowly to avoid getting tongue tied. Do not lick your lips in front of the audience.
Tense muscles	Use platform movement and gestures.
Cramps, butterflies, or stomach noises	Remember that the audience is ordinarily not aware of such symptoms. Ignore them as much as possible.
Wanting to return to your seat	Resist this feeling at all costs. The best way to control stage fright is by having experience in public speaking.
Feeling inferior	Try dressing for the speech in the outfit that makes you look your best. Naturally, it must be appropriate to the audience and occasion.

Application: Controlling symptoms of stage fright

Have a class discussion about ways you have found helpful to control particular symptoms of stage fright. Notice during this discussion how many different methods your classmates use to control stage fright symptoms.

Speak as often as you can

Confidence in public speaking is built more by the experience of giving speeches than by anything else. This class will provide you with several opportunities to deliver speeches, but it may not provide enough experience to make you truly confident of your abilities on the platform. If you genuinely want to feel at ease about public speaking, look for speaking opportunities outside the classroom. Many organizations that you are eligible to join sponsor speech contests each year. The Future Business Leaders of America (FBLA) is one such organization, as is the Future Farmers of America (FFA). Most local Optimist Clubs have speech contests for high school students. Scout organizations give merit badges for public speaking. In addition, your school may have a debating team or a speech club which sponsors tournaments with nearby schools. By getting involved in these kinds of activities you can gain valuable experience in public speaking as well as develop a much greater sense of confidence.

The more often you speak publicly, the better your delivery will become. Here a student is speaking at a meeting of the Future Farmers of America.

How did Maritza Cifré, 17, and Danny Washington, 18, feel when a television crew suddenly arrived at their high school to film them in a special performance they had been preparing for?

They felt jittery and wondered if they would remember their lines. They were distracted by the bright television spotlights and by people moving around behind the cameras. Danny laughed and joked with his friends, but inside, his stomach churned and he felt uncomfortable.

Danny and Maritza are members of the "The Matchless Players," a special cast of students from a high school in New York City, which performs anti-smoking skits at other city schools. The skits are funny and lighthearted, but their main purpose is to warn of the hazards of cigarette smoking.

The players, all nine of them, work well together. They sometimes improvise on the lines that their teacher/director, Steve Chenek, has written for them. When a television station heard about the group it sent over a crew to tape a performance, which was aired that night on a national network.

"At first I was really nervous," Danny said. "But then, just before I stepped on, I turned the nervousness into energy. I stopped shaking and it came out right. I said to myself, 'I can do it.' And I did. In fact the more nervous I am, I think, the better I am."

Maritza knew what to do if she forgot a line because her teacher had warned her, just in case. "If you forget a word," she said, "say something that's in context with what you meant to say. And just keep on— don't stop—because if you stop, then everybody will realize you made a mistake. Otherwise they'll never know."

Danny used another trick: "I imagined that all those people out there in the audience were my friends, because I'm always more relaxed around my friends. Once I got started and the audience was responding wonderfully, I felt great. My lines came just like that.

"I've always liked to entertain people," Danny added. "In elementary school I used to play the tamborine. Whenever people cheered me, it felt great. The feeling you get when people clap for you, it's like 'Wow! That's for me?' "

Another way to cut down on nervousness in front of an audience is to be well prepared. Both Danny and Maritza knew their speeches backwards and forwards, and once they got into the pattern of their act, they forgot to worry. And guess what? The performance came off without a hitch.

Checklist for building confidence

■ 1. Do I remember that stage fright feels worse than it looks?

■ 2. Do I prepare thoroughly for my speeches?

■ 3. Do I practice various relaxation techniques before speaking?

■ 4. Am I developing a positive attitude toward public speaking?

■ 5. Do I concentrate on getting my message across to my listeners?

■ 6. Do I know how to handle any symptoms of stage fright that I might have?

Summary

Understanding the true nature of stage fright and learning how to control it are two of the most important things you can do as a beginning public speaker.

UNDERSTANDING STAGE FRIGHT. Stage fright is a problem that affects the great majority of public speakers, as well as the majority of other people who perform in public. While both experienced and inexperienced speakers suffer from it, those with experience generally handle it more effectively.

Stage fright starts in your mind. A strong psychological tension urges you to do well and at the same time reminds you that you might not do very well at all. This tension triggers physical reactions such as sweaty palms, a queasy stomach, a dry mouth, and shaking limbs. Such symptoms of stage fright can prevent a successful speech if allowed to get out of control. At a controlled level, however, it can be helpful and can actually promote a successful speech by "supercharging" your body and sharpening your thinking.

CONTROLLING YOUR NERVOUSNESS. One of the best methods for dealing with stage fright is thorough preparation. Knowing that you are completely ready for a speech can greatly reduce most nervousness. Practicing various relaxation techniques while waiting your turn to speak is helpful in relieving the physical symptoms of nervous tension. If you remember that audiences are sympathetic and that a little tension is good you will be developing the right mental attitude for public speaking. Concentrating on your topic and the audience rather than on yourself is particularly useful in controlling excess tension. A speaker who is making sure that the audience is "getting the message" has little time to worry about the impression his or her performance is making.

In addition, injecting humor into your speech helps both you and your audience to relax, and using communicative body movements during your delivery dissipates a lot of your physical tension. In the process of learning to handle the specific symptoms of stage fright you will build your confidence. Finally, there is no substitute for actual speaking experience as a cure for stage fright.

Vocabulary

stage fright

tension

controlled stage fright

runaway stage fright

lack of confidence

overconfidence

platform movement

Review questions

1. What are two conflicting emotions which cause the tension that leads to stage fright? What additional factor sometimes increases this tension?

2. How can controlled stage fright be helpful to a speaker?

3. What are two causes of uncontrolled, or runaway, stage fright?

4. What are some ways that stage fright can show itself during a speech?

5. How will an audience usually react to a speaker's stage fright?

6. How does preparing thoroughly for a public speech reduce a speaker's nervousness?

7. How can a speaker relax her or his body before giving a speech?

8. What three attitudes toward stage fright can help a speaker overcome it?

9. How can physical movements help in reducing stage fright?

10. Give a solution for each symptom of stage fright: trembling hands and rattling manuscript, getting tongue twisted, unwillingness to look at the audience, cold hands, dry mouth?

Discussion questions

1. Talk about experiences you have had with stage fright in non-speech situations (before a concert, dance recital, or sports event, for example). What did you do about the feelings of stage fright? Did your feelings of stage fright work for or against you?

2. Think about which kind of audience would be most likely to give you stage fright: your class, a school assembly, a public gathering in your town or city? Which kind of subject would be more likely to give you stage fright: a personal-opinion topic about which you feel very strongly or a factual report? Discuss the reasons for your answers and try to determine why you would experience stage fright.

3. Discuss effective and ineffective uses of humor in public speaking. For specific examples draw on assembly speeches, introductions by TV hosts, sermons, and so forth.

4. Observe a talk show or news broadcast for a week. What kinds of body movements do the professional public speakers use and how do they use them?

5. Sometimes things do go wrong in public speaking situations. How do talk show hosts or news broadcasters react when mistakes are made (for example, when someone misses a cue or the wrong person responds to it, when the wrong news clip is shown or none is shown at all, or when a guest makes an embarrassing comment)? Discuss especially those techniques you and your classmates can use in your own public speaking. How can a knowledge of such techniques reduce your own stage fright?

At-home activities

1. Write a short paper (several paragraphs) about how stage fright affects you. Your teacher may ask you to read your paper to the class.

2. Keep a diary as you give speeches in this class. Enter your feelings before, during, and after each speech. Indicate whether you achieve greater control over your stage fright as the weeks go by.

3. Interview several students in your school who give public performances (cheerleaders, athletes, student government officers, musicians, debaters). Ask them whether they experience nervousness before appearing in public. What are their feelings about the effects of their nervousness on their performances? Do they plan in advance any methods of handling nervous symptoms that may arise?

In-class activities

1. Invite a noted person in your city or town who frequently gives public speeches to visit your class. Prepare with your classmates a list of questions you will ask to find out (a) whether he or she experiences stage fright prior to or during speeches, and (b) what techniques he or she uses to control it.

2. If your school has videotape recording equipment, tape one of your speeches. Watch the playback for symptoms of stage fright. Did you notice some symptoms less than you did while you were delivering the speech? Which are your most noticeable symptoms? How can you reduce them during your next speech?

Careers

DRAMA TEACHERS instruct students in all aspects of theatrical production at the high school or college level. High school courses such as English, drama, speech, and psychology are helpful. A bachelor's degree is necessary. For employment at the college level, a master's degree or Ph.D. is required.

TRAVEL GUIDES show tourists around particular areas describing points of interest. There are no specific educational requirements, but high school courses should include speech, history, and foreign languages. College is recommended for those who wish to move into positions of authority. Guides should enjoy speaking to groups of people and must be confident and calm when problems arise. Most tour guides work for travel agencies, but government positions (for example, in national parks and at historic sites) are also available.

7

PREPARING YOUR SPEECH

When you have completed this chapter you should be able to

List the essential qualities of a good speech topic.

Analyze the background, attitudes, and interests of an audience.

List the various forms of proof you can use to back up the ideas you present.

Record your evidence effectively.

Choose the most appropriate pattern of organization for a particular speech.

Write a speech outline.

Rehearse your speeches aloud, on your feet, and in the most suitable place.

Time your rehearsal sessions to conform to an expected time limit.

In order to construct a solid and functional house, builders must start with a set of plans. The process of drawing up the plans is, in some ways, as important as the actual construction process itself. Many critical questions must be answered in the plans: "Will the foundation be adequate to support the weight of the house? Are the rooms arranged properly for maximum convenience? Is the structure placed in the best possible position on the lot?" By first building the house in their minds and on paper, the builders can save great amounts of time and money. A mistake at this early stage is easily fixed; mistakes made after construction has started are generally very expensive to correct.

Wise speakers will build their speeches in much the same manner that builders construct houses—first in their minds and on paper. Each speaker's preparation, like the builder's, should answer many critical questions: What strategy best suits the particular audience I will be addressing? Where can I locate the best sources of information and supporting evidence? In what order should I present my ideas? Without ample time to answer these questions beforehand, a speaker runs a great risk of having the speech crumble into a disorganized jumble of words. On the other hand, a well-prepared speaker goes into a speech confident of the outcome. This chapter will deal with the preliminary steps in giving a speech—those important steps prior to the actual delivery of the speech that will determine whether the speech sounds smooth and natural or halting and awkward.

Developing your topic

The first part of speech preparation involves selecting your topic. As you consider possible topics, ask yourself these questions: Does this topic interest me? Will this topic interest my audience? Can I develop this topic adequatcly within the time limit set for the speech? Is this topic timely? And finally, will I be able to research this topic adequately?

Choose a topic that fascinates you

In certain situations you will be asked to speak on a particular subject. The specific occasion or your knowledge in a certain area will determine the topic of your speech. You may be asked to make a nominating speech for a friend who is running for Student Council or to speak to new members of the Audio-Visual Aides Club on how to run a movie projector. In each of these cases the topic will be a natural one and you won't have to ask yourself the question, "What shall I talk about?" As a student in a speech class, however, you will probably have more freedom in choosing a subject. It may be left entirely up to you to decide what speech topic is best.

You should make this decision carefully because the choice of topic can make or break your speech. Begin by making a list of topics that really interest you. These need not be full titles at this point. A word or phrase to indicate the general subject matter, such as horseback riding, pro-football rules, last summer's job, or making an omelette is sufficient. Be certain that only topics of genuine interest to *you* find their way onto this list.

Sometimes speech students think they must come up with a brand new or highly unusual topic if they want their speech to succeed. Not at all. As long as you are enthusiastic about your topic, you will be able to generate enthusiasm among your listeners. Throughout history the speeches that have made the greatest impact have been given by speakers totally wrapped up in their topic. Martin Luther King, Jr.'s "I Have a Dream" speech was given by a man whose life was dedicated to attaining civil rights for all of the citizens of the United States . In his "Ich Bin Ein Berliner" speech (see page 408), John F. Kennedy's challenge "Let them come to Berlin" grew out of his deep love of freedom and his admiration for the brave citizens of West Berlin. Similarly, most student speakers who have won national speech contests have been those who chose a topic that genuinely concerned them and not those who simply latched onto any topic just to enter a contest.

Even though you may have acquired quite a bit of knowledge about topics that fascinate you, nearly every speech you give will require some additional research before you are ready to deliver it. With this in mind, be certain to choose your topic far enough in advance of your speaking date to allow for this additional preparation. Two weeks is not too much lead time, even for brief speeches, since choosing one's topic is just the first step in a long list of speech-preparation tasks. Following is a list of general topics. Some of them may be interesting to you. They are only a small sample of possible speech topics.

Airplanes	Energy	Equality
The Outdoors	Crime	Health Care
Music	Hobbies	Banking
Work	Freedom of the Press	Disease
Sports	TV	Dating
Politics	War	Air Travel
School	Stereotyping	Investment
Skiing	Smoking	Space
Civil Rights	Free Enterprise	Farming

Analyze your audience

With enough enthusiasm you should be able to make any topic interesting to anyone. It will be more difficult to interest audiences in some topics than others, however. For example, someone speaking on

Martin Luther King, Jr.'s historic speeches ignited the imaginations of audiences across the country.

dressmaking patterns may have a tough time interesting classmates who do not sew, and someone speaking about football plays may have a similar problem with those not interested in that sport. Therefore, immediately after choosing a topic ask yourself "How can I make this topic interesting and acceptable to all the members of my audience?" Answering this question involves **audience analysis**, one of the most important steps in speech preparation.

Audience analysis includes discovering everything you can about the background, attitudes, and interests of the listeners who will hear your speech. It also means uncovering how those listeners' attitudes and interests relate to your speech topic. You will want to ask yourself questions such as these:

- *Do they already know much about this topic?*
- *What can I tell them about the topic that they do not know?*
- *Will my topic interest some audience members more than others?*
- *How can I make my topic more interesting to all?*
- *If I take a stand on an issue, will my audience agree with me?*
- *If not, what interests or needs do they have through which I might change their minds?*

Audience analysis for a classroom speech is relatively easy. After a few weeks in a speech class you will become acquainted with most of the class members who will form the audience for your speeches. You

"What kind of audience will I face?" The student above is questioning a member of a future audience. The more a speaker knows about the audience, the better the speaker will be able to tailor the speech to the listeners' special needs and interests.

can readily guess what their interests and attitudes are. Whenever you are unsure, you will have frequent opportunities to ask them directly.

Outside of the classroom, however, audience analysis usually demands more work. When the President of the United States prepares to make a major policy speech on television, for instance, a huge staff ordinarily goes to work weeks in advance, trying to determine the feelings and attitudes of the American people about the issues to be discussed in the speech. Often they rely on the results of national polls; occasionally they conduct their own polls. What the polls tell them determines in a major way the strategy the President will employ in the speech.

Few speakers have a staff available for such audience analysis. Therefore, the speaker must learn to perform this part of speech preparation personally. Usually it is best to start by questioning the person who issues you the invitation to speak to a club or organization. At the time you accept the invitation, take the opportunity to ask some questions like the following about the composition of your audience and their attitudes:

- *Approximately how many persons will be in my audience?*
- *Will they be mostly male, female, or a fairly equal balance of each?*
- *How much do you think they know about my topic already?*
- *What are their views about my topic?*
- *Do they generally agree with my position, disagree with it, or are they neutral?*
- *If they are neutral, would you say it is because they know very little about the issues involved or because they are uninterested?*

- *Will the audience members be largely business people? Professionals? Blue collar workers? A mixture?*

- *What are their religious affiliations?*

- *Their political views? Their age range?*

- *How much formal education have they had?*

- *What strong interests and goals do they consider important as a group?*

If you personally know one or two people who will be in your audience, discuss your speech and analyze the audience with them as well. They can probably give you insights into the knowledge and interests of your future listeners. You may also want to talk to other speakers who have addressed the same group in the past. Ask them how they were received. The more you can learn about the nature of your audience at this early stage of your speech preparation, the better chance you have of tailoring your speech to suit the particular needs and interests of your listeners. Each audience has its own characteristics. A speech that is highly successful with one group may fail with a different set of listeners unless it is adapted to their special circumstances.

Application: Choosing topics for a class speech

Hold a round-table discussion of speech topics that the members of the class would find interesting. Keep a list of topics you would like to consider for your next in-class speech.

Consider your timing

Two other factors to consider when selecting a speech topic involve time. Your speech must fit within an expected time limit and fit the "times" in which it is given. Many a speech that could have been highly successful died because of poor timing.

As soon as you begin to focus on a speech topic that interests you, decide whether you can cover it adequately in the speaking time available. Some topics are too broad for a short speech. For example, you could not do justice to a topic such as "The World's Major Religions" in a five-minute speech, since you would have time for only a few sentences about each religion. Without time to include more interesting details you would not be informing your listeners of anything they did not already know. Sometimes one part of a broad topic fits better within the allotted time. For example, a subject such as "Major Beliefs of the Hindu Religion" could be better covered in five minutes than the previous topic dealing with all the world's religions.

In class, your teacher will usually set the time limits for your speeches. Outside of the classroom, you should always inquire of anyone inviting you to speak: "How long do you wish me to talk?" Once you know the time limit you can narrow your topic to fit within that limit. Some speakers make the mistake of deciding first how much they want to say, then trying to cram it all, somehow, into a very limited amount of time. This backwards process is much like trying to shove toothpaste back into the tube—it's a very frustrating experience. If the time you have available is not sufficient for you to cover a complete topic, choose the most fascinating portion of that topic, which you can cover nicely in the allotted time.

The second "time" question to ask yourself is "Is this a topic of interest *now*?" Some topics eventually get too old or too overworked to remain interesting. Others, such as "Who Should Be Our Next President?", may be fascinating until election day arrives but become about as tantalizing as stale bread as soon as the election is over. The topic "Baking a Cake" is likely to be of interest to your Home Economics class only if most members do not already know how to bake a cake. Be sure to consider the **timeliness** of your topic.

Become an expert

By the time you are ready to deliver your speech, you should be an expert on your subject. This does not mean, however, that you should only choose topics about which you are *already* well informed at the time you make your choice. When Betty Furness first decided to become an expert on consumer affairs, she undoubtedly knew very little about the subject compared to what she discovered after beginning her re-

Consumer affairs reporter Betty Furness has become an expert on her subject through the thorough research she has done for her broadcasts.

search. You, too, can choose speech topics about which you know very little. So long as you know enough about a topic to want to look into it further, you can make yourself an expert through research.

Being an expert when speaking on a topic does not mean you must be one of the top five most knowledgeable people in the world about that subject. It simply means that you should have sufficient knowledge by the time you face your audience to give your listeners certain information or insights that most of them did not already possess. If you do not give your audience something new through your speech, you have not earned the right to speak to them. You are wasting both their time and your own.

Here is a sampling of current topics on which you might become an expert. Notice that the topics given here are much more specific than those given earlier in the chapter. Part of choosing the right topic is finding one that is narrow enough to develop adequately in the time given you to speak.

The Problems of Commercial Airlines
How to Enjoy the Outdoors
Different Views of Music: Pop, Rock, Western, Jazz
How My Part-Time Job Has Helped Me
Are High School Sports Too Competitive?
Should Capital Punishment Be Abolished in the U.S.?
How to Do Decoupage
How High School Students Can Become Politically Involved
What It Means to Be the Principal's Daughter
The Thrill of Water Skiing
Learning How to Cross-Country Ski
Where Is the Civil Rights Movement Going in the 1980's?
Are We Meeting the Energy Crisis?
Solar Energy Versus Atomic Power
My Theory Regarding the Equal Rights Amendment
Should the United States Institute Socialized Medicine?
The Confidentiality of News Reporters' Sources Must Be Assured
Do Americans Watch Too Much TV?
The Horror of War: Can Our Generation Avoid It?
How It Feels to Be Stereotyped
Smoking May Not Stunt Your Growth—But Think of Your Lungs!
All Hail to the Free Enterprise System!
The Day-to-Day Life of a Bank Teller
Is There a Cure for Cancer?
The Joys and Sorrows of Dating
Why I Hope to Become an Airline Flight Attendant
Playing the Stock Market: Legalized Gambling?
What Will the Space Shuttle Program Cost?

Organizing your thoughts

Once you have settled on a topic that is right for you, for your audience, and for the occasion, you need to begin organizing your thoughts so that you can produce a speech that is well researched and clearly arranged. This means taking stock of what you already know, conducting research to discover additional facts, and then organizing your material into a pattern that will be easy for both you and your listeners to follow.

Start with what you already know

The best way to begin organizing your thoughts is to take stock of what you already know about your topic. For a few speeches—"My Exciting Vacation Last Summer," for example—you will find you already have 90 percent of the information you need to interest and inform your audience. For more meaningful speeches, taking stock of what you already know will only scratch the surface of the total amount of information needed. If you find your topic demands a minimum of research, you may want to outline your speech before doing your research (see pages 165-170 on outlining). However, if you know very little about your topic, you must usually do some preliminary research before you can even begin an outline. Then the research and outlining can be completed together.

At least some research is necessary for nearly every topic to assure the listeners that the speaker is not just "shooting off his or her mouth." No one is credited with being the only authority on a given topic; even noted scientists and Presidents of the United States regularly use examples, statistics, and the opinions of other people to support their own ideas in their speeches. For example, such a personalized speech as "My Exciting Vacation Last Summer" can be spiced up with statistics noting how many visitors passed through the area you saw or a reference to the time the Queen of England visited the same place.

Know what you are looking for

Whether the purpose of your speech is to provide information or to persuade your audience to adopt new views, what you are looking for in your research is **support** for the various statements you will be making in your speech. Support is needed mainly to prove the accuracy of your statements, but it can also be used to illustrate points and make them more interesting. Audiences are accustomed to listening for distinct kinds of support. Among the most common types are facts, statistics, testimony, narrative, examples, and comparisons.

For backing up the accuracy of your statements, facts offer the strongest form of support. **A fact** is an event or a truth that is known to exist or has been observed. A fact is very difficult to contradict or refute, especially if it has been witnessed by a large number of people. Here are examples of facts:

> Beethoven's Ninth Symphony was written when the composer was totally deaf.
>
> The population of the U.S. is over 200 million.
>
> Gertrude Ederle was the first woman to swim the English Channel.

Notice, a fact is always something that has occurred in the past or is presently occurring. No future event can be used as a fact, since something could happen to cancel or alter it.

Statistics are a second useful form of support for accuracy of statements. **Statistics** are collections of facts stated in numerical terms. They can be used to present facts in percentages, rank order, and averages. The following are examples of statistics:

> Approximately one out of three marriages in this country currently ends in divorce.
>
> Roughly 52 percent of the world's population is female, and 48 percent is male.

Another form of support, **testimony,** is the quoting or restating of another person's opinion to support a point. Often the person quoted is a recognized expert in the field. Here is an example of testimony:

> As Helen Keller once wrote, "No barrier of the senses shuts me out from the sweet, gracious discourse of my book friends. They talk to me without embarrassment or awkwardness."

Naturally, testimony can consist of quotations of various lengths. In one of his own speeches, Edward Kennedy used a longer example of

You don't need to know everything about a topic to give a good speech, but it helps to have facts and statistics handy. Here students are studying background material which will support knowledge of the subject they already have.

testimony by quoting from a speech that had been given at an earlier time by his brother Robert:

> A speech he made to the young people of South Africa . . . sums it up best . . . "Some believe there is nothing one man or one woman can do against the enormous array of the world's ills. Yet, many of the world's great movements, of thought and action, have flowed from the work of a single man. A young monk began the Protestant Reformation, a young general extended an empire from Macedonia to the borders of the earth, and a young woman reclaimed the territory of France. It was a young Italian explorer who discovered the New World, and the 32-year-old Thomas Jefferson who proclaimed that all men are created equal.
>
> "These men moved the world, and so can we all. Few will have the greatness to bend history itself, but each of us can work to change a small portion of events, and in the total of all those acts will be written the history of this generation. . . ."

Testimony is not as strong a form of support for accuracy as facts are since testimony is merely opinion. Even when a quoted source is considered an expert, that expert can make a mistake. However, testimony is frequently very useful, especially if you think your audience is likely to respect the views of the person quoted.

Narrative is supporting material in the form of a story, either real or imaginary. Besides being enjoyable and interesting, narratives are often used in a speech to help make a point that has already been or will soon be supported by facts or statistics. Here is an example of a brief story that might be told by a speaker who wishes to make a point about dissatisfaction:

> A story is told of Ali Hafed who sold his farm and set out in search of a diamond mine. He searched over the entire world without success and finally drowned himself in despair. Meantime the man who had purchased his farm spotted a glittering object in his creekbed one day and soon became the owner of one of the world's richest diamond mines.

Examples are specific instances or occurrences of a situation or principle you are attempting to describe. Examples may be stated in the form of facts, statistics, testimony, or narrative. Thus examples are general kinds of support that may include any one of several other forms. Three examples are used to support the following sentence:

> Some of this century's most noted speakers have been American presidents. Woodrow Wilson, Franklin D. Roosevelt, and John F. Kennedy are generally considered to have been excellent public speakers.

Comparisons involve the equating of essentially unlike ideas or phrases. They highlight the similarities that exist between basically dissimilar situations. Like examples, comparisons may take different forms. They may include facts, statistics, testimony, or narrative. They may also include the speaker's own opinions if the opinions seem to offer a useful means of illustrating the views being presented. The following is an example of a comparison based on opinion:

> The way some people shop at a sale reminds me of a swarm of bees clustered around a hive, each seemingly unaware of all the others crowded about.

After preliminary research, you can begin to build an outline. As you develop main heads and subheads (see page 165 for a discussion of outlining) you will begin to recognize what forms of support you need. This will help you as you proceed with more detailed research. For example, in a speech on "Land Pollution: Desecrating Our Landscape," a main head might read "How Efficient Have We Become at Littering?" Obviously you will need to find an example or some statistics to answer this question. The answer might be:

> Fifty years ago the average American threw away every day a little over two-and-one-half pounds of garbage. Today each of us will create six pounds of trash. . . .

Find good sources of supporting material

For many topics, the natural place to begin researching is in a library. If you don't know much about your subject, begin your research by consulting general reference books. If, for example, you know almost nothing about beekeeping except that it seems like a fascinating topic for a speech, begin by checking an encyclopedia, such as the *Encyclopaedia Britannica* or the *Encyclopedia Americana,* under the headings "Bees" and "Beekeeping." The encyclopedia articles will help you to begin forming a speech outline, and the references at the end of the articles might lead you to more detailed sources about beekeeping.

Once you have a general notion of the direction in which you wish to go with your topic, you will find more detailed discussions of it in periodicals, newspapers, and books. Several handy reference works list articles in periodicals under general subject headings. The *Readers' Guide to Periodical Literature* lists articles in current magazines, such as *Newsweek, Reader's Digest, Time,* and *U.S. News & World Report.* If your topic deals with education, *Education Digest* lists articles that have appeared in education journals. The *International Directory of Little Magazines and Small Presses* lists lesser-known publications, such as literary magazines and scholarly journals that cover a wide variety of topics.

The library is a good place to start if you don't know much about your subject. General reference books, such as encyclopedias, may lead to more detailed sources of information.

Feel free to browse in the periodical section of your library. Looking at pictures in magazines can stimulate your interest in topics you might not have considered otherwise. Regular reading, especially of magazines dealing with current events and issues, can provide you with a constant source of information on numerous topics. Though you can't be expected to read a dozen magazines every month, becoming familiar with one or two of them and reading them regularly will keep you abreast of current events and serve as a storehouse of support information whenever you need to deliver a speech. Any of the magazines in the list below could be used for this purpose:

Atlantic Monthly	*New Republic*
Business Week	*New Yorker*
Commonweal	*Newsweek*
Ebony	*Popular Science Monthly*
Fortune	*Reader's Digest*
Harper's Magazine	*Saturday Review*
The Nation	*Scientific American*
Nation's Business	*Smithsonian*
National Geographic Magazine	*Sports Illustrated*
National Wildlife	*Time*
Natural History	*U.S. News & World Report*
Negro History Bulletin	

Stories in newspapers are additional sources of information. Most major news stories are indexed in *The New York Times Index*. Even if your library does not store back copies of *The New York Times*, the stories in that newspaper were probably carried in other major metropolitan newspapers on the same dates as those indicated in *The New York Times Index*.

Almanacs and atlases can serve as handy guides to specific items of support for a speech. The *World Almanac* contains statistics and facts on many topics, for example, and geographical and environmental information is frequently available in helpful table or graph form in an atlas.

The library card catalog is your best place to search for material to be found in books. If you know the name of an author who has written on your subject or the title of a book, you simply look under that author's last name or the first main word of the title. If you don't know any authors' names or any titles, look under the subject heading, generally in red at the top of a card. All cards are filed in alphabetical order in the catalog. Examples of these cards appear on page 160.

In addition to magazines, newspapers, and books, most libraries have a documents section, where bulletins and pamphlets published by state and national governments, religious institutions, business organizations, and universities are kept. You may want to check this section of the library for information on certain topics.

Speakers can also find quotations to support their ideas in sources such as Bartlett's *Familiar Quotations, Brewer's Dictionary of Phrase and Fable, Granger's Index to Poetry,* and the *Oxford Dictionary of Quotations*.

Finally, do not forget about reference librarians. They are there to aid you in locating the materials you need. If you are having difficulty, do not be embarrassed to ask for help.

Although the library will often provide you with much of the information you need for a speech, do not overlook other valuable sources of information. Interviews with people knowledgeable about your topic can prove very helpful. If your topic concerns business, why not interview a teacher in the business department of your school or a local business leader? If your speech deals with anatomy, talk to a biologist or a physician.

Other frequently overlooked sources of support for speeches are television and radio—particularly news programs. Since the main purpose of local and network news teams is to gather and sort out facts and testimony, their reports are a gold mine of current information with which to support your ideas. Keep up with world and local news and jot down the date of the program as well as the source of the information whenever you hear an item that might prove useful. Since newspapers are available for reading at any time, they possess an advantage over television and radio as sources of supporting materials. If you happen to miss a particular news broadcast, you often fail to obtain the information later. A newspaper can be retrieved and read months after the event has occurred.

Taking your own informal survey of public opinion among friends or neighbors can prove an effective type of support for a speech, particularly when you speak on local issues. Audiences are impressed when

629.434
Se420

    Seifert, Howard S
        Orbital space flight; the physics of satellite motion ₍by₎
Howard S. Seifert ₍and₎ Mary Harris Seifert. New York,
Holt, Rinehart & Winston ₍1964₎

        139 p.   illus., map, ports.   20 cm.   (Holt library of science, ser. 2
₍no.₎ 19)
        Bibliography: p. 129-130.

        1. Artificial satellites—Orbits.   2. Astrodynamics.   I. Seifert,
Mary Harris, joint author. II. Title.

    TL796.6.E2S3   629.434   64-23014

    Library of Congress   ₍5₎

Author card

629.434   Orbital space flight
Se420

    Seifert, Howard S
        Orbital space flight; the physics of satellite motion ₍by₎
Howard S. Seifert ₍and₎ Mary Harris Seifert. New York,
Holt, Rinehart & Winston ₍1964₎

        139 p.   illus., map, ports.   20 cm.   (Holt library of science, ser. 2
₍no.₎ 19)
        Bibliography: p. 129-130.

        1. Artificial satellites—Orbits.   2. Astrodynamics.   I. Seifert,
Mary Harris, joint author. II. Title.

    TL796.6.E2S3   629.434   64-23014

    Library of Congress   ₍5₎

Title card

629.434   Artificial satellites — Orbits
Se420

    Seifert, Howard S
        Orbital space flight; the physics of satellite motion ₍by₎
Howard S. Seifert ₍and₎ Mary Harris Seifert. New York,
Holt, Rinehart & Winston ₍1964₎

        139 p.   illus., map, ports.   20 cm.   (Holt library of science, ser. 2
₍no.₎ 19)
        Bibliography: p. 129-130.

        1. Artificial satellites—Orbits.   2. Astrodynamics.   I. Seifert,
Mary Harris, joint author. II. Title.

    TL796.6.E2S3   629.434   64-23014

    Library of Congress   ₍5₎

Subject card

a speaker is sufficiently enthusiastic about the issues to conduct such a survey; they enjoy hearing what people living in their own town think about a topic.

Record your evidence

As you discover facts, statistics, testimony, and other forms of support for your speech, be sure to write them down. Even though you are not certain you will use a particular piece of evidence in your speech, record it and the source where you discovered it while it is before you. Always take down more than you plan to use to avoid making extra trips to the library or rescheduling an interview.

It is best to establish a consistent system for recording speech evidence. Most speakers prefer to take their notes on 3 × 5 index cards, recording only one item of information on each card. These can be arranged later in the best order for presentation and are easy to handle on the platform. When you discover an item of information you feel might be useful, first record a general heading under which it falls at the top left-hand corner of the card. In the center of the card place the quotation, example, statistic, or fact. Sometimes the evidence may spill over to the back of the card, or even to a second card. Finally, below the evidence, write the source from which you obtained it. Here is an example of a note card.

Civil Rights:

"Let us not seek to satisfy our thirst for freedom by drinking from the cup of bitterness and hatred. We must forever conduct our struggle on the high plane of dignity and discipline. . . ."

Martin Luther King, Jr., from "I Have a Dream" (Speech given Aug. 28, 1963, Washington, D.C.)

Typing the cards you decide to use during delivery is useful, since it makes them easy to read on the platform. However, if your handwriting is clear and legible, typing is not necessary.

Even when not preparing for a specific speech, you may find it helpful to keep a general file of favorite topics for future use. You can build a storehouse of information to support these topics by gathering quotations, statistics, and other forms of evidence from books, magazines, newspapers, television, or conversation. A student interested in current events can usually spot information that may prove useful the next time a speech is needed.

Select a pattern of speech organization

The final step in organizing your thoughts consists of selecting a general organizational pattern for your speech. Though you are free to arrange your speech materials in any manner you choose, over the years certain methods of arrangement have proved effective for certain occasions and audiences. This section will outline organizational patterns most often used.

One common pattern for speeches is the **chronological pattern.** This arrangement proceeds from past to present to future; in other words, the speech develops in the same order that the events developed in time. One of the best known speeches using a chronological pattern is Abraham Lincoln's "Gettysburg Address." Notice how the first portion of the speech is about events that occurred in the past, the middle portion is about events of the present, and the last few sentences express Lincoln's hope for the future:

> Fourscore and seven years ago our fathers brought forth on this continent a new nation, conceived in liberty, and dedicated to the proposition that all men are created equal.
>
> Now we are engaged in a great civil war, testing whether that nation, or any nation so conceived and so dedicated, can long endure. We are met on a great battlefield of that war. We have come to dedicate a portion of that field as a final resting place for those who here gave their lives that that nation might live. It is altogether fitting and proper that we should do this.
>
> But, in a larger sense, we cannot dedicate—we cannot consecrate—we cannot hallow—this ground. The brave men, living and dead, who struggled here, have consecrated it far above our poor power to add or detract. The world will little note nor long remember what we say here, but it can never forget what they did here. It is for us, the living, rather, to be dedicated here to the unfinished work which they who fought here have thus far so nobly advanced. It is rather for us to be here dedicated to the great task remaining before us—that from these honored dead we take increased devotion to that cause for which they gave the last full measure of devotion; that we here highly resolve that these dead shall not have died in vain; that this nation, under God, shall have a new birth of freedom; and that government of the people, by the people, for the people, shall not perish from the earth.

Abraham Lincoln's famous "Gettysburg Address" followed the chronological pattern of speech organization. Lincoln began by mentioning events of the past, proceeded to an analysis of the present, and concluded movingly with a challenge to future generations.

Of course a speech in chronological order need not always contain all three time periods: past, present, and future. The essential feature of this pattern is that the ideas or events in the speech move forward according to a time sequence.

When the parts of a speech are tied together by space arrangements rather than by time sequence, the organizational pattern is called **spatial.** It is useful in speeches in which the speaker describes a place for the audience. If you wish to give a speech on "My Vacation Trip to Disney World," you might choose a spatial pattern of organization in which the four major sections of the speech would be about *Frontierland, Tomorrowland, Fantasyland,* and *Adventureland.* You would pinpoint the location of each "land" in the overall Disney World layout and describe the features of each section of the park.

A third organizational pattern, called **topical,** is also frequently used. This is a broadly defined pattern in which the subject is broken down into its natural parts. An example would be a speech about "The United States Congress" divided into Senate and House, then subdivided into Democrats and Republicans. A speech on "Modern Modes of Travel" might contain three divisions: monorail, wide-bodied jet, and space shuttle. A speech on "My High School Career" could be divided into sections about the naive freshman, the know-it-all sophomore, the know-nothing junior, and the mature senior. A speech topic may often be divided topically in several different ways. As long as the divisions represent natural parts of the whole topic, the organizational pattern is called topical.

The **problem-solution pattern** is still another pattern used in speeches. Here the speaker devotes roughly the first half of the speech to describing a problem that exists, or is about to occur, and the second half developing one or more solutions. Presidential addresses on national television generally follow this format. If, for instance, the problem is the energy crisis, the President might spend the first half of the time proving how serious the problem is and the second half calling on the American people to conserve energy in various ways. Sometimes speakers misuse this organizational pattern by spending nearly the entire time discussing the problem and then barely mentioning the solution in the final sentences. It is best to devote approximately equal time to the problem and the solution.

Another pattern used especially by salespersons is called **Monroe's Motivated Sequence.** This pattern was originally suggested by Alan H. Monroe for use in persuasive speeches. It consists of five separate steps:

> The Attention Step
> The Need Step
> The Satisfaction Step
> The Visualization Step
> The Action Step

The first step is an obvious one. Gaining the audience's attention is always the first task of any speaker. It is a step necessary in every type of speech situation. Once the listeners are paying close attention, the second step for the speaker is to show them that they have needs not being met by the way things are at present. The third step for a speaker using Monroe's Motivated Sequence is to present the opinion or solution that will satisfy these unmet needs of the audience. In the fourth, or visualization, step, the speaker must help the listeners actually see the change that will occur if they adopt his or her views. The final step involves telling the listeners what action they must take to bring about the improvement the speaker has promised. Salespersons, as well as speakers trying to persuade an audience, often use the five steps of Monroe's Motivated Sequence to organize their presentations.

Another organizational pattern, used mainly for after-dinner speeches or entertaining, is called the **string-of-beads pattern.** This pattern consists of a series of stories, jokes, or anecdotes strung out like beads on a string and tied loosely to some weak central theme. The jokes or anecdotes themselves usually carry the main impact in this kind of speech, and the topic or theme is less important. The famous comedian Will Rogers often used the string-of-beads pattern when addressing his audiences. Nowadays Joan Rivers often follows this pattern when doing her monologues. An advantage of this pattern for an after-dinner speaker is its flexibility. Should a speech run overtime, the speaker can easily dispense with several anecdotes without the audience's feeling the speech is unfinished. This pattern does not ordinarily work well, however, for other types of speaking.

Outlining the speech

A good outline is like a tree without its leaves. All the basics are present in the tree—the overall direction, the necessary support, the division into branches. Only springtime is needed to fill it out with leaves. Your speech outline also needs a basic purpose or direction, supporting materials, and appropriate subdivisions. When time for delivering the speech arrives, you will be ready to fill it out with the necessary words.

By the time you have chosen a topic, researched it, and selected your general organizational pattern, you may often find yourself already engaged in making a speech outline. These processes of speech preparation often occur simultaneously. Whatever order you follow for a particular speech, the beginning of your outline is critically important to the success of your speech.

Start with a purpose

If your speech outline is to have any order about it, you must know clearly what your purpose is in making this speech. The best way to assure that your purpose is clear in your own mind is to write it down in a single sentence (called the **purpose sentence**) at the top of your outline. This purpose sentence states exactly what you hope to accomplish by giving the speech: what you hope your listeners will know, think, believe, or do as a result of hearing your speech. Imagine you wish to tell your listeners something about airplanes. You could have a number of widely different purposes in mind for such a speech:

> The purpose of this speech is to inform the listeners about the safety of commercial airline travel.

> The purpose of this speech is to inform the audience regarding the history of commercial aviation.

> The purpose of this speech is to tell the listeners about my most memorable airplane ride.

> The purpose of this speech is to compare and contrast six different styles of commercial aircraft.

Notice that each of these purpose sentences states a specific idea about which a person might wish to speak. A purpose sentence such as "To inform my audience about airplanes" is useless. It is not a sentence. But more important, it shows that the speaker does not have a *specific purpose* in mind—only a general topic area. By the time you begin outlining you must have a specific purpose in mind. The purpose sentence serves to guide you as you complete the outline.

Sometimes speech students think a purpose sentence is a key sentence phrased for use at the beginning of the speech. Though you may often express the same general idea at the start of your speech, the

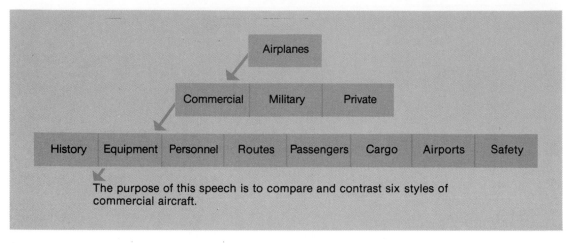

General topics must be narrowed down to a specific purpose statement before a speech outline can be written.

purpose sentence itself is a *written* sentence only meant to guide your outlining process. When a speaker states the purpose aloud to the listeners, it is usually reworded in a much more conversational style.

Application: Developing purpose sentences

Read John F. Kennedy's speech "Ich Bin Ein Berliner," in the Appendix of Speeches. Then hold a class discussion to decide what President Kennedy's purpose sentence would have been for the speech. You may wish to put various class members' suggested sentences on the board and compare them.

Develop main heads and subheads

The major divisions of a speech outline are referred to as **main heads.** Ordinarily the fewer main divisions you make of your topic the better. Most speeches should only have two or three main heads, though there are exceptions. A topic with eight or nine main divisions, however, becomes too difficult for the audience to follow or remember and hard for the speaker to fit into the time limit. If it seems impossible to avoid dividing your topic into a large number of main heads, you should consider narrowing the scope of your topic or combining several heads into one.

Suppose you are outlining a speech on "Capital Punishment." Your purpose sentence could read: "The purpose of this speech is to persuade the audience that capital punishment should be declared illegal in the United States." If this is the case, your main heads might be:

    I. Capital punishment does not deter crime.
   II. Innocent people are sometimes convicted.
  III. The "eye-for-an-eye" philosophy is cruel.

As shown in the example above, each main head should directly support the purpose sentence and be approximately equal in importance.

Subheads relate to main heads in the same manner that main heads relate to the purpose sentence. They subdivide the main head into parallel parts. Notice how the following subheads A, B, and C support the first main head in a speech titled "Skydiving":

  I. Skydiving is safer than most people imagine.
    A. Only highly qualified personnel may serve as trainers.
    B. Extensive training is mandatory before a "live" jump.
    C. Chutes must be checked and rechecked before a jump.

All subheads under a given main head must be of approximately equal importance.

While it is possible to further subdivide the ideas of the outline under sub-subheads, this is not ordinarily done. Most of the subdivisions below the subheads are reserved for supporting details rather than for concepts or ideas. Notice in the example on page 168 how the level below the subheads consists primarily of supporting details (examples, statistics, narratives, comparisons).

Use complete sentences for main heads and subheads

Main heads and subheads in speech outlines should be stated as complete sentences. Although experienced speakers sometimes use word or phrase outlines, full sentence outlines are best for beginning speakers. Writing down the basic ideas in complete thoughts forces you to think through the ideas and also helps set them in your memory. This does not mean, however, that the sentences should be long. Actually, you should strive to keep them as brief and simple as possible, as long as they are grammatically complete.

Once you get below the level of subheads, words or short phrases may be adequate for some supporting details. A simple reminder, such as "Narrative about dog" or "Statistics on smoking," will often be sufficient to remind you of the complete piece of evidence you wish to use.

Notice how the sentences and phrases in the sample outline on pages 168 and 169 show the relative importance of levels of ideas by the way they are arranged on the paper. As you can see this is done in two ways. First, different letter and number designations are attached to different levels of ideas. Main heads have Roman numerals (I, II, III), subheads have capital letters (A, B, C), supporting details have Arabic numerals (1, 2, 3). Second, the outline shows you at a glance which ideas are more important and which are less important through the use of indentation. Main heads start near the left margin, with the various subheads indented in step fashion to show that each level is less important than the one above. The whole outline becomes a picture of the way in which each idea relates to each of the other ideas.

A sample outline

Now that you have considered each part of a speech outline separately, let's put them all together in a complete sample outline. A speech contains three main sections: introduction, body, and conclusion. These represent the three basic sections of your outline. Suppose you have chosen "Playing Tennis" as your speech topic. Your completed outline might look something like this:

PURPOSE SENTENCE The purpose of this speech is to inform my listeners about the basic techniques used when playing tennis.

INTRODUCTION

I. Answer the following multiple choice question: According to last week's television special, what is the fastest growing participation sport in this country today? (a) polo, (b) soccer, (c) tennis.
    A. If you answered "tennis" you were correct.
    B. If you don't yet play, you're a member of a rapidly shrinking group.

II. My "vast" experience of three years on the courts only qualifies me to speak to you about the basics.

BODY

I. Holding the racket correctly is crucial.
    A. Grasp it as if you were shaking hands with the handle for forehand shots.
        1. Most tennis instructors recommend this technique.
        2. This grip will help keep your shots level.
    B. Use this same grip for serving, except for special types of serves.
    C. Turn your hand slightly counter-clockwise from this position for backhand shots if you are righthanded (clockwise if you are lefthanded).

1. You should be able to lay your thumb flat along the back edge of the grip.
2. Many players like to support their backhand grip with their other hand.

II. Stance is also very important.
    A. Most beginners face the net directly when hitting the ball.
      1. I did it this way for four months before someone "clued me in."
      2. My shots showed me something was wrong.
    B. The better method is to stand with your side facing the net for forehand and backhand shots.
    C. When serving, you should not face the net directly but on a 45-degree angle:
      1. Notice the pros on television.
      2. Television camera angles sometimes render this difficult to see clearly.
    D. Sometimes when running for a ball, it is impossible to get in the correct position in time.
      1. I find this especially difficult.
      2. Evonne Goolagong doesn't seem to find it so difficult, however.

III. The swing is extremely important.
    A. You should begin with a wide backswing.
      1. Using a short backswing will rob your shots of power.
      2. Chris Evert Lloyd's backswing
    B. Try to contact the ball when it is waist high and slightly in front of you.
      1. Keep ball level.
      2. Avoid "scoop" shots.
    C. Keep the racket level as you continue with your follow through.
      1. John McEnroe's form
      2. Tracy Austin's form
    D. Except for special shots and serving, the swing should be horizontal, not vertical.
      1. The overhead smash is a special shot for which you use a vertical swing.
      2. The lob is another special example.

CONCLUSION

I. You probably won't become an overnight Jimmy Connors or Chris Evert Lloyd with what I've told you today.

II. What you can do is start enjoying the fastest growing sport in America as a participant and not just as a spectator.

When the time for delivering your speech arrives, your teacher may allow you to take your outline to the podium. If not, you will want to transfer the major ideas from the outline to note cards. Using 3 × 5 cards makes it easy to insert the same-sized evidence cards you prepared earlier into the deck of outline cards at appropriate places. You then will have only a small stack of cards to handle on the platform. These will include the major ideas of your speech as well as statistics, examples, quotations, and other forms of evidence.

Rehearsing

Rehearsal is the crowning point of speech preparation. Without rehearsal a speaker is like a beginning golfer entering the U.S. Open after having read all the golfing manuals but never having actually played. Nothing can take the place of thorough practice, and if well done, rehearsal can put you in top form for a successful speech.

Recognize the importance of thorough rehearsal

One or two brief run-throughs does not constitute thorough rehearsal. Start preparing your speech well before the speaking date. Allow time for several rehearsal sessions. Rehearsal that is crammed into one evening is ineffective compared to three or four rehearsal sessions on successive nights.

In order to thoroughly prepare yourself for a speech, you must progress through several rehearsal stages, developing gradually from the stage in which ideas are simply listed on your outline or note cards to the point where they are firmly implanted in your mind. Since people's brains work subconsciously on such ideas between rehearsal sessions, you need time for well-spaced rehearsals if you are to have total command of the speech material.

Find a place for rehearsal

Since the actual speech will be spoken aloud, you need a place for rehearsal where you can speak aloud. Simply saying the speech to yourself, or whispering it quietly, only allows you to practice the mental parts of the speech—the ideas. But public speaking demands a number of physical skills as well. You need to rehearse proper breathing and voice projection, clear articulation, good timing, and correct synchronization of words with body movements. The ancient Greek orator Demosthenes is reported to have rehearsed his speeches on the seashore where he had to speak over the roar of the surf. It is also said that he practiced with pebbles in his mouth to make himself conscious of the need for clear articulation. Don't risk choking by using pebbles, but do consider practicing outdoors. It offers a very good place for speech rehearsal since you are forced to speak above the noise of wind and traffic. If you cannot find a suitable place outdoors, the next best place is a room similar in size and acoustics to the one in which you will give the actual speech.

Plant the pattern of ideas in your mind

Begin by reading your outline over silently to yourself several times, trying to set the **pattern of ideas** in your mind. Often the major segments of the outline will already be fixed in your mind since you are the one who wrote the outline. Your teacher may or may not allow you to use the outline during the actual speech, and even if you are permitted to use it you will want to depend on it as little as possible.

Once you feel you have the ideas firmly planted in your mind, stand up and say the ideas aloud to an imaginary audience. Speak the ideas in whatever words come to you as you are rehearsing. Try to go completely through, filling in details of the outline without starting over. Your speech will be halting at first with long pauses in places, but it will begin to smooth out with repeated practice. The second, third, and fourth times, do not try to say the ideas in exactly the same words you used the first time. Remember, what you are doing is planting the pattern of ideas in your mind, not a memorized pattern of words.

Have your outline or note cards handy (whichever you plan to use during the actual speech), and refer to them if you forget an idea. Run through the entire speech five to ten times or until you are certain you can go from beginning to end without hesitation.

It is said that in ancient Greece Demosthenes practiced his speeches by the sea. Competing with the crash of waves helped improve his voice power. Modern-day microphones have done away with a speaker's need to roar, but rehearsing a speech out loud is still the best way to prepare for its actual delivery.

Robert W. Pratt is a speech writer. One of his major jobs has been writing for Ella Grasso, during her years as governor of Connecticut. Carrying out this work, he has prepared speeches on a wide variety of subjects for Grasso to give at banquets or before special interest groups ranging from veterans' organizations to senior citizens' organizations.

When Pratt worked as a volunteer in the governor's campaign, he wrote hundreds of speeches, none of them longer than ten minutes. Brevity, he believes, is one of the keys to a good speech.

Speech preparation for Pratt is not so much a matter of writing as of thinking and organizing beforehand. When told that a speaker would like a speech written on a particular subject, Pratt resists the impulse to race off immediately to the library to do research. Instead he generally begins by asking himself some questions about the audience to which the speech is to be addressed.

"Basically I want to know 'Who will be in the audience?', 'What issues are members of the audience interested in?', and 'Why do members of the audience want to hear about these issues?'" he says. "If you apply these three questions to a speech before starting your preparation, you'll know more about how to write it. It's a very, very quick way of organizing yourself, of setting an objective."

Answers to the three questions, he says, will provide solutions to three of the most difficult problems that every speech writer faces: "What do I want to say?", "How do I want to say it?", and "Why do I want to say it?"

Only after Pratt identifies the audience does he proceed with his research. Then he studies in the library or gathers information from other sources available that deal with the particular subjects to be covered in that speech. "I don't do a lot of writing," he says. "I gather as much information as I need and then I use the tape recorder. By using the tape I can play the information back. I pick up bits and pieces and fit them together. Later, I begin to put words in certain areas which will have emotional impact."

If a speech requires many statistics, facts, or quotations Pratt sometimes isolates these in a series of "bullets," or short chunks of information, at the bottom of a page. From there, the speaker can use them as they are needed, working them extemporaneously into the body of the speech.

Ella Grasso is an excellent speaker and frequently provided ad lib humor for her speeches herself. Occasionally Pratt helped her out by writing some in. "Humor is the most effective vehicle for getting people's attention," he says. "Everybody enjoys laughing. It's probably the master stroke in giving a speech well."

Rehearse alone and with friends

Most people prefer to rehearse a speech alone, at least until they have it pretty well smoothed out. Once you feel you have the speech under control, however, rehearsing with a friend or two as your audience can improve your preparation. Having a dress rehearsal of this type can give you ideas about possible audience reactions you cannot obtain through a solo rehearsal: Are you speaking loudly enough to be heard in all parts of the room? Do the listeners react in an unexpected way to a particular portion of your speech? Do they understand all of the message? Do they agree or disagree with all or part of your message? Knowing the answers to these kinds of questions beforehand can allow you time to make changes and produce a better effect on your real audience.

Time rehearsals

Time yourself as you practice. Using a kitchen timer that shows how much time has been spent and how much is left can be helpful. The timing will probably not be too precise the first few run-throughs, but by your final practice session you should be able to conclude your speech within 30 seconds of your time limit.

For most brief classroom speeches your timing will need to be precise. Later, when you give 20- or 30-minute speeches to groups outside the classroom, timing will still be important, but two or three minutes leeway will probably be permissible. Any speaking you do on radio or television, of course, must be timed very closely and usually demands a manuscript for rehearsal rather than an outline.

Checklist for rehearsal

The day before a speech, run through the following rehearsal checklist to assure yourself you are ready:

1. Have I rehearsed in an appropriate place?

2. Have I practiced each time in a voice loud enough to be easily heard when I give the actual speech?

3. Have I practiced on my feet, rehearsing body movements as well as words?

4. Have I planted the pattern of ideas firmly in my mind?

5. Have I run through the entire speech at least five to ten times?

6. Have I obtained the reactions of one or two friends?

7. Have I practiced any adjustments my rehearsal audience suggested that I make in my presentation?

8. Have I timed my rehearsals?

Summary

Speech preparation is the process of building your speech in your mind. Planning it in every detail beforehand can help you avoid embarrassing mistakes during the actual delivery.

SELECTING YOUR TOPIC. Whether speaking in or outside of the classroom, both your speech preparation and the speech itself will be easier if your involvement with your topic is great. Choose a subject that fascinates you. Do not worry about whether other speakers have spoken on that topic or whether other students will choose the same topic for their speeches. Audience analysis is a key part of speech preparation. To increase your chances of success you must discover beforehand the background, attitudes, and interests of your audience. Exactly how you approach a chosen subject may depend greatly on these factors. Audience analysis for classroom speeches is relatively easy since the audience is readily available for questioning. Speeches to be made outside of class may call for formal or informal polls, surveys, and perhaps a questioning of the person who invited you to speak as well as acquaintances who plan to be in the audience. A speech topic must fit within the given time limit and also fit "the times" in which it is delivered. Many a speech has been unsuccessful because the speaker bored the audience by talking too long or by choosing an untimely subject. A topic that was fascinating to people last month may be a dead issue this month. Remember, too, that even though a topic is interesting and current, it may lose some of its charm if spoken about for too briefly or too long a time. In addition to considering matters of timing, you must also earn the right to speak to the audience by becoming somewhat of an expert about the subject.

ORGANIZING YOUR THOUGHTS. Organizing your thoughts for a speech begins with a survey of what you already know about the topic. For most significant speeches, however, this is just a starting point. Thorough research is necessary to discover support for the ideas you will express in your speech. Support takes a variety of forms, the most common of which are facts, statistics, testimony, narratives, examples, and comparisons. These may be found in books, magazines, and newspapers; in interviews with people expert in your topic area; by listening to television specials and news broadcasts; and through surveys and questionnaires. Record all your evidence and the sources from which you obtain it on 3 × 5 index cards for later reference. As you do research, form a pattern of organization for your speech. Typical patterns are chronological, spatial, topical, problem-solution, Monroe's Motivated Sequence, string-of-beads, and various combinations of these.

OUTLINING THE SPEECH. Your speech outline should always be guided by a purpose sentence. Write this sentence, which states precisely what you wish to accomplish in your speech, at the top of your outline. Every main head in the outline should be a major subdivision of that specific topic. Similarly, every subhead divides each main head into parallel subdivisions. All main and subheads should be written in complete sentences. Below the level of subheads, words or phrases may be sufficient for some supporting details.

REHEARSING. Rehearsal is the crowning part of speech preparation. All the earlier parts of the speech preparation process are brought together and perfected during rehearsal. Find a place for rehearsal that forces you to project your voice, and rehearse the speech aloud, on your feet. Use your outline to plant the pattern of ideas in your mind, then speak the ideas aloud to an imaginary audience. Force yourself to speak completely through the outline without starting over or backtracking. Concentrate on remembering the pattern of ideas rather than a pattern of words. Repeat your practice at least five to ten times to smooth out rough sections of the speech. Once you feel confident about solo rehearsal, hold a dress rehearsal with a friend or two to obtain a sample of audience reaction. You may want to make minor adjustments. Time your later rehearsal sessions to make sure you will meet the time expectations of your audience.

Vocabulary

audience analysis	example	string-of-beads pattern
timeliness	comparison	purpose sentence
support	chronological pattern	main heads
fact	spatial pattern	subheads
statistic	topical pattern	pattern of ideas
testimony	problem-solution pattern	
narrative	Monroe's Motivated Sequence	

Review questions

1. What five things should influence your choice of a speech topic?

2. What are three things you should know about your audience before you begin to prepare a speech?

3. How will the time available affect the topic you choose?

4. What are the two basic purposes of research in preparing a speech?

5. What are the six kinds of support most commonly used in preparing a speech?

6. What are some typical patterns of organization used in developing a speech?

7. What function does a purpose sentence serve for the speech writer?

8. What is the best place to rehearse a speech? The next best?

9. Why is it important to rehearse a speech several times with time between rehearsals?

10. Besides establishing your pattern of ideas, what physical skills should you work on during rehearsals?

Discussion questions

1. Choose a speech from the Appendix of Speeches following Chapter 16. Decide what the speaker's purpose sentence was. Compare your choice with those of your classmates.

2. Discuss the organization patterns and methods of proof used in the speech you chose in Question 1. Discuss what other patterns and methods of proof could have been used effectively by a different speaker who might have chosen to speak on the same topic.

3. Make a list of timeless topics—those that will always be of concern to people. Narrow at least two of the larger topics into ones that would be appropriate for twenty-minute speeches and for five-minute speeches.

4. Choose a topic and a time span from Question 3. Work with your classmates to determine the organizational pattern and methods of support to use in developing such a topic.

5. Discuss the reasons why it is better to plant a pattern of ideas in your mind than to try to memorize your speech.

At-home activities

Preparing a speech means building the speech in three stages: in your mind, on paper, and aloud. These at-home exercises will give you practice in each of these areas.

1. Select an audience in your community that you might someday be invited to address (a service organization such as a Rotary or Lions Club, a scout troop, a PTA or school board, or a religious group). Choose an imaginary topic that you could speak about to this group. Then go through all the necessary steps of audience analysis to fit your topic to that group. This may involve making phone calls, reading about the group's history and traditions, or writing letters. Write an essay showing how you would approach this particular group when speaking on the topic you chose.

2. Ask your teacher to supply you with a list of topics that are too broad for a stated time limit. Examples might be "World War II" (10 minutes) or "Hobbies" (5 minutes). For each topic on the list, write several purpose sentences that could reasonably be covered within the time limit.

3. Using one of the purpose statements you wrote for Exercise 2, find supporting proof that could be used in a speech with that purpose statement. Include at least one example of each type of proof: facts, statistics, testimony, narrative, example, and comparison. Be sure to include the source of each item of your support (see page 161).

4. Read a speech from a copy of *Vital Speeches of the Day* or a speech that has been reprinted in your local newspaper. Outline it as you read. Come prepared to read your outline to the class and tell what patterns of speech organization the speaker was following (chronological, spatial, topical, problem-solution, string-of-beads, or some combination).

5. Be prepared to tell in class which of the following source materials are in your school library:

> *Readers' Guide to Periodical Literature*
> *The New York Times Index*
> *U.S. News & World Report*
> *Familiar Quotations*
> *Sports Illustrated*

6. When rehearsing for an in-class speech, choose a friend from your speech class to listen to your speech. Then switch roles and you listen to his or her speech. Sharing speaking and listening roles in this way will give both of you a greater appreciation for the task of fitting your speech to your audience.

In-class activities

1. As a class, select a speech topic and word a purpose sentence. Then build a speech outline on the blackboard, with various class members suggesting main heads, subheads, and supporting evidence.

2. Your teacher will place a general topic on the board—for example, "Pets." Each member of the class should write one purpose sentence for a speech about that general topic. Then list all the purpose sentences on the board. Notice how many different purpose sentences can be generated on the same topic. Can you classify the speech each purpose sentence describes as informative, persuasive, or entertaining?

3. Play the following "Identifying the Support" game in class. Your teacher will read aloud selections of supporting materials from various speeches. Write down the type of support each selection represents (fact, statistic, testimony, narrative, example, or comparison). At the conclusion of the readings, your teacher will give you the correct answers. The student with the greatest number of correct answers will be declared winner.

4. During one round of in-class speeches, try to outline each speech as it is delivered. Several other students should also outline these speeches. At the conclusion of the round, each speaker should be given all the class outlines to compare with her or his own. This will provide each speaker with some feedback as to how clearly the speech was outlined and delivered.

Careers

MEMBERS OF THE CLERGY (MINISTERS, PRIESTS, RABBIS) are spiritual leaders of congregations and are responsible for the members' spiritual welfare. They counsel groups and individuals and speak to large groups of people. High school courses such as sociology, psychology, English, and speech are helpful. Graduation from a seminary is necessary, and in most cases a college degree is required. Advanced theological degrees may also be necessary.

COMMENTATORS analyze news and write commentary for broadcast. They base stories on personal knowledge and experience with the subject matter. Commentators select material most pertinent to the subject and organize it into proper form. High school subjects such as English, speech, sociology, economics, psychology, and typing are helpful. Junior colleges offer training. A bachelor's degree in English or journalism is usually preferred.

8

CHOOSING EFFECTIVE LANGUAGE

When you have completed this chapter, you should be able to

Explain why written language and spoken language are different.

List five characteristics of clear language.

Explain the difference between *concrete* and *abstract* words.

Explain the difference between *specific* and *general* terms.

List five ways in which you can create different levels of emphasis in your speeches.

Define and give an example of each of the following language devices: simile, metaphor, personification, hyperbole, understatement, and irony.

Recognize and avoid five problems in choosing language for your speeches.

Words are the garments with which speakers clothe their ideas. Choosing effective language for a speech is like choosing the right clothes for a special occasion. Words can be courageous or timid, commanding or pleading, persuasive or entertaining, hurtful or kind. Their effect on the listeners can be enormous or microscopic, depending on how well the words clothe the ideas. Once when referring to Winston Churchill's speeches to the English people during World War II, John F. Kennedy stated: "He mobilized the English language and sent it into battle." Churchill's words may well have done more for the Allied cause than fifty planes or a dozen ships.

Speeches are made of ideas, but unless those ideas are expressed in carefully selected language, they may be overlooked. In this chapter you will find a number of suggestions that can help you choose the kind of language that will best express your ideas to audiences.

You will explore five qualities of spoken language that make it different from written language. Being aware of these differences will help you state your message clearly. Then the chapter will show you ways to emphasize important points in your speech. Speakers must know how to highlight important ideas so listeners will remember them. Finally, you will find a list of certain problems to avoid. The use of effective language involves four points—clarity, emphasis, interest, and caution. By following the suggestions in this chapter, you should find it easier to get your message across to your audience.

Differences between written language and spoken language

The first step in choosing effective language for public speaking is to realize that language that is appropriate for writing is not always appropriate for speaking. In part, this is because the tasks of reading and listening are so different. Readers can set their own pace, stopping and reviewing anything that is hard to understand. Listeners, on the other hand, must try to keep up with the speaker. If they miss an idea, it is often gone for good. Effective language for speaking must therefore be immediately clear to the listener.

In conversation, most people recognize this need to make spoken language immediately clear. In general, spoken language possesses five specific qualities that make it very different from written language:

Spoken language makes greater use of short and simple words.

Spoken language tends to be more concrete, less abstract.

Spoken language is usually specific.

Spoken language makes greater use of restatement.

Spoken language generally includes fewer unnecessary words.

The receiver of sign language used by the deaf must keep pace with the signer if the ideas expressed are to be understood. People listening to spoken language must also keep pace with the speaker to understand the message.

The next part of this chapter will focus on these five qualities of spoken language. Although they are a natural part of spoken language, they are too often forgotten when it comes to giving public speeches.

Making spoken language clear

A listener runs a much greater risk of missing ideas that are poorly stated than a reader does. If an audience fails to understand even a small part of a speaker's language, that part of the message will be lost to them. The world's great speeches have always been characterized by the clarity of their language. Language for public speaking must be simple, brief, and clear enough that listeners can easily understand it.

Keep wording short and simple

Spoken sentences need to be shorter and simpler than written ones. A great number of long sentences make a speech difficult for listeners to follow. They also make it harder for an audience to pay attention for any length of time. Spoken language calls for more short, simple sentences.

Similarly, spoken language calls for simple words. The use of simple words has long been considered a sign of clear language. Simple words are not always short words, though many are short. Rather, they are those that are among the ordinary vocabulary of your particular audience on any given occasion.

When speaking to your peers, people in your own age group with a similar level of education, your selection of language is relatively easy.

Simply choose words you would typically use in conversation. When speaking to a much younger group or a less educated audience adjust your language level downward appropriately. Watch the listeners' feedback carefully for signs of lack of understanding.

If you address a special group with a vocabulary of its own—a sports group, a religious group—it is permissible to use the special words of that group as long as the entire audience will understand the language used. The same is true when addressing groups composed of audience members from a specific region or cultural group. As long as you are a member of that group and nearly all your listeners understand the special regional or cultural terms, you should feel free to use them. Actually, you compliment such an audience by using language that is special to you and them. Do not, however, try to use the regional or cultural language of a special group if you are not a member of the group, or if there are many non-members in your audience.

Use concrete language

Language for public speaking must not only be simple, it must also be concrete. **Concrete words** and phrases are the kind that let the listener "see" the idea as well as understand it. A word such as *girl* is concrete since it stands for something that can be perceived by the senses. A word such as *beautiful* is **abstract** (the opposite of concrete), since you cannot see, touch, feel, smell, or taste *beautiful*. Compare the two following sentences and decide which one gives you a clearer mental picture of the ideas expressed.

Abstract: John seemed nervous, yet determined.

Concrete: John was shaking, but his jaw was tightly set.

The two sentences express essentially the same ideas, but the second sentence allows you to "see" those ideas. You can't see *nervous*.

Notice how Debra Morris, a high school student, makes excellent use of concrete language in her award-winning speech "Those Happy Days."

> I saw a commercial the other day in which an inconspicuous girl with glasses and an armful of books walks right through a huddle of football players—and the quarterback doesn't even make a play. I felt a little sorry for the girl, although there was certainly no need to. After she takes off her glasses, lets down her hair, and shows up in a pleated skirt and a sweater with a megaphone on the front, the quarterback starts fumbling . . . but finally makes the right pass. The commercial ends with the two sitting on the bleachers, enjoying the soft drink that "adds life to everything that makes her living nice." High school students know that it isn't the soft drink . . . it's the sweater!

Application: Choosing concrete words

Decide which words in the following list are concrete and which are abstract. Can some words be either abstract or concrete? Discuss in class.

pines	wild
justice	decision
honor	circus
automobile	house
person	home
poodle	picture
gracious	art

Use specific words

A public speaker also needs to use specific words. **Specific words** are words that refer to a limited class of objects. For example, the word "hobo" is a more specific word than "traveler" since there are many travelers in the world who are not hobos. The class "traveler" is larger than the class "hobo" since hobos are just one form of traveler. A given word cannot be labeled general or specific. It will merely be more general or more specific than some other word. We just said that "hobo" is more specific than "traveler." But "traveler" is more specific than "person," which includes the class "traveler." Notice the progression from general to specific in this list:

> galaxies
> solar systems
> planets
> Mars

The trick when preparing a speech is to pick the most specific word you can find to tell your audience just what you have in mind.

Application: Being specific

Name more specific words that are included in each of these general groups:

stars	human race
war	dancing
builders	theater
precipitation	animals

When you aren't sure which word to use, consult a dictionary. When you prepare a speech, pick the most specific word you can find to tell your audience just what you have in mind.

Restate main ideas

Restatement is a natural speaking device. It assures that the listener does not miss or forget a part of your message. Writers have less need to restate, since the reader can carry out any necessary review by simply rereading a phrase or sentence. Since listeners do not have this opportunity, public speakers typically restate their main ideas a good deal, using somewhat different terms each time to make sure everyone gets the idea.

Notice how Frank Knox, Secretary of the Navy under President Franklin D. Roosevelt from 1940 to 1944, used restatement in a speech in order to make clear his belief that a nation must be willing to fight to preserve liberty and peace:

> The only peace in which the world can put any confidence, for at least one hundred years to come, is the kind of peace that can be enforced by the peace-loving nations of the world. . . .
>
> You cannot preserve liberties such as we enjoy, save by willingness to fight for them if need be.
>
> The currency with which you pay for peace is made up of manly courage, fearless virility, readiness to serve justice and honor at any cost, and a mind and a heart attuned to sacrifice.
>
> We must also remember that it is only the strong who can promote and preserve a righteous peace. . . .
>
> A powerful national defense, especially on the high seas, is a prerequisite of a peace-promoting, justice-loving America. . . .

Remove unnecessary words

In life, being economical means not wasting money or other resources. In public speaking, being economical means not wasting words. Part of clear speaking consists of using only as many words as necessary to get the message across. Once you have accomplished that—stop! Did you know that on the same day that Abraham Lincoln delivered the Gettysburg Address, another speaker, Edward Everett, gave a speech that lasted nearly two hours? Lincoln's speech, only ten sentences in length, took about two minutes to deliver. Probably you have never heard of Edward Everett or his speech, but Lincoln's Gettysburg Address is known around the world. Part of the reason for the lasting effect of Lincoln's speech was undoubtedly his economy of language. Afterwards, Everett wrote Lincoln a letter in which he declared that he wished he could have done as much justice to the occasion with his two-hour speech as Lincoln did with his two-minute one.

One of the best ways of achieving **economy of language** is by chopping needless words from individual sentences. The speaker who says: "We must take into consideration the fact that this property comes under certain zoning restrictions" could save words (and energy) by shortening the wording: "We must consider certain zoning restrictions on this property." Let's look at several other examples:

Uneconomical: Regarding the situation in the flooded area, we must make a concerted effort to aid the local residents.

Economical: We must try to aid the residents in the flooded area.

Uneconomical: A period of sunny weather set in and remained for a whole week.

Economical: We had sunshine for a whole week.

In each of these examples many of the words in the uneconomical version are not needed. They do not add anything to the meaning of the sentence. They are unnecessary and should be left out.

✔ **Checklist for using clear language**

□ 1. Am I planning to use a number of short and simple sentences?

□ 2. Have I chosen words that my audience will understand?

□ 3. Have I tried to express my ideas in concrete language?

□ 4. Am I planning to use specific terms in my speech?

□ 5. Have I considered restating my main ideas so the audience won't miss them?

□ 6. Have I removed any unnecessary words from my speech?

Creating levels of emphasis

So far we have considered the importance of using clear language when speaking in public. But language should do much more for a speech than make it clear. Listeners will be more likely to remember your message if you choose language that will emphasize important points of your speech.

Several language devices can be used to create levels of emphasis. Their purpose is to highlight certain parts of your speech and thereby downplay the other parts where they are not used. Among the most common of the devices used to create emphasis are contrast, rhetorical questions, repetition, and climax. Before you consider these devices, however, consider the most basic way of creating different levels of emphasis—the use of variety.

Variety sets the stage

Without variety in words and types of sentences, a speech quickly forms a repetitious language pattern. Any kind of regularly recurring pattern quickly distracts an audience, causing them to pay less attention to the speaker's message. But when there is variety in word usage and sentence length, certain points will stand out; others will recede into the background. Thus language variety can be of great use in creating levels of emphasis.

Varying one's vocabulary, sentence length, and sentence structure can also help maintain listener interest. It can enliven your speech. Speeches which repeatedly use the same words to refer to a given idea soon become monotonous. Speakers who use all short, simple sentences begin to sound like machine-guns clattering. Those who use just long sentences quickly lose the attention and interest of their listeners. A basic key to successful speaking is variety.

By using variety in vocabulary, sentence length, and sentence structure, a speaker can spark up a speech and avoid losing the interest of the audience.

Contrast sticks in the listener's mind

The language device called contrast has long been used to make important statements stick in listeners' minds. The following examples come from three speeches by the same person. Do you know who spoke them?

"Let us never negotiate out of fear. But let us never fear to negotiate."

"In the election of 1860 the great issue was whether this country would remain half slave and half free; in the election of 1960 ... the great issue is whether the *world* will remain half slave and half free."

"Ask not what your country can do for you—ask what you can do for your country."

Each of these uses of contrast by President John F. Kennedy became widely repeated statements. **Contrast,** a language device Kennedy used frequently, begins with two balanced phrases, clauses, or sentences. The words containing the ideas the speaker wishes to emphasize are the only words changed or rearranged in the second part of the statement. Notice how, in the second example above, Kennedy changed only three things: the date *1860* to the date *1960*, the word *country* to *world*, and the verb *would* to *will*. Thus he highlighted what he considered one of the most important issues in the 1960 election year. Had he stated only "The great issue in 1960 is whether the world will remain half slave and half free," his statement would not have carried as much emphasis, nor been remembered as long. Contrast is a language device that seems to stick in the listener's mind. The better your audiences remember some of your key statements, the greater the overall impact your speech is likely to have.

Contrast is not an easy device to create. Ordinarily, speakers do not spout forth well-balanced statements of contrast on the spur of the moment. Such statements usually grow from extended thought and careful planning. Therefore, contrast is usually found when a speaker has had ample time to plan precise language. If you plan to use contrast, you will need to think it out before the speech and then use manuscript or note cards showing the statements of contrast you wish to make. The time spent is not likely to be wasted. Well-planned use of contrast can prove effective in most speeches.

Contrast, however, is a device that can be easily overused. Since it is generally saved to emphasize one of the major points in a speech, overusing it can make several points sound most important. The audience may become confused and forget all of them. One or perhaps two well-placed statements of contrast are ample, even in a lengthy speech.

Rhetorical questions demand attention

Ideas in a speech can also be emphasized by putting them in the form of rhetorical questions. **Rhetorical questions** are questions that are not meant to be answered out loud. It is difficult, however, for most people to ignore a question put to them. Thus, they will generally try to answer it in their minds. A speaker can sometimes capitalize on this fact by occasionally asking rhetorical questions of the audience. Notice how Dr. Martin Luther King, Jr., used rhetorical questions in his speech "I've Been to the Mountaintop," delivered in Memphis, Tennessee, just before his assassination. He was urging the members of the clergy who were his listeners to join with striking sanitation workers:

> That's the question before you tonight. Not, "If I stop to help the sanitation workers, what will happen to all of the hours that I usually spend in my office every day and every week as a pastor?" The question is not, "If I stop to help this man in need, what will happen to me?" "If I do not stop to help the sanitation workers, what will happen to them?" That's the question.

Dr. King did not expect out-loud responses from his listeners to these questions. Rhetorical questions demand an answer in the mind of each individual listener. They are difficult to ignore.

Repetition highlights important points

Repetition is another effective device for highlighting important points. Listening to TV commercials, you might wonder whether modern television advertising ever makes use of any device other than repetition. Public speakers also make great use of repetition. Sometimes their basic purpose in using it is to persuade, to create an emotional reaction, or to aid listener recall. In many cases, however, the basic purpose is to emphasize important points. When used in this way its effect is like holding up a large sign stating: "Don't miss this! It's one of the most important points of my speech."

Repetition is different from restatement. Restatement (stating the same idea several times using different words) aids listener recall, but ordinarily does not drive a point home to the same extent that repetition does. **Repetition** (stating the same idea several times using the same words) is much more effective in signaling the important point for the audience.

Attending a women's rights convention in 1851, Sojourner Truth, a freed slave, used the repetition of a rhetorical question for emphasis while speaking for women's rights and against slavery:

That man over there says women need to be helped into carriages and lifted over ditches.... Look at my arm. I have ploughed and planted and gathered into barns, and no man could head me—and ain't I a woman? I would work as much and eat as much as a man—when I could get it—and ain't I a woman? I have borne thirteen children, and seen most of them sold into slavery, and when I cried out with my mother's grief none but Jesus hear me—and ain't I a woman?

A variation of repetition consists of beginning or ending sentences with the same single word or short phrase. This device, called **parallelism,** was used by President Franklin D. Roosevelt in a fighting speech during World War II:

From Berlin, Rome, and Tokyo we have been described as a nation of weaklings—"playboys"—who would hire British soldiers, or Russian soldiers, or Chinese soldiers to do our fighting for us.
Let them repeat that now!
Let them tell that to General MacArthur and his men.
Let them tell that to the sailors who today are hitting hard in the far waters of the Pacific.
Let them tell that to the boys in the Flying Fortresses.
Let them tell that to the marines!

But repetition should be used sparingly. It serves as a highly effective means of achieving emphasis only as long as it is not overused.

Climax emphasizes the last item in a series

When a speaker lists three or four items in a series, the item spoken of last carries the greatest emphasis. Suppose you wished, for example, to emphasize how seriously wrong you consider someone's behavior to be. The expected order would look like this: "His behavior is wrong, it is immoral, it is actually criminal." This is called **climax ordering**—moving from less significant to more significant, and ending the series with whichever item is most important. If, in the example above, a speaker were to arrange the items in any other order, the audience would most likely become confused. Since audiences usually expect to hear climax ordering whenever items spoken in a series differ in importance, speakers can emphasize the last item strongly by using it. General Douglas MacArthur in a speech to the cadets at West Point used climax ordering twice in succeeding paragraphs to describe the "American man-at-arms." These examples appear here in italics:

But when I think *of his patience under adversity, of his courage under fire, and of his modesty in victory,* I am filled with an emotion of admiration I cannot put into words. He belongs to history as furnishing one of the greatest examples of successful patriotism. He belongs to posterity as the instructor of future generations in the principles of liberty and freedom. He belongs to the present—to us—by his virtues and by his achievements.

In 20 campaigns, on a 100 battlefields, around a 1,000 campfires, I have witnessed that enduring fortitude, that patriotic self-abnegation, and that invincible determination which has carved his statue in the hearts of his people.

As is the case with most language devices used for creating levels of emphasis, climax must be used sparingly. Well-placed usage of such devices, however, can make the difference between a twenty-cent speech and a twenty-dollar one.

Using figures of speech

Language in a speech must sometimes be rich and imaginative; other times plain and straightforward. The plainer parts help emphasize the richer ones. Few speakers can produce clever, imaginative language constantly, and even if they could the listeners would soon sicken of it. It would be much like eating steak every day, without the faintest hope of some ordinary hamburger now and then. The careful use of imaginative language can, however, add a great deal to your speeches. Knowing ways of creating rich language can help you make your meanings clear to your listeners.

In this section we'll look at several methods of making speech more imaginative, methods that are called figures of speech. **Figures of speech** are phrases and sentences that make a point by stating something that is not literally or exactly true. They rely on such things as comparison, contrast, and exaggeration to make meanings clear.

Similes and metaphors

Two special forms of comparison, the simile and the metaphor, are frequently used to make ideas memorable for the listeners. A **simile** is a brief comparison of two basically unlike things, using the word *like* or *as.* When Adlai Stevenson lost the presidential election in 1956, he used a simile to express his feelings: "I feel like a little boy who has just stubbed his toe. I'm too big to cry, but it hurts too much to laugh." Very likely, few people would have remembered Stevenson's remark had he simply said, "Well, I'm too old to cry, but I certainly don't feel like laughing either."

A **metaphor** is a more direct comparison of two things than a simile, because it omits the word *like* or *as.* When Muhammad Ali said "I am king!" he was using a metaphor to express his feeling that he had some of the same kind of power and authority that a king would have. If Ali had said, "I feel like a king," it would have been a simile.

"I am king!" Muhammad Ali made use of a metaphor to express his feeling of superiority over other boxers.

Similes and metaphors usually are only one sentence in length. The often heard retort of a jokester whose joke has fallen flat is a one-sentence simile: "Well, that went over like a lead balloon!" At other times a simile or metaphor may consist of several sentences. Hubert Farbes won a national high school speech contest with a speech containing this combination of metaphor-simile:

> For there is a parasite in the minds of men today. It grows like a leech, taking its morbid existence from the strength of its host, warping his mind and character.

Whenever a comparison grows beyond two or three sentences, however, it is ordinarily labelled an extended comparison, or an **analogy.** Similes and metaphors gain part of their impact from being short and pithy.

Similes and metaphors may be used quite frequently in a speech. Using them freely generally does no harm, as long as the speaker does not flood the listener with such devices. Keep in mind that a substantial portion of your speech must consist of vanilla ice cream, so that the hot fudge portion may be appreciated.

Personification

Personification is a figure of speech by which a speaker gives human qualities to inanimate objects, ideas, or non-human creatures. An effective use of personification was contained in a speech by President Franklin D. Roosevelt. When his political enemies accused him of wasting taxpayers' money by sending a naval destroyer to pick up his dog Fala on an Aleutian island, Roosevelt gave human emotions to the dog in his reply. Notice how he gradually builds up to the personification:

> These Republican leaders have not been content with attacks on me, or my wife, or on my sons. No, not content with that, they now include my little dog, Fala. Well, of course, I don't resent attacks, and my family doesn't resent attacks, but Fala *does* resent them. You know, Fala is Scotch, and being a Scottie, as soon as he learned that the Republican fiction writers in Congress and out had concocted a story that I had left him behind on the Aleutian Islands and had sent a destroyer back to find him—at a cost to the taxpayers of two or three, or eight or twenty million dollars—his Scotch soul was furious. He has not been the same dog since. I am accustomed to hearing malicious falsehoods about myself—such as that old, worm-eaten chestnut that I have represented myself as indispensable. But I think I have a right to resent, to object to libelous statements about my dog.

By focusing attention on the dog's feelings, Roosevelt was able to express some of his own feelings about the charges that had been made, but in a humorous way.

Personification may also be used to set a general mood. Consider the effect of an opening narrative that begins with these words: "It was

In a humorous reply to critics, Franklin D. Roosevelt expressed his own feelings by using personification to attribute human emotions to his dog Fala.

a dark and gloomy winter's day, with stubborn clouds threatening us every moment...." You might expect suspense, mystery, intrigue, or devilment of some sort to follow. Part of the mood is created by the words "stubborn" and "threatening." Since these are qualities of human beings, and not of clouds, attributing them to clouds gives greater liveliness to a speech.

Hyperbole

Hyperbole is perhaps the most commonly used figure of speech in everyday conversation. It consists of intentionally exaggerating in order to emphasize a point. Because most of us engage in hyperbole so regularly, much of our everyday use of it has become subconscious. Ordinarily we are exaggerating subconsciously when using common expressions such as:

She's the greatest!

I'm completely exhausted.

I'm dead!

I jogged a thousand miles today.

Such statements are rarely true, of course, but the listener understands that the exaggeration is only intended to underscore the speaker's feelings.

In public speaking, hyperbole must be used sparingly, since in emphasizing too many points, a speaker winds up emphasizing none. Ralph Zimmerman, a student speaker, used hyperbole to describe the terrible pain he had experienced as a hemophiliac:

> But what I remember most of all is the pain. Medical authorities agree that a hemophilic joint hemorrhage is one of the most excruciating pains known to mankind. To concentrate a large amount of blood into a small compact area causes a pressure that words can never hope to describe. And how well I remember the endless, pounding, squeezing pain. When you seemingly drown in your own perspiration, when your teeth ache from incessant clenching, when your tongue floats in your mouth and bombs explode back of your eyeballs; when darkness and light fuse into one hue of gray; when day becomes night and night becomes day—time stands still—and all that matters is that ugly pain. The scars of pain are not easily erased.

Of course, bombs do not actually explode back of the eyeballs, and time does not really stand still, but these hyperboles strongly emphasize the excruciating nature of the pain.

Understatement

Understatement is the opposite of hyperbole. Its purpose is to highlight something by playing down its importance or making what is significant sound insignificant. If a multi-millionaire is asked about the extent of her wealth, she might use understatement in her reply: "Let's just say I'm not terribly worried about where my next meal is coming from."

Irony

Irony is a figure of speech in which the literal meaning expressed by a person's words is the opposite of the meaning intended. If you wished to show your dislike and lack of respect for another person, you might exclaim "Oh, she's a fine person!" with a sarcastic tone in your voice that indicates you mean to convey the opposite of *fine*. Robert G. Ingersoll was a nineteenth-century speaker who used irony effectively in many of his speeches. Here is an excerpt from one of his speeches in which he wished to emphasize the inequity of male and female roles in the households of his day:

> ... Think of the intellectual strain that must have been upon that man, and when he gets home everybody else in the house must look out for his comfort. A woman who has only taken care of five or six children, and one or two of them sick, has been nursing them and singing to them, and trying to make one yard of cloth do the work of two, she, of course, is fresh and fine and ready to wait upon this gentleman—the head of the family—the boss!

Avoiding common problems

Language can be a public speaker's greatest asset. Unfortunately, it sometimes traps a speaker into saying what is not meant or meaning what is not said. Following are several problems encountered in choosing effective language. A couple of these should always be avoided. Others may prove helpful or harmful, depending on how you use them.

Watch out for unintentional connotations

All words have a standard, dictionary meaning. This is a generally accepted, objective meaning known as a word's denotation. Words may also have connotations—special meanings for different people or different groups of people. If, for instance, a speaker were to use the word *gold*, the denotation would be "a heavy, yellow metal." The connotation,

Next time you see a candy bar commercial on television or read a glossy magazine advertisement for typewriters, take a closer look. It may be that Vanessa Levin had something to do with writing them.

Vanessa Levin is an advertising copywriter with one of the leading international advertising agencies. She could be called a "wordsmith." Her job is to find words to describe products. She just might say how "indescribably delicious" a particular candy bar tastes or explain exactly how the latest model typewriter works.

The words she chooses for her advertisements are important. If she doesn't write clearly enough or if her phrases are boring, no one will buy the product. Like a speechwriter, she uses words to convey ideas, convincingly and precisely. She hopes her audience will not only understand what she is saying but might be convinced to go a step farther and buy the product.

Levin has three rules of thumb in mind when she writes an advertisement. The first is to keep her words and sentences simple, but innovative. "I try to use words and phrases people recognize, also word combinations that have a chance of sneaking into the English language, or ones that people can easily associate with the product," she said.

Second, Vanessa Levin uses colorful word images which will convey a real picture to the minds of her audience. "When you are doing an advertisement for travel, you sometimes talk about 'water so clear you can see right down to the coral,' or 'beaches that go on forever,'" she said. "A really good copywriter can write food advertisements that make your mouth water.

Levin's third rule is economy of language. She writes advertisements for television, radio, and publications, but in all three mediums the length of an ad or commercial is extremely brief. "I can use up to 60 words for a 30-second television commercial," she said. "Magazine ads are brief because some advertisers believe that consumers won't bother to read a large mass of type," she said.

Other variables Vanessa Levin must contend with to produce good copy are the audience toward which the product is directed, and the television, radio, and publication mediums themselves. When writing, she tries to imagine the kind of people to whom the product is most likely to appeal and write directly to them. Words and phrases which will appeal to someone in, say, a candy bar advertisement, are different from those which will catch the attention of someone being persuaded to buy a different type of product.

When she writes commercials for television or radio, Vanessa Levin's style turns conversational, since her audience will be listening to the words. Copy for magazine advertisements is written more formally. "We always have to be careful with grammar, but print is even more demanding because it's there forever."

Vanessa Levin may not be writing speeches, but many of the rules governing a "good speech" and a "good advertisement" are, by her own admission, the same.

for some audience members, might include ideas of wealth or beauty. Speakers must be aware of the possible connotations the words they use are likely to carry for the bulk of their audiences. If the connotations would be likely to cause strong negative reactions, it is usually wiser to choose other language.

Use euphemisms carefully

Euphemisms are gentle or softened expressions for harsh or unpleasant realities. People often say "He passed on" for "He died," or "She enjoys tilting the bottle" for "She is an alcoholic." Euphemisms are often helpful, since they allow a speaker to be tactful and avoid insulting an audience. Avoid using them so frequently that your message becomes clouded with soft terms, however. A speaker should not become as euphemistic as the woman whose friend told her "Hilda, I believe you could find something positive to say about the devil himself!" Hilda quickly replied "Well, you must admit he's a hard worker."

Avoid clichés

Clichés are expressions that at one time expressed a truth or idea clearly and briefly, but have become so overused as to be almost meaningless. Examples of clichés are "A stitch in time saves nine," "Where there's smoke there's fire," "Green with envy," and "As pretty as a picture." The use of clichés generally bores an audience. It also causes listeners to lose a certain degree of respect for the speaker, since using clichés makes it appear that the speaker lacks originality.

Don't stereotype

Stereotyping is assigning qualities to people or objects because they are part of a general group, without considering their individual differences. Stereotypes may be based on a person's appearance, type of employment, nationality, religion, race, or age. "All bus drivers are rude" and "Young people are lazy" are examples of stereotyping. Using words or phrases which stereotype greatly harms a speaker's image. They should always be avoided.

Use slang sparingly

Slang consists of contemporary words and phrases that come in and go out of style very rapidly. Because the majority of expressions have a short life, using them in your speeches will confuse listeners who have never had a chance to become familiar with them. Some years ago *cool* and *groovy* were "in" words. Today the person who uses them sounds neither "cool" nor "groovy." You should also remember that many slang expressions, current among young people, never get picked up by older people at all.

Be very thrifty in your use of slang even when talking to your classmates. You may wish to use it once in a while to produce an informal atmosphere, for novelty or humor, but beware of using it often in public speaking. Look at the high school student's speech on page 000. Notice how little slang the speaker used in the speech she gave as a finalist in a national contest. Slang dates your speech, and if overused shows a limited vocabulary.

Summary

Words are the garments with which speakers clothe their ideas. Wise speakers choose their language very carefully in order to display their ideas effectively.

DIFFERENCES BETWEEN WRITTEN LANGUAGE AND SPOKEN LANGUAGE. Realizing that language used in writing is different from language spoken aloud can be helpful. Spoken language contains more short, simple sentences than does written language. It also uses simpler words, is more concrete and specific, has more restatement, and contains fewer unnecessary words. These qualities of spoken language help listeners understand the messages they receive.

MAKING SPOKEN LANGUAGE CLEAR. Clarity ranks as the most important quality of spoken language. Without clear language a speech is doomed to certain failure. Clarity means using reasonably short sentences and simple words—words immediately understandable to the audience being addressed. It also means using concrete and specific language—language that paints pictures in the listeners' imaginations. It calls for the restatement of the main ideas in a speech so that the speaker can be sure the listeners have not missed anything important. Finally, it requires the removal of unnecessary words. Language that is simple and direct makes the best impact on an audience.

CREATING LEVELS OF EMPHASIS. Language in a public speech may also be used to emphasize certain points more than others—to create levels of emphasis. Variety of vocabulary, sentence length, and sentence structure is one method of achieving this. Other devices are contrast—the use of balanced phrases; rhetorical questions—questions that need no answer; repetition—repeating the same words, phrases, or sentences; and climax—saving the most important item in a series until last.

USING OF FIGURES OF SPEECH. Figures of speech can also help you get your meaning across to your listeners. They make use of such things as comparison, contrast, and exaggeration to highlight ideas and make them memorable. Similes and metaphors compare two essentially unlike things. Personification is a way of giving human qualities to nonhuman things. Hyperbole emphasizes through intentional exaggeration. Its opposite, understatement, highlights a matter by downplaying its importance. Irony makes the literal meaning of the spoken word the opposite of the intended meaning.

AVOIDING COMMON PROBLEMS. Language problems to be avoided, or approached cautiously, include unintentional connotations, euphemisms, clichés, stereotypes, and slang. While some of these traps should always be avoided, others can sometimes be helpful, if used sparingly.

Vocabulary

concrete words	simile
abstract words	metaphor
specific words	analogy
restatement	personification
economy of language	hyperbole
contrast	understatement
rhetorical questions	Irony
repetition	euphemism
parallelism	clichés
climax ordering	stereotyping
figures of speech	slang

Review questions

1. What are five ways in which spoken language differs from written language?

2. What are the four characteristics of clear language?

3. Why is it important to restate main ideas when speaking?

4. What is the best way to achieve economy of language?

5. What three aspects of language should you vary in order to keep your speech lively?

6. In your own words, define or give an example of each of these devices for creating levels of emphasis: contrast, rhetorical question, repetition, parallelism, climax ordering.

7. What is the name of each figure of speech below?
    - (a) "I feel like a little boy who has just stubbed his toe."
    - (b) "He is a prince."
    - (c) "The stars cry for justice."
    - (d) "Your tongue floats in your mouth and bombs explode back of your eyeballs."

8. Define *euphemism* and give an example of a euphemism.

9. What are five problems to avoid in using spoken language?

10. How and when can slang be used effectively in a speech?

Discussion questions

1. What are some ways in which knowing your audience can affect the way you use language in public speaking?

2. Suppose that you were speaking before both an audience of your classmates and a panel of adult judges in a speech contest. How would this "double audience" affect your choice of language?

3. Why is it risky to "ad lib" parallelism or an analogy? What would be a better way to incorporate such devices into your speech?

4. Discuss the language devices used in advertisements that you find particularly effective. Tell how they create an image of the product.

5. Develop a TV commercial for one of the products listed below. Include such language devices as contrast, repetition, climax, simile, and understatement. Try to use at least one phrase that the audience will identify with the product.

| a beverage | a breakfast cereal |
| a motor bike | a health club |

At-home activities

1. Write a speech introduction in abstract language; use big words and long sentences. Then rewrite the same introduction in concrete language; use simple words and shorter sentences. Read both aloud to the class. Ask why the second is more effective.

2. Write an introduction and conclusion for your next in-class speech. When you finish, go over the words carefully again. See if there are places where you can use more concrete words, eliminate needless words, or just use simpler, clearer words. Insert language devices for emphasis if you have not already done so.

3. Read the student speech by Beth Simmons on page 409. How many of the following devices can you discover in her speech?

contrast	personification
repetition	rhetorical question
simile	hyperbole
metaphor	understatement
irony	climax

Do you think she used enough of these devices in her speech? Did she overuse them?

4. Read the following excerpt from an essay written during the mid-nineteenth century. Note the long sentences and stilted phrasing. Rewrite this excerpt in spoken-language style so that it applies to both men and women. Use only five or six fairly brief sentences, while retaining the main ideas.

Again, as health ought to precede labour of the body, and as a man in health can do what an unhealthy man cannot do, and as of this health the properties are strength, energy, agility, graceful carriage and action, manual dexterity, and endurance of fatigue, so in like manner general culture of mind is the best aid to professional and scientific study, and educated men can do what illiterate cannot; and the man who has learned to think and to reason and to compare and to discriminate and to analyze, who has refined his taste, and formed his judgment, and sharpened his mental vision, will not indeed at once be a lawyer, or a pleader, or an orator, or a statesman, or a physician, or a good landlord, or a man of business or a soldier, or an engineer, or a chemist, or a geologist, or an antiquarian, but he will be placed in that state of intellect in which he can take up any one of the sciences or callings I have referred to, or any other for which he has a taste or special talent, with an ease, a grace, a versatility, and a success, to which another is a stranger. In this sense then, and as yet I have said but a very few words on a large subject, mental culture is emphatically useful.

In-class activities

1. Your teacher will read several selections aloud to the class. Some selections will be from speeches, others from essays. Your teacher will not identify the source before reading it. Discuss each selection and tell why you think it is from a speech or an essay. Note differences between the spoken and written styles.

2. Take part in an in-class streamlining activity. Change the wording of the following sentences to make them suitable for speaking and be prepared to read them aloud to the class. The student that streamlines a sentence best (while retaining the meaning) gets one point. The decisions of the judge (your teacher) are final.

We need to reconsider again the unusually unique matter of the falling of Skylab.

It is my considered opinion that a period of continuous precipitation is about to begin in the weather.

Moving and traveling over rocky and poor roads has made me exhaustingly tired.

Whereas teachers and students sometimes appear to be opposed to one another and at loggerheads, in reality they actually share a number of common purposes.

Meaning to let them in on our opinion as soon as possible, we made every effort to try to meet with them as soon as possible.

3. Your teacher will tape record a class discussion for about five minutes. Listen to the results and discuss the style of language used. What language devices in the conversation would be appropriate in a public speech? Which inappropriate? Why?

4. During the next round of in-class speeches look for and write down any language devices the speakers use that enliven their speeches—devices such as repetition, contrast, similes, and metaphors.

5. At the conclusion of the next round of in-class speeches, take part in electing one of the class members "best stylist." This should be the speaker who has shown the most effective uses of all the language techniques discussed in this chapter. You may wish to vote for second and third place also.

Careers

INTERPRETERS translate spoken passages from one language into another. They provide consecutive or simultaneous translation of languages. High school subjects such as English, foreign languages, speech, and social sciences are helpful. There are no standard educational requirements. A college degree in foreign languages is highly recommended. Interpreters usually find employment in metropolitan areas.

PRESCHOOL TEACHERS instruct children in activities designed to promote social, physical, and intellectual growth. They plan individual and group activities. High school subjects such as English, speech, social studies, math, art, music, and psychology are helpful. A bachelor's degree is required. Preschool teachers should be patient, enjoy working with small children, and possess pleasant speaking voices.

SPEECH WRITERS write copy for use by individuals or companies. They write preliminary drafts and correct copy until approved by a supervisor. High school subjects such as English, speech, social studies, and typing should be helpful. Usually a bachelor's degree is required. Speech writers must communicate well with others and should have extensive vocabularies, creativity, and imagination. Many speech writers are self-employed, while others work for individuals or large companies or agencies.

9

DELIVERING YOUR SPEECH

When you have completed this chapter you should be able to

List the advantages and disadvantages of different methods of delivery.

Describe several ways of combining delivery methods effectively.

Recognize the importance of nonverbal aspects of delivery.

Describe the importance of volume, pitch, speaking rate, and voice quality in speech delivery.

Practice correct articulation and pronunciation in your speaking.

Speak with or without a speaker's stand.

Get maximum benefit from a microphone.

Guard against distractions and interruptions during delivery.

Handle a heckler.

Delivering a speech is not the same as delivering the mail or a loaf of bread. Generally, the mail and the bread are neither improved nor harmed during the process of being delivered to their destination. On the other hand, a speech can be made much better or much worse by the manner in which it is delivered. Although delivery is not the most essential part of giving a speech, it is very important. Good delivery can make a weak speech seem a bit better. Poor delivery can ruin an otherwise excellent speech. This chapter begins by examining several different methods of speech delivery.

Using different methods of delivery

Over the years, four basic methods for delivering public speeches have developed. One might be called the **manuscript method.** Using this method, speakers write down everything they plan to say to their listeners, then bring their manuscripts to the podium and read them to the audience. A second method, called the **memorization method**, also begins with a written manuscript but differs in that the manuscript is memorized word-for-word and not used during the delivery. Using a third method, the **extemporaneous method**, speakers prepare outlines of the *ideas* of their speeches beforehand, but do not memorize an exact pattern of *words*. They choose the words with which to clothe their ideas as they are speaking. Outlines or note cards may or may not be used. The fourth method, called the **impromptu method**, is used on occasions when people must speak "off the cuff," with no chance for previous preparation. This method demands that the speakers both organize their ideas and choose their words as they proceed through their speeches.

Comparing methods of delivery

Each of the four methods has advantages and disadvantages. Let's take a moment to compare them. The manuscript method has an advantage in that there is no danger of forgetting a part of your speech. Unless a sudden wind blows away your manuscript, about the worst thing that can happen is momentarily losing your place while reading. The manuscript method also allows you plenty of time to choose the most effective language for your speech beforehand. Presidents of the United States and other heads of state often read from manuscripts when making major policy statements. This helps assure that they do not make any "slips of the tongue" that could result in embarrassment for their countries or in an international incident. Speeches read from manuscript often sound smoother than those delivered extemporaneously. The use of a manuscript also assures precise timing of a speech, a factor

President Reagan read from a manuscript when he addressed Congress. This method of delivery assured the accuracy of his statements. Yet because he was well prepared, President Reagan was still able to make occasional gestures and eye contact with his audience.

of great importance for televised speeches. Unfortunately, many speeches read from manuscript *sound* as if they are being read. The audience is aware of the manuscript, and it prevents the speech from sounding natural. How many times have you had to listen to a speaker read from manuscript and felt like screaming at the speaker: "Stop reading *at* us and start talking *to* us"?

Memorized delivery has some of the same advantages as manuscript delivery. You may choose the most effective language beforehand, and your speech may be timed precisely. Memorized delivery often sounds prepackaged, however, as indeed it is. Word-for-word memorization also puts a tremendous burden on your memory for any speech longer than four or five minutes. This method of delivery is used rarely nowadays.

The major advantage of the extemporaneous method is that it sounds natural—much like ordinary conversation. Imagine for a moment that you and a close friend are planning to attend a big basketball game. At the last minute your friend is prevented from going, so she asks you to tell her all about the game later. How would you go about preparing your "speech" for your friend? You could make a strong effort to remember all the important plays, the score, the poor calls by the referees (you might even make a few notes to help you remember), but you definitely wouldn't write out your description of the game word-for-word and later read it to your friend. She would get bored listening to your "reading" about the game instead of "telling" her about it. To an audience, extemporaneous speaking sounds more like "telling" your speech than like "reading" it. No audience likes a speaker to read a message that can be told. They will usually become bored and lose interest, even if the reader reads well. However, they are very tolerant of a speaker who looks them in the eye and addresses them directly, even if the flow of words is a bit halting.

The extemporaneous method also gives you, the speaker, the best opportunity to make use of positive and negative feedback from your audience. By constantly monitoring the listeners' reactions and making necessary adjustments, you will improve your chances of maintaining a high level of audience interest and enthusiasm. Since the manuscript and memorization methods prevent this, they fall far short of the extemporaneous method of speaking.

The only advantage of impromptu delivery is that it sounds natural—much like ordinary conversation. Its major drawback, of course, is its tendency to sound unprepared. Unless a speaker has had considerable experience at impromptu speaking, this kind of delivery is likely to sound jumbled and awkward.

Combining methods of delivery

In Chapter 7, you prepared an outline or a set of note cards to use for reference when delivering a speech. You concentrated on planting a pattern of ideas in your mind, rather than on preparing a speech manuscript to read or memorize. Thus you were really preparing to deliver an extemporaneous speech.

This speaker has found that using a combination of delivery methods is the most effective way to present a speech. The introduction and conclusion can be memorized and note cards can be used to jog the memory during the body of the speech.

Of the four methods you have been comparing (manuscript, memorization, extemporaneous, and impromptu), extemporaneous delivery appears to have the greatest number of advantages. Many of the best speakers, however, find they are most effective when they combine methods. One of America's greatest public speakers, President Franklin D. Roosevelt, often prepared manuscripts for his major addresses, and then regularly departed from them during delivery, speaking extemporaneously instead. Although this practice annoyed newspaper owners who had sometimes already printed the advance text in their papers, it was extremely effective with Roosevelt's audiences. By combining the methods in this way, he was able to gain the advantages of each, while avoiding their pitfalls.

Combining methods of delivery in this way requires a certain degree of skill and experience. The listeners should not be able to detect which parts are being read from manuscript, which are memorized, and which are being spoken extemporaneously. Combining methods effectively also requires skill in the use of the extemporaneous method, since the extemporaneous parts must sound as fluent and well prepared as the manuscript sections. However, you can begin to use a combination of methods in small ways.

You will probably find it helpful, at this point, to memorize your introductory remarks and your conclusions. Memorizing the introduction gets you off to a smooth start, sounds impressive, and helps build your confidence for the body of the speech. A carefully worded, memorized conclusion can make a lasting impression on the audience and end your speech effectively. Major transition sentences within the body of the speech may also be memorized. Most of the body of the speech can then be prepared using the extemporaneous method. The manuscript method may be used for brief sections of the body where you wish to insert a direct quotation in the original author's language or present a set of statistics, too complex to memorize. These kinds of material can be written out fully on 3 × 5 note cards or a manuscript page and read at appropriate points in your speech. Beware of preparing lengthy sections of the speeches you are now giving by the manuscript or memorization methods, however. Your main concentration should be on learning the extemporaneous method, since it will serve as the backbone for any combination of methods you may later wish to use.

Recognizing nonverbal aspects of delivering a speech

People often think of a speech as a set of words spoken aloud. Actually you communicate with an audience as much through nonverbal means as through words. Eye contact, gestures, platform movements, appearance, and the motions you make as you begin and end a speech will "say" a great deal about you and your message to the listeners.

Beginning your speech

You may think that your speech begins when you speak the first word. The audience, however, makes judgments about you from the moment you rise from your seat to approach the speaking platform. You nonverbally communicate self-confidence, poise, and leadership, or nervousness, disorganization, and timidity simply by the manner in which you approach the platform and take command of it.

Walk to the platform vigorously, but not hastily. Arrange any notes on the lectern. Turn your face up toward your listeners, and look about at various sides of the audience for several seconds before beginning to speak. This unhurried beginning assures those present of your confidence and command of the situation.

Making eye contact

As you speak, establish eye contact with your listeners. Look directly into the eyes of various audience members. This causes most listeners to feel as if you are devoting your attention to them personally in the same way you would if you were conversing with just one person. The greater the proportion of your speaking time you devote to eye contact, the deeper and more positive this impression becomes.

Looking at your listeners also performs a second important function. It makes it possible for you to monitor the feedback. Feedback is simply the total of all the visible and audible reactions of the audience to the speaker. It can consist of yawns, smiles, boos, nodding heads, hisses, questioning looks, and even fidgeting in the seats. When you use extemporaneous delivery, you are largely free to read your listeners' feedback and then adjust your approach to maintain positive feedback.

When making eye contact, look at one audience member for several seconds as you speak, then turn your head slightly to look at another. Don't forget the people at the sides of the room near the front. Because speakers must turn their heads farther to look at them, these listeners are often cheated out of eye contact.

Some beginning speakers report that looking directly at their listeners makes them nervous and confused. If this happens to you, let your teacher know, and he or she will probably allow you to look at your audience in general for awhile, rather than directly into individuals' eyes. Beware of getting into a habit of doing this, however. Eye contact is so important for both speaker and audience that lack of eye contact can sometimes ruin an otherwise good speech. Once you have gained some experience and have learned to relax on the platform, you should be able to maintain real eye contact without difficulty.

Using gestures

Communicating nonverbally through gestures is a natural part of human communication, yet many beginning speakers freeze up when giving a public speech, taking on the appearance of a totem pole. Never-theless, because we all gesture naturally, the urge to gesture will or-dinarily return once a speaker has gained platform experience.

Books on public speaking used to include long lists and extensive illustrations of gestures, showing in detail how they should be made. The problem with that approach was that it was like telling a speaker which words to use. Each person has his or her own style of nonverbal communication, just as each chooses his or her own words. When you gesture during a speech, it should be because it feels natural at that point. If, for instance, you are describing a far distant place, and it seems appropriate to extend your arm to indicate how far away it is, then you should extend your arm. If you refer to that same distant place later in the same speech, and this time it does not seem appropriate to extend your arm, then you should not do so. It is basically a matter of what feels appropriate at the moment without any lengthy thought about it. While it is helpful for beginning speakers to make some ges-tures while speaking, it is not good to force gestures. Certainly it is not wise to decide during rehearsal that you are definitely going to make a certain gesture at a particular place in your speech. It would probably look rehearsed if made during the live speech.

While discussing the subject of gestures, student speakers some-times ask: "What should I do with my arms and hands when I am not using them to gesture?" Unfortunately, no single answer can be given. As with gestures, basic hand and arm positions must be both natural to you and well suited to the audience and the total speaking situation. Here are some commonly used positions that you may want to consider:

One or both arms hanging naturally at your side.

One or both hands resting on (not grasping) the speaker's stand.

One or both hands held several inches in front of your stomach.

These positions will look quite natural for some speakers but not for others. You can learn from the reactions of your teacher and classmates which suit you best.

Audience members ordinarily pay more attention to a speaker's head and facial gestures than they do to arm or hand movements. Smiles, frowns, nods, and any other movements of the head, eyebrows, chin, lips, or brow can create an impression of a dynamic and enthusi-astic speaker, as long as they are appropriate to the spoken message. As with any gestures, head and facial movements must be natural. They must come from your inner enthusiasm about your message and not be practiced or tacked on for show.

Many beginning speakers show too somber a face to their audi-ences. Of course, some topics demand a serious countenance, but many do not. A speaker describing "How to Shoot Rapids in a Canoe" need not look overly solemn to the listeners. A generally pleasant look, alter-

Facial expressions can help a speaker communicate the enthusiasm she feels about her topic to the audience.

nated with some facial expressions showing the adventure and thrill of canoeing, will make a better impression on the listeners.

Variety is the spice of public speaking, just as it is of life. Like all other parts of a speech, gestures (whether arm-hand or head-face) must be varied regularly to maintain audience attention and interest. A speaker who makes the same gesture repeatedly distracts the audience with that gesture. Pretty soon many listeners are wondering when the gesture will occur again and are paying little attention to the message. Although he was a first-rate speaker, President John F. Kennedy occasionally overused a gesture with his right arm during his campaign speeches. It became so characteristic of his speaking style that mimics began imitating the movement. But because Kennedy possessed so many outstanding qualities as a speaker, it was easy for listeners to excuse this overworked gesture. Unknown speakers, however, must be doubly careful of any gesture that becomes a regular pattern in their speech. While taking care not to overuse any one gesture, you must also remember that using no gestures at all is just as deadly. In addition, a speaker's face is an area that particularly needs variety. Facial gestures such as raising the eyebrows, smiling, frowning, and widening the eyes, indicate your involvement with your topic and generate interest and enthusiasm in your audience.

Using platform movement

The way in which a speaker uses platform movement (movements involving the entire body) can also project a certain image to the audience. In Chapter 6 you read about the basic forms of platform movement and the dangers of falling into distracting forms. (Remember the Ping-Pong Pacer, for instance?) The question here is, how can one make the best use of positive forms of movement? Like gestures, platform movement should look and feel natural. The best way to achieve this is to move when there is a reason to move and to remain still at other times. Legitimate reasons to move during a speech are similar to reasons for moving during a one-to-one conversation. Ask yourself: "When do I ordinarily move about if I'm having a conversation with a friend?" Your answers are likely to include at least two or three of the following reasons:

To whisper something confidential or intimate to the other person.

To compensate when the listener shifts his or her position.

To change to a new topic or to change the mood.

To provide variety.

Reasons for platform movement during a public speech fall into the very same categories. You may want to get closer to the audience to show greater confidentiality or intimacy, to compensate for audience members' fidgeting in their seats, to emphasize change to a new topic or section of your speech at major transition points, or to create a bit of visual variety.

Making the most of your appearance

Much of Diana Ross' appeal comes from her appearance—the carefully styled hair, the stylish gowns, the glittering jewels. Speakers, too, are often judged as much by how they look as by what they have to say.

Diana Ross' stylish appearance is an important part of her performances.

A speaker's appearance should be suited to the speaker's own personality, the audience being addressed, and the occasion for which the speech is being given. The way speakers dress says a great deal about their attitudes toward their listeners and how much importance they attach to the speech itself. Speakers who radically violate the audience's expectations concerning clothing and general appearance have two strikes against them before they say their first sentence. You can improve your chances of creating a good impression by asking yourself: "What is the most appropriate thing to wear for this particular audience and set of circumstances?"

A speaker's appearance is more than clothing, however. No matter what your personality, the audience, or the occasion, *neatness* is always necessary when giving a public speech. Even when the most informal mode of dress is called for, clean hair, nails, face, and hands are a must. A sloppy appearance automatically communicates to your audience: "I'm not very interested in giving this speech, so I didn't spend much time getting ready to meet you."

Application: Discussing appearance

Discuss with your classmates what each of you would consider to be appropriate dress for the following audiences and speaking situations:

Audience	Occasion
Classmates	Pep rally
Senior citizens group	Banquet
First graders	School assembly
College professors	Political rally
Family members	Family reunion
Athletic team	Fund raising drive

Concluding your speech

Just as the speech begins at the moment you rise from your seat, it cannot be said to have concluded until you have regained your seat. You do not want to create the impression that you wish to leave the platform as quickly as possible, so an unhurried departure is called for. Once you have spoken your final word, pause momentarily while still facing the audience to let the impact of your conclusion sink in. Then walk to your seat in a manner appropriate to your topic.

If your speech was serious in nature, a grave and solemn return is indicated. If the topic was light or entertaining, a more cheerful mode is appropriate. Above all, do not ruin the effect of a good presentation by showing you felt it was a poor job as you depart from the platform. Let the audience be the judge of that.

Using your voice effectively

A good deal of emphasis is placed on the visual aspects of speech delivery—what an audience *sees*. A large part of the message of a speech, however, is carried by the voice—what an audience *hears*. How you control and use your voice can make the difference between a well received and a poorly received speech. Before you read this section, review the section "Vocalizing" in Chapter 2 (page 43), to recall the way in which vocal sounds are produced. Then you can proceed to consider a number of different factors involved when using your voice for public speaking.

Speak with the right volume

No matter how well organized, researched, and practiced a speech may be, if the listeners cannot hear what is being said, the speech cannot possibly succeed. Although it is possible to speak too loudly for a given room or audience, most beginning speakers have the opposite problem. They speak too softly and cannot be heard in the rear of the room. This may be due to nervousness; more often, inexperienced speakers simply do not realize they are not using sufficient volume.

Volume is controlled primarily by the amount of air a person forces through the vocal cords. By inhaling you obtain a supply of air in your lungs that can then be used to produce vocal tones (sounds) as you exhale, forcing the air across your vocal cords. If you are going to speak very loudly, you must have a considerable supply of air in your lungs. If you need to speak loudly for an extended period of time (as in a public speech), you need a constant, large supply of air. Research has found that people use sixty-six times as much energy addressing a large audience in a large room as they do in ordinary conversation. So the manner in which you inhale while speaking becomes very important. Inhale deeply through your nose, sucking in air by expanding your diaphragm. Upper chest breathing does not provide enough air for an extended sentence in a large auditorium. Diaphragmatic breathing, however, provides plenty. Besides, filling the lower lungs with air does not really take much longer than shallow inhalation.

How you exhale is also important in sustaining sufficient volume. If you let all the air out as you say your first few words, one of two problems will occur. Either the ends of your longer sentences will be too soft to be heard, or you will need to inhale so often you will begin to sound like an air compressor at work. As you gain experience in public speaking, you will learn to pace your exhalation, saving enough air for emphasizing important ideas with extra force.

Variety in volume is important too. A speaker who is constantly loud makes everything sound important. Eventually, nothing sounds important. One who is constantly soft is difficult to hear. Listeners eventually give up straining to hear such a speaker. Important or key ideas must always be spoken with sufficient force so that those in the back row can hear them easily. Transitions to new sections of a speech, the start of the conclusion, and the parts where you wish to be dramatic with a kind of "stage whisper" may be spoken more softly, but should still be audible for listeners in the rear of the room.

Vary your pitch

Pitch refers to the tone of the voice on the musical scale. Words or syllables to be emphasized are usually spoken in a higher key. Strong emotion is generally indicated by great differences in pitch among words or syllables used together. Think, for example, of the way you might pronounce the following sentence: "I certainly don't think that!"

Changing pitch as you speak comes naturally to you in conversation, but beginning public speakers often fail to maintain their pitch variety when speaking from a public platform. Speaking in a **monotone**, with no ups and downs in pitch, can quickly give an audience the impression the speaker is not enthusiastic or sincere about the topic. Of course, pitch changes should not be affected. The enthusiasm must first be present. Then pitch variety will naturally follow.

Each of you has a general pitch—that portion of your range in which your voice usually hovers when you speak. For public speaking, each person needs to discover his or her optimum pitch, that pitch which can be used most comfortably without strain for extended periods of time. The most comfortable tones are found most often in the lower half of a person's range.

Watch your speaking rate

Normal speaking rate varies from 120 to 150 words per minute. Some people regularly speak more rapidly or more slowly than others, and nearly everyone varies his or her speaking rate for different situations. Barry Goldwater once said of the late Hubert Humphrey, former vice president and senator from Minnesota: "Hubert has been clocked at 280 words per minute with gusts up to 340." A good average rate for speaking, however, is in the 120 to 150 words-per-minute range.

Many times inexperienced speakers speak too rapidly due to nervousness. If your teacher says you are speaking too quickly, force yourself to slow down by concentrating on the problem. Changes in rate are brought about in two ways: by varying the number and length of pauses between words or by varying the length of time it takes to pronounce each syllable. If you are told that you are speaking too rapidly, the best place to start correction is with your pauses. Some speakers feel they must constantly be emitting some kind of sound every second they are before their audience. They fear periods of silence, however brief. This is a false feeling. A well-timed pause, supported by appropriate gestures, movement, and eye contact can often say much more than several

Cheerleaders must learn to project their voices without strain.

sentences. Pause especially for several seconds between major segments of your speech and more briefly between sentences.

A specific problem, common to many speakers, is called the **vocalized pause.** This is the habit of filling in pause time with "uh," "er," "like," "you-know" or similar non-meaningful sounds. If these sounds become numerous they can be very distracting to the listeners. Here are two methods for handling the vocalized pause.

1. Make a list of transition words to use between sentences and vary them regularly during your speech.

2. Rehearse your speeches with a tape recorder and listen to yourself.

Hearing a great number of vocalized pauses in one's own speech can often motivate a person to concentrate seriously on solving the problem.

Use crisp articulation and correct pronunciation

As you know, you are capable of producing vocal sounds that are not words. You can use your vocal cords to make sounds like those of a dog or cat, an airplane, automobile, or nearly any sound you choose to imitate. Crisp articulation and correct pronunciation are needed to turn these vocal sounds into recognizable words and verbal symbols.

"Watcha doin ta-day, Sam?" "I dunno. Wudder you?" This kind of talk may communicate very well during informal conversation with your friends, but clearer articulation is definitely called for in a public speech. **Articulation** refers to the way in which the tongue, teeth, palate, and lips are moved and used to produce the crisp, clear sounds of good speech. Most people are capable of producing vowel and consonant sounds clearly, but fall into lazy habits. They become unwilling to exert that extra bit of effort needed to produce clear speech, especially during conversation. Unfortunately, when such bad habits are carried over into public speaking, an audience may show little respect for the speaker who sounds sloppy or mushy. When practicing your speeches, therefore, concentrate on moving your tongue, lips, and lower jaw vigorously enough to produce crisp, clear sounds. Be especially careful of the consonants that can be slurred or dropped altogether. Don't use "madder" when you mean "matter," "pacific" for "specific," or "gonna" for "going to."

Pronunciation can also play a role in determining the degree of respect given a speaker by the audience. **Pronunciation** means selecting the correct sounds and the proper syllable stresses. What makes a certain pronunciation correct and another incorrect is usage. Once enough people agree to pronounce a word in a certain way, that becomes the correct way. But you cannot assume that your friends, or even all the people in your school, have cornered the market on correct pronunciation. The two best sources for discovering the accepted pronunciation of words are (1) the dictionary and (2) the prominent speakers of the day, such as national news commentators and noted government officials.

If you need to use proper names or technical terms in a speech, be certain you know the accepted pronunciation before beginning your rehearsal. Using the correct sounds and stresses during rehearsal will usually assure correct pronunciation during the live performance. When you pronounce unusual words with authority and without hesitation, your audience is likely to be impressed by the thoroughness of your speech preparation and to feel you have genuinely earned the right to speak to them.

Application: Using effective vocal delivery

Hold a class contest to determine which class member can read the following excerpts from noted speeches with the most effective vocal delivery. Decide what caused you to vote for the winner.

> You ask what is our aim? I can answer in one word. It is victory. Victory at all costs—victory in spite of all terrors—victory, however long and hard the road may be, for without victory there is no survival.
> *Winston Churchill*

> I know not what course others may take; but as for me, give me liberty or give me death! *Patrick Henry*

> It is rather for us to be here dedicated to the great task remaining before us—that from these honored dead we take increased devotion to that cause for which they gave the last full measure of devotion—that we here highly resolve that these dead shall not have died in vain—that this nation, under God, shall have a new birth of freedom—and that government of the people, by the people, for the people, shall not perish from the earth. *Abraham Lincoln*

Checklist for evaluating nonverbal and verbal delivery

☐ 1. Did I approach the speaker's platform and begin my speech with poise and confidence?

☐ 2. Did I look directly into the eyes of various members of the audience during the delivery of my speech?

☐ 3. Did my gestures and platform movements seem natural? Did they aid me in getting my message across to the listeners?

☐ 4. Was my appearance appropriate for the audience and the occasion?

☐ 5. Did I speak with enough force to be heard by all my listeners?

☐ 6. Did I show enthusiasm for my topic by varying the pitch of my voice?

☐ 7. Was my speech delivered at a reasonable speaking rate? Did I avoid vocalized pauses?

☐ 8. Did I articulate crisply? Was my pronunciation of difficult words correct?

☐ 9. Did I conclude my speech and return to my seat in an unhurried manner?

Special problems of delivering a speech

Delivering a speech frequently involves dealing with special problems and situations. Among these are the use of a speaker's stand and microphone and coping with distractions and interruptions. Practice at handling these matters can aid you when you encounter them as a speaker.

Using the speaker's stand

In the majority of places where speeches are given a **lectern** (speaker's stand) is available. One can probably be found in your school's speech classroom. On occasion, however, you may encounter a situation in which a lectern is not available. Therefore, you need to know both how to use a speaker's stand effectively and how to get along without one.

The basic purpose of a lectern is to hold a speaker's notes or manuscript. It was never intended to serve as a support for speakers with weak backs or as a hiding place for those with wobbly knees. A person who uses the speaker's stand to lounge upon or to obviously hide behind immediately reveals apathy or extreme nervousness to the audience. Allowing one or both hands to rest on the stand occasionally is acceptable, as long as one does not *grasp* the stand so desperately that the knuckles turn white. A foot should never be placed on the base of the stand either. It should be left flat on the floor behind it. In general, the less the lectern is grasped, leaned on, caressed, or tapped on, the better the overall impression will be.

Usually the top surface of a lectern is tilted at an angle to allow a speaker to read note cards or manuscript pages with ease, but at the same time keep them out of sight. The best way to handle papers, when using a lectern, is to lay them on the stand at the start and *leave them there throughout the speech*. The audience should be as unaware of your notes as possible, so you must avoid picking them up and putting them down or carrying them in your hands. In addition, cards or manuscript pages should be brought to the lectern in a prearranged order. Try to avoid using paper clips or staples that will require removal or the flipping of pages. When the top card or page has been used, you want to be able to slide it gently and quietly to one side, exposing the next card or page. Picking up a stack of cards in order to place the used one on the bottom of the stack can be very distracting to the listeners, as is the flapping of stapled manuscript pages over the front of a speaker's stand.

Your teacher may ask you to give at least one of your classroom speeches without using the lectern. This can help prepare you for later occasions when no lectern is available. If you want to use note cards but know you will have no stand on which to place them, remember that the easiest size to hold is a 3 × 5 card. As each one is used, you can quietly slip it to the back of the deck, making the next card ready for reference. A full-sized manuscript is more difficult to handle without a speaker's stand. Thus, if you intend to read from manuscript, you should always find out whether or not a stand will be available.

One advantage of having no lectern when you are using note cards is the additional freedom you have to move about on the platform. Not feeling tied to the stand allows you to walk a few steps more often, reducing your tension and generating greater audience attention.

Adjusting the microphone

When you are speaking to more than 80 people, or are in a room where the acoustics are poor, you will find a microphone helpful. A microphone must be properly used, however, if it is going to enhance the communication rather than harm it. The first step in its proper use comes before the speech begins. Test the microphone if at all possible! Probably more speeches have gotten off to weak starts due to untested, faulty microphones than due to any other single cause. It only takes a moment to make certain (1) the microphone is turned on, (2) there is no electronic feedback, and (3) it is set at the proper distance and height.

Students often ask: "How far should the microphone be from my mouth?" Microphones vary somewhat, but an average of 10 to 12 inches (25 to 30 centimeters) works well for most microphones. Of course you must keep this "mouth-to-mike" distance fairly constant while speaking. You cannot weave or move your head very much, or your voice will begin to fade in and out like a siren. One advantage of a **lavalier microphone**—the kind that hangs around your neck—is greater freedom to move about on the platform.

Occasionally a speaker will look at the microphone rather than at the audience. This can create a comical effect, since it appears to the

Communicator close-up

Beverley Edwards is a minister in Rhode Island. Through her weekly sermons, she is able to develop the themes of her ministry. Therefore, her method of delivery, how she acts when she speaks and how well she speaks, are very important in getting her messages to her congregation.

One of the ways the Rev. Edwards inspires the members of her congregation is by showing them that she is personally interested in them, and interested in talking *with* them, rather than *at* them. She prepares and practices her sermons carefully beforehand so that she doesn't worry during the sermon about what she is going to say. This preparation also gives her a chance to later apply her energy toward the delivery of the sermon.

"Delivery of a sermon is so personal that you want to provide as much animation, and as much eye contact, as possible," she said. "It's really a dialogue with the congregation. A sermon should appeal to the intellect, but it should also go beyond the rational and appeal to the heart. You have to use methods which will touch people."

The Rev. Edwards, who was ordained in 1975, is still working on these methods which include learning to control the tone of her voice, the rhythm of her language, and her use of hand gestures. "You have to do everything with a little bit of exaggeration to make it sound right," she said. "At first, I found I was too stiff, too afraid of gesture and of changing my voice, too prim. My greatest admiration is for Martin Luther King, Jr. He knew how to use his voice so well, not only cadence and pitch, but also volume and the rise and fall of emotion. It's hard to do. I practice breathing on the beach. If you can breathe from your diaphragm, then you can speak better. In fact, all the techniques of public speaking work in a sermon. The question is learning to control them."

When she speaks, the Rev. Edwards keeps herself constantly alert for reaction from her congregation. By using eye contact, she senses immediately when some people grow restless or when points she is making are not being understood.

"The worst thing for me," she said, "is realizing I'm not making sense to people. I wouldn't mind if they got mad." One of the hardest things to do when speaking publicly, she added, is to change, or clarify, a speech in midstream. "I'm still not good enough to do that well," she said. That's why the Rev. Beverley Edwards prepares and rehearses all her sermons thoroughly before delivering them.

This minister has discovered that to speak to a congregation in ways that will enable them to understand her message correctly, she must prepare and rehearse the verbal aspects of a sermon in advance in order to be free to respond later to the congregation's feedback as she delivers it.

Experienced speakers, such as Hank Aaron, have learned to adjust their distance and to pronounce words carefully when using a microphone.

audience that the speaker is addressing remarks to the microphone rather than to them.

Certain consonant sounds are easily distorted if spoken with too much force into a microphone. Some of the worst offenders are *t, p, b, s, sh, z, g, k,* and *d.* You will want to avoid blasting your listeners by using too much force when uttering these sounds.

Since the presence of a microphone makes certain demands upon a speaker, it is wise to rehearse with a live microphone, particularly before your *first* microphone speech. If at all possible, secure the room or auditorium in which the microphone will be used for a practice session. Run through your speech several times with the microphone on, and have another person stand or sit at various locations. Even an untrained listener can tell you whether you are coming across clearly or not. Your speech teacher may be the ideal person to help you during such a practice session if his or her schedule permits.

Dealing with distractions and interruptions

During the delivery of a speech unexpected events sometimes occur that cannot be planned for beforehand. Although the list of such potential distractions and interruptions is large, it is a rare speech in which more than one such problem arises. Speakers, therefore, should not fear that a string of major disasters is likely to occur every time a speech is to be delivered. On the other hand, being aware of the problems that may arise can prepare you to deal with one confidently if it does occur.

Some interruptions distract the audience's attention only briefly. Noisy jets may fly over the building. A latecomer may interrupt to find a seat. You may lose your place or stumble over words, or people may cough or shuffle their feet. These do little harm to the listeners' basic interest in you and your topic. The best way to handle such noises and distractions is just to pause briefly until the room is quiet, then proceed as if nothing had happened. Making a comment about this kind of interruption simply increases the distraction and usually does more harm than good.

Other interruptions—the kind that create a major breakdown in the audience's concentration on your speech—need to be handled differently from minor distractions. If a group of people arrives late, for instance, and their attempts to find seats distract a good portion of the audience, the speaker should fall silent and remain quiet until the entire group is settled. The speaker may even aid people in finding seats by pointing out empty chairs, thereby shortening the length of the disturbance. Should a loud noise begin and appear likely to continue for the remainder of the speech, the speaker should first attempt to be heard over the noise, or ask the audience to move closer to the speaker's stand, if possible. If it proves impossible to overcome, the speaker may have to abandon the attempt to deliver the speech.

If a heckler should begin to yell at you from the audience, handle the situation with dignity and poise. First, remember that the audience came to hear *you* speak, not the heckler, and their sympathy is basically with you. For a time it is usually best to ignore a heckler, attempting to be heard in between the interruptions. If the heckler's comments are too frequent or too loud to permit the audience to hear you, members of the audience may attempt to quiet the heckler themselves. As the speaker you should provide sufficient time for this to occur, since a heckler soon loses heart when it becomes obvious the audience does not support the disturbance. Only when all this has failed should you address the heckler directly, with a calm and dignified comment, such as: "Sir (or Madam), I will be happy to try to field any questions or comments from the audience as soon as I have finished my prepared remarks." Under no circumstances should you ever engage in a shouting match with a heckler, since this gives the intruder precisely what was hoped for—a major share of your audience's attention.

Summary

The way a speech is delivered is quite important. Good delivery will improve almost any speech, while poor delivery will ruin an otherwise excellent one.

USING DIFFERENT METHODS OF DELIVERY. A speaker may choose from four different methods for delivering speeches—manuscript, memorization, extemporaneous, and impromptu. While each has certain advantages and disadvantages, the most helpful one for a beginning speaker to master is the extemporaneous method, where the pattern of ideas is prepared beforehand, but the exact wording is chosen during delivery. Once speakers have gained some experience with this method, they can begin experimenting with various combinations of the methods until each speaker discovers his or her own most effective style.

RECOGNIZING NONVERBAL ASPECTS OF DELIVERING A SPEECH. Remember that your speech begins when you rise from your chair and approach the speaker's platform. Move vigorously, but not hastily; arrange any notes you may have; and look at your audience for several seconds before speaking. Other nonverbal aspects of speech delivery include eye contact, gestures, platform movement, and appearance. Finally, you should remember that your speech is not truly over until you have regained your seat. When you have concluded your speech, look around your audience, then leave the platform in a confident, unhurried manner, and return to your seat.

USING YOUR VOICE EFFECTIVELY. Effective use of your voice is very important in speech delivery. Since being heard is basic to giving a speech, you must learn to breathe deeply and maintain enough volume to be heard easily in all parts of the room. Varying your volume is also helpful, mainly to create interest or change a mood. Pitch refers to the tone of the voice on the musical scale and must also be varied along with force to relay to your audience your interest and enthusiasm for the topic. Speaking rate ordinarily hovers in the 120-150 words-per-minute range, but again some variety will make a speech more interesting. Articulation and pronunciation both play an important part in forming sounds into recognizable words and verbal symbols. Avoid "lazy-lips" and be certain you know the correct pronunciation of each word and name you use in a speech.

SPECIAL PROBLEMS OF DELIVERING A SPEECH. As a speaker, you must know how to deal with a number of special situations. First, you must know how to handle a lectern, as well as how to get along without one. The basic idea to keep in mind is that a speaker's stand is intended to provide a convenient place to lay notes or a manuscript. When one is not available, notes must be held inconspicuously in the hands. You must also be able to handle a microphone. A microphone can be very helpful when speaking to a large audience. In order to get the maximum use from a microphone, however, you should rehearse with it, test it shortly before the speech, and keep your mouth a constant 10 to 12 inches (25 to 30 centimeters) from the head of the microphone at all times. If distractions or interruptions occur during a speech, they must be handled calmly and with poise. If the interruption is minor, it is usually wise to ignore it; if it creates a major disturbance, you must handle it decisively and with authority.

Vocabulary

manuscript method

memorization method

extemporaneous method

impromptu method

monotone

vocalized pause

articulation

pronunciation

lectern

lavalier microphone

Review questions

1. What are the four different ways of delivering a speech?

2. Which method requires planting a pattern of ideas in your mind?

3. In using a combination of methods, which parts should be memorized? Where would manuscript be used?

4. When does an audience begin making a judgment about a speaker?

5. What are the two main values of eye contact with an audience?

6. Why does a speaker's face most need variety of movement?

7. What are four reasons for platform movement during a speech?

8. When is a speech ended? Is there more than one way to end a speech?

9. What are four aspects of vocal delivery? Briefly define each one.

10. How should a lectern be used? What two things should a speaker *not* do in relation to a lectern?

Discussion questions

1. Discuss thoroughly your personal feelings about the various methods of speech delivery. Give advantages and disadvantages for each and try to decide which you would feel most comfortable using.

2. Discuss ways of varying your rate of delivery. Experiment with various methods. See if your classmates can detect which method you are using and how often you change.

3. Recall a professional speaker (newscaster, actor, emcee, for example) you have heard. Discuss with your classmates how that person does or does not use his or her voice effectively and what would improve the presentation.

4. Discuss appropriate and inappropriate ways of handling interruptions, distractions, and hecklers. Include a speaker's consideration of posture, gestures, and voice in dealing with such problems.

5. Take part in a class discussion on the topic "What I find most difficult about speech delivery." Notice during this discussion how many of your classmates have the same problems you experience.

At-home activities

1. Practice walking from your seat to a speaker's platform and saying the first few sentences of a speech you are preparing to deliver in class. Be certain your approach is unhurried, shows confidence, and suits the mood of your speech. Also rehearse the last part of your conclusion and the manner in which you will return to your seat. Look back in the chapter for additional tips on beginning and concluding a speech.

2. Say each of the following tongue-twisters as rapidly as you can, three times in succession. Go only as fast as accuracy will allow. To see if your articulation improves, time yourself on each tongue-twister, then try to improve your time.

Remember—they must be spoken accurately to count!

"Sally Sunshine sews her socks. When Sally Sunshine sews her socks, the seams she sews seem sealed like stocks."

"Peter and Paul play paddle ball. Peter plays perfectly, as does Paul. A perfect pair playing paddle ball."

"Mary Macer makes many messy meals. Since most of Mary Macer's meals are messy, Mary Macer's mother makes Mary make her meals less messy."

"Brother Brather bothers mother. Mother bothers brother Brather. Brother Brather's brother, Baffer, baffles Brather and his mother."

In-class activities

1. Join other classmates in taking turns standing in front of the class and speaking the following line three times: "The entire world is not large enough to satisfy my curiosity." The first time use gestures appropriate for speaking to five or six friends; the second time for speaking to a classroom of 30 to 40 persons; the third time for addressing a large auditorium of 300 to 400 listeners.

2. The sentence in the previous exercise can also be used to help you and your classmates improve your vocal volume. Again take turns saying the sentence three times. The first time say it with sufficient volume to be heard by a group of 5 or 6, the second time by a group of 30, the third time by 80 audience members (without a microphone).

3. During one round of classroom speeches, note the distractions that arise. After the speeches, discuss how well each speaker followed the advice in the chapter about dealing with such distractions.

Careers

HOTEL FRONT OFFICE CLERKS greet guests, rent rooms, issue keys, handle mail, and answer questions. High school courses such as business, English, speech, psychology, and foreign languages are helpful. There are no basic educational requirements. Hotel front office clerks must be courteous, friendly, and patient. They must possess good speaking voices.

FUND RAISERS raise money for causes or institutions. They contact potential contributors and persuade them to contribute funds. High school courses in English, drama, speech, and business are helpful. Fund raisers work for educational institutions, religious groups, hospitals, museums, libraries, theaters, charities, and health organizations.

10

SPEAKING TO INFORM

When you have completed this chapter you should be able to

Identify the main characteristics of a speech that is meant to inform.

Know the special functions of each of the main parts (introduction, body, and conclusion) of a speech given to inform.

Gain audience attention and build interest in your topic during your introduction.

Effectively maintain attention, react to feedback, and execute smooth transitions during the body of an informative speech.

Conclude informative speeches in an effective manner.

Conduct an effective question-and-answer period.

Decide correctly when visual aids should be used in a speech.

Know the types of visual aids available.

Although occasionally a speech may be given to inspire, to entertain, or to eulogize a person, most speeches are given for one of two basic reasons: to inform or to persuade. This chapter discusses speaking to inform. Chapter 11 is about speaking to persuade.

When you give a speech to inform, your basic purpose is to provide the listeners with information they do not already have. Even though the audience may have some general knowledge of your topic before you begin, an **informative speech** will impart new knowledge or more in-depth information on that topic.

Speeches given to inform serve many useful functions in everyday life. Reports at business meetings, classroom lessons and demonstrations, reports to labor unions, tours through state and national parks, speeches given at civic clubs—all are examples of informative speeches. Notice that a speech is considered informative whenever the speaker's *primary* purpose is to impart new knowledge. In some cases a speaker may have a mixed motive for addressing an audience. Along with imparting new information the speaker may also wish to persuade listeners by influencing their beliefs, attitudes, or behavior. Teachers, for example, speak to their classes with such mixed motives. Along with showing you how to work with decimals, a math teacher might wish to persuade you to accept the importance of knowing how to work with decimals. Since the teacher's main purpose in speaking is to impart new knowledge, however, you would call this math lesson an example of informative rather than persuasive speaking.

If you are like most people you will give more speeches to inform during your life than for any other purpose. Let's take a close look at each of the parts of the informative speech.

Beginning an informative speech

Many speech authorities consider the introduction the most important part of any speech. Listeners quite often base their opinions about a speech on their first impressions. Thus, the quality of the introduction may determine the effect of an entire speech. Because of the importance of an introduction, a large portion of this chapter is devoted to ways you can make your introductions most effective. There are five important things to remember when introducing an informative speech. Each one of these will be discussed separately.

Gain the audience's attention

Perhaps the first and most important way you can use an introduction is to attract the audience's attention. If a speaker fails to gain the listeners' attention at the beginning of a speech, it is highly unlikely that the speech will ever fulfill its purpose. Gaining the audience's attention is a crucial function of the informative speech's introduction.

In most businesses, being able to share information with others effectively is an important skill.

Audience members will mentally test a speaker for the first few moments of a speech. If the material sounds dull or uninteresting, their attention will quickly turn to other matters—the dance Saturday night or what will be served for supper. So one of the speaker's first tasks is to demand the listeners' attention by using special material as an **attention device.** Over centuries of speechmaking, certain types of material have proven effective and become widely accepted for this purpose.

One of the most widely used attention devices is **humor.** Nearly everyone enjoys a good joke, so most audiences will automatically pay attention to a speaker who uses humor. Humor that is closely related to one's speech topic, the occasion, or the audience is usually more effective, however, than just a standard joke. The speaker who relates a funny incident that serves as a smooth transition into the main body of the speech insures against losing the listener's attention as soon as the joke is over.

Some people are more effective at being funny than others. Before attempting to use humor in a public speech, ask yourself whether you are an effective humorist. If you are able to make friends laugh in private conversation or at a party, you have probably developed an ability to be humorous. If you seldom get a laugh when you wish to, it is wiser to wait until you have had a chance to develop this technique before using it in a speech introduction. Attempting humor in a public speech and having it fall flat wounds the speaker's confidence and does more harm than good.

If you are one of those people who is an effective humorist, you may be strongly tempted to overuse humor in your public speeches. Do not give in to this temptation. Humor acts as a spice in public speaking—a little bit is helpful; too much can destroy the "flavor" of your speech. Audiences respect a speaker who can be both humorous and serious, but if the purpose of the speech is to inform, the listeners expect to be informed, not merely entertained. Use humor sparingly as an attention device.

Finally, make sure any humor you use is in good taste. Though some members of your audience may laugh at offensive humor, their respect for you will decrease. Since a speaker's character in the listener's eye has always been considered one of a speaker's most potent means of influence, a joke that is offensive will be harmful rather than helpful.

An attention device similar to humor is **narrative.** A story does not need to be funny to be fascinating and to secure attention. Speakers who use narrative in their introduction are almost sure to capture their listeners' attention. As with humor, a story that has a natural connection with the speech topic is far better than one without any connection. Notice how Belinda Moyers, a student speaker, gained audience attention with the following narrative introduction in a speech on runaways:

> Twelve year old Rita is missing. While shopping with her older sister, she locked herself in the local department store restroom and refused to come out. Her sister, after pleading for nearly an hour, went for help. While her sister was away, Rita slipped out. After she was gone all night, her parents became extremely worried and searched her room. In her room they found a note explaining her plans to run away and why she was so unhappy. Her parents, like those of one million other kids who run away each year, were frantic. Stop and think about it for a minute. What would you do if you were Rita's parents or what would you do if you were Rita? Did you ever consider running away?

Avoid the temptation to make the story too detailed or too lengthy. Many stories need to be shortened and adapted to a particular speech, especially if the entire speech is rather short. A five-minute story as an attention device in a ten-minute speech is too long. Keep in mind the general rule that speech introductions should usually account for only about ten percent of the total speech.

The **common ground technique** is another widely used means of gaining listener attention. When using this device, speakers begin by identifying hobbies, interests, careers, experiences, or preferences that they share in common with their listeners. They might note similarities in political or religious background, ethnic heritage, or interest in certain sports. The common ground technique includes anything that highlights the fact that speaker and listeners share common interests. When Princess Margaret of the United Kingdom visited the Kentucky Derby and was asked to present a cup to the owner of the winning horse, she began her presentation speech by noting the similarity between the Kentucky Derby and the English Derby.

The common ground technique gains listener attention most effectively when the similarities between the speaker and listeners are greatest. If there are few real likenesses between you and your listeners on a given occasion, you would be better off choosing another attention device. Do not try to force weak similarities.

The attention device called **shock technique** is used to demand quick, almost instantaneous attention from an audience. Shock technique consists of mentioning an unusual, frightening, or hard-to-believe fact, statement, or statistic. It usually is used at the very beginning of a speech. The idea is to blow away any mental "cobwebs" in your listeners' heads and startle them into instant mental alertness. Thom Mayer, a student speaker, made excellent use of the shock technique in a speech on "The Population Bomb":

> If I were to tell you that there are 3.6 billion people on the earth, with more arriving at the rate of 132 per minute, these figures would probably do nothing more than bore you. If, on the other hand, I were to say "There's a bomb in this room and it could explode at any second!" it is likely that I would have your attention, and you would realize the urgency in what I had said. The cold facts, however, are that the bomb I warned you about and the figures I cited are actually one and the same thing. That bomb is known as the Population Bomb, and it is ticking right now in this room and all over the world.

Not only did Thom Mayer assure listener attention from the first words of his speech, but the statistics led naturally into the main body of his speech on overpopulation. As with humor and narrative, the shock technique works best when it is closely tied to the main message of the speech. Speakers using the shock technique must always have evidence to prove the shocking statements they make.

Suspense is another device useful for developing rapid listener attention in an introduction. Usually suspense is developed by withholding one's theme or topic from the audience for several moments and by hinting at its importance or uniqueness. A speaker who is building suspense talks "around" the topic for several moments, teasing the audience into trying to guess what the topic will be. Marie Ransley, a student speaker, used suspense in the following manner at the beginning of a classroom speech:

"Warning: the green slime is here." It sounds like a creature out of a grade-B horror movie. But unfortunately it's more real than that. The *New York Times Magazine* warns: ". . . a monster has been loosed among us. In . . . countless incidents around the world, one can almost hear the sloshing of the algae as they grow and expand like the mucid mutations of the late-night horror movies, crawling everywhere and smothering life beneath the slime of cells gone beserk."

Yes, algae is the monster and the immediate victims are the country's lakes.

When used as an attention device in an introduction, suspense must be built quickly. A brief amount of suspense makes an audience curious and expectant, but suspense drawn out beyond several moments rapidly loses its effect. The listeners begin to resent the speaker for not "letting them in on" the speech topic.

Application: Choosing attention devices

Refer to the sample speech topics in Chapter 7, page 153. Suggest as many effective attention devices to introduce each as you can. Try to include examples of each of the techniques that have been suggested.

Build interest in the topic

Besides gaining the listeners' attention, a speaker should build their interest in the speech topic during the introduction. Some topics are naturally more fascinating to certain audiences than others are. A speaker who has analyzed the audience beforehand will know if she or he must build audience interest in the topic.

Building interest in one's topic is not the same as gaining attention, but many of the same devices may be used to accomplish it. Earlier in this chapter it was mentioned that humor as an attention device works best if it is easily tied to the speaker's topic. Telling a humorous incident unrelated to your topic may gain your listeners' attention, but it does nothing toward building their interest in your topic. A topic-related joke, however, can fulfill both these important functions at once. The same can be said of the narrative, common ground, shock, and suspense techniques.

There are other methods of building interest in the speech topic which have also been found effective. One is the practice of starting the speech with questions related to the topic. A speech dealing with furniture-making, for instance, might begin with a series of questions: "Do you know which is the hardest wood in existence? Do you know which

A humorous story that has been prepared and rehearsed beforehand can prove to be both an effective attention-getting and an interest-building device.

is the most expensive hardwood still used for making furniture? Which is the most commonly used wood for furniture construction?" You read in Chapter 8 that these are called rhetorical questions. The speaker does not expect an "out-loud" answer from the listeners. Rather, it is intended that the listeners will mentally try to answer the questions. The speaker thereby generates attention and builds interest in the speech topic. Occasionally, speakers will ask *real* (not rhetorical) questions, which they expect audience members to answer aloud. This can sometimes be done by a show of hands or by inviting specific listeners to answer aloud. This technique can build topic interest as well as arouse attention, but it is a bit risky. Since the speaker may not receive the expected answer, he or she may be caught off guard and become confused. If you plan to use real questions, prepare to react to various kinds of responses.

Another interest-building technique consists of beginning a speech with a quotation that highlights an important aspect of your topic. Audiences are usually interested in the thoughts of others, particularly if quoted from some well-known or well-beloved person. One way to build listener interest in a patriotic speech, for example, would be to introduce your topic with John Kennedy's famous quotation "Ask not what your country can do for you,—ask what you can do for your country." The use of a quotation from the Bible or another religious work in introductions has long been a favorite interest-building device of members of the clergy. The quotation identifies the general topic area for the listeners and creates a mild suspense about how the speaker will develop the particular topic within the area.

Directly challenging your audience is still another means of building topic interest. Notice how effectively student speaker Belinda

Moyers challenged her audience through rhetorical questions in her introduction on page 225. Read the introduction to Beth Simmons' speech (page 409) and decide whether she captured your attention effectively.

Preview the topic

On the covers of many paperback books you will find intriguing hints about the contents of the book. These are meant to help sell the book. A speech introduction serves a similar function prior to the main body of the speech. Audiences have learned to expect the speaker to "clue them in" on the speech topic, its purpose, and often the main points that will be covered. Thus, previewing the topic is a significant function of most speech introductions.

The most obvious and straightforward method of previewing the topic consists of simply stating your speech purpose to the audience during the introduction. Sometimes, however, this type of introduction may fail to fulfill the other important functions of an introduction at the same time. An introduction that merely previews the topic, without at the same time generating attention and building interest in the topic, might be labeled a clear but dull introduction. The approach used by Caroline Bird in a speech on "What Do Women Want?" not only previews the topic but also attracts the audience's attention and interest:

> What . . . do women want? The question stumped Sigmund Freud, the psychiatrist who knew what you wanted when you didn't know what you wanted yourself. Simpler men have never been puzzled. They *know* what women want without ever asking them.
>
> I've been coping with this certainty for a long time now.
>
> Twenty years ago, when I worked for a public relations firm, I asked why our automobile clients couldn't make car doors so that little kids couldn't open them from the inside. If you want to sell women, I said, you have to sell safety.
>
> The men on the account smiled indulgently. The only thing women care about in cars, one of them told me, is the color and whether the upholstery goes with their clothes.
>
> I said *I* wasn't all that interested in colors.
>
> "Which just goes to show," the man said, "that you don't know what women want."

Caroline Bird's introduction previews her ideas about the status of women. It illustrates how the opinions of women often have not been taken seriously in the past. The example from her own experience in public relations work helps build up interest in the topic.

Again, as you can see, the previewing of the topic is a very important function of the introduction in speeches given to inform. Because the principal purpose of the speech is to teach, the speaker must make sure the message is received. To insure audience understanding, good public speakers use several opportunities to restate their message. Previewing the topic in the introduction is the first opportunity to give the listener the basic message in a brief form. If the audience hears the topic previewed in the introduction, is told the complete message in the body of the speech, and then hears the same message summarized in the conclusion, most of them are likely to receive the message.

Apply the message to the audience

A third function of the introduction is a natural follow-up to previewing the topic. As soon as you tell your listeners what you propose to talk about, show them how that topic applies to them. Applying the message to the listeners means showing the audience what they stand to gain from hearing the message, why the topic should be of particular interest to them, and why it has significance for them.

Louis Housman applied his message in a speech on "Older Americans" by showing that the speech dealt with a significant topic and by implying that his listeners stood to gain from hearing about this topic:

> There are 31 million Americans 60 years and older. They constitute the single largest minority in the nation. There are more of them than there are blacks or Chicanos of all ages.
>
> This minority, since 1900, is growing at twice the rate of our total population.
>
> The way in which these older Americans are viewed by society as a whole, by younger persons, and by themselves, has important implications for all of you concerned with the well-being of older persons.

Establish ethos

The ancient Greek rhetorician Aristotle claimed that three forces influenced an audience—the speaker's logic, appeals to the listeners' emotions, and the character of the speaker. He wrote that the speaker's character, which he called **ethos,** was the most powerful of the three. Although Aristotle was writing about persuasive speaking, and though some modern speech authorities would disagree with his ranking of the three elements, no one would claim that the speaker's character and credibility is unimportant, even in informative speeches. You have undoubtedly noticed how you accept what some people tell you much more readily than you accept the words of others. Ethos is also the basis for the old adage among salespersons: "You have to sell yourself first."

Since listeners more readily accept information from a source they believe and have confidence in, establishing one's ethos is an important

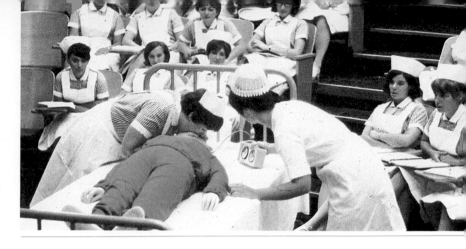

"You may be able to save a life." The audience at this demonstration of coronary pulmonary resuscitation will be more attentive throughout the speech if they realize how important it could be for them to be able to restart a heart that has stopped beating.

task for a public speaker to accomplish during the introduction of an informative speech. Of course, not all speakers need to begin by establishing their expertise and sincerity. Well-known personalities or speakers fortunate enough to be introduced to their audience by someone else are usually wiser to accept their reputation in modest silence. Most speakers, however, must themselves fulfill the job of convincing the listeners of their knowledge, sincerity, and likeability. When this job is left up to you, as it will be in most of your speeches, you should establish your ethos early, preferably during the introduction.

Ethos exists in the minds of your listeners. It consists of their inward answers to three unspoken questions: "Is this speaker thoroughly familiar with the subject?" "Is this speaker being completely open and honest with me?" "Do I enjoy listening to this speaker?" Many of the techniques useful for gaining audience attention and building interest in the speech topic may also aid in building speaker ethos. Humor for instance, usually increases an audience's enjoyment when listening to a speaker. Devices such as narrative and the shock technique can show listeners the speaker has done research and is informed about the topic.

Several specific techniques for building ethos can be used on occasions when you feel a special need to "sell your credentials" to your audience. One of these is straightforwardly mentioning some of the research and preparation you did for the speech. This can be worked into your introduction not in a bragging way but simply to show the listeners you have earned the right to speak to them. A similar technique of ethos-building consists of mentioning some experience you have had that qualifies you as an "expert" on your topic. Here is an example of such an ethos-builder:

> "Perhaps the process by which soft drinks are bottled sounds like an awfully dry and humdrum topic for a classroom speech. Last year I probably would have considered it boring too, but my job last summer in a bottling plant showed me that, far from being humdrum, it's exciting and sometimes even dangerous. This afternoon I'd like to share with you some of the experiences...."

Such an introduction, besides building interest in the speaker's topic, shows the listeners they are listening to an eyewitness—someone who has earned the right to speak to them on this particular topic.

On occasions when you are introduced to the audience prior to your speech, you ordinarily will not want to attempt much, if any, ethos building of your own at the start of your speech. Usually a simple "Thank you, Bob" or "Thank you for that kind introduction" is all that is needed. If the introducer has been extremely flattering, you may want to insert a humorous comment to show modesty, such as "My generous introducer got so carried away, I found myself sitting here trying to imagine who was going to give this marvelous speech!" If, on the other hand, your introducer should fail to give you enough credit, you should modestly supply some of the missing facts yourself during the speech introduction. This should be done very matter-of-factly, as an attempt to fill in some information the introducer overlooked. Here is an example:

> Thank you, Sharon, for that introduction. Something Sharon did not mention was my two years as a Little League umpire. I bring this up because that experience gave birth to many of the ideas I will be expressing in my speech tonight.

Imparting the message of an informative speech

The central part of an informative speech, sandwiched between the introduction and conclusion, is called the body of the speech. The body contains the essential message of the speech, completely developed. The speech outline, of course, plots the speaker's individual approach to the topic, and the way in which the subject unfolds during delivery is unique to each individual speaker and speech occasion. Still, certain general rules must be followed while imparting the message if the informative speech is to have its maximum impact.

Maintain attention

A basic function of the introduction is to gain the initial attention of the audience. Gaining attention at the start, however, does not automatically give the speaker a guarantee of unbroken attention for the rest of the speech. Since people's attention usually focuses on one person or idea only briefly and shifts constantly from one object to another, a public speaker must make a constant effort to keep the listeners focused on the message.

Most of the attention devices that are useful during the introduction of an informative speech may also be sprinkled throughout the speech to maintain listener attention. A humorous anecdote, an occasional story, a set of shocking statistics, or a bit of suspense during the body of the speech can regain flagging attention and renew audience interest.

Careful preparation regarding nonverbal attention-factors can also help to capture audience attention effectively. The way your audience is seated is one of these nonverbal attention-factors. Speakers have found that audience attention generally remains at a higher level the closer the audience members are to one another. Audience members generate attention among themselves, thus relieving the speaker of part of the task of keeping their attention. Whenever you find yourself facing a sparse or scattered audience, with numerous empty chairs between your listeners, invite the audience to sit more closely together in front rows. Maintaining their attention throughout your speech will prove considerably easier.

A second nonverbal attention-factor relates to listening conditions. The more you, the speaker, can assure comfortable conditions for effective listening, the more likely you will be to have the continuous attention of your audience. Whenever possible, arrive at the speaking location before your audience to arrange for proper listening conditions.

React to feedback

As you proceed through your speech, be alert to audience reactions and respond to them whenever necessary. Reacting to audience feedback is not a technique a beginning speaker can acquire all at once during a first or second speech. It is an important skill to develop, however, since a public speech involves two-way communication just as a conversation does. To never show any reaction to audience feedback may cause some listeners to feel you are ignoring them. Many audiences may find this lack of response insulting.

In order to respond to feedback, you must first learn to interpret it. As you begin giving speeches you will notice that some listeners react more vigorously than others do. Some people will appear more interested, more alert, and more intense in their reactions. Pay closer attention to these individuals as you speak, and look for signs of understanding, puzzlement, agreement, or disagreement in their faces, their posture, and their eyes. Once you have developed the ability to recognize positive and negative reactions, you can begin to adjust your message, language, and delivery techniques a bit to lessen negative reactions and increase positive forms of feedback.

Adjust especially to an audience reaction if it comes from a sizeable proportion of your listeners. If only one or two listeners frown, for instance, their action may mean that only they did not understand or did not agree with something you just said. However, if thirty or forty percent of your listeners frown, whatever you just said probably needs repeating or clarifying.

Make smooth transitions

A transition is like a switch on a railroad line. It allows a speaker to change from one aspect of the topic to another. Well-planned transitions go unnoticed by the listeners but give them an impression of a smoothly flowing speech. Not planning one's transitions results in jerky shifts from one main point to another, making the speech sound like a series of disconnected mini-speeches.

Transitions between major points (the main heads of your outline) may consist of only a sentence or two that relates what you have just finished saying to what you will say next. Transitions between minor points (subheads) can often be made with just a word or phrase, such as "First . . .," "Second. . . ." In either case they all must be thoroughly planned and rehearsed, not left to chance. Word-for-word memorization may be useful when rehearsing transitions to assure they will tie the parts of the speech together clearly.

Speakers commonly plan major transitions (those between main heads) by selecting a key word or phrase used to make the previous point to reuse in making the next point. Notice how President John F. Kennedy, in his inaugural address, tied together two different kinds of "summonses" by focusing on that word in a transition:

> Since this country was founded, each generation of Americans has been summoned to give testimony to its national loyalty. The graves of young Americans who answered the call to service surround the globe.
> Now the trumpet summons us again—not as a call to bear arms, though arms we need—not as a call to battle, though

John F. Kennedy used the words summoned *and* summons *in his inaugural address to provide a smooth transition from speaking about the past to speaking about the present.*

embattled we are—but a call to bear the burden of a long twilight struggle, year in and year out, "rejoicing in hope, patient in tribulation"—a struggle against the common enemies of man: tyranny, poverty, disease and war itself.

Concluding an informative speech

Speech conclusions are typically brief, accounting for only about five percent of the total speech. However, the conclusion may represent the most important part of many speeches. Since the audience hears the conclusion last, they are likely to remember it the longest. A concluding summary is usually the third time the listeners have heard the basic speech message, so the greatest learning might be expected to occur at this point.

Include a summary

The **summary** is the main part of a speech conclusion. Though a conclusion may have other functions as well, its principal function is summarizing the major ideas, especially in an informative speech. Summarizing means presenting the basic message again in very brief form. This is generally accomplished by using the device called restatement— repeating the same ideas again, but in different words. Observe how two student speakers summarized their informative speeches.

The following conclusion is from a speech entitled "Africa: Continent of Change" by Joseph Palmer:

> I have spoken of an Africa that has problems—large, complicated, immediate and stubborn. To a large extent they bear the imprint of outsiders, are peculiar to the environment in which they are found, and are rooted in the past. But in most respects, they are part of the problems which face all mankind: past errors, change, adaptability, progress, and peace— and look to the future.

The second conclusion is from "The Life and Death of Our Lakes" by Marie Ransley:

> In all these ways—sewage, polluted run-off, and landfill— man accelerates the eutrophication process in terms of millennia. Scientists estimate that Lake Erie has aged 15,000 years since 1920. And Madison's Lake Mendota is believed to be in worse shape than Lake Erie. Thus there is reason to hear the plea "Save Madison's lakes!" What a pity it would be if we, in our unthinking way, caused the early death of Madison's lovely lakes. The green slime is caused here.

In each of the above summaries, the main ideas of the entire speech were again presented in brief form. Even without reading the entire speech, you were able to perceive the topic of the speech and its main points.

Consider other ideas for conclusions

Depending upon the nature of the topic, the audience, or the occasion, you may need to accomplish more than a simple summary with your speech conclusion. Below is a chart of concluding purposes you may wish to accomplish and techniques appropriate for each.

PURPOSE	METHODS
To cause the listeners to remember a single, most important principle or idea from your speech.	Insert a brief analogy or story highlighting the principle or idea in the conclusion.
To stimulate further interest in your speech topic among your listeners.	End with a question, which the speech has not fully answered.
To plant a theme, slogan, or key phrase in your audience's minds.	Begin the speech with the phrase or slogan, then repeat it word-for-word in the conclusion.
To stir the feelings of the listeners.	Conclude with a pertinent quotation from a well-known and respected individual.

Remember, every informative speech needs some form of conclusion. Never end with your last main point. The audience expects you to "put it all together" before you sit down. Conclusions need not be lengthy—as a matter of fact, they should almost always be brief—but they must always be there!

Conducting a question-and-answer period

At the conclusion of your in-class informative speeches, your teacher may ask you to remain at the lectern for a brief question-and-answer period with the class. This gives class members an opportunity to ask about points in your speech that are unclear to them. They can ask for additional information or simply delve more fully into your topic. Question-and-answer periods are also helpful for you in several ways. For one thing, they provide an opportunity for you to learn to think on your feet by forcing you to form answers without preparation beforehand. This should not alarm you if you know your subject thoroughly. A second reason for practicing question-and-answer periods stems from their frequent use following speeches given outside of the classroom. A large number of informative speeches given to civic clubs, church groups, or business groups call for the speaker to respond to questions from the audience about the speech topic.

Invite questions

You will generally know whether or not a question-and-answer period is likely to follow a speech. Some clubs and organizations consider such a session traditional. Or you may anticipate your topic arousing enough interest to cause a number of audience members to ask questions. Whenever you expect a question-and-answer period to follow a speech, it is a good idea to invite such a session when you begin your speech. Mentioning at the start that you will be happy to respond to any questions when you have finished gives the listeners a chance to develop questions during your talk. When a speaker ends the speech with "Now, are there any questions?" without giving any prior warning, the audience is caught off guard and often cannot form any significant questions quickly.

Once a question-and-answer session has begun, the speaker must be as impartial as possible in recognizing listeners who have questions. Naturally, preference should be given to the first hands raised over the later ones and to those who have not yet asked a question over those who have already had a turn. If there is a pre-arranged time limit for questions or if you feel that the audience is getting bored or that the questions are becoming repetitive, you can provide a warning that you are about to close the session. For example, you might make a comment such as "I believe we have time for only two more questions. I'll recognize the woman in the second row, then the man in the rear."

Answer questions

If you are thoroughly prepared and knowedgeable about your speech topic, you will be able to answer most questions easily. Occasionally, of course, a question will be raised to which you do not know the answer. When this occurs, simply respond "I'm sorry, I can't answer that question." For informative speeches you will not appear to be avoiding the question, but merely indicating a lack of knowledge on your part. Audiences do not expect speakers to be all-knowing on any topic, so using this response occasionally causes no one embarrassment.

In the next section you will learn about using visual aids during your speeches. If you have used one or more of these aids during an informative speech and someone asks a question related to an aid, be certain it is again brought into full view of the audience before responding to the question. This allows listeners to perceive your answer through two channels, verbal and visual. You may also wish to point to a particular part of an aid while responding, if the question relates specifically to that part.

When you are asked a question requiring both a direct answer plus some explanation, provide the direct answer first, then the explanation. Usually the questioner is more interested in the factual answer than in a list of reasons or causes, and making the person wait for the core of the answer can irk the questioner. Occasionally, you may feel there is strong justification for reversing this order, but ordinarily give the direct answer first followed by the explanation.

Finally, be complete and concise in answering questions. Avoid, on the one hand, single word answers such as "Yes" or "No." On the other hand, once you have answered the question, stop. Do not be tempted to ramble on with fascinating information that strays too far from the topic and which may only bore your listeners. If the matter is fairly technical in nature and requires some explanation for a complete answer, by all means give the explanation, then stop. Often there may be several others anxiously waiting to ask a question that is very special to them.

Using visual aids

Dr. Ray Birdwhistell, one of the foremost scholars in nonverbal communication, claims that words account for only thirty-five percent of what we communicate; the remainder is largely accomplished by body motion. Though the figure may be exaggerated, it emphasizes an important concept for public speakers. As a public speaker, you can accomplish communication through what the audience *sees*, as well as through what the audience *hears*.

Visual aids have been found very helpful both for the speaker and the listeners, especially during informative speaking. For the speaker they provide a natural excuse to move about on the platform, to gesture, and to point. They can also help the speaker to remember details of the presentation. If the speaker is giving a demonstration, they may be an essential part of it. Members of the audience find that visual aids deepen their perception and understanding of the speaker's message and help them remember the details of the speech.

While visual aids, well used, can better a speech in a number of ways, they can also turn a speech into a disaster if a speaker attempts to use them without thorough preparation and practice. Because speaking with visual aids involves doing two things at once—maintaining the verbal flow and handling physical objects—it is never easy. So more careful preparation is called for than for a speech without visual aids.

"Could you go over that once again, Gene? Just in case any of us don't understand it."

Deciding when to use aids

One of the first questions that will arise is "How do I know when to include visual aids in an informative speech?" During this course, your teacher may answer that question for you by saying "Your next speech should include visual aids." This is especially likely to happen if you are asked to give a demonstration. On other occasions, however, you will have to decide for yourself whether one or more visual aids should be used. Ask yourself these two questions: "If I use a certain aid, will its presence make it easier for me to get my point across? Will using a certain aid make the point more meaningful for my audience?" If the answer to either question seems to be "Yes," then you should include the aid. Suppose, for example, that you are asked to give a speech on "How to Thread a Motion Picture Projector." Using a side-view drawing that shows the working parts of a projector, or even better, an actual projector to thread with film as you talk, will save you an enormous number of words and much time. If you are giving a speech on "My Trip to the Grand Canyon," using several color slides will surely deepen the impression on your audience.

Once you have decided to use visual aids in a speech, beware of the temptation to overuse them. Visual aids in public speaking should always remain in the role their name implies—aids. Once they become the main center of audience interest and attention they have ceased to be aids and have turned a speech into a presentation of the aids themselves. Using five or six of your best slides as aids in a speech on "My Trip to the Grand Canyon" greatly enhances your speech, but showing twenty-five or thirty slides during a six- to eight-minute presentation means you are no longer giving a speech with visual aids; you are giving a slide show with a brief commentary.

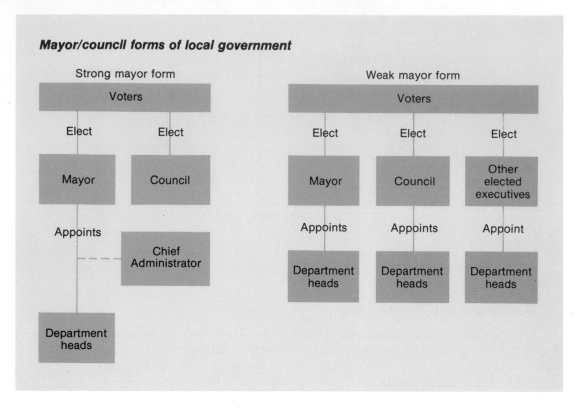

Mayor/council forms of local government

A sample line-staff chart

A sample line graph

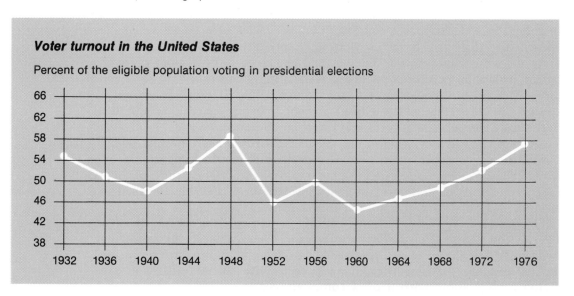

Voter turnout in the United States

Percent of the eligible population voting in presidential elections

Types of visual aids

At times you will want to use a series of aids, at other times only one will be necessary. It all depends on your speech topic and the relationship of the aids to it. Following are brief descriptions, with examples, of aids that are available to a speaker.

CHARTS. A drawing showing the relationships among the parts of a whole is a **chart.** The drawing usually includes lines and words and can deal with almost any subject. One commonly used type of chart is the *line-staff* chart showing the relationships among members of an organization. An example appears on page 240.

GRAPHS. A second common type of aid is the **graph.** Graphs picture large amounts of information (usually quantitative or numerical) at a single glance. They consist primarily of lines with occasional words and numbers. One frequently used type is the line graph on page 240. When the area under the peaks and valleys in a line graph is darkened to provide greater visual contrast, the graph is called a profile graph.

The bar graph is an alternate form of the line or profile graph, often used to show the same kind of information. A bar graph is shown below.

A circle graph, or pie graph as it is sometimes called, is used to indicate parts of a whole. On page 242 is a typical circle graph.

Picture graphs are similar to bar graphs in basic design, but include pictorial materials to heighten visual appeal. Since they demand

A sample bar graph

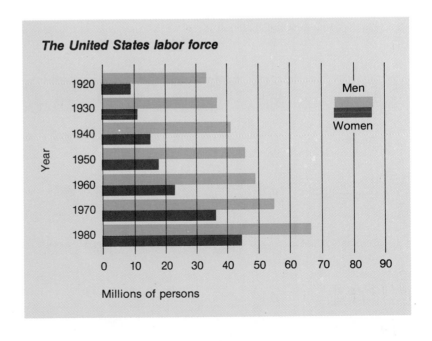

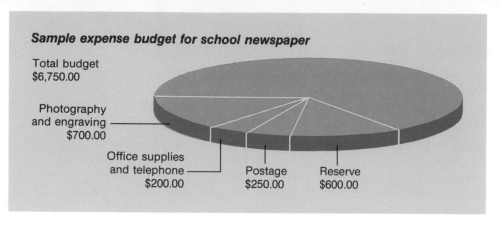

A sample circle or pie graph

more artistic ability, they are more difficult and time-consuming to prepare. At the bottom of page 242 is a picture graph.

DIAGRAMS. Like a chart and a graph, a **diagram** is used to show the relationship of a part to a whole. Diagrams, however, generally rely more on drawing and less on words and numbers than charts and graphs do. Diagrams may range from very simple line drawings to very

A sample picture graph

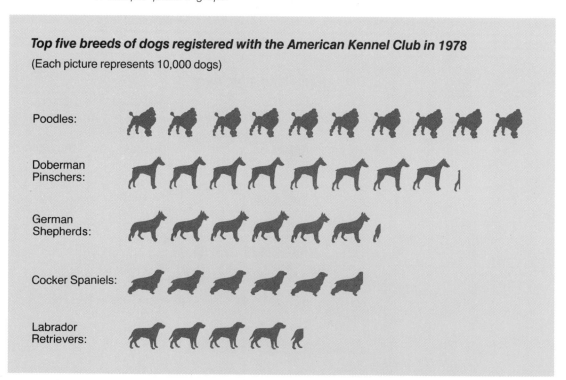

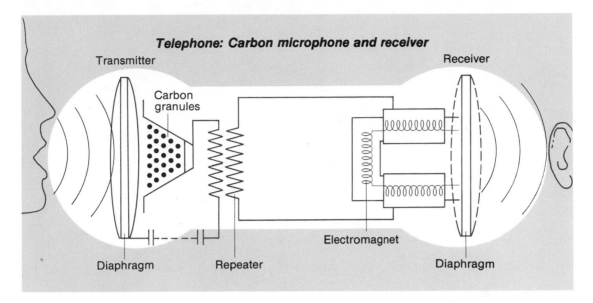

Telephone: Carbon microphone and receiver

A sample diagram

complex pictures with shading and perspective. The above figure is an example of a diagram.

MAPS. A **map** shows information that is geographical in nature. Some maps are used simply to indicate location, whereas others show location as it relates to elevation, weather at a given time, agricultural production, or any number of other items. The figure on page 244 is a map showing land use in China.

POSTERS. A relatively easy type of visual aid to prepare is one consisting of print or lettering on a **poster.** Lists of important points in your speech, key phrases, slogans, and humorous sayings can all be visually presented through print. Simply printing the main ideas of a speech on a large sheet of paper and showing it to the audience does not make an effective visual aid, however. Printed visual aids should be genuinely attention-getting or essential memory aids. The lettering must be imaginative, with attention given to spacing, color, size of letters, and their type style.

CARTOONS. Cartoons turn humor into a visual aid. A **cartoon** is simply a funny or satirical drawing used to make a point. Though cartoons demand a certain artistic ability to be effective, their impact on an audience can be great when they are well prepared.

PICTURES. Whether simply printed or in the form of a photograph, slide, filmstrip, or film, a **picture** can be a very effective visual aid. Two cautions, however, must be observed when using pictures. First, they must be large enough to be easily seen by the whole audience. If

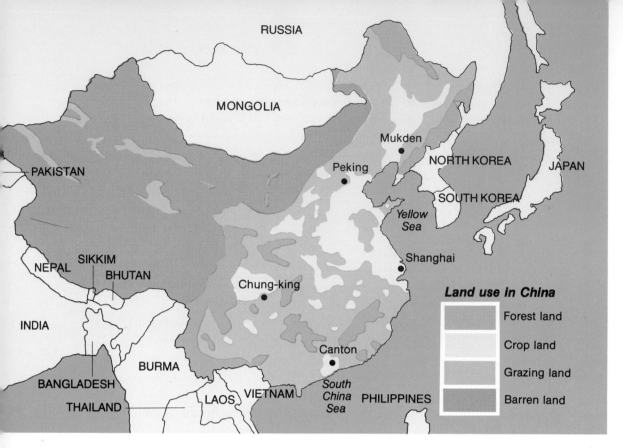

A sample map

necessary, they must be enlarged through projection. Second, the pictures themselves can easily become the center of attention and distract the audience from the speaker and the message. They must, therefore, be used sparingly. When these cautions are observed a picture can, indeed, be worth a thousand words.

OBJECTS. The aids discussed thus far are two-dimensional aids. A three-dimensional **object,** however, will make a deeper impression than a picture or representation. One of the great sales advantages of an auctioneer is being able to present the object being sold as he or she talks. Thus using a collection of Indian arrowheads, rather than drawings of them, as visual aids in a speech will gain greater audience attention and interest. At times it may be possible for audience members to handle as well as to see actual objects.

MODELS. Sometimes, an object is too large to be conveniently brought to a speech presentation. Then a scaled-down version, called a **model,** may be used instead. A two-foot (88-centimeter) plastic model of a rocket, for example, enables the speaker to show parts and views not possible with either a real rocket or a two-dimensional drawing. Models of many large objects may not be readily available, but often an inexpensive one can be made from cardboard or papier-maché.

CUTAWAYS. A model with a section of the outer covering removed to show interior parts is called a **cutaway.** A model of an internal combustion engine with part of the casing removed to show the valves and pistons, would be an example of a cutaway.

HANDOUTS. Something prepared ahead of time to give to each member of your audience is a **handout.** It can contain explanations, directions, maps, charts, or other material. Handouts are especially useful to present information to your audience that they will want to refer to after your speech is over. Be sure to have enough copies of your handout available so that each member of your audience can have one.

Handouts and the other aids mentioned here are not the only types of visual aids available; they are simply the ones most commonly used. Anything that can visually support the verbal part of a speech and is appropriate for the speaker, audience, and occasion may be used as a visual aid.

Following these guidelines will help you produce an effective visual aid.

Lettering visual aids: problems and solutions

STYLES — Styles that are too fine are difficult to see.

Styles that are too fancy are difficult to read.

SIMPLE, block styles are best.

SIZES — Lettering that is too small to be seen by your audience will not help get your message across.

½" letters (12.7 millimeters) cannot be seen from more than about ten feet (3 meters) by people with normal eyesight.

1" letters (25.4 millimeters) can be seen from about 30 feet (9.1 meters) by people with normal eyesight.

COLORS — Light colors on a light background cannot be seen easily.

Dark colors on a dark background cannot be seen easily.

Use colors that contrast with your background colors.

Preparing speeches using visual aids

Because speeches containing one or more visual aids are more difficult to deliver than speeches without visual aids, precise preparation and practice is called for when aids are to be used. Speakers usually prepare their own aids, but even in cases where the aid is readily available (objects, for example) careful rehearsal of the speech with the aid is essential to achieve perfect timing and handling.

A first principle regarding the selection and preparation of any aid you plan to display is that it must be capable of being seen easily from all parts of the room. Elementary as this may seem, it is one of the most frequently violated rules regarding the use of visual aids. For graphic aids such as charts, graphs, diagrams, maps, cartoons, and posters, this means that letters, numbers, and lines should be large and heavy and have sufficient contrast with the background on which they are mounted to be easily seen by all audience members in the back rows. The best way to ensure this is by stepping to the back of the room in which the speech will be given and checking the aid during its construction. Pictures cut from newspapers or magazines are rarely large enough for even a classroom audience of thirty people to see details without projection. Snapshots almost always require projection. Occasionally actual objects or models are too small for easy viewing of details. Remember, however, that it is only necessary for the audience to see whatever degree of detail you consider important. If minute details of the aid are not essential to your speech, then it is not essential that they be large.

A second necessary element in a visual aid is that it be neat and attractive. It need not be a work of art, but it should never be sloppy. One of the major problems with drawing an aid on a blackboard or easel while you are speaking is that most people who are not artists cannot produce an aid in a neat and attractive way under pressure. Preparing well-proportioned aids ahead of time, on the other hand, can greatly enhance your prestige with your audience. It gives listeners the impression that you were concerned enough about the reception of your speech to take pains to create attractive visual aids. When preparing them, the stress should be on neatness, but don't overlook the opportunity to highlight important items through the use of various colors and varied media. Felt tip pens, crayons, pre-made lettering, ink, and many other elements can be combined to produce an aid that is both informative and appealing.

You will also need to plan prior to the speech how to display the visual aid. Small objects, models, and cutaways can be held in the hands and shown to the audience with relative ease. Most good graphic and pictorial aids, however, will be so large that holding them while speaking will appear clumsy and awkward to the audience. If an easel is available, it can be very useful in displaying this type of aid, as long as

Visual aids need not be great works of art, but they should be prepared in advance so they will be neat and attractive.

you make sure that it is placed at the proper angle to be seen from all parts of the room. When an easel is not available, you may want to bring masking tape to help you properly display the aid. When displaying it by attaching it to the wall, be certain it is placed high enough so that the audience can see it. You should also make sure it is far enough from the lectern, so your body will not block the listeners' views. Finally, if you decide to lean the aid against something—an easel, the lectern, or a blackboard—you must use cardboard that is heavy enough to remain in place without being held.

Naturally you will need to point to various details on your aid at certain points in your speech. Pointing with your hand often means your arm blocks part of your audience's view of the aid. Thus you should use a pointer if at all possible. When using a pointer, hold it in whichever hand is closer to the aid so you do not have to reach across your body to point. Look at the aid only long enough to locate the spot to which you wish to point. Then, with your pointer held on that spot, turn your eyes immediately back to your audience. If your aid is such that you will be pointing to it repeatedly, continue holding the pointer in your hands during that portion of the speech in which you are making frequent reference to the aid. If, on the other hand, you plan to refer to the aid at only a few widely separated times during the speech, lay the pointer aside and pick it up again the next time it is needed.

Two other important matters to consider are the point at which you first wish to display an aid and the length of time you will want to continue to display it. If the aid will be referred to off and on throughout most of the speech, you want to show it to the audience when you first make reference to it and then let it remain in view until the speech

Inside Sarita Spears' head is stored a book of information about the United Nations. Sarita Spears is a tour guide at the U.N. in New York City, and there isn't much she doesn't know about the workings of that institution. She tells her tour groups, for instance, how many countries are represented in the General Assembly room and which flag belongs to which nation. She knows where the language interpreters sit as they transcribe English into French, or Chinese into Russian, and what the delegate, who is being applauded at that particular moment, just finished speaking about.

Tours last about an hour. During that time, Sarita Spears, who was born in Turkey but whose parents come from India, speaks constantly. She tries, on the one hand, for absolute accuracy of fact, although this is sometimes difficult because of the enormous amount of information she must store in her head. (U.N. tour guides speak extemporaneously, without benefit of notes.) On the other hand, her presentation must be interesting to listen to, fluent, and even dramatic at times to catch visitors' attention and hold it. In giving her speech, Sarita Spears attempts to find a happy balance between fact and flavor. A long barrage of facts would muddle a visitor's mind.

"All the information which we learn about the U.N. during our training can't possibly be delivered at one time," she said. "I think the main satisfaction we get is being able to vary what we say."

U.N. tour guides (there are presently 52 of them) go through an intensive three-week training period before making their debut before a group of visitors. Reading and learning facts about the U.N. is just the first step in this training. In classes, the guides are then taught to organize this material. "They ask us to prepare small speeches on the Security Council or the General Assembly and to give them in class the next day," Sarita Spears said. As a guide successfully masters the information and its presentation concerning one area of the U.N., she or he moves on to other areas—for instance, the Trusteeship Council or the gifts that nations have given to the U.N. Slowly new guides build up a repertoire of speeches which, strung together, make up the complete tour they eventually conduct.

But that's not all. The U.N. is not a static place where facts are always the same. Decisions are made and votes taken. Problems arise on a daily basis, and it is Sarita Spears' job to stay informed about issues the various councils are discussing. Every morning before work, the guides congregate in a small room for a 15-minute briefing session on the latest turn of events. They are expected to integrate the new information into their tour speeches, sometimes only minutes after the briefing has ended.

In addition, tour guides are expected to keep up with world events generally by reading newspapers and other publications on foreign affairs. The ability to assimilate information rapidly and then to speak about it is a crucial one for each guide. It is one of the reasons all U.N. guides must have a university degree to qualify for the job. In addition, guides must be fluent in at least two, but preferably three, languages.

Sarita Spears, who has lived in Argentina, Kenya, Brazil, Turkey, and India, speaks Portugese, Spanish, and two Indian languages besides English. She may conduct a tour in any one of these languages.

is completed. If the aid is to be referred to only once, or for the final time long before the speech is completed, you should put it aside or cover it immediately after your last reference to it. Otherwise, it will distract the listeners by remaining in view. Aids mounted on cardboard may be turned face down on a desk or table. Objects, models, and cutaways can be covered with a piece of cloth.

Practicing your speech while handling a visual aid is very important. In order for a speech involving visual aids to look smooth and professional, you must coordinate the verbal and the visual elements. The best place to rehearse is in the same room in which you will give the actual speech. If that is impossible, then a room similar in overall shape should be used. Practice when to first display the aids, how to display them, for what length of time, and when and how to remove them from view. Be certain that your body does not block the audience's view of visual aids.

Some aids are used to make a single point in a speech. They are displayed for only a few seconds. If you plan to use one or more aids of this type be certain to give the audience sufficient time to view the aid. Inexperienced speakers often work hard to produce a neat, attractive aid, then lose its effectiveness by displaying it for only two to three seconds. If the audience is going to have just one opportunity to see an aid, they will ordinarily need about ten to twelve seconds to familiarize themselves with the content of the aid. It is perfectly acceptable to display an aid in silence for several seconds after you have said what is necessary about it.

Using equipment with visual aids

Some visual aids can best be presented through the use of some form of equipment—an overhead projector, an opaque projector, a videotape unit, a movie projector, or a slide projector. When equipment is

 Checklist for visual aids

■ 1. Will using this visual aid help make my message more meaningful to my audience?

■ 2. Is it large enough to be easily seen from all parts of the room?

■ 3. If it includes letters, numbers, or line drawings, is there sufficient contrast between foreground and background colors for it to be easily seen?

■ 4. Is it neat, well-proportioned, and attractive looking?

■ 5. Can it be easily displayed before the audience?

■ 6. Have I planned at what point during my speech I will display the aid and for how long?

to be used, rehearsing with the equipment is as crucial as rehearsing with the aids themselves. Most projectors require a darkened or semi-darkened room, so you must be certain this can be arranged before choosing an aid requiring projection. Many times it is best to arrange for a friend or classmate to run the equipment during your speech and to turn the lights on and off at the proper times to relieve you of having too many responsibilities all at once. Naturally, such preparations must all be rehearsed in advance.

The day of the speech itself, carefully set up the equipment and check it prior to the speech. Don't assume that the projector bulb is all right or that the videotape player is working properly. More good speeches have probably been ruined by burned-out bulbs than by any other single cause. Finally, it is wise to plan how you will handle the situation if a piece of equipment malfunctions during your presentation. Perhaps you can prepare handouts in advance to use in case other materials cannot be used. It may be possible for you to explain verbally the material you had planned to display. Remember that audiences are usually sympathetic, so don't panic.

Application: Considering visual aids

Look at the sample speech topics listed in Chapter 7, page 153. Decide, for each topic, whether a visual aid or aids would be appropriate, and if so, what type of aid or aids could be used.

Summary

The main purpose of speeches given to inform is to impart new knowledge to the listeners. Informative speeches are used every day in situations as varied as business meetings, classroom teaching, and reports to labor unions. As long as the speech's primary purpose is to tell the listeners something they do not already know, a speech may be labeled an informative speech.

BEGINNING AN INFORMATIVE SPEECH. The functions of the introduction in an informative speech include gaining initial audience attention, building interest in the speech topic, previewing the topic for the listeners, applying the topic to the audience, and establishing ethos as a speaker. A number of time-tested techniques exist for carrying out these functions—humor, narrative, common ground, shock, suspense, the use of rhetorical and real questions, quotations, challenges, stating the speech purpose directly, and noting what the audience stands to gain from the speech.

IMPARTING THE MESSAGE OF AN INFORMATIVE SPEECH. While the body of an informative speech will inevitably follow each speaker's individual approach, several functions must be fulfilled during this main part of a speech. A speaker should maintain audience attention through the occasional use of some of the same devices used to gain initial attention in the introduction. Giving attention to seating arrangements and listening conditions before speaking can help assure continuous listener attention. A speaker must also react to audience feedback through careful monitoring of listener reactions and make smooth transitions during the body of the speech.

CONCLUDING AN INFORMATIVE SPEECH. The conclusion of an informative speech is ordinarily brief, but can fulfill several important functions. Chief among these is that of summarizing the major points made during the body of the speech. Speakers typically achieve their summary through restatement—saying the same ideas more briefly in different words. Other functions of the conclusion include planting a theme or key phrase in the listeners' minds and stirring the feelings of the listeners.

CONDUCTING A QUESTION-AND-ANSWER PERIOD. Question-and-answer periods often follow speeches. You should anticipate such a session by preparing for it during rehearsal and by promising to answer questions as the speech begins. This gives the listeners a chance to prepare questions and increases their level of participation in the speech itself. You should try to be impartial in recognizing questioners and aware of any pre-arranged time limit for the question-and-answer session. If you do not know the answer to a question, say so, rather than trying to bluff your way through an answer. If a question relates to a visual aid used during the speech, you should display the aid while answering that question. Answer questions directly and completely, but avoid unnecessarily long answers that stray from your topic.

USING VISUAL AIDS. Visual aids can be extremely effective tools for informative speaking. You can maximize their impact by carefully planning and meticulously rehearsing their use. The first decision—whether to use aids—should be made by answering the question "Will the use of this aid (or aids) make it easier to get my point across or make the speech more meaningful for my audience?" Once you have decided to use aids, the most appropriate ones may be chosen from a wide variety of types—charts, graphs, diagrams, maps, posters, cartoons, pictures, objects, models, cutaways, and handouts. Be sure that aids you plan to display can be seen easily from all parts of the room and are neat and attractive. Rehearse with each aid to find the best method for displaying it, how and when to point to it, and when to remove it from view. Handling visual aids requiring special equipment dictates even greater care during preparation.

Vocabulary

informative speech	chart
attention device	graph
humor	diagram
narrative	map
common ground technique	poster
shock technique	cartoon
suspense	object
ethos	model
transition	cutaway
summary	handout

Review questions

1. What is the primary purpose of an informative speech?

2. Name the five functions of an introduction.

3. Name five devices you can use to capture the audience's attention in your introduction.

4. What is the main purpose of the body of an informative speech?

5. What nonverbal factors affect the audience's attention to a speaker?

6. Why may the conclusion be the most important part of a speech?

7. What should a summary include?

8. What are some examples of two-dimensional and three-dimensional visual aids? (Give at least five.)

9. When should visual aids be used?

10. How and when should visual aids be used during the question- and-answer period?

Discussion questions

1. Discuss the various attention-getting techniques that can be used in an introduction. Suggest topics with which each technique would be especially appropriate.

2. Talk with your classmates about the problems of interpreting and reacting to audience feedback. Discuss ways of recapturing listeners' attention when it wanders.

3. Discuss the problems involved in a question-and-answer period following a speech. What are some things you can do to try to predict what questions you may be asked? How can you prepare to answer them? How would you deal with someone who attacked you or your speech? How would you deal with a question you couldn't answer?

4. Make a list of topics that lend themselves to the use of visual aids. What types of visual aids are especially appropriate for each topic?

5. Discuss the use of visual aids (background photographs, charts, videotape footage, and so on) on a TV news program. When are the visual aids critical in understanding content and when are they just "window dressing"?

At-home activities

1. Read the introduction of some well-known informative speech assigned by your teacher. Make two columns on a sheet of paper. In the left-hand column list the functions of an informative-speech introduction that the speaker fulfilled (gaining attention, building interest in the topic, previewing the topic, applying the message to the audience, establishing ethos). In the right-hand column opposite each function list the device or devices the speaker used to accomplish that function (humor, narrative, common ground, suspense, shock technique, rhetorical question, real question, quotation, challenge, stating the speech purpose directly). This same exercise could also be carried out on the body of a speech or the conclusion.

2. After rehearsing for an informative speech, write a list of any questions you are likely to receive during a question-and-answer period. Do not try to memorize word-for-word answers, but rehearse the kind of answers you would give. You will not anticipate every question, but you will answer completely and effectively those you did practice.

3. Prepare a visual aid for an in-class speech. Check to see if your aid meets all criteria in the checklist on page 249.

In-class activities

1. As you listen to some in-class informative speeches, write a list of the functions of the introduction each speaker fulfills and the devices used to accomplish those functions. You may be asked to turn in these lists for a listening grade or to give them to your classmates as reactions to their speeches.

2. Discuss whether or not the aids used in several class speeches seemed appropriate for the topics, how well they were prepared, and how effectively they were handled during the speech. Give constructive opinions only.

3. Take part in a class discussion dealing with the question-and-answer periods held at the end of a presidential news conference. How well do you feel the President invites and answers questions? What rules seem to be followed both by the President and the reporters? In what ways could presidential news conferences be improved?

Careers

PUBLIC INFORMATION OFFICERS act as links between organizations and the public by collecting and directing information through the media. They prepare written and oral messages. High school courses in English, speech, social studies, psychology, and business are helpful. Knowledge of public speaking is essential, since much time is spent speaking to groups. A bachelor's degree is the basic educational requirement. Public information officers work for small and large companies, as well as public agencies such as police departments and social welfare organizations.

COUNTY AGRICULTURAL AGENTS organize and conduct cooperative extension programs to advise and instruct farmers and others about applications of agricultural research findings. They advise on related problems and demonstrate practical procedures. High school courses in math, science, and speech are helpful. A bachelor's degree in agriculture is required.

11

SPEAKING TO PERSUADE

When you have completed this chapter you should be able to

Describe the difference between informative and persuasive speaking.

Explain three ways people can be persuaded.

List characteristics of positive, neutral, disinterested, and opposed audiences.

Use the most effective persuasive strategies for different kinds of audiences.

Explain how evidence and reasoning work together to create logical persuasion.

Choose the most appropriate forms of evidence for different kinds of audiences.

Describe and practice the three ways of building prestige.

Explain what is meant by *responsible persuasion.*

Much of public speaking has as its primary purpose providing information to listeners—informing them about subjects the speaker knows more about than they do. But another purpose which accounts for a great number of speeches is that of persuasion. A speech given to persuade has as its primary goal the influencing of the attitudes, beliefs, or behavior of the listeners. Political figures try to secure votes through persuasive speaking. Lawyers use persuasion to secure a jury's decision. Legislators speak persuasively for or against a pending bill. All citizens have numerous opportunities for persuasive speaking. You might want to convince members of your PTA to take a certain stand on the school budget, tell your city council why you believe they should vote for an ordinance you favor, or explain to other members of your investment club why you feel a certain stock should be bought. All would be exercises in persuasion.

Each one of the general principles of public speaking discussed in earlier chapters applies to persuasive speaking. Persuasive speaking, however, is more difficult than speaking to inform. It demands additional skills which will be discussed in this chapter.

Three sources of persuasion

Before people will believe, think, or do something, they must *want* to do it. **Persuasion** is simply a means by which one person can cause another to *want* to believe, to think, or to do. You adopt new beliefs, attitudes, and actions constantly. Think for a moment why you might decide to accept a certain date, admire a certain singer, or learn to drive a car. Basically, each decision is made only when *you want* to make it. Whenever someone else tries to convince you to decide a certain way, that person is using the process of persuasion.

Three major factors are likely to influence people when they adopt an attitude, belief, or behavior pattern: (1) their personal drives, needs, and desires, (2) their own thinking processes, and (3) the character and personality of others. Persuaders must concentrate on each of these factors. They must know their listeners' needs, build logical arguments that others can follow, and establish their own prestige when attempting to influence listeners. A knowledgeable, logical, sincere speaker stands an excellent chance of successfully persuading others.

Analyzing the needs of your listeners

Most people like to consider themselves very logical creatures. They prefer to think they make decisions and behave in certain ways based solely on logic. But if they were to make an honest analysis of the reasons for much of their behavior and many of their decisions, they would probably be forced to admit that they are sometimes not logical at all. Unlike Mr. Spock of *Star Trek*, people frequently believe, decide, or act in particular ways simply because they want to or need to, rather than because reason or logic points to these choices.

If you plan to persuade people, you must appeal to the needs and desires of your listeners as well as to their brains. Some people consider this beneath the dignity of a persuader. This is not the case at all, as long as the needs and desires to which you appeal are legitimate, and you honestly believe in the cause you are promoting.

Discover the needs of your audience

The effective persuader seeks out the special needs and attitudes of each audience prior to a speech in order to plan the strategy most suited to that group of listeners. Remember the section on audience analysis in Chapter 7? Knowing the particular needs and attitudes of an audience is especially important when you are speaking to persuade. In a persuasive speech the success or failure of your entire speech can depend on how well you know your audience beforehand.

Audiences may have hundreds of special needs and attitudes depending on the subject of a given speech and the listeners' previous experiences with the topic. These many different needs can be grouped according to how they affect the audiences' reception of you and your topic. An audience's attitude toward you and your topic will fall somewhere on a scale between "very positive" and "very negative." Essentially, audiences fall into four basic categories: the positive audience, the neutral audience, the disinterested audience, and the opposed audience. Each has a different set of needs and must be approached differently by the speaker. You will want to try to place your audiences' pre-speech attitudes as carefully as possible on this scale.

Scale of audience attitudes

Yes, I agree.   I'm not sure. Maybe.   Ho-hum.   No. You're wrong!

← Positive ———— Neutral ———— Disinterested ———— Opposed →

The **positive audience** is one that already agrees with your basic persuasive purpose. If you are speaking to librarians about the need to raise money for the local library, most of your listeners are likely to be in favor of your idea before you begin. If you are speaking to students about the need to oppose a curfew for young people in your community, most of your audience will again be likely to support your idea. Of course, this is the easiest type of audience to persuade. Your only persuasive task is to deepen their feelings about the topic. Their basic need is simply for a "recharging."

The **neutral audience** has a different need. They are neither for nor against your topic—they simply do not know very much about it. Their basic need is for information that will make it possible for them to form an opinion. Suppose you are trying to sell a brand new dishwashing detergent, and the people in your audience have never heard of it before. If you are going to persuade them to buy it, you must first give them some information about it. You might, for example, tell them that it washes more dishes per bottle than brand X, it smells better than brand Y, it cleans better than brand Z, and it is easier on the hands than all three!

The **disinterested audience** knows about the topic but couldn't care less. They consider it a dull issue or an unimportant one, not particularly relevant to them or their needs. This kind of audience needs to be "electrified." They need to be shown the seriousness of the problem, the closeness of the danger, or the way in which they will be affected. Before they can be persuaded to do anything, they must be motivated to care.

The **opposed audience** is the most difficult kind of audience for a persuasive speaker to face. It is composed of people who disagree with your stand on the topic. They feel as strongly about the issues as you do, but they have opposing opinions. Sometimes they may distrust you simply because you hold a viewpoint different from theirs. Their need is first for open-mindedness, then for conviction. You must first succeed in getting a fair hearing for your side, then attempt to convince them of your view.

How do you discover whether you will be facing a positive, neutral, disinterested, or opposed audience? Usually by the same methods mentioned under "Audience Analysis" in Chapter 7 starting on page 148. Ask the person who invites you to speak about the attitudes and needs of the listeners. Ask friends and acquaintances who know your future audience members. Talk to other speakers who have addressed the same group in the past. In each case, ask questions designed to tell you about the attitudes of the audience toward your topic and about their needs in relationship to the topic.

If you are planning a speech that strongly advocates greater freedom for editors and reporters on your school newspaper, appropriate questions to ask about members of your future audience might include the following:

- *How many of my audience members will be fellow students?*
- *How many will be teachers and school administrators?*
- *What is the attitude of our organization of parents and teachers towards the school paper?*
- *Are there certain opinion leaders among the group? If so, what are their views on freedom of the press?*
- *Have any of the audience members been bothered in the past by insistent school reporters?*
- *Do some of the school administrators feel our school press is too liberal in its editorial views?*

Questions of this kind should enable you to make an educated estimate of the attitudes and needs of the particular audience you will be facing. Once you know those attitudes and needs you can begin planning your persuasive strategy. Strategies differ, depending on the type of audience.

Use different approaches for different audiences

For the positive audience, your job is a relatively easy one—keep them happy or make them even happier! Since the positive audience already is in basic agreement with you, you have probably been invited to speak either to rededicate or remotivate them or talk about means rather than ends. A common example of a speaker facing a positive audience is that of a coach giving a pep talk to a team before the big game. The team members form a positive audience in the sense that they share the same goal as the coach—they all want to win. The coach's job as a speaker, then, is not to convince them that they should win, but to "psych them up" and to convince them that certain tactics will work better than others.

The neutral audience needs information. Certain kinds of information, especially factual information, can be convincing in itself, particularly when fact is piled upon fact. The strategy for handling a neutral audience, then, is one of presenting the listeners with information from which they can reach only one conclusion—the conclusion you want them to reach. Beth Simmons, a high school student, shows how to apply this strategy in her speech called "It's Hard to Be Human."

From early America's melting pot to today's claim that "Everybody Needs Milk" our differences have been homogenized to produce an era of paper people. Now you take a society, fold it into convenient sizes, cut carefully, unfold, and PRESTO! Nameless, faceless, expressionless silhouettes meaninglessly holding hands.

Your first task as a persuasive speaker facing any audience is to win a fair hearing for your arguments.

Whoever you are, today's horoscope will apply; the message in any fortune cookie is universally didactic. Dial a prayer, dial an inspiration, or if you need a friend, phone dial-a-smile to hear continuous laughing for three minutes, only interrupted by a voice reminding you that it is just a recording. It's easy to become satisfied with having things done for us by our computers and tape recorders. And, just as easy, to slip into the efficiency of automatic communication.

Notice how Beth Simmons used specific examples and experiences common to most of her listeners. In this manner, she increased her chances of persuading her audience to agree that it is difficult to be an individual in an increasingly impersonal world.

Facing a disinterested audience is harder than facing a neutral one. When an audience is aware of an issue, but considers it unworthy of any mental strain on their part or too dull to bother getting excited about, the speaker's main persuasive task is somehow to light a fire under those listeners. Often this can be done by showing the audience how the topic will affect them directly. President Jimmy Carter used this technique when appealing to his listeners' basic need for survival in a speech on "Nuclear Arms Reduction" delivered to the United Nations General Assembly:

If we are to have any assurance that our children are to live out their lives in a world which satisfies our hopes—or that they will have a chance to live at all—we must finally come to terms with this enormous nuclear force and turn it exclusively to beneficial ends.

Dealing with the opposed audience requires a double strategy. First, the listeners must be "softened up" to the point where they will really listen to your arguments and consider them fairly. Second, you must present sound evidence to back your position. Imagine that you have discovered some "shady dealings" during your school's most recent election for class officers. You plan to expose these practices in your next classroom speech, to be titled "Whatever Happened to Integrity?" You know you will face an opposed audience, since most of the members of your speech class were very active and involved in the election process either as candidates or campaign workers. Starting your speech with a direct attack on the issue would be an almost certain way to lose that kind of audience right at the beginning:

> Student politics and student government in this school are riddled with graft and corruption. The recent election showed me quite clearly that we cannot trust either the winners or the losers. In an election where vote buying occurred and campaign workers tampered with ballot boxes . . . .

Such an opening will only deepen the negative feelings of an opposed audience. Even with facts to back up your claims, it is unlikely that you would achieve a fair hearing for your case. A better approach for this kind of audience would be:

> This school has always had good student leadership. I think you will agree that since our first year here we have been fortunate in the people we have elected as our class officers. I know many of you are dedicated to good student government here, as I am. I was very surprised and shocked, therefore, to discover some irregularities in our recent election process. Please listen as I recount some facts that have come to my attention. . . .

This approach may not persuade your listeners to believe you any more than they would have with the first approach, but at least, in the second case, your audience is likely to listen to your arguments and consider them. If the arguments you then present in the body of the speech are strong enough, the listeners may actually be persuaded.

Of course, positive, neutral, disinterested, and opposed audiences do not always occur in pure form. Many times an audience is composed of people who disagree among themselves. When an audience is made up of positive listeners and neutral listeners, the speaker's task is not too difficult. Giving persuasive information to such a group satisfies the neutral listeners and recharges those who already agree. The same approach can also be used effectively with an audience of neutral and opposed listeners but should be preceded in this case by some "mind-opening" tactics before presenting the factual information. For a disinterested and opposed group, the approach suggested for opposed listeners alone may prove effective. Perhaps the worst combination to face is an audience of positive and opposed listeners. Here, too, the safest approach might be to use the strategy for opposed listeners. By appealing mainly to them, you may gain some converts from your opposed listeners and are unlikely to lose any of the positive ones. The next section will present specific kinds of evidence that can be useful in dealing with these different types of audiences.

Being logical

Have you ever been in an argument with someone and found yourself saying, "You're not being logical!" If you have, you probably still remember how frustrated you felt because the other person wouldn't argue according to the rules of logic. People frequently make decisions based on their needs and desires, but they like to feel they have decided logically. A persuasive speaker's job is to show listeners through logic how to fulfill their needs and desires. Logic, then, is a powerful tool of persuasion.

Use valid evidence and correct reasoning

Being logical in persuasive speaking means using valid evidence and correct reasoning. **Evidence** is the raw material with which you must begin. **Reasoning** is the process of putting this raw material together into a logical argument, which in turn may be used to reach a logical conclusion. The process of building a logical argument to use in a persuasive speech can be compared to the way in which mighty rivers are formed. Rivers begin in the mountains and hills in tiny rivulets and creeks (evidence), which then flow together (the reasoning process) to form larger streams. Finally, these larger streams run together in a mighty river (the conclusion). Imagine that you wish to persuade your fellow townspeople that your city desperately needs a new hospital. In the diagram on page 262 the creeks represent your evidence, the paths taken to form streams represent the reasoning process, and the entire process results in a river—your conclusion.

To reach this conclusion, you must begin with good evidence. In Chapter 7, you studied a number of different types of evidence that can be used to support your arguments: facts, statistics, testimony, narrative, examples, and comparisons. The most persuasive evidence you can use generally consists of facts or statistics. Testimony, when the opinions are based upon facts, is also a very persuasive type of evidence. Notice how, in the diagram, the pieces of evidence are either statements of provable fact or opinions that can be backed by facts. Since support for a conclusion almost always begins with such evidence, a good persuader must be certain of the correctness of the evidence which is used throughout the argument.

Once you have chosen your evidence, use the process of reasoning to make sure that the evidence flows together logically to produce the conclusion you wish to reach. If you have given equally persuasive facts

Twenty-four people who could not get beds in our present hospital died last year.

Dr. Jones feels twenty of those people would probably have recovered had they been able to get into a hospital.

Proper treatment for their ailments was available in our present facility.

Neighboring Jamestown has twice the number of hospital beds that we have to fill its needs.

No one was denied a hospital bed in Jamestown last year.

When people are dying simply because enough hospital beds are not available, something needs to be done.

We should have at least as many hospital beds available as does a smaller, neighboring town.

The state fire marshall, during his visit last month, said our present hospital is not safe from fire.

Our city electrical inspector has said our present hospital is not safe from fire.

Our present hospital is a firetrap.

OUR TOWN NEEDS TO BUILD A NEW AND LARGER HOSPITAL.

"Our town needs a new and larger hospital." You will need evidence and correct reasoning to turn a statement such as this into a valid conclusion.

for and against your conclusion, you cannot expect your audience to agree with your conclusion. If your conclusion is based on three arguments but you have supported only one of them with evidence, you will also have difficulty in convincing your audience. If your evidence is weak or contrary to the practical experience of the audience, you are again likely to fail. To succeed, your reasoning must show how each piece of evidence works with the other pieces of evidence, how all of them together lead to one very definite conclusion—the conclusion you wish the audience to reach.

Make your evidence suit your audience

Certain forms of evidence have been found to be especially suitable for various kinds of audiences. The following chart gives the four basic types of audiences and the kinds of evidence that may be especially effective with each.

TYPE OF AUDIENCE	KINDS OF EVIDENCE
Positive	Narrative, Examples, Comparisons
Neutral	Facts, Statistics, Testimony, Examples
Disinterested	Facts, Statistics
Opposed	Narrative, Facts, Statistics, Examples, Comparisons

The positive audience needs recharging, not convincing. Narrative, examples, and comparisons seem most effective with such listeners. The neutral audience lacks information. They find examples helpful, but are likely to be more impressed with facts, statistics, and testimony. The disinterested audience must be given facts and statistics. They must be shown that a serious problem exists or is about to become critical and that it affects them. The opposed audience needs all the tools at the speaker's command. A speaker is wise to start with humor, common-ground devices, or compliments. A narrative can also work well at the beginning. Once the listeners have decided to give the speaker a fair hearing, these can be followed with the harder forms of evidence (facts, statistics, examples, and comparisons). Mixed audiences react best when the speaker analyzes their needs correctly, then applies the various kinds of evidence in the best proportions. Correct reasoning is important no matter what type of audience you face. Logical reasoning is especially important, however, when facing an opposed audience.

Application: Using logic that will suit your audience

Assume you have been asked to give a speech on the topic "This School Needs a New Gymnasium." Discuss in class how you would approach each of the following audiences:

The student body
A group of parents and teachers
The school board

Which of these audiences would you consider positive, neutral, disinterested, or opposed? What types of support would you use with each?

Use a logical framework

Two of the speech patterns discussed in Chapter 7 provide an especially logical framework for persuasive speeches. These are the problem-solution pattern and Monroe's Motivated Sequence. You may want to review that section of Chapter 7, giving particular attention to these two patterns. Both offer certain ideas that may be useful in developing a logical strategy for your own persuasive speeches.

Whatever pattern you use, your persuasive speeches must have an introduction, a body, and a conclusion. These three basic parts of a speech, which were discussed in Chapter 10, serve similar functions in almost every speech. However, a special emphasis should be given to several specific functions in persuasive speeches. In the introduction, building your ethos becomes particularly important. In the body, it is essential to use valid evidence and correct reasoning. In the conclusion, you must reestablish your ethos and clearly indicate the response you desire from your audience. As you can see, building ethos, or establishing **prestige**, is especially important in persuasive speaking. The next section should help you accomplish this.

Establishing your prestige

At the beginning of this chapter it was stated that speakers must rely on their knowledge of the listeners' needs, logic, and their own prestige in any attempt to persuade. Having looked at the first two of these, you are now ready to turn to the matter of prestige.

In Chapter 10 you read that the ancient Greek rhetorician Aristotle used the term ethos to describe a speaker's prestige. He felt it was the most powerful form of proof a speaker could possess. No matter how logical a speaker, no matter how well that speaker appeals to the needs of the listeners, if those listeners do not respect the speaker's character, there is little chance of successful persuasion. Thus, as a speaker, you must establish ethos, especially when attempting to persuade an opposed audience. This is done by showing listeners you are well prepared and competent, by being sincere in what you say, and by appearing genuinely interested in your audience.

Competence: Let your preparation show

If a persuader ever hopes to convince listeners of anything, that speaker must show a high degree of **competence** and **confidence.** Audiences do not follow frightened or hesitant speakers. Only speakers who know their topic thoroughly and feel confident in their preparation are likely to succeed at persuasion. If your preparation has been shallow or haphazard, you will find it almost impossible to convince your audience of anything. Abraham Lincoln's well known saying applies aptly to persuasive speaking: "You can fool some of the people all of the time, and all of the people some of the time, but you cannot fool all of the people all of the time." Incompetence and lack of confidence will usually become obvious to most audiences after a very short period of time.

While audiences seldom fail to notice incompetence, they may occasionally fail to recognize a truly competent speaker. If no one points out a speaker's knowledge, preparation, and ability to the listeners, they can misjudge the true qualities of that speaker. Sometimes a speaker's competence is mentioned when someone introduces him or her to the audience before the speech begins. In such introductions the audience is informed about the speaker's qualifications to speak on the topic. When a speaker has already established a national reputation in a given field or is well known to a local audience, it is unnecessary to remind listeners of the speaker's competence. Unfortunately the speakers most needing this kind of "prestige-boosting," the unknown or inexperienced speakers, are the ones who least often receive it. This leaves them with the task of building their own ethos during their speeches.

One of the most effective methods of assuring your audience of your competence is to let your speech preparation show during the speech. This can be accomplished in several ways. One way is by frequent use of evidence and supporting materials. The use of facts, survey results, statistics, and quotations from known authorities in the field says several important things about your knowledge and preparation. First it assures the audience that you are not simply "putting your mouth in motion." Listeners who hear sufficient amounts of evidence will recognize that you have backing for what you are saying and are not merely expressing your own unsupported opinions. Second, referring to outside sources of evidence shows the audience you have taken the time and effort to discover that evidence. Even though they may be an opposed audience, they will admire you for doing thorough research to support your point of view. They will realize you have earned the right to speak to them about your topic.

A second way of showing your competence is by referring to your own experience with your topic, particularly during the introduction of your speech. Audiences have learned to expect this kind of self-competence building from unknown speakers and do not consider it bragging, as long as it is done in a subtle and sophisticated manner. Notice how Bart Wojciehowski accomplished this in his speech dealing with the right to die with dignity. His speech won fifth place in a national high school speech contest:

> This past year held two unique events for me. The first involved my oldest friend, an elderly man forewarned of his impending death of malignant cancer. At that time, with the Socratian wisdom of someone who had fought the good fight for eight decades, my friend requested of his wife and family that he be allowed to die as comfortably as possible in the security of his own home. Family members rallied to provide the attending support and health care for his last few remaining months.

The audience soon learns that this friend was the speaker's own grandfather. Bart's use of this kind of personal experience undoubtedly went a long way toward earning him respect and a good response from his audience.

You can also show experience or preparation by mentioning a part-time job you have had, by describing an informal survey you have taken, or simply by saying, "While researching for this speech, I noticed...." So long as you do not overdo this kind of reference, your ethos will grow in the minds of your listeners.

If they are to be successful, politicians must be able to convince voters of both their competence and their sincerity.

Sincerity: Don't fake it!

Sincerity is the second part of a speaker's prestige. Like competence, it must be genuine to make a lasting positive impression. Insincere speakers can impress audiences for a time, but eventually most are exposed as "fakes." What is meant by **sincerity** in persuasive speaking? Basically, it means that the speaker's motives for advocating a particular attitude, belief, or behavior must originate from a genuine concern for the best interests of the audience rather than from self-interest.

If a politician speaks to the people about a solution to a problem during an election year, the listeners sometimes find it hard to believe that the politician is attacking the problem unselfishly. A natural question in their minds is "Is the purpose of this speech to help solve the problem or to assure election?" A politician speaking under such circumstances needs to make a special effort to convince the audience of her or his sincerity. Audiences will more readily accept a speaker they consider somewhat incompetent than a speaker they consider insincere. The slightest hint of insincerity will turn many listeners against a speaker instantly.

Good will: Show a genuine interest in your audience

Audiences will be more open and receptive to a speaker who shows an interest in them or **good will** toward them. Particularly with opposed audiences, persuaders need to first open the minds of their listeners to assure a fair hearing for their side of the issue. Getting an audience to like you as a person can lead to its members liking and accepting your arguments.

One commonly used method of showing an interest in one's audience is the practice of expressing appreciation for the invitation to speak to the group. The first thing ordinarily done by many speakers is to voice an appreciation for the privilege of addressing the audience.

Closely related to thanking one's audience is complimenting them. If you genuinely believe "This club represents the leaders in our community," then do not hesitate to tell the club. If you consider your audience to be a fair-minded group of people of sound judgment, tell them that, especially if your topic is likely to demand that they be fair as they listen: "This group has a reputation for being open-minded and fair in its decisions. I feel confident you will listen to what I have to say today in that same spirit." An opening such as this compliments the listeners and challenges them to be fair-minded as they listen to your speech.

Another way to show interest in your audience is to speak directly to various individuals in the group. If you are well acquainted with members of your audience, you may want to call them by name during your introductory remarks: "I see my friend Charles Stevens here today. I'm glad you could be here, Charlie." This sort of public recognition flatters Charles and probably puts him in a more receptive frame of mind toward you and your message. But calling audience members by name can be risky. If you call one friend's name, you'd better call all of your friends by name; otherwise, those left out may feel slighted. If you see twenty-eight of your friends in the audience, however, you'd better avoid such a roll call! Take care also not to identify someone as a friend if that person is only a nodding acquaintance. This comes across as false and insincere.

To show interest in your audience in another way, you might identify interests and experiences you and your listeners have in common. The use of the common-ground technique (see page 225) is a good method for demonstrating a genuine interest in your listeners as people. Audiences appreciate this. Effective use of humor (see page 224) also makes the speaker seem a likeable person. If you can make your listeners laugh with you, they are more likely to listen receptively to your serious, persuasive message.

Application: Analyzing ethos

Hold a class discussion in which you analyze the ethos of some well-known speakers. Which components of ethos—competence, sincerity, or good will do you consider each speaker's strongest asset? Which do you consider the weakest?

Being responsible

Persuasive speaking is, in many ways, more difficult than speaking to inform. It demands detailed audience analysis, considerable research, and a well-planned strategy for building your prestige, particularly in the face of an opposed audience. For these reasons and others, persuasion has long been considered the highest level of public speaking. A speaker who can effectively persuade wields great influence over the minds of others. With this influence comes heavy responsibility as well.

Persuasive speaking is one of the major ways in which decisions are reached in a free society. The President of the United States attempts to persuade the American public to adopt a plan for fighting inflation. Members of Congress attempt to persuade one another to vote for or against the passage of an important bill. Business leaders work constantly to persuade customers to buy. Citizens have the opportunity to persuade each other to vote for particular candidates in each election. Responsible persuasive speaking is necessary if such a society is to function well.

This lawyer is trying to persuade the judge to make a decision in favor of his client. What tactics would you use in such a situation?

Being a responsible persuader does not guarantee you will always be right in what you advocate to an audience, but it does mean you honestly *believe* you are right. If you try to convince your neighbors to vote against a property tax increase, for example, you should sincerely believe that a tax increase is unwise at the moment, and not just wish to avoid paying higher taxes. If you are asking a group of people to vote for you, you should believe honestly that you are the best qualified candidate, and not wish simply to increase your own personal power.

Responsible persuasion can mean different things to different people. For centuries, however, most persuaders have agreed on certain ethical standards, without which the process of persuasion loses much of its value. At the top of the list is the belief that any form of deception is wrong. You should be honest. Don't present false evidence. Don't present the ideas of others as if they were your own. Don't appeal to the emotions of your listeners without any basis in fact. Don't pose as an authority if you are not. These forms of deception are considered both irresponsible and unethical. Responsible persuasion means telling the truth as you have discovered it.

 Checklist for the responsible persuader

■ 1. Do I believe in the ideas, products, or services I am attempting to sell to others?

■ 2. Do I make an effort to become thoroughly informed before persuading others to accept my opinions?

■ 3. Do I listen with an open mind to others when they attempt to persuade me?

■ 4. Do I avoid falsifying evidence?

■ 5. Do I always present what I believe to be the truth?

■ 6. Do I avoid presenting the ideas of others as if they were my own?

■ 7. Do I have a factual basis for any emotional appeals that I make to my audience?

■ 8. Do I avoid posing as an authority when I am not?

When college student John Bennett heard that a subcommittee of the House of Representatives in Washington, D.C. would hold hearings on the question of land conservation in Alaska, he wrote the subcommittee and asked to testify.

Bennett, who had recently returned from a year of living and working in Alaska, felt his experiences there equipped him to speak on the subject. He favored Alaskan land conservation and wanted to persuade the members of Congress to support a bill that would make a considerable amount of Alaskan land a part of our national conservation system. In due time, the subcommittee responded, and John Bennett was invited to appear in Washington on a Monday morning.

Bennett wrote the testimony, a little nervously he confessed, after considering for weeks the tactics he would use to present an effective argument. He knew, for instance, that most of the subcommittee seemed already to favor the bill. "It was considered by many to be a 'safe' environmental vote," he said. "It would look good on their voting record since it was something that many Americans seemed to support." Having identified his audience as basically a positive one, Bennett tried to write a speech that would reinforce their support.

Since he considered his personal experience in Alaska a strong point and one which would establish his credibility as a witness, he introduced himself by explaining exactly where he had lived and what he had done during his year in Alaska.

Next, he launched a logical, two-part argument. The first part stated his concern for the survival of native Alaskan culture. The second cited facts supporting his view that the economic benefit from a more intensely developed Alaska was questionable.

In writing the speech, Bennett tried to use language that would fire the imaginations of his audience while it persuaded with logic. The trick was to strike a balance. He wanted to speak primarily to the issue at hand, but added a few flourishes for color and interest. "I think it's a mistake to over-emphasize style in your speech. I would definitely advise against using flashy language at the expense of simplicity and logic," he said.

Bennett had planned to read from his carefully composed manuscript. For one thing, he was worried that he might forget what to say without the words directly under his nose. Fortunately, Bennett had rehearsed his speech thoroughly, for when, speech in hand, he rose to speak, he decided to change tactics.

"I saw that the majority of the people were reading from their speeches. There was something about their impact that was a bit less effective than it could have been. So I read only the first paragraph of my testimony, and then spoke extemporaneously from a few notes I had prepared. I felt that if I could look into the representatives' eyes it would help me to convey the message of the speech on a more personal level. Speaking extemporaneously helped me relax too, because when I could actually look at the members of the subcommittee, they seemed more human. And, of course, it's simply a lot easier to articulate and be heard if you aren't looking down at your notes."

Were the members of the subcommittee persuaded? After hearing Bennett's speech, and hundreds of others advocating a similar position, the committee agreed to recommend the conservation bill to the House of Representatives for action.

Summary

Persuasive speaking has as its primary goal the influencing of the attitudes, beliefs, or behavior of the listeners. To do this, a speaker must combine the skills needed to give an informative speech with a number of additional skills that are special to persuasive speaking.

THREE SOURCES OF PERSUASION. Persuasive speaking involves making an audience want to think, believe, or do something they might not have done otherwise. The three major factors that are most likely to influence people are their own needs, their own thinking processes, and the character and personality of others. Thus, a persuasive speaker must appeal to personal needs and logic, while stressing his or her own prestige.

ANALYZING THE NEEDS OF YOUR LISTENERS. To appeal to listener needs you must first discover what those needs are. Knowing whether you face a positive, neutral, disinterested, or opposed audience—or some combination of these four—can help you determine what strategy to use.

BEING LOGICAL. Logical appeals consist of the proper use of evidence and reasoning. Evidence is the raw material upon which arguments are based. Reasoning is the process of putting evidence together into larger conclusions which in turn prove the main points of your speech. Certain forms of evidence may prove more effective with different kinds of audiences. Narratives, examples, and comparisons work well with positive audiences. A neutral audience is generally most impressed by statistics, facts, and testimony. Disinterested listeners also need facts and statistics. The opposed listener usually requires all forms of evidence at the speaker's command.

ESTABLISHING YOUR PRESTIGE. The speaker's prestige (ethos) has long been accepted as a powerful persuasive influence. In order to achieve this kind of prestige a speaker must be seen as competent and sincere. A speaker must also appear to be acting with good will toward the audience. Methods of building speaker prestige include frequent references to evidence, noting your experience in your topic area, being convinced of the truth of your point of view, the use of the common-ground technique, and sincerely thanking and complimenting your audience.

BEING RESPONSIBLE. The ability to persuade others is a powerful tool and carries with it a heavy responsibility. Decisions in a free society are regularly reached through persuasive speaking. Therefore, those who wish to persuade must not only know the best techniques but must practice them ethically. Any form of deceit in persuasion will be discovered eventually and does harm to the democratic decision-making process.

Vocabulary

persuasion

positive audience

neutral audience

disinterested audience

opposed audience

evidence

reasoning

prestige

competence

confidence

sincerity

good will

Review questions

1. What is the primary goal of a persuasive speech?

2. What three factors cause people to adopt attitudes, beliefs, or behavior patterns?

3. Why is analysis of the audience especially important for a persuasive speaker?

4. What are the chief characteristics of each kind of audience: positive, neutral, disinterested, opposed?

5. What approach should a speaker use to persuade each kind of audience?

6. What are the two components of logic? Define them.

7. What are the differences between evidence and reasoning?

8. What types of evidence are especially well suited to each type of audience? Can you give reasons why each type is required?

9. What are three means of establishing prestige as a persuasive speaker?

10. What are the characteristics of a responsible speaker?

Discussion questions

1. Some audiences are a mixture of two or more of the four basic types. Discuss with your classmates effective ways of combining approaches and types of evidence to persuade such mixed audiences.

2. Imagine that you are a community leader intending to give a speech before an election. Your topic is the duty to vote and to vote responsibly. What do you think the attitudes of the audience you face might be? What approaches and types of evidence would be most effective?

3. Do you agree or disagree with the notion that a persuasive speech is more difficult to give than an informative one? How are the two types of speeches similar? How do they differ?

4. Imagine that you are to give a series of persuasive speeches favoring the adoption of an honor system in your school. You are to speak separately to your fellow students, to the teachers and administration, and to the parents. Which do you think would be the most difficult audience to persuade? In what ways should each speech be the same? In what ways should each one differ?

5. Advertising is essentially the business of persuasion. Select five current TV commercials and discuss them with your classmates. Try to determine the audience, approach, evidence, and reasoning for each. Discuss whether the ads are effective or not.

At-home activities

1. Make a list of the times you personally use the process of persuasion during a single day (with one or more listeners). Come to class prepared to discuss your list with your classmates.

2. Prior to your next speech, rehearse ways in which you can compliment your audience or identify interests you share with your listeners. Plan to use these or other ethos-building techniques in class.

In-class activities

1. At least a week before a round of in-class persuasive speeches, exchange purpose sentences with your classmates. Rank yourself as a positive, neutral, disinterested, or opposed listener on each topic. Give these rankings back to each speaker to enable each to prepare for whatever type of audience he or she will face.

2. Take part in a class discussion of the speech by Bart Wojciehowski given on page 410. What type of audience do you suspect he faced? Were his appeals based mainly on needs, logic, or his own prestige? Which particular appeals did you consider especially effective?

Careers

SALESPEOPLE sell merchandise or services. They explain features and demonstrate in stores or retail establishments. High school courses should include English, speech, math, business, and psychology. A high school diploma is usually the minimum educational requirement. Salespeople should have numerical and verbal skills, drive, initiative, diplomacy, and tact in dealing with people.

PUBLIC RELATIONS REPRESENTATIVES plan and conduct public relations programs designed to create and maintain a favorable public image for their employers or clients. They serve as in-house staff members or outside consultants. Public relations representatives prepare and distribute news releases to media. They purchase advertising space and prepare exhibits and tours. They represent employers at public gatherings. High school courses in creative writing, speech, and English are helpful. For most positions a bachelor's degree is the minimum requirement.

Debate and parliamentary procedure   unit four

12

DEBATE

When you have completed this chapter you should be able to

Explain the major differences between debate and discussion.

List the responsibilities of the affirmative and negative sides in a debate.

Analyze a debate proposition.

Find evidence to support logical reasoning when building a debate case.

Question an opponent's arguments with tests of evidence and reasoning.

Question and respond effectively during cross-examination.

Practice effective delivery during debate presentations.

Describe different strategies that can be used by each side in a debate.

Correctly follow the order of speakers in the standard and cross-examination debate formats.

Once, in the midst of debate in the English Parliament, a woman member snapped at Sir Winston Churchill: "Sir, if you were my husband, I would put arsenic in your tea!" In a flash, Churchill retorted: "Madam, if you were my wife, I would drink it!" Although true debate deals with issues and not with personal quibbling, this incident points out the competitive nature of this form of oral communication.

The ancient Greeks were among the first to recognize the value of placing ideas in open competition in order to arrive at decisions about important matters. This same practice is followed today in legislatures and law courts. Debating is perhaps the most challenging form of oral communication in which you can engage.

This chapter will introduce you to debate as a decision-making process and as a means of persuasive argument. Although this chapter will focus on **formal debate**—the kind used in school contests—you should be aware that any time you argue the strengths of two political candidates with your neighbor, speak for or against increasing the school budget, or take a stand on the energy issue, you are debating informally.

The nature of debate

The formal debates held in schools and colleges throughout the country are contests. Each can, in fact, be seen as a mental tug-of-war. There is an issue to be decided with two sides holding opposite views. At the end a judge will usually decide who is the winner. The purpose of formal debate is to determine the set of arguments which seem more convincing by testing both sides under pressure. No other form of oral communication discussed in this book has these characteristics. Conversation is certainly not a contest. It is built on a basis of cooperation. Group discussion is also built on cooperation. It is not a contest but a cooperative search for the truth about a matter. Nor is public speaking a contest. Instead the speaker informs or persuades the listening audience. Only debate pits one side against another in order to discover the best answer through mental and verbal battle. By bringing the best evidence on each side out in the open, debate enables those listening to judge wisely as to the best solution, the best candidate, or the best course of action.

The clash of ideas

Not every issue is debatable. Debate is restricted to issues which have only two sides. Thus a question such as "What should be done about inflation?" is not debatable. There may be numerous answers. In order to assure only two sides in a debate, and a direct clash of ideas between the two, debate issues are stated in the form of a **proposition.** A formal debate proposition is a statement that can be answered by yes and no. It also generally demands that some specific action be taken or not taken. Here are several examples of debate propositions:

> Resolved, that the United States should adopt a system of national health insurance.

> Resolved, that more on-site job experience be incorporated into the high-school curriculum.

A well-worded formal debate proposition has several features:

1. It is worded as a statement, not a question.

2. It is worded to permit only a *for* and *against* response.

3. It is worded so that each side has an equal opportunity to argue its position successfully. In other words, the proposition is not slanted to favor one side.

4. It is worded to address a current, controversial issue.

5. It is worded to call for a change from present policy.

6. It is worded using specific, concrete language that does not make judgments about the topic.

Application: Discussing debate propositions

Discuss the following debate propositions in class. Tell what is wrong with each and then try to reword it to make it debatable.

> Resolved, that the Civil War was caused primarily by slavery.
> Resolved, that we should keep the high school curriculum just as it is.
> Should state legislatures meet annually or bi-annually?
> Resolved, that the brutal sport of football should be abolished.
> Resolved, that energy conservation is more important than the economy is.

The opposing sides

The two sides in a formal debate are called the **affirmative** and the **negative.** Each side may be represented by any number of speakers, but usually either one or two people argue each side. The affirmative has two basic tasks: attacking the way things are at present (the **status quo**) and arguing that a specific change should occur. Suppose the debate proposition reads "Resolved, that compulsory education should end after the eighth grade." The affirmative side must show that there are serious problems with the present requirement that young people stay in school until age 16 or older. They must also argue that many of these

"I don't agree." A discussion between friends in which differing views are expressed is a form of debate.

problems could be solved by allowing people to leave school after the eighth grade. The basic structure of an affirmative argument might go like this:

There is a serious problem (or series of problems) caused by the present situation.

The affirmative proposes an alternate plan of action that will solve the serious problems of the *status quo* and will be in and of itself beneficial.

The affirmative side in a debate is the side proposing a change from present policies. Thus, it has the responsibility of proving that a problem exists and that the solution stated in the proposition would work better than the present system. This affirmative responsibility is called the **burden of proof.** Just as in court trials defendents are presumed innocent until the prosecution proves them guilty, so in a debate the *status quo* is presumed the best way of continuing until the affirmative proves another plan better.

The basic task of the negative side in a debate is to disprove, or **refute**, the attacks on the *status quo* made by the affirmative side. The negative side must prove the *status quo* is satisfactory or that the plan for change proposed by the affirmative side will not work.

The opposing sides take turns presenting their arguments. Because the affirmative side is the one proposing a change from present conditions, it always presents the first and the last arguments. In some debates both sides are also given the chance to **cross-examine**, or question, the other side about their statements.

Formal debate requires careful preparation in advance. You must analyze the proposition thoroughly, find evidence, and develop logical arguments to support your case.

Preparing to debate

Formal debate, with a set order of speakers and usually an audience, demands careful preparation. This means you must carefully analyze the debate proposition. You must prepare sound evidence and reasoning to build an organized case. Then you must plan with your debate partner so that you will work well together. All of this takes time. Political candidates will tell you that they never prepare for a debate overnight. You, too, must prepare carefully in advance.

Analyze the proposition

Your first step in preparing for any formal debate is to begin with the proposition. It is the written source that dictates the direction the debate must take. Analyze it carefully. Decide upon the words or phrases which need to be defined, and write down the definitions you consider fair. The first affirmative speaker will begin the debate by defining the terms. If the negative considers certain definitions to be unfair, it should provide its own definitions in its first speech.

Discover the background that has caused the proposition to become a debatable issue. Find out as much as you can about the opinions on both sides of the question. It doesn't matter whether you will be debating affirmative or negative. You will need to know the possible arguments of the opposition as thoroughly as you do your own.

Focus on the **issues.** The issues in a debate are the major points of disagreement. They are the key arguments on which acceptance or rejection of the debate proposition hangs. In most debates there will be only three or four main issues. Often you can discover major issues by asking questions such as these about the topic:

- *Are serious problems being created by the present system? Can these problems be better solved by some other approach?*
- *What other approach, if any, would better solve the problems? Is such an approach feasible? Practical? Too expensive?*
- *Is the proposed solution the best solution?*
- *Will another solution to the problems have certain disadvantages? Will these disadvantages be as serious as those of the proposed solution or the present system?*

Once you have located the main issues of the proposition, you are ready to begin searching for evidence. Then you must put that evidence together with sound reasoning.

Support your case

The kinds of evidence and reasoning which you use to support a debate case are the same as those used for support in a public speech. Begin by reviewing "Know What You Are Looking For" on page 154 and "Finding good sources of supporting material" on page 157 in Chapter 7. Then review "Being Logical" on page 261 in Chapter 11. These will remind you of places to look for evidence. They will also show you how to put that evidence together to form a convincing argument.

WORKING WITH EVIDENCE. How much evidence is sufficient? There is no magic answer to this question. It would be nice if you could be sure that a combination of three direct quotes, four sets of statistics, and two individual examples would always beat an opponent. But, it's never that simple. In a debate, the team with the greater amount of sound evidence will usually win. Therefore, the wise team will gather as much evidence as possible.

The methods of recording evidence for use in debate are slightly different from those of recording evidence for a public speech. For one thing, a public speaker will ordinarily not record much evidence beyond what will actually be used during the speech. A good debater, however, should have on hand about three times the number of evidence cards expected to be used in the debate. This is always necessary because neither team knows beforehand what kind of approach to the topic the other side will take.

Quotations, statistics, and examples are recorded on 3 × 5 cards, as for a public speech. For debate, each card heading should list the way in which the card can be used and the debate issue to which it relates. Under the heading, the quotation, statistic, example, or other form of evidence is recorded. At the bottom you should note the exact source from which you obtained the information. Following is an example of an evidence card from a debate dealing with ways to reduce crime. The first part of the heading, "Plan Meet Need," shows that this piece of evidence could be used to help refute one of the possible solutions the other side might propose. The rest of the heading shows that the card deals with the plan to give lie-detector tests to more criminals in order to reduce crime.

PLAN MEET NEED: Guilty knowledge (lie detector) test
not always possible

"... the guilty-knowledge test (with a polygraph) cannot be used in all cases. The police have to have enough privileged information to design a test."

which means: Lie detector test cannot be used in all cases because police sometimes do not have access to information they need to prepare questions for the test.

David T. Lykken, Professor of Psychology at the University of Minnesota, Psychology Today, March, 1975, p. 58.

USING REASONING.   Reasoning is the mental process of forming logical conclusions from one's evidence. Through reasoning a debater builds an affirmative or a negative case. Reasoning enables a debater to refute arguments of the opposition during a debate. For centuries several forms of reasoning have been considered valid. Among these are induction, deduction, cause to effect, effect to cause, and analogy.

Induction is reasoning from specific facts or cases to general principles. Here a person begins by stating a number of facts that are similar. If these similarities are consistent enough, the reasoner concludes that they represent a general principle. For example, if you wish to prove that having smoke alarms in homes can save lives, you could give statistics for the last five years comparing the number of deaths caused by fires in homes with smoke alarms versus the number in homes without smoke alarms. From these statistics you could conclude that having smoke alarms in homes can save lives.

In **deduction** you reason from general principles to specific cases. In using deduction a debater attempts to prove a specific case is true because it falls under a general principle or law. Thus, if you wished to show that an affirmative team's plan should be rejected because it could lead to greater inflation, you would start with the general principle, "Any plan that causes greater inflation is undesirable." Next you would give evidence to show that the plan of the affirmative side would cause higher prices. Your conclusion, then, is "this plan will very likely lead to more inflation. Therefore, it should be rejected."

Reasoning from what began something to its result is reasoning from **cause to effect.** If you show that one event will take place as a result of another event, you are using cause to effect reasoning. In attempting to prove that jury trials should be done away with, one of your arguments could be that serving on juries causes hardship on the jurors. The cause would be serving on juries. The effect would be hardship on the jurors.

Reasoning from a result back to what started it is reasoning from **effect to cause.** In arguing the other side of the jury system topic, you would be using effect to cause reasoning if you showed that the excellent record of court decisions in this country is largely due to the jury system.

An **analogy** is a comparison. When using analogy, you prove the truth of something by showing its similarity to something else. For example, in debating the safety of nuclear power plants you might argue: "Building and operating a nuclear power plant today is about as safe as lighting one's campfire within three feet of a wooden keg of gunpowder. As long as you exercise extraordinary caution, everything is fine. But take your eyes off that fire for just a few minutes, and the results can be unbelievable!"

For reasoning to be successful, of course, it must be supported by sound evidence. If you think of reasoning as a steel bridge that can carry an argument from start to finish, evidence can be seen as the individual girders that support the bridge itself. Without the support of examples, statistics, and quotations, the structure of reasoning collapses. Beware of going into a debate armed with reasoning, but without having researched enough evidence to support that reasoning.

Application: Using evidence and reasoning

Choose one of the debatable propositions you wrote for the Application on page 278. Working with your classmates, list questions you would want answered about the proposition and the sources you might use to locate this information. What words or phrases in the proposition would need to be defined? What might be the main issues in a debate on this proposition? If you were to represent the affirmative side in a debate on this proposition, what types of evidence and reasoning might best support your argument? If you were to debate on the negative side, what types of evidence and reasoning would you need to refute the other side?

Build a case

In debate, the term **case** refers to a team's total argument on any given proposition, set down in writing. There are at least two methods for outlining a debate case, either of which can be effective, depending on the side which you will be debating and on your own personal preference.

A **brief** is a complete outline of your case, written in complete sentences. It contains, as main heads, what you consider the major issues in the case. The subheads are the evidence and proof for those issues. Specific examples, quotations, and statistics are sometimes written out fully as sub-subheads. They may also be placed on individual evidence cards and then referred to by number in the brief. Affirmative teams usually find it easier to prepare a case in the form of a brief than negative teams do. Since the negative often does not know the specific plan the affirmative will use, preparing a complete brief is difficult. However, negative teams sometimes prepare several briefs. During the debate, the negative chooses the one that presents the case that works best against the issues raised by the affirmative team.

The second method of preparing a case is to outline it on evidence cards. This is often simpler for negative teams. Particular cards may be inserted into the case, deleted, or rearranged, depending on the approach taken by the affirmative. The method for building a case on evidence cards consists of numbering the individual pieces of evidence (one on each card) in the order in which they will be presented during the debate. Additional evidence cards must be handy for use whenever the opposition inserts an unexpected issue into the debate. Thus, evidence cards are more flexible and adaptable than a complete brief.

The brief includes all the debater's analysis and reasoning. Evidence cards contain only the evidence. Inexperienced debaters will probably find it helpful to prepare both. Preparing the brief firmly establishes the logic of the case in one's mind. The evidence cards are simpler and easier to handle during the actual debate.

Work with your partner

Most school debates involve two-person teams. Even in the courts, it is not unusual for more than one attorney to represent one side in a case. Debating, then is usually a team effort.

Teamwork in preparation and consistency in the team's presentations are very important in debating. If you are going to debate with a partner, prepare for the debate with that partner. This does not mean that each of you cannot do research independently. The overall planning of your strategy, deciding on the major issues, writing the brief, and rehearsal, however, must be done as a team. Each person must be certain which issues the other will deal with. Each must know how the team will handle unexpected points brought up by the opposition. Thor-

Debating is often a team effort. Partners must consult frequently to avoid contradicting or disagreeing with one another during the debate.

ough rehearsal is also important in order to get used to your partner's speaking style and to be certain all parts of the case mesh properly. Nothing can hurt a team's chances of winning a debate as much as a contradiction or disagreement between team members.

During the actual debate, listen carefully as your partner is speaking. Everything you say should agree with your partner's presentation. Any disagreement between team members must be resolved either beforehand or privately during the debate. You will need to recognize one of your team members as leader. When a disagreement arises during a debate about the team's strategy, the matter must be settled quickly. There is not time for extended discussion. After a brief private exchange of views on the matter, the recognized team leader should decide.

 Checklist for debate preparation

☐ 1. Have I analyzed the debate proposition carefully?

☐ 2. Have I defined any words or phrases in the proposition that need definition?

☐ 3. Have I researched the proposition and identified the basic arguments that can be made to support either side of the proposition?

☐ 4. Have I gathered and recorded enough sound evidence to support my position?

☐ 5. Have I used valid reasoning in my arguments?

☐ 6. Have I prepared the brief(s) or evidence cards needed to present the arguments I intend to use?

☐ 7. Have I worked with my partner to decide on main issues, plan strategy, write the brief, and rehearse?

☐ 8. Am I prepared to agree with everything my partner plans to say during the debate?

Meeting the opposition

Once a debate begins, your two primary tasks are to present your own case in the most favorable light possible and to refute the arguments of the opposition. This section will discuss methods of testing the evidence and reasoning presented by your opponents, the process of note-taking during a debate, cross-examination techniques, and delivery of debate speeches.

Look for weaknesses in the opposition's evidence

The foundation on which any argument rests is its evidence. A good debate team will first be certain that its own evidence is valid. Then, as the debate progresses, it will constantly look for weaknesses in the opponents' evidence.

Have your opponents presented sufficient evidence? Occasionally, debaters will make statements they wish to have accepted as fact, but provide no supporting evidence. These statements are called **unsupported assertions.** Obviously, unsupported assertions represent the weakest form of argument. Suppose your opponents claim "Socialized medicine has worked effectively in other countries. There is no reason it cannot work effectively in the United States as well." They have made an unsupported assertion. Unless your opponents supply at least several examples of particular countries where socialized medicine has been effective, you should vigorously attack their argument as an unsupported assertion.

It is obvious that without evidence it is impossible to win a case, but remember that the quality of a debater's evidence is just as important as the quantity. Here are several questions you can ask yourself to test the quality of your opponents' evidence:

- *Is my opponent's source of evidence reliable? Is the person who is being quoted someone who is trustworthy? Knowledgeable in the field? Unprejudiced on the matter quoted?*

- *Are the statistics being presented sound? Have they been carefully gathered? Are they being reported accurately? Do the people questioned in the sample accurately represent the entire population?*

- *Are the opposition's examples appropriate? Has each individual case been reported by an eyewitness? Are there enough individual examples to support the debater's conclusion?*

- *Is the evidence being offered up-to-date? On certain debate topics, where rapid change is not occurring, older evidence is acceptable. On a topic such as the energy crisis, however, statistics and examples from 1970 are no longer valid.*

Watch out for faulty reasoning

Sometimes debaters use sound evidence but still arrive at the wrong conclusion through faulty reasoning. Here are a few questions that can be used to test your opponents' reasoning:

- *When reasoning by induction, has the opposition given enough examples? For instance, can a debater who cites three examples of dogs that have bitten children logically conclude "dogs make dangerous pets"? Obviously not.*

- *When arguing by deduction, have my opponents considered all reasonable alternatives? Consider this argument from a debate on socialized medicine: "To improve health care in this country we must institute a system of socialized medicine." The flaw in this argument is the failure of the debater to consider alternative solutions (other than socialized medicine) for improving health care, such as methods for easing the shortage of doctors in some areas of the country.*

- *When arguing by cause and effect, has the opposition shown that an event was actually* caused *by a preceding event or did it simply occur later? Suppose someone said, "We had baked apples for dessert last night and everyone in the family got sick. We'll never eat baked apples again." This person has blamed the baked apples when they may not have been the cause of the illness at all.*

- *When arguing by analogy, did my opponents overlook any essential differences in the two things being compared? A Russian once claimed to an American visitor that his system of government was as democratic as ours by arguing that they held elections, just as we do. The American found the flaw in the analogy and retorted that in the United States there is more than one party from which the voters may choose their candidates.*

Take notes and keep a flow sheet

During a debate, you should take notes of your opponents' arguments. Be sure to include notes about any weaknesses you find in their evidence or reasoning. Include only those key points you want to respond to. In a typical debate, your opponents will bring up a much greater number of arguments than you will have time to answer. The approach of one high school debater was to begin a speech: "The negative team has asked us to answer a long list of quesions. We are more than happy to do so, so here goes: yes, no, no, maybe, you've got us there, maybe, no, yes, yes...." Although this method may have secured a laugh from the judge, it probably did not win the debate for its user. A good debater will respond only to key arguments that apply directly to the case.

A partial flow sheet from a debate on energy in the United States

1st. Aff. Con.	1st. Neg. Con.	2nd. Aff. Con.
	Theme Status quo can solve any problems.	
	Topicality NO PLAN TO SOLVE	
	Sig. NO QUANTIFICATION OF SOLVENCY	
	Harm - Economic harms are not → reserves are not reliable pragmatic.	
	- SQ can decrease dependence Fossil Fuels Oil demand is decreasing → Exxon evidence is biased We have enough Alaska's Oil North Slope Oil } → Must compare to Arab reserves.	
I. U.S. is dependent on oil (must import) A. Are dependent. B. Imports will increase (36% needed)	- PRESENT SYSTEM CAN DECREASE DEPENDENCE	
II. Harms (personal) A. Purchasing power decreases ($45 - $60 bill) B. Oil Crisis likely (only have enough reserve for 60 days) C. Problems will continue.	→ No harm to Arab investment → Doesn't hurt economy → OPEC can't afford embargo	→ Doesn't apply → Bad housing (deaths)
III. Harms (other) A. Trade deficit is caused by oil. B. Will get worse.	→A. No sig. impact B. Deficit must allow for investment C. Deficit doesn't devalue dollar.	→ Oil prices will increase
IV. Harms (economic) A. The dollar devaluates B. LINK - (Economy is tied to Energy.) C. Inflation leads to higher oil prices D. Inf. will continue.		PLAN I. National Coal Gasification Board II. Enforcement III. Funding ADV: - Less pollution A. 65% sulfur and ash removed. B. Coal can't be under- mined by OPEC.

One useful method for selecting the key arguments to refute is to construct a flow sheet as the debate progresses. **A flow sheet** is your own summary outline written in a continuous manner to show how the arguments on each issue progress throughout the debate. It is written during the debate, usually in vertical columns on a large legal pad or art pad. Each column represents one speech that is given. If you record, in brief sentences or phrases, the essence of each argument and the response to it in a

2nd. Neg. Con.	1st. Neg. Reb.	1st. Aff. Reb.
——————→ X	No Sig.	
————→ X (Plan in 2 AC is unfair)	No Inh.	
————→ X	NO IMPACT TO HARM	
—→ Energy demand is slower		
—→ Best (only) evidence given —————————		—→ Aff. evidence is better.
—————————————————		—→ X
——————————→ goes both ways		
—→ Difficult link ——————→ X		
—————————————————		—→ X
————————→ X		
————————→ X		
* Trade deficit not shown to be the same as devaluation of the dollar.		
————————→ Extra topical ————————		—→ Can't deny the advantage.

subsequent column, you will have a picture of the debate at any point along the way. This enables you to see the arguments you have not responded to thus far in the debate and helps you to select arguments for refutation that seem to be key points. Another advantage of keeping a flow sheet is being able to see which of your own arguments your opponents have been able to refute. The part of a sample flow sheet illustrated on pages 288 and 289 will give you an idea of how yours can be constructed.

Make effective use of cross-examination

The brief cross-examination periods included in many high-school debates can be the most exciting part of a debate. These questioning sessions, modeled on courtroom cross-examination, give each team a chance to expose weaknesses in the opposition's case through clever questioning. Though skill at cross-examination requires some experience, here are suggestions for both the questioner and the respondent to consider:

For the Questioner

Prepare general questions on each of the major issues before the debate. During the debate, try to tie your questions as closely as possible to the specific arguments actually used by your opponents.

Never ask a question for which you think the opponents might have a strong answer. If their response is strong you only score points for the opposition by giving them a free chance to state it.

Keep questions brief and clear. Do not attempt to confuse your opponent with long or complicated questions. You will also confuse the judge.

Demand brief answers. You cannot demand a simple yes or no. If the respondent begins to give a little speech, however, you may cut it off.

Do not comment on the responses you receive during the cross-examination period. This should be done in your, or your partner's, later speeches. You may, however, use follow-up questions during the cross-examination period.

For the Respondent

Be constantly on guard. The purpose of the questions is to make your case look weak and foolish.

Remember that you do not have to answer an unreasonable question. If you are asked, "Are all your examples as bad as that one?" you may point out that this is a loaded question and refuse to answer it.

Keep your answers brief, but complete. You cannot be forced into single word answers. Briefly giving a reason or qualification for your answer is always permissible.

If you do not know the answer to a question or are not familiar with the context of the question, say so immediately.

If you do not have a strong answer to a particular question, it is better to yield the point immediately rather than offer a weak response. A weak response gives the questioner a chance to make you look bad with a series of embarrassing, follow-up questions.

Speak persuasively

All the rules of good public speaking and persuasion explained in Unit 3 apply in debate. Since a debate is a special kind of speaking situation, a few special rules need to be mentioned.

You are not trying to convince your opponents, but the judge. Direct your arguments and your eye contact to the judge.

Be thoroughly familiar with your evidence cards. This will enable you to maintain a large measure of eye contact with the judge while reading them.

Do not develop the tendency of many debaters to try setting a speed record. A good speaking rate for any kind of persuasive public speaking is also a good speaking rate for debate. The judge is not interested in how many arguments you can squeeze into eight or ten minutes, but in how effective your arguments are.

Do not forget the value of gestures, platform movement, and facial expressions. Be dynamic and forceful in your delivery.

Maintain variety in vocal expression. Changes in pitch, rate, and volume give persuasive impact to your message.

Never allow yourself to get angry with your opponents. No matter how silly or false their arguments sound to you, stick to the issues. Do not attack the debaters.

Remember that the most important aspects of a debate are your arguments. But poorly delivered arguments rarely carry the impact of those presented well. In debate, as in any kind of public speaking, the most effective delivery is the kind with which you feel at ease and which does not call attention to itself.

Using different strategies

Each side in a debate is responsible for certain tasks. You read about these tasks on pages 278 and 279. How each side goes about fulfilling their responsibilities depends on the strategy each chooses to use as well as the format of the debate.

Fulfilling responsibilities of the affirmative side

The first task of the affirmative in carrying its burden of proof is that of presenting a **prima facie case.** A *prima facie* case means an overall argument that would convince any reasonable judge who has not yet heard the response of the other side. Say the proposition being debated is "Resolved, that the federal government should provide a guaranteed annual income for all U.S. citizens." If the affirmative fails to show that harm comes from U.S. citizens not being guaranteed an income, and merely claims it would be helpful for everyone to have the money, it has failed to present a *prima facie* case. The argument is too weak to deserve a response. In such an instance, a judge could decide in favor of the other side even before hearing any of its arguments.

The affirmative side always opens a debate. If you are the first speaker for the affirmative, you should begin by stating the debate proposition. You should also define any terms in the proposition that need definition. Then you must present your proposal for change by proving that there are serious weaknesses in the *status quo*. These are often needs that are not being met (or cannot be met) by the present approach to the problem. If the debate proposition calls for changing the jury system, for example, you might argue that the present jury system causes undue hardship through lengthy delays. You might also argue that the present jury system is terribly expensive. Once a speaker from the other side has had a chance to respond, the second affirmative speaker generally presents the team's plan for change. This speaker shows the advantages of the plan over the *status quo*. In this case, the second affirmative might argue for a team of six professional jurors whose experience would enable them to decide cases much more efficiently, thus hastening trial dates and saving money in the long run.

The responsibilities of the affirmative team are frequently divided along the following lines:

First affirmative	Second affirmative
States proposition	Presents affirmative plan
Defines terms	Shows advantages of plan
Attacks *status quo*	Summarizes entire affirmative case

If there is only one debater on each side, then all of the above tasks fall to the single affirmative speaker.

This form of affirmative argument based on need → plan → advantages has long been the most common approach to building an affirmative case. It has usually been called the **needs case.**

In recent years, however, a slightly different type of affirmative reasoning has often been used instead of the needs case. This other form of affirmative case is called the **comparative advantages case.** Instead of the typical need → plan → advantages form of arguments, this affirmative case consists of agreed goals → plan → comparative advantages. With certain debate topics, it is sometimes more useful than a needs case. An example would be a debate proposition that reads, "Resolved, that the state's sales tax should be abolished." In using a comparative advantages case to debate this topic the affirmative would begin by calling upon the negative to agree that everyone should be allowed to keep as much of their personal income as possible to spend as they see fit. The negative can hardly disagree with that idea. It would be an **agreed goal.** The debate then revolves, not around the goal of personal economic freedom, but around a comparison of two means by which to achieve that goal. The affirmative would then argue that their plan—say to reduce certain state services—would prove better for citizens than paying the sales tax to get those services. A good affirmative debater will carefully analyze a debate proposition. Then the debater will decide which strategy—a needs case or a comparative advantages case—will work better for a given topic.

The use of a comparative advantages case generally calls for a division of speaking responsibilities quite different from that used with a needs case:

First affirmative	*Second affirmative*
States proposition	Responds to attacks of first negative speaker
Defines terms	Reinforces plan
Presents goals negative will have to agree with	
Presents plan for meeting goals	
Outlines advantages of plan	

Fulfilling responsibilities of the negative side

The basic task of the negative side is to disprove the attacks on the *status quo* made by the affirmative. There are several ways the negative may do this. Any one of these may win the debate for the negative if done well enough. One way is by attacking the affirmative's arguments

Abraham Lincoln challenged Stephen A. Douglas, his opponent in the Illinois senatorial race, to a series of debates in 1858. Although Lincoln lost the election, the debates established him as a national figure, and Lincoln went on to win the presidency in 1860.

of need. The negative may claim that the *status quo* is completely satisfactory or that the affirmative has failed to prove it unsatisfactory. There is no need for a change.

Another possibility is for the negative to center its attacks on the affirmative plan. Here the negative argues that the affirmative plan would create problems more serious than those currently being experienced under the *status quo*. This is usually the best strategy to use against an affirmative comparative advantages case.

A third option is the **need-plan wedge case.** When using this approach, the negative does not attack the affirmative's need or plan directly. Rather the negative attacks the logical link between the two. The negative argues "even if the need the affirmative claims did exist (which is doubtful), and even if their plan were a workable one (which is doubtful), their plan is incapable of satisfying the need they have outlined."

A fourth approach, and perhaps the most common one, is called the **running-refutation negative case.** Here the negative side attacks all parts of the affirmative case. It claims that the *status quo* is handling the situation satisfactorily and that the affirmative has failed to show a need for a change. It also argues that the affirmative plan is not workable, that the plan would not produce any significant advantages, and that it might produce some disadvantages.

Unlike the affirmative side, which begins the debate knowing its own strategy, the negative has the disadvantage of having to wait until the debate has begun to decide its specific plan of attack. However, this does not mean the negative cannot prepare beforehand. Thorough preparation for the negative consists of researching all of the major issues the affirmative might use. Then the negative must prepare a response to whatever kind of case the affirmative might choose. The affirmative team's strategy will become evident during their first speech. Then the negative side can insert its most appropriate proofs and its most appropriate case.

The duties of the first and second negative speakers differ according to how the affirmative case is presented as well as according to how they decide to disprove the affirmative case. If the affirmative uses a needs case, the first negative speaker will generally refute the affirmative needs. The second negative will generally attack the plan and its advantages. If the affirmative has chosen to use a comparative advantages case rather than a needs case, the negative response will be different. In that case, the first negative will generally attack the affirmative advantages. These will have been heard in the first affirmative speech. The negative will usually try to show that the affirmative plan cannot produce the advantages claimed, that the advantages are not significant, or that they can be gained without the affirmative plan. The second negative will generally refute the plan itself and try to show it unworkable. The argument will usually be that the plan will produce disadvantages that outweigh any advantages.

The responsibilities of the negative speakers might be summarized as in the following list.

If the affirmative uses a needs case:

First negative	*Second negative*
Agree with, or redefine affirmative's definitions	Attacks affirmative's plan
Refutes affirmative's needs	Refutes advantages

If the affirmative uses a comparative advantages case:

First negative	*Second negative*
Agrees with or redefines affirmative's definitions	Attacks affirmative plan
Attacks advantages of affirmative plan	

Debate formats

Many different formats can be used for conducting debates. The format which is used depends on the time available, the seriousness of the issue, and the number of debaters on each side. Here the discussion will focus on two formats widely used in high school debates when there are two debaters on each side.

In the **standard format**, two different kinds of speeches are made by each of the speakers during a single debate. Each speaker gives both a constructive speech and a rebuttal. The **constructive speeches** are lengthy, usually ranging from eight to ten minutes each in length. They are used to present and develop the major points of each team's case. **Rebuttals** are briefer speeches, typically lasting four to five minutes each. They are given after the constructive speeches. The main purpose of rebuttals is to refute the opposition's major arguments. Rebuttals also answer the main objections to one's own case.

In the standard format this is the order of speakers:

Speaker	*Number of minutes*
First affirmative constructive speech	10
First negative constructive speech	10
Second affirmative constructive speech	10
Second negative constructive speech	10
First negative rebuttal	5
First affirmative rebuttal	5
Second negative rebuttal	5
Second affirmative rebuttal	5
Total time	60

Debate is the form of public speaking with which Marvin Arrington is particularly familiar. Arrington is one of nine elected members of the City Council in Atlanta, Georgia. He is also a lawyer with a private practice so he is frequently in court to argue cases.

As a politician, Arrington uses debate techniques to match viewpoints and wits with political opponents who seek his council seat at election time or who disagree with a political position which he supports. As a lawyer, Arrington takes part in debate against other lawyers, as they vie for favorable judgments for their clients from presiding judges. Arrington draws on experience gained from his high school debate team and from debate training he received in law school, in order to argue his positions effectively.

When preparing for a political debate or an argument in court, Arrington starts by acquiring, and then offering, the facts (pro and con) of the position he will argue. "The first thing you have to do is face, squarely, the particular issues," he said. This sounds easier than it really is. Issues, like facts, have a way of gaining or losing importance according to priorities held by the audience set to hear them.

For example, if Arrington is to prepare for a political debate on ways to stop crime rates from rising in downtown Atlanta, he considers first which one of several issues to choose as his main issue for argument. One issue could be the effectiveness of police patrols. Another could be the availability of additional city funds for employing more police officers for better patrolling. Still another could be the condition of the downtown area itself, the extent to which the environment does, or does not, encourage criminal activity. Arrington must decide which issue his audience is most concerned about. Then he can proceed to design an argument, either pro or con, around the points of the issue.

Next in importance to Arrington is what he calls "being able to deliver." By this he means the debater's ability to speak effectively. Political debate resembles public speaking in many ways, but with one major exception. Arrington attempts, like any good speaker, to use clear and persuasive language and to balance logic with appeals to the audience's emotions. He must be ready at a moment's notice to change his argument as his opponent's arguments are revealed and be prepared to answer unexpected questions or charges, even if they are about material not included in his original argument. But he must also be ready to respond and to reweave the thread of the discussion back into his main argument.

"You've got to know when to highlight some issues and when to capitalize on the interest of your audience. You've got to know when you've got their attention," Arrington said. Debate is a competitive, give and take form of discussion in which a speaker can never be sure of what facts or arguments the other side will bring up. The ability to respond quickly and clearly to an opponent's thrust comes in part from experience and from learning how to speak well under pressure. It also comes from knowing the subject thoroughly. "And that," Arrington said, "comes from hard work and hard research. There is no substitute."

While these speaking times are common for contest debate, they may be shortened for classroom use. Constructive speeches of seven minutes and rebuttals of four would permit a debate to fit within most class periods.

Notice that the order of affirmative and negative speakers switches in the rebuttal period. This is done to assure that the affirmative team both opens and closes the debate.

The **cross-examination format** is currently the most popular in high school debates. In this format, cross-examinations follow immediately after each constructive speech. A member of the opposite team attempts to expose weaknesses in each speaker's arguments by asking questions for the speaker to answer. High school cross-examination periods usually last about three minutes. The order of speakers in the cross-examination format looks like this:

Speaker	*Number of minutes*
First affirmative constructive speech	8
First negative speaker cross-examines	3
First negative constructive speech	8
Second affirmative speaker cross-examines	3
Second affirmative constructive speech	8
Second negative speaker cross-examines	3
Second negative constructive speech	8
First affirmative speaker cross-examines	3
First negative speaker's rebuttal	4
First affirmative speaker's rebuttal	4
Second negative speaker's rebuttal	4
Second affirmative speaker's rebuttal	4
Total time	60

The times for each presentation may again be shortened to insure that a debate will fit within a class period. Constructive speeches may be shortened to five minutes each. Cross examinations may be two minutes. Rebuttals may be three minutes. The total time would then be forty minutes.

Summary

Debate is perhaps the most challenging form of oral communication. It is used daily in courts and legislatures as a means of arriving at decisions about important issues. It has also been used in schools for centuries as a means of mental discipline and training for responsible decision-making.

THE NATURE OF DEBATE. A formal school debate begins with a proposition—a statement that something should be considered or done. Unlike a discussion question, a debate proposition is a statement, answerable by yes and no. There are only two sides in a debate, the affirmative, which upholds the proposition by demanding that the *status quo* be changed, and the negative which argues against such a change. At the end of the debate, a judge renders the decision. The affirmative has the responsibility of proving that a problem presently exists and that its plan for solving the problem would work better than any other approach. This responsibility is known as the affirmative's burden of proof. The basic task of the negative side is to refute the arguments of the affirmative side. The opposing sides in a debate take turns presenting their arguments. In some debates, speakers may cross-examine their opponents about their arguments.

PREPARING TO DEBATE. Preparing to participate in a debate demands careful analysis of the debate proposition, gathering sound evidence, the development of clear reasoning, the writing of a fully outlined case, and close work with your debate partner. Analyzing the proposition includes deciding what terms need definition, obtaining background information about the proposition, and focusing on the issues (the major points of disagreement). Evidence to support your side on the issues consists of such things as examples, statistics, and quotations. These are usually recorded on 3 × 5 index cards for later use during the debate. Reasoning is the process of forming conclusions from one's evidence, and may take several forms. It may include induction, deduction, cause and effect, and analogy. In order for you to have a firm grasp of your total case it must be put in writing. The two most common ways of doing this are to prepare a brief or to work with numbered evidence cards. All of these forms of preparation (except the actual research) should be carried out together with your partner.

MEETING THE OPPOSITION. When a debate begins, you must continually test the evidence and reasoning used by your opponents. Taking careful notes on your opponent's arguments is also essential during a debate. This is usually done by means of a flow sheet. A flow sheet gives you a quick picture of how the arguments on each issue are progressing throughout the debate.

Cross-examination can be the most exciting part of a debate. Each questioner should prepare questions on the major issues before the debate. Never ask a question if you know there is a strong answer. Keep questions brief and clear, and demand brief answers from the respondent. Respondents should be constantly on guard. They should keep their answers brief and admit immediately if they do not know an answer. They cannot be forced into yes or no answers, but must answer any reasonable question.

All the rules of speech delivery apply in debate. There are also special delivery considerations during debate. You should try to convince the judge, not your opponents, and maintain eye contact as much as possible when reading evidence cards. You must avoid the temptation to speak too quickly, while still remaining dynamic, both in voice usage and body movement.

USING DIFFERENT STRATEGIES. A debate is always opened by the affirmative side, whose first task is that of presenting a *prima facie* case—an overall argument that would convince any reasonable person who has not also heard the response of the negative side. Typically, the affirmative's case consists of showing serious needs in the present situation, presenting a plan to meet those needs, and showing the advantages of that plan. A popular alternate approach is the comparative advantages case in which the affirmative does not present needs, but rather goals on which both sides can agree (agreed goals) followed by a plan which they then attempt to show is more advantageous than the negative's approach to solving the problem.

The basic task of the negative side is to disprove the attacks of the affirmative. The negative may do so in several ways. They may attack the affirmative's claims of need, the affirmative plan, or the logical link between the needs and plan. A fourth way is for the negative to attack all parts of the affirmative case—needs, plan, and advantages. This is called the running-refutation negative case.

There are many formats for debate. One common format for high school debate is called the standard format. This includes two types of presentations from each of the two-person teams. Constructive speeches are used to present and develop the major parts of each team's case. Rebuttals are used to refute the opposition's major arguments and answer their objections to one's own case. In the cross-examination format, the speakers are also given a chance to question the opponents at the end of each constructive speech. These cross-examination sessions are used to expose weaknesses in the other side's case.

Vocabulary

formal debate	deduction	comparative advantages case
proposition	cause to effect	agreed goal
affirmative	effect to cause	need-plan wedge case
negative	analogy	running-refutation negative case
status quo	case	
burden of proof	brief	standard format
refute	unsupported assertion	constructive speech
cross-examine	flow sheet	rebuttal
issue	*prima facie* case	cross-examination format
induction	needs case	

Review questions

1. What is the purpose of formal debate?

2. How are debate issues stated?

3. What are the characteristics of a well-worded debate proposition?

4. What steps should you take in preparing to debate?

5. What are five forms of reasoning that may be used to support a case?

6. As a debate progresses, what three things should you be doing to prepare yourself to meet the opposition during rebuttal or cross-examination?

7. What are the responsibilities of the affirmative side in a debate?

8. What are the responsibilities of the negative side in a debate?

9. What are the differences between standard format and cross-examination format?

10. How should a questioner proceed during a cross-examination?

Discussion questions

1. Discuss ways in which debate and discussion are similar and how they differ.

2. Pick three current issues and discuss ways to develop a solid debate proposition about each of them.

3. Choose one of the propositions developed in your class in Question 2 and discuss the arguments you might use in debating the affirmative position.

4. Consider the affirmative case you built in Question 3. Discuss with your classmates the arguments the negative side might use to refute these affirmative arguments.

5. As a class, discuss the importance of delivery in debate. Consider the elements of public speaking discussed in previous chapters and relate them to delivery in a debate. Be sure to discuss nonverbal as well as verbal elements.

At-home activities

1. Prepare to participate in a classroom debate. Analyze the proposition you discussed in the Application on page 283 and decide on the issues. Conduct research to discover sound evidence to support your reasoning.

2. Prepare a set of cross-examination questions for use in one of your classroom debates. Develop questions that you think the opposition will find difficult to answer. Make certain your questions are brief and clear, and touch upon major issues in the debate. Be ready to adapt your questions to meet the changing needs of the live debate situation.

3. Attend a debate held in a court, at a city commission meeting, at a school board meeting, or in some other public forum. Note similarities to and differences from the techniques of debate described in this chapter. Report to the class on the debate you attended. What part did thorough preparation in advance play in the outcome of the debate?

4. Maintain a file of evidence cards on any debate topic you research. Many high-school debaters have discovered a renewed interest in debate in college, and often the same or similar topics appear again.

In-class activities

1. Take part in preparing for a series of formal team debates for presentation in class. Each debate should involve four class members (two affirmative, two negative) who will spend about a week in preparation and then conduct their debate on a selected topic before the class. Participate in a class discussion after each debate.

2. During a classroom debate, listen with particular care to the arguments of one of the four speakers and apply the tests of evidence and reasoning. Jot down the essence of each argument as it is spoken and note any weaknesses. After the debate, compare your results with those of other students who have listened to the same speaker.

3. Keep a flow sheet during a classroom debate. Use brief phrases and abbreviations in order to allow time to record all major points. Your completed flow sheet should contain eight columns, headed 1st Aff., 1st Neg., 2d Aff., 2d Neg., 1st Neg. Reb., 1st Aff. Reb., 2d Neg. Reb., 2d Aff. Reb.

4. To practice cross-examination, try the following in-class exercise: Research both sides of an agreed-upon debate proposition for a week. Then take turns with other class members in delivering constructive speeches followed by cross-examination. You may wish to hold several such cross-examination sessions on the same speech. After several speeches, take part in a discussion of effective cross-examination.

Careers

POLITICIANS serve by appointment or election. They govern countries, states, counties, cities, or towns. The ability to write and speak effectively is necessary. High school courses in English, speech, drama, government, history, and psychology are helpful. No educational requirement exists, but many politicians are lawyers.

LAWYERS assist people with legal problems. They advise clients of their rights and defend them in courts. They conduct lawsuits, and draw up many types of legal documents. High school courses in English, speech, psychology, and social studies are helpful. Lawyers must possess both a college and a law school degree. They must also pass a state bar examination before they can practice. Lawyers are found in private practice, companies, and government agencies.

13

PARLIAMENTARY PROCEDURE

When you have completed this chapter you should be able to

Explain the purposes of parliamentary procedure.

Describe five of its basic principles.

List the correct order of business for a meeting.

Explain the duties of the chair.

Present a motion correctly during a meeting.

Describe the purposes of each of the four types of motions.

Explain the order in which motions may be made.

Have you ever attended a meeting with more than five people present? Have you been frustrated by everyone talking at once? Did it seem to take forever to arrive at a decision? **Parliamentary procedure** is a set of rules designed to reduce that kind of frustration. Probably you have attended meetings of clubs, student government organizations, or other groups which use these rules to conduct their business. Parliamentary procedure makes discussion at such meetings more efficient and productive. The rules are also designed to protect the rights of the individual. These include the right to be heard, the right to remain silent, and the right to full and free discussion of every issue presented. While parliamentary procedure provides for majority rule, it also protects the rights of the minority.

Parliamentary procedure did not suddenly spring into existence fully developed. Years ago a few basic rules were formed in the early English Parliament. They were gradually expanded and changed to fit the needs of that growing body and other democratic groups and societies where it came to be used. Today a number of standard codes of parliamentary procedure are in wide use throughout the world. *Robert's Rules of Order, Newly Revised* and *Sturgis Standard Code of Parliamentary Procedure* are the two most commonly used in this country. This chapter will not make you a **parliamentarian** (an expert on parliamentary procedure). It will, however, explain the fundamental points of parliamentary procedure. Copies of these codes are readily available for anyone wanting to learn more.

This scene showing the House of Lords of the English Parliament was painted in 1823. Rules developed by earlier English Parliaments have since evolved into the rules of parliamentary procedure now used by political and nonpolitical groups throughout the world.

Rules of parliamentary procedure make it possible for large groups to work together efficiently as well as democratically.

Basic principles

Several fundamental principles form the basis of parliamentary procedure. Once you have these in mind, all of the lesser rules, regulations, and motions will seem logical.

One question at a time

Order can be maintained in a group by debating and voting on only one issue at a time. The members may not always vote on an issue before moving on to another one. But this principle dictates that they must dispose of a pending issue *in some way* before considering another.

Majority rule

In bodies following parliamentary procedure, each member automatically agrees to abide by the decision of the majority. A **simple majority** is at least one more than half the people who voted. In special situations at least two-thirds of those voting must vote favorably in order for the issue to pass.

Protection of minority rights

Voting members of an organization who make up the minority group on an issue are not necessarily wrong. Voting with the **minority** means only that on that particular vote less than half the members agreed with them. The rules of parliamentary procedure protect the rights of the minority. One of the rights protected is the right to continue to be heard and to try to change the minds of members in the majority group.

Equality of rights and responsibilities

In a body following parliamentary procedure, everyone is equal. Each has an equal right to speak or to remain silent, to vote or not to vote. At the same time each has the same responsibility to take an active part in discussion, to cast her or his vote, and to serve as an officer of the organization when called upon to do so. Though some members may be more active than others in exercising their rights and in fulfilling their responsibilities, all are equal in their possession of those rights and responsibilities.

Free debate

Free debate is essential to enable members of an assembly to vote intelligently on issues. Parliamentary procedure attempts to guard open discussion of every issue, so long as a reasonable number of those present want it to continue. Motions to limit debate or to cut it off entirely require consent of two-thirds of the members to pass. Free debate also means that ordinarily only one person may speak at a time, and only after having obtained the floor by recognized procedures.

Checklist for responsible membership in an organization

1. Do I attend meetings regularly?
2. Do I take an active part in discussion?
3. Do I remain silent when I have no constructive suggestions to make?
4. Do I listen carefully to the proposals and discussions of other members?
5. Do I know and abide by the rules of parliamentary procedure?
6. Do I consider issues carefully before casting my vote?
7. Am I willing to abide by the decisions of the majority?

Holding a meeting

Parliamentary procedure provides a number of very specific rules for holding meetings. These rules allow meetings to be efficient, productive, and democratic. They regulate the way meetings are announced and the number of members that must be present to conduct business. They also regulate the manner in which the business is conducted and the duties of the presiding officer.

Notice

When an organization plans to hold a meeting, notice must first be given to all of the members. **Notice** means that all of the members are told about the meeting far enough in advance so that they can plan to participate. Ten days notice is normal. Failure of the officers to give adequate notice can invalidate decisions made at a meeting. If it can be proven that the officers conspired to hold a "secret meeting," they can be removed from office. Notice should ordinarily be given in writing. It is often routinely given for regularly scheduled meetings by mailing out to the membership beforehand the list of items to be discussed (the **agenda**) with the date, time, and place of meeting.

Quorum requirements

Once the time for the meeting has arrived, the presiding officer must determine whether a quorum is present before calling the meeting to order. A **quorum** is the number of members that *must* be present before any meeting can be held or any official business conducted. Though each organization can set its own quorum requirements in its bylaws, the standard requirement is a majority of all members in good standing. Suppose an organization had 100 members in good standing on its membership role. Following the standard requirement, that organization would need 51 members present before it could hold an official meeting and conduct any official business.

An organization may, of course, set its quorum requirements at less than a majority in its bylaws. This assures that business may be conducted when attendance is low. However, it is dangerous to set the quorum too low. This would make it possible for a very small minority to set policy and decide important matters for the entire organization. Setting quorum requirements too high should also be avoided. It might become difficult to secure enough attendance to conduct business.

Order of business

The **order of business** for a meeting is an agenda. This is a listing of the various items of business in the order in which they will be taken up during the meeting. This is generally the agenda followed:

Call to order
Reading and approval of the minutes of previous meetings
Reports of officers, boards, and standing committees
Reports of special committees
Unfinished business
New business
Announcements
Adjournment

Ordinarily, an organization will follow this regular order of business unless its bylaws call for a different order. Occasionally, though, if a special reason exists it is possible to shift around certain items.

Application: Planning an agenda

Assume that you and your classmates represent members of a club, a business organization, or a civic group. Plan an agenda for a meeting of this make-believe organization. Be sure to include at least one item under each section of the standard order of business.

Duties of the chair

The **chair** is the name given to the person presiding over a meeting of an organization. Ordinarily this duty is exercised by the president of the organization. The vice-president usually presides if the president is absent. The chair has the same right to vote that any other member has. A number of other duties are also fulfilled by the person in this position.

MAINTAINS CONTROL. The chair's main task is to maintain control over the meeting, continually making sure that each member's rights are protected. The chair is not the ruler of the assembly, however; she or he serves the organization.

MAINTAINS ORDER. The chair must maintain order at all times. He or she should prevent debate that takes the form of personal attack rather than a discussion of the issues. The chair must also guard against the railroading of matters through to a vote without time for sufficient thought and discussion. Sometimes members of a group try to prevent a vote on an issue by making long speeches to waste time. This is called **filibustering.** The chair should discourage such stalling tactics and must always restore order at the first sign of any form of disturbance.

ACTS IMPARTIALLY. The chair should not take sides on issues being discussed. If, on rare occasions, the chair wishes to speak for or against a particular measure, another officer should be asked to preside for as long as the chair takes part in debate. If the chair possesses information about a matter that is unknown to the other members, he or she may state such information impartially without relinquishing the chair.

RECOGNIZES SPEAKERS IMPARTIALLY. The chair must be especially impartial in allowing members to speak. This process is called **recognizing** members and follows certain rules. When a particular member has made a motion, the chair should always give that member the right to speak first about the proposal. Then, the chair should alternate between those speaking against and for the topic. If there is uncertainty about who is in favor and who against, the chair should ask before permitting a member to have the floor. The chair should also recognize those who have not yet had a turn to speak on the subject before those who have already had an opportunity.

ASSURES UNDERSTANDING. The chair should be sure that every member understands each matter being discussed. All members should know what they are voting on and what effects their vote will have.

KEEPS THE MEETING MOVING. The chair must insure that the meeting moves along at a good pace. Members will then be more likely to pay attention and be enthusiastic. At the same time, the chair must not deny members their parliamentary right of full discussion.

As you can see, the chair must be constantly alert in exercising these duties. Much of the responsibility for a productive meeting rests squarely on the shoulders of the presiding officer.

Application: Discussing qualifications for presiding officers

Hold a class discussion about the role of the chair in a parliamentary meeting. What personal qualities and skills does the chair need to run an efficient and orderly meeting?

Methods of Voting

There are several ways in which members may show how they wish to vote on an issue. These methods of voting include voice votes, rising, raising hands, roll calls, and secret ballots.

The most common method of voting is a voice vote. The chair usually calls for a voice vote by saying "All those in favor say aye," and then "All those opposed say no." If the vote is a close one, or if the motion requires a two-thirds vote to pass, the chair may instead ask members to rise or to raise their hands. The wording is similar: "All those in favor please rise (or raise your hands)." This is followed by a count of the votes in favor. Then the chair asks those opposed to rise or to raise their hands for a count.

Roll-call votes are required in the bylaws of some organizations. A roll call may also be necessary if guests who don't have the right to vote are present at the meeting. A roll-call vote is announced by the chair in the following way: "Those in favor will answer aye as their names are called. Those opposed will answer no. The secretary will call the roll."

Voting by secret ballot is required in elections of officers and when voting on important issues. The chair should be sure that each member has a ballot and understands how aye and no votes are marked before the vote is taken.

When a large number of people are voting, having them raise their hands to indicate their votes rather than asking for a voice vote leads to more accurate results.

When a meeting is being conducted according to parliamentary procedure, business is handled through the making of **motions.** A motion is a formal suggestion or proposal made by a member for consideration and action by the group. Before any new business can be discussed in a parliamentary meeting, someone must make a motion. Without a motion on the floor the group cannot accomplish anything. It is as if they were all sitting in an automobile ready to start a trip and no one bothered to turn the ignition key.

Once a motion is made, the members must act on it in some way. They may vote for it or against it. They may postpone consideration of it. They may refer it to a committee or handle it in any of several other ways. But they may not simply forget about it.

How motions are made

What should you do during a meeting when you wish to make a motion? First you must obtain recognition from the chair to speak. This may be done by holding your hand in the air until you are called upon by the chair, standing until recognized, or whatever the local custom demands. The chair will recognize you by calling your name or by pointing to you. Then you may state your motion. Always begin with the words "I move." Never begin with "I suggest" or "I recommend" or "I think that we should." The words "I move" are a signal that you are making a motion—a formal proposal that you wish the group to debate and act upon.

Formal motions require a **second**, which is an indication by one other member of the assembly that he or she wishes to see the matter debated and acted upon. This is accomplished by someone's saying "Second" or "I second the motion" immediately after it has been made. Though a second is usually made by a member who agrees with the intent of the motion, it is not necessary that the seconder agree. The second only indicates that she or he also wishes to have the matter considered and acted upon. The seconder may actually intend to vote against the motion.

Immediately following the second, the chair restates the motion by saying "It has been moved and seconded that we (do such and such)." Then, if it is a debatable motion, the chair says, "Is there any discussion?" This restatement by the chair officially puts the motion on the floor and makes it a **pending motion.** A pending motion is one that is under consideration.

Here is an example of a motion being made:

LIZ, a member:	(raises hand)
CHAIR:	Liz
LIZ (rises):	I move that we hold a pancake breakfast to raise money for the scholarship fund. (Liz sits down.)
NICK, a member:	I second the motion.
CHAIR:	It has been moved and seconded that our club hold a pancake breakfast to raise money for the scholarship fund. Is there any discussion?

Motions are divided into four types. These are main motions, subsidiary motions, privileged motions, and incidental motions. Let's look at each type of motion and some of the rules governing them.

"I second the motion." Before most motions can be discussed they must be seconded. This indicates that the motion is of interest to others as well as the member who suggested it.

Main motions

Main motions are those which deal directly with the items of business being considered. They are directly concerned with the issues before the group. Here are a few examples of main motions:

"I move that this club donate $100 to our college scholarship fund."

"I move that we initiate a new membership drive immediately."

"I move that we raise our local dues by $1.00, starting May 1."

"I move that we accept Evan Lee as a new member of this board, to complete the unexpired term of Wanda Malik."

Main motions introduce items of new business to an assembly. They must ordinarily be made first, before any of the other classes of motions would make any sense. Main motions are the foundation of parliamentary business.

Main motions require a second before they may be debated. They are debatable motions, and they require a simple majority vote to pass. A simple majority means fifty percent plus one of those present and voting. Suppose thirty members are present for a meeting, and only twenty decide to vote on a particular motion. The majority required to pass that motion would be eleven. When the vote is taken, the chair must always ask for both the affirmative and the negative sides of the vote.

Subsidiary motions

Subsidiary motions allow members to change the nature of main motions or to handle them in some way other than ordinary debate and a vote. They allow such things as postponements, amendments, and limitations on debate. Following are seven commonly used subsidiary motions in the order in which they may be made following a main motion. You will see the purpose of each, whether each is debatable, and what size vote is required to pass each. Subsidiary motions are always proposed after the main motion to which they apply. They must be debated and voted on before the group returns to debate on the main motion.

POSTPONE INDEFINITELY. The purpose of making the subsidiary motion to **postpone indefinitely** is to prevent any further discussion or voting on a pending main motion. By not allowing the main motion to come to a direct vote, you can assure that it will be defeated. Assume, for example, that the following main motion is pending: "I move that this club donate $100 to our local college's scholarship fund." A member who wishes to see this motion defeated might get recognition to speak and state, "I move that we postpone this motion indefinitely." If there is a second, this subsidiary motion may then be debated and voted upon. If a simple majority votes in favor of the motion to postpone indefinitely, the main motion to donate the $100 is defeated or killed. If the majority votes against postponing indefinitely, the assembly returns to the debate on the main motion.

AMEND. The purpose of a motion to **amend** is to change a main motion in some way. Again assume the pending main motion is to donate $100 to the college scholarship fund. Someone may propose an amendment such as "I move that we change $100 to $50 in the main motion" or "I move we add 'by this coming weekend' to the main motion." Although amendments may change a main motion, they must be **germane** to the main motion to which they apply. Being germane means they must be logically and directly connected with the subject of the main motion. Suppose someone tried to amend the main motion to donate $100 by adding "and raise the salaries of all our club officers." The chair would have to rule the amendment out of order since it is not germane. Raising the officers' salaries is not directly connected with the matter of donating $100 to a scholarship fund.

As is the case with all subsidiary motions, debate and voting on an amendment occur before returning to the main motion. A simple majority vote is required to pass an amendment. If an amendment passes, the assembly returns to debate on the amended version of the main motion. If the amendment fails, the group debates on the main motion in its original form.

REFER TO COMMITTEE. The motion to **refer to committee** is used when a group wants to save time by allowing a small sub-group to discuss a complicated matter. It is also used when the assembly wishes to insure privacy on a delicate matter. Referring to a committee can put off a decision until later, or it can defeat a matter if the committee is hostile. This motion may be made in the simple form: "I move that we refer this motion to a committee." When makers of this motion wish, they may include any pertinent details they desire in the motion. Details may include how many members should be on the committee, who the members should be, and when the committee should report back to the main assembly. Another detail could be whether the committee may only recommend action or whether it has the power to make a decision for the entire assembly. If a motion to refer to a committee passes, any such details not given in the motion are then decided by the chair of the assembly.

The motion to refer to a committee may be debated briefly. Debate is restricted to selection of the committee, instructions to it, its membership, and duties. A motion to refer to a committee requires a simple majority vote to pass.

POSTPONE DEFINITELY. Whenever it is desirable to put off consideration of a pending motion, with the intention of bringing it up again at a later time, a motion to **postpone definitely** should be used. Unlike the motion to postpone indefinitely, the motion to postpone definitely includes a specific time when the pending matter will again come up for consideration. Suppose the main motion to donate $100 is pending. Someone might move "to postpone consideration of this matter until after we have heard our annual budget report at the next regularly scheduled meeting." This motion to postpone definitely assures that the motion on the $100 donation will again be on the table following the budget report at the next meeting. Matters may also be postponed definitely until a time later in the same meeting in which the motion is made.

As in the case with all formal motions, the motion to postpone definitely requires a second. It may be debated briefly. Debate is restricted to the reasons for and the time of postponement. It requires a simple majority vote for passage.

LIMIT OR EXTEND DEBATE. The motion **to limit or extend debate** either restricts the time to be devoted to debate on a pending motion or removes any limitation placed upon it. Its most common use is to limit, rather than to extend debate, however. There are a number of ways to make such a motion:

"I move that we limit debate to a total of fifteen minutes."

"I move that we limit debate to one minute per speaker."

"I move that the debate on this motion cease at 2:30 p.m."

Since the very purpose of the motion to limit debate is to restrict further discussion, the motion to limit debate itself may be debated only briefly. Debate must be restricted to the type and time of the limitation. Limiting debate violates a basic principle of parliamentary procedure. This principle is complete and free discussion of every issue. Therefore, this motion requires a two-thirds majority rather than a simple majority to pass.

VOTE IMMEDIATELY. This motion, if it passes, instantly cuts off debate on a pending motion and brings it to a vote. Assume that the main motion to donate $100 has been placed on the floor for debate. Either right away, or after some discussion on it, a member gets recognition and says: "I move that we **vote immediately** on this motion." The purpose could be to prevent further discussion which the member feels would damage her or his side of the case. The purpose could also be simply to move business along more speedily. In any case, if there is a second, the chair stops debate and immediately takes a vote on the motion to vote immediately. Since its purpose is to stop debate, it is not a debatable motion. Also, since, like the motion to limit debate, it cuts off further discussion, it requires a two-thirds majority to pass. If it passes, the chair then takes an immediate vote on the pending motion. If it fails, the assembly returns to debate on the pending motion.

"All who thought my little joke very funny say 'Aye.'"

POSTPONE TEMPORARILY. The subsidiary motion to **postpone temporarily** sets aside consideration of a pending matter until some time later in the same meeting. It is sometimes called a motion to lay on the table. It differs in two ways from the motion to postpone definitely. First, its effect applies only during the same meeting in which it is made. If a matter postponed temporarily during a meeting is not again brought up later in that same meeting, it dies. Second, no definite time is stated in this motion for again discussing the postponed matter.

One reason for making a motion to postpone temporarily is to secure more information about a pending matter before voting. Another reason is to set aside an unwelcome motion in the hope that it will not be brought up again. This motion is not debatable. It requires a simple majority vote to pass.

Privileged motions

Three motions are considered to be of such an urgent nature that they form a class called **privileged motions.** Unlike subsidiary motions, they do not relate to the items of business before the assembly. They refer instead to the organization and its members. Because of their urgent nature, they may be made and considered ahead of any of the other classes of motions. They are the motions calling for question of privilege, recess, and adjournment.

QUESTION OF PRIVILEGE. Though called a motion, the **question of privilege** is really a request made by a member and granted or denied by the chair. A question of privilege may be made to secure immediate action on some urgent matter that relates to the comfort, convenience, rights, or privileges of the assembly, or one of its members. It may also be made to secure permission to make an urgent motion while some other matter is pending. The following example shows how a question of privilege may be presented:

MEMBER: Mr. Chairman, I rise to a question of privilege.

CHAIR: State your question of privilege.

MEMBER: I ask that we send someone to check the public records in the courthouse before we vote on this current matter.

If the courthouse records are likely to have a direct bearing on the assembly's decision on the pending matter, the chair would probably grant such a request.

RECESS. If a motion to **recess** passes, it calls a halt to a meeting without ending it. A motion to recess must always include a time when the body will resume the meeting. Though recesses are usually brief, they can last for days. The time of the recess cannot extend beyond the time for the next regularly scheduled meeting of the group, however. The motion to recess requires a second. It may be debated briefly regarding the time or need for the recess. It needs a simple majority vote to pass.

ADJOURNMENT. Passage of a motion to **adjourn** ends a meeting. Unlike the motion to recess, which only calls a halt in a meeting, the motion to adjourn legally concludes a meeting. When an assembly meets again following an adjournment, they do not take up at the point where they left off on their agenda (as in the case of a recess). Rather they begin a new meeting with a new agenda. Business that was interrupted or left unfinished by an adjournment comes up on the agenda of the next meeting under the heading "Unfinished Business." Since it would defeat the purpose to debate a motion to adjourn, it is not debatable. It requires a simple majority vote to pass.

Incidental motions

The last type of motion relates to procedures having to do with the conduct of parliamentary business. Some of these are true motions, requiring a second and a vote. Others are simply requests, granted by the chair. Here are the names, purpose, and vote required (if any) of the eight most common **incidental motions:**

APPEAL. An **appeal** motion allows a member who disagrees with a ruling by the chair to put that ruling to a vote. This is a true motion requiring a second and a simple majority vote.

SUSPEND THE RULES. A motion to **suspend the rules** is also a true motion. It allows the assembly to set aside some procedural rule so the members can do something not ordinarily allowed by that rule. Only procedural rules may be suspended. Suppose the bylaws of an organization call for a particular order of business, but the officer who should make the next report has not yet arrived. A member may make a motion to suspend the rules and allow that officer to report later so the group may proceed with other business in the meantime. Such a motion would require a second and a two-thirds majority vote.

OBJECT TO CONSIDERATION. This allows an assembly to entirely avoid debate and a decision on a pending motion. The assembly may believe it to be embarrassing or unprofitable or may have some other good reason for not wishing to consider it. Since it completely avoids consideration of an issue if it passes, **object to consideration** is a motion requiring a second and a two-thirds majority to pass.

POINT-OF-ORDER. This is a request used to call to the attention of the chair and the assembly that an error is being made. Perhaps a procedure is being violated. A member must gain attention by calling "**Point of order**" immediately after the error has occurred. After stating what she or he believes the error to be, an immediate ruling is given by the chair. No vote is taken.

PARLIAMENTARY INQUIRY. **Parliamentary inquiry** is a request that gives a member an opportunity to ask the chair questions about parliamentary procedure dealing with a motion under consideration at that time. Because it is a request addressed to the chair and not a motion, it does not require a second. The chair answers the inquiry, so no vote is necessary.

WITHDRAW A MOTION. **Withdraw a motion** enables a member who has made a motion to remove it from consideration before a vote is taken. Such a motion may be withdrawn by simple request of its maker if (a) the chair has not yet restated the motion to the assembly or (b) the chair has restated it, but no one objects to its being withdrawn. If just one member objects in the second case above, however, the request to withdraw becomes a motion requiring a majority vote.

DIVISION OF QUESTION. A **division of question** is used to separate a motion having two or more independent parts into separate motions for purposes of separate debate and voting. This is ordinarily a request, granted by the presiding officer, unless a member objects. Then, like the motion to withdraw a motion, it must be voted upon and requires a simple majority to pass.

DIVISION OF ASSEMBLY. If a vote has been taken by voice, and anyone is unsure about which side has the majority, a member may request a **division of assembly.** This is simply a method of retaking such a vote by a show of hands or by having members rise in their places to be counted. Such a request is ordinarily granted by the chair as long as there is a reasonable question about the outcome of the voice vote.

Precedence of motions

All of the motions discussed, except the incidental motions, must be dealt with in **order of precedence.** This is a ranking system that tells you the order in which you must vote on each of the motions. There are two rules that govern the order of precedence:

1. When a motion is pending, only motions above it in the order of precedence may be made.

2. When motions have already been made, they must be debated and acted upon in the opposite order from that in which they were made. In other words, the motion made most recently is acted upon first.

Earlier in this chapter when you read about the different kinds of motions, they were presented in the order in which they could be introduced. The order of precedence reverses that order because it lists the motions in the order in which they would be acted upon. The order of precedence looks like this:

Privileged Motions	1. Adjourn
	2. Recess
	3. Question of Privilege
Subsidiary Motions	4. Postpone Temporarily
	5. Vote Immediately
	6. Limit Debate
	7. Postpone Definitely
	8. Refer to Committee
	9. Amend
	10. Postpone Indefinitely
Main Motion	11. Any Main Motion

The chair must understand the order of precedence in order to conduct a meeting correctly.

"I move that we amend the motion." Members of this mock political convention according to the order of precedence, must debate and vote on the amendment before discussion of the main motion itself can resume.

The first rule of precedence means that only motions of higher rank may be made while another motion is pending. Suppose, for example, that a member has made the main motion to donate $100 to a scholarship fund. While this main motion is pending, someone else moves to amend the amount to $50. This motion to amend is permissible, or in order, since the motion to amend (9) is of higher rank than the main motion (11). During the debate on the amendment, however, someone attempts to make a motion to postpone indefinitely (10). The chair must rule this motion out of order. This means it cannot be made at that time. This is because the motion to postpone indefinitely (10) is of lower rank than the pending motion, amend (9).

The second rule of precedence means that members must always first dispose of the last motion made. Then they can proceed backwards to the first one proposed. Suppose, for instance, they start with a main motion. A member proposes an amendment to the main motion. Then someone moves to limit debate. The assembly must first decide on whether or not to limit debate before returning to debate on the amendment to the main motion.

The incidental motions have no order of precedence. They may be made at any time they are appropriate and must be acted upon immediately. The charts below summarize these and other motions, giving all the basic information you need to deal with motions made during a typical meeting.

Rules governing motions with order of precedence

(r = restricted)

	CAN INTERRUPT?	REQUIRES SECOND?	DEBATABLE?	AMENDABLE?	VOTE REQUIRED?
Privileged motions					
1. Adjourn	no	yes	no	no	majority
2. Recess	no	yes	yes^r	yes^r	majority
3. Question of privilege	yes	no	no	no	none
Subsidiary motions					
4. Postpone temporarily	no	yes	no	no	majority
5. Vote immediately	no	yes	no	no	two-thirds
6. Limit debate	no	yes	yes^r	yes^r	two-thirds
7. Postpone definitely	no	yes	yes^r	yes^r	majority
8. Refer to committee	no	yes	yes^r	yes^r	majority
9. Amend	no	yes	yes	yes	majority
10. Postpone indefinitely	no	yes	yes	no	majority
Main motions					
11. The main motion	no	yes	yes	yes	majority

Rules governing motions with no order of precedence

	CAN INTERRUPT?	REQUIRES SECOND?	DEBATABLE?	AMENDABLE?	VOTE REQUIRED?
Incidental motions					
Appeal	yes	yes	yes	no	majority
Suspend rules	no	yes	no	no	two-thirds
Object to consideration	yes	yes	no	no	two-thirds
Point of order	yes	no	no	no	none
Parliamentary inquiry	yes	no	no	no	none
Withdraw a motion	yes	no	no	no	none
Division of question	no	no	no	no	none
Division of assembly	yes	no	no	no	none

Murry Zweben is the United States Senate's parliamentarian. In the Capitol, in Washington, D.C., he presides over a small, but extremely busy, staff whose job it is to see, through advising the Chair and members, that Senate proceedings are conducted according to parliamentary rules of order and the interpretations of those rules which the Senate has developed over the years.

Many of the rules date back to 1789, the year the American Constitution was drafted. Such leaders as Thomas Jefferson and James Madison helped to establish not only the democratic principles which would govern America but also the rules by which the two legislative bodies, the Senate and the House of Representatives, would govern themselves. Without parliamentary rules, the Senate, which now has 100 members, and the House, with over 400 members, could not act effectively.

"The rules were established to give the majority (within the Senate) the right to work its will while at the same time protecting the rights of the minority," Zweben said. "If a body like the Senate, which is passing laws by which people live their lives, does not pass those laws in a fair and orderly way, it would not be regarded as a responsible legislative body."

In theory, Zweben's job appears simple. Sitting at a desk just in front of the Senate's president, who is referred to as "the Chair," Zweben answers questions of procedure which individual senators bring up. He is the authority on the Senate's standing rules and the various historical interpretations of these rules. These are the rules by which all senators are bound during discussions. "*Point of order*! *Point of order*!" a senator may shout in the thick of a session. The call means that the senator has a question about what is happening. Perhaps the senator wishes to object to the consideration of an amendment which may be out of order. Once recognized by the Chair, the senator states the question. The parliamentarian is consulted, in whispers by the Chair, if the question is a difficult one. The Chair then reports the answer to the Senate at large, and proceedings continue, governed by the rule the parliamentarian has cited.

In practice, Zweben's job is tricky. Over the years, the Senate has accumulated, by vote, a staggering number of rule interpretations. Zweben, backed by his staff, is under constant pressure to cite them correctly for the Chair. The Chair then announces the ruling. The Chair's rulings can be challenged, however, and if enough senators, a majority, vote to change what has been cited, or the interpretation of it, it can be changed. Unlike standard parliamentary rules followed by councils and boards, Senate rules must constantly be interpreted following decisions that have been made over the years.

Most of the points of order or parliamentary inquiries Zweben is called upon to answer involve the Senate's own interpretations of rules whose implications may not be totally clear. Most senators know the Senate's standing rules and abide by them, but a senator who knows the rules as well as the ways they have been applied over the years fares best, Zweben said. Such a senator can use that knowledge to delay discussion of a matter or to speed a bill's passage.

"Look at it this way," Zweben said. "I played tennis for an hour and a half this morning. If I hadn't known the rules of the game, my opponent definitely would have had the advantage."

Summary

Parliamentary procedure is a set of rules designed to streamline the conduct of business at meetings and at the same time protect the democratic rights of the participants. It began in the English Parliament and has developed over the years as a set of basic principles.

BASIC PRINCIPLES. Five basic principles form the basis of parliamentary procedure. Only one question may be considered at a time. The majority rules. The rights of the minority are protected. All members share equal rights and responsibilities. Every issue may be subjected to free debate.

HOLDING A MEETING. Holding a meeting according to parliamentary procedure begins with giving notice. This means informing members about the meeting, usually about ten days in advance. When the time for the meeting arrives, the chair must determine whether a quorum is present before beginning. The usual order of business consists of the call to order, approval of the minutes, reports of officers, reports of standing and special committees, unfinished business, new business, announcements, and adjournment. During a meeting the chair's duties include keeping order, recognizing members to speak, insuring that all members understand the issues, and moving the meeting along. Methods of voting on issues include voice votes, rising, raising hands, roll calls, or secret ballots.

MOTIONS. Business is handled during meetings by the making of motions. Motions are formal proposals made by members for consideration and action by the assembly. Motions fall into four major types. Main motions deal directly with the issues before the assembly. They are the foundation of a parliamentary meeting. Subsidiary motions allow members to change the nature of main motions, or to handle them in some other way than by ordinary debate and a vote. The class of subsidiary motions includes motions to postpone indefinitely, amend, refer to committee, postpone definitely, limit or extend debate, vote immediately, and postpone temporarily. Privileged motions relate to urgent matters dealing with the organization and its members. The three motions in this class involve questions of privilege, recess, and adjournment. Incidental motions have to do with procedural matters and the conduct of parliamentary business. This class of motions includes requests for and motions to appeal, suspend the rules, object to consideration, point of order, parliamentary inquiry, withdraw a motion, division of question, and division of assembly. Motions are arranged in an order of precedence, a ranking system that indicates the order in which each motion must be voted upon. There are two rules of precedence. One states that when a motion is pending only motions of higher precedence may be proposed. The other requires that motions be debated and acted upon in the opposite order from that in which they were made.

Vocabulary

parliamentary procedure
parliamentarian
simple majority
minority
notice
agenda
quorum
order of business
chair
filibustering
recognizing
motion
second

pending motion
main motion
subsidiary motion
postpone indefinitely
amend
germane
refer to committee
postpone definitely
limit or extend debate
vote immediately
postpone temporarily
privileged motion
question of privilege

recess
adjourn
incidental motion
appeal
suspend the rules
object to consideration
point of order
parliamentary inquiry
withdraw a motion
division of question
division of assembly
order of precedence

Review questions

1. What are the five principles that form the basis for parliamentary procedure?

2. What are the two most commonly used codes of parliamentary procedure?

3. What is a simple majority?

4. What are the seven guidelines for responsible membership in an organization?

5. What is a quorum?

6. What is the usual order of business for a meeting?

7. What are the duties of the chair?

8. What are the four types of motions?

9. What is the purpose of each of the four types of motions?

10. What is the order of precedence for the various types of motions?

Discussion questions

1. What are the reasons behind the number of votes required to pass a motion? Consider with your classmates the types of motions that require a simple majority and those that require two thirds. See if you can determine why some motions require more votes than others.

2. Discuss the reasons why you think some motions are debatable and others are not. What relationship, if any, do you think exists between your findings here and those in Question 1?

3. Discuss the circumstances under which it is advisable to table a motion.

4. Decide with your classmates under what circumstances it is advisable to refer a question to a committee.

5. Study a newspaper account of a town or city council meeting. How does it or doesn't it conform to what you have learned in this chapter? How could it have been improved?

At-home activities

1. Suggest to the other members of a club or organization you belong to that the group begin conducting its meetings according to the rules of parliamentary procedure. Explain the advantages of using these rules to conduct meetings. You might wish to volunteer to serve as parliamentarian. (A parliamentarian advises the chair on matters of parliamentary procedure.)

2. Memorize the order of precedence of motions for use in a mock parliamentary assembly.

3. Work with a friend in your speech class to memorize the purpose of each type of motion. You should also memorize what vote is required for each. (Hint: Only four require a two-thirds majority. All others require a simple majority.)

In-class activities

1. Take part in an election to choose a chair, a parliamentarian, and a secretary, and then participate in an in-class meeting. Follow the agenda you prepared in the Application on page 307. Use as many types of motions as possible during this meeting.

2. During a mock meeting, take turns with various class members serving as chair. After the meeting, discuss the problems each of you had while acting as chair.

3. Participate in the following "Identify the Motions" game in class:

Stand with your classmates in line as you would for a spelling bee. Your teacher will then name one of the motions discussed in the chapter. The first person must state whether it requires a second, whether or not it is debatable, what vote it requires, and what other motion is directly above it in the order of precedence. (For incidental motions, the correct answer is "No order of precedence.") A student missing any of these responses must be seated. The teacher will continue naming one motion per student in rotation until only the winner remains standing.

Careers

CITY MANAGERS are the administrative heads of city governments. They must be experts both in administration and in government. City managers meet with people formally and informally and conduct government meetings. High school courses in English, speech, history, government, and economics should be useful. A bachelor's degree is becoming a necessity. A master's degree in public administration is necessary for positions in larger cities.

14

ORAL INTERPRETATION

When you have completed this chapter you should be able to

Define oral interpretation.

Identify occasions for oral interpretation.

Describe the value of oral interpretation.

List different types of literature available for oral interpretation.

Make well-informed choices of material for oral presentations.

Analyze a piece of literature for understanding.

Prepare an introduction for an oral interpretation.

Practice your selection making good use of your voice to reinforce your meaning.

In order for you to hear a piece of music someone must play it. It is a musician's job to transform what is written on a sheet of music into what is played on an instrument. But more than just playing notes, a good musician must interpret the music. What you hear is really a musician's understanding of *how* the music should be played. By interpreting a piece of music a musician is said to *perform* it. People attend concerts not only to hear the music but also to experience a particular musician's performance of that music. *How* the music is played is just as important as *what* music is played.

A good speaker can perform literature just as a good musician performs music. By transforming written words into spoken sounds the speaker can provide a way for you to hear literature. Just as a good musician does not simply play notes, a good speaker does not simply read words. To perform a piece of literature a speaker must interpret it orally. **Oral interpretation** is the process by which a speaker performs literature aloud for an audience.

In this chapter you will study some of the methods used to turn literature into a successful performance. These are the techniques of oral interpretation. First, however, some background information may be in order. How has oral interpretation been used in the past? When is it performed today? What is its value in daily life? What types of literature can be used? With the answers to these questions in mind, you will find it easier to choose selections and prepare to perform.

A brief history of oral interpretation

Oral interpretation is one of the oldest of human social activities. Before writing, people communicated primarily by word-of-mouth. Because there were no newspapers, magazines, or books, ideas were handed down orally from one generation to the next. In this way, literature was preserved in memory rather than on paper. Some of the greatest literature survived for hundreds of years in oral form before it was finally written down. Professional storytellers, known as **minstrels** or **bards,** traveled from village to village bringing news and entertaining people with their stories.

As writing became widespread and people learned to read, the oral tradition did not end. Great writers in the nineteenth century not only read their work to audiences, but expected their novels to be orally interpreted by others. In homes where their stories were popular the best oral interpreter in the family would read aloud a chapter every evening. In the early twentieth century professional oral interpreters traveling through America on reading tours were a common source of entertainment. Young children today are first exposed to literature when their parents orally perform stories and poems for them. Thus the tradition has endured from earliest times to the present.

Occasions for oral interpretation

You will probably encounter many occasions in your lifetime when you will be able to orally interpret some type of literature. In school you may be called upon to read part of a story or to recite a poem. At home or while babysitting, you may find yourself reading to younger children. And during religious services you could be asked to read prayers or other religious passages aloud. Many professions also call for an ability to perform oral interpretations. Teachers, lawyers, religious leaders, librarians, and broadcasters are only a few of the people whose jobs demand that they read aloud skillfully.

The value of oral interpretation

You may ask: Why study oral interpretation? What value does it have? What are its benefits? In order to answer these questions you must consider two separate points of view—the speaker's and the listener's.

For the speaker, there is often a sense of personal pride associated with reading orally. Aside from the enjoyment of reading something well, it makes people feel good to share their experiences of literature with others. Sometimes people take on the characteristics of the material they orally interpret. It may not be just a joke that is amusing, but

This picture of an engraving made in 1840 shows a family listening to the father read a favorite story.

also the way it is told. Another person may become more interesting to others when reading an interesting newspaper article aloud.

Oral interpretation also provides a number of other benefits for the speaker. By carefully preparing for a performance, you can develop a better understanding of a piece of literature. The process of developing an oral interpretation encourages you to read carefully and think about the literature to be performed. This extra effort not only helps to improve your study skills, but can also help to clarify meanings and may often lead to new insights.

From the point of view of the listener, oral interpretation is primarily a source of entertainment. When literature is performed, it seems to come alive for the audience. As a listener you not only experience the reader's enthusiasm for the material being performed, but you also benefit from the speaker's understanding of that material. An oral performance may offer you new insights into what you have read before, or it may serve as an introduction to literature you have not previously experienced. Oral interpretation also helps to develop your listening skills. By listening to different interpretations, you become better able to judge a good performance from a bad one. Finally, by giving speakers your full attention, you will not only appreciate others for their skill in communicating literature, but will also discover new ways to improve your own oral performances.

Types of material for oral interpretation

One of your responsibilities as an oral performer is to recognize what types of materials are available for interpretation. Just because something is written does not necessarily mean that it is suitable for oral performance. You would, for example, have difficulty performing a grocery list, a set of directions, or the ingredients listed on the back of a soup can. Essentially, your task is to distinguish literature from other types of writing.

Literature says something of lasting value and says it well. The literature used for oral interpretation in this chapter falls into two very broad categories: prose and poetry.

Prose

Compared to poetry, **prose** is closer to the language of everyday use. When an author writes in prose, he or she generally tries to duplicate the way someone would speak aloud. Although it wasn't a popular literary form until the sixteenth century, prose is now, by far, the most common form of literature. Every time you read a book or a magazine article you are reading prose. Prose is used by authors to tell or describe something. The two types of prose are fiction and nonfiction.

FICTION. Basically, **fiction** is material created in the imagination. The author of fiction has complete freedom to add, subtract, or change any of what is being written. Fiction deals with imaginary characters and events. Novels and short stories are the two most common types of fiction. Do not be misled if an author includes some facts in a work of fiction. In order to make their stories more believable, many authors create their fiction around actual events or real people. These facts, in a sense, serve as a background for the author's imagination. They suggest what did, could, or would happen. For example, a story about the bombing of London during World War II would be based on actual events of history. But by introducing imaginary characters in imaginary situations, the author creates a work of fiction.

NONFICTION. **Nonfiction,** on the other hand, is based entirely on truth as the author understands it, on real people, and on actual events. Nonfiction is written to inform the reader and is usually the result of an author's research. A biography, for example, is a work of nonfiction about someone's life. Its very nature demands accuracy and truth. An autobiography is simply a biography written by the person it is about. If you were to do an oral interpretation of an autobiography you would try to speak and act like the person who wrote it. The quality of your performance would depend upon your ability to show by your interpretation what this person is really like. Another interesting type of nonfiction is the essay. Essays are used to state a position, to analyze, or to interpret something. In constructing an essay, an author makes a statement and uses facts to support it.

Poetry

Poetry, the oldest of the literary arts, can trace its roots directly to the very beginnings of the oral tradition. Most of the oldest literature in existence today, which includes such works as *Beowulf*, *The Odyssey*, and *The Iliad*, is poetry. The bards were really the first poets. Each one of their stories contained a specific rhythm and rhyme. The rhythm helped them to remember the number of syllables in each line, and the rhyme gave them clues as to the actual words. The result was a kind of chanted story-poem.

Poetry can be described as communication of thought and feeling through the careful arrangement of words for their sound and rhythm as well as their meaning. Poetry has not only survived as literature for thousands of years, it is considered by many people to be the most noble form of literature. As an oral performer you will be concerned with two major types of poetry: the narrative poem and the lyric poem.

NARRATIVE POETRY. **Narrative poetry** is poetry that tells a story. It usually describes something that has happened. Narrative poetry is not as popular as it used to be. Most modern writers prefer to use prose to tell stories.

What factors should this student consider when choosing a selection to interpret orally?

LYRIC POETRY. While narrative poetry concerns events, **lyric poetry** deals with what happened or is happening inside the poet. Used mainly to express deep thoughts or feelings, lyric poetry frequently takes the form of a sonnet, ode, hymn, or elegy. Lyric poems are usually very musical. In fact, the word *lyric* means "song-like." If you stop to think about it, a song is really just a poem put to music.

Choosing material for oral interpretation

The first step in oral interpretation is to choose your material. If you are not assigned to perform a particular piece of literature, then your choices are practically limitless. It is always wise to approach the oral interpretation process with an open mind. You shouldn't be afraid to read something by an unfamiliar author or to consider a type of literature you have not read before. A good library may be your best source since it can provide you with anthologies of poems and prose passages from many different authors and types of literature. Do not hesitate to spend some time carefully examining a poem or a prose passage before making a choice. The range of literature is so wide that it is difficult to suggest specific methods for choosing literature for oral interpretation. However, it is wise to consider some of the basic characteristics of good literature.

Universal appeal

As you examine a piece of literature keep your audience in mind. Ask yourself: Will this piece be interesting to others? Does it deal with feelings or ideas that are common to all people? Stories and poems that can be appreciated and enjoyed by many people at many different times are said to have **universal appeal.** In other words, they deal with problems or experiences that everyone can easily recognize and identify with. Some of the more popular universal themes include growing up, loneliness, parent-child relationships, and love.

In choosing a selection for oral interpretation, it is usually best to choose a work with universal appeal, a work whose theme is likely to appeal to almost any audience. Consider Emily Dickinson's lyric poem "I'm Nobody! Who Are You?"

> I'm nobody! Who are you?
> Are you nobody, too?
> Then there's a pair of us—don't tell!
> They'd banish us, you know.
>
> How dreary to be somebody!
> How public, like a frog.
> To tell your name the livelong day
> To an admiring bog!

Dickinson's poem can be appreciated by many people because almost everyone has, at one time or another, had the desire to be "somebody." You need not belong to a certain group of people or possess a special kind of knowledge to appreciate the meaning of this poem.

Insight

Good literature also deals with important ideas. It provides a new way of viewing life by drawing your attention to everyday things and helping you to see them in a different light. In this manner, good literature increases your range of experience. As an oral interpreter, you will find it easier to arouse and maintain the interest of your audience if you choose a poem or a prose passage that offers this kind of experience, that goes beyond the obvious to suggest a new and exciting way of looking at something. Literature with this particular quality is said to offer insight. Having **insight** means that you have a particularly clear understanding of something. In the following prose story from *The Tarot of Cornelius Agrippa* by Frederick Morgan, the author gives the reader insight by having the main character come to a new understanding of something. What did the stonemason think he saw in the mirror? What do you think this experience taught the stonemason about death that he had not realized before? What do you think a reader might gain from this story?

A stone mason who in the course of one winter lost his wife, his son and his best friend, put aside the tools of his trade and went out in search of DEATH, whom he conceived as a tall pale man dressed in black, with a face like a skull.

Setting forth from his house, he brought with him only the money he had saved through the years, and his old trusty musket, with which he intended to execute his enemy. "For," he said to himself, "if I find him and kill him, I shall not only have avenged myself—I shall have bestowed the greatest possible blessing on my fellow men and women."—And so he went traveling methodically through the land, searching for his victim in lonely farmsteads, in the streets of great cities, in the homes of rich and poor. But nowhere did he find Death, though he found many who had been marked by him.

Late one night in the tenth year of his quest, when he was staying over at a small inn in a country village, he was awakened suddenly from a dream in which he was being pursued by serpents. Coming slowly to himself, he got down from the bed, stood erect, and opened his eyes. The first faint light of dawn came palely in through the window—and by it he could see a figure that stood at the far side of the room, watching him. The body was that of a skeleton, the head was his own . . . He reached for his musket and was about to fire, when he realized that the person confronting him was his own reflection in a tall standing mirror. As he approached, it became more and more commonplace and recognizable. The sun was rising, he put down his gun.

It was only a mirror—yet he could not escape the conclusion that he had at last come face to face with his enemy. He gave up his search, went back home, and resumed his old ways. But for the remainder of his life he turned his thoughts more and more inward.

Beauty

Another quality to look for in good literature is *beauty*. These lines from Henry Thoreau's *Walden* offer a good example:

> If a man does not keep pace with his companions, perhaps it is because he hears a different drummer. Let him step to the music which he hears, however measured or far away.

In only a few words Thoreau suggests a way of understanding people who do not think and act like the majority. Keep in mind that the best writers are often able to explain difficult ideas in very simple terms. Their skill lends a sense of beauty to literature.

Of course, people disagree about what is, or is not, beautiful. The sounds you find pleasant may not be enjoyed by others. A description may seem well-stated to you but not to your listeners. There are no rules in such cases, but there are guidelines. Look for literature that has noble ideas presented in language that is pleasant to the ear. Avoid poetry that stresses sound too much and has few good ideas. Avoid prose that has many ideas but sentences that are unclear. Literature that achieves a harmony between words and ideas can be truly beautiful.

Application: Finding beauty in a selection

Read the following passage taken from "A White Heron," a short story by Sarah Orne Jewett. A young girl, Sylvia, has just climbed to the top of a tall pine tree:

> Sylvia's face was like a pale star, if one had seen it from the ground, when the last thorny bough was past, and she stood trembling and tired but wholly triumphant, high in the treetop. Yes, there was the sea with the dawning sun making a golden dazzle over it, and toward that glorious east flew two hawks with slow-moving pinions. How low they looked in the air from that height when before one had only seen them far up, and dark against the blue sky. Their gray feathers were as soft as moths; they seemed only a little way from the tree, and Sylvia felt as if she too could go flying away among the clouds.

Discuss with your classmates how the author of this passage uses words and ideas to create beauty.

Technical quality

The way a piece of literature is put together—its **technical quality**—is another thing you should consider when choosing material for oral interpretation. Are the author's ideas expressed clearly? Can they maintain a person's interests?

The way an author introduces an idea to a reader is one aspect of the technical quality of literature. When you read orally, be sure that you choose material that quickly provides your listeners with enough detail to get them involved in the material.

Young children listen with rapt attention to a selection chosen to appeal to their interests.

The way an author approaches the high point of a story or poem is also important. Many passages in literature describe events leading up to and passing some critical stage. This is usually called a climax. The point at which the climax occurs is a measure of an author's ability to arrange events properly. Examine passages for climaxes and ask yourself: Does the climax occur in the middle or toward the end of the piece? If it occurs in the middle, does the second half of the material seem less interesting than the first? On the other hand, a selection that drags on and on, finally arriving at a climax that should have occurred earlier, is equally undesirable. Look for prose and poetry selections that will keep the attention of your listeners from beginning to end.

Your preference and the occasion

The most important thing to remember when choosing literature for oral interpretation is to choose something you truly like. If you do this, your audience will be more likely to share your enthusiasm for the selection and you will have more fun sharing it with them.

The occasion for a performance, your purpose in performing, and the type of audience are all important considerations in choosing material for oral interpretation. If you were babysitting and you wanted to entertain a young child, your choice of material would be vastly different from the choice you would make if you were asked to give an oral interpretation of a literary work at your high school.

Finally, you should be very conscious of the amount of time that you have to interpret a work. Avoid selecting a short story, for example, that you suspect will require more time to perform than you are given. Your oral interpretation will be spoiled if you have to speed up halfway through in order to finish on time. Besides making you nervous, the need to quicken your speaking rate could annoy your audience. If you have a choice between a piece of literature that is too long and one that is too short, choose the shorter one, and do it well. Be aware that you don't always have to perform an entire piece of literature. In fact, most literature is much too long to be read in one performance. It is perfectly acceptable to cut a piece of literature down to a manageable size as long as you make your listeners aware that they are not hearing the whole piece, and as long as you do not change any of the words.

Interpreting your selection

There are many different ways to orally interpret any piece of literature. Just as two musicians who perform the same musical piece do not sound exactly alike, no two people who perform the same piece of literature interpret it in exactly the same way. A story about "Old Weird Harold" would sound different if Bill Cosby did not perform it.

Young children learn that different people interpret the wolf in "Little Red Riding Hood" in different ways.

It is important to remember that there is never a single "correct" oral interpretation of a poem or story. Everyone experiences literature differently. Although a piece of literature can have many "correct" interpretations, some interpretations are better than others. It is therefore important that you carefully develop the skills necessary for good oral interpretation.

In order to prepare a good oral interpretation you should know all you can about the literature you have chosen to perform. You must understand your selection thoroughly. You must also consider some of the elements within the literature that will affect your performance. These include the person speaking in the selection, the imaginary audience being spoken to, and the setting in which it occurs.

Understand your selection

When you choose a selection to perform, be sure you understand the meaning of every word it contains. A dictionary can help you with the meanings of unfamiliar words. Your selection may also contain references to real people or events from history or to imaginary characters from other pieces of literature. Look in encyclopedias, biographical dictionaries, or other reference books to see why these people and events have been mentioned in your selection.

While concentrating on meaning, remember the importance of pronunciation. Don't take a chance on pronouncing words incorrectly during your performance. Look up and practice the pronunciation of any words you are unsure of. Feel free to mark accents in your manuscript (as long as you are not using a book).

You may also find it helpful to know something about the author of your selection and why he or she wrote it. Perhaps the piece has some particular meaning based on the time or place in which it was written. Knowing the background of your selection can make your interpretation of it more meaningful for your audience.

Know the fictional speaker

You should be aware of who is speaking in any piece of literature you perform. Sometimes the authors themselves speak directly to the reader. Sometimes, however, in order to provide a specific point of view, an author uses a **fictional speaker.** The voice you hear telling the story or poem when you read silently is the voice of the fictional speaker. Quite often, the fictional speaker is one of the main characters in the story or poem.

Consider the speaker in the following passage from Mark Twain's *The Adventures of Huckleberry Finn.*

"What do the words mean? How are they pronounced?" These are important questions to be answered before interpreting any selection orally.

You don't know about me without you have read a book by the name of *The Adventures of Tom Sawyer*, but that ain't no matter. That book was made by Mr. Mark Twain and he told the truth, mainly. There was things which he stretched, but mainly he told the truth. This is nothing. I never seen anybody but lied one time or another, without it was Aunt Polly or the widow, or maybe Mary. Aunt Polly—Tom's Aunt Polly, she is—and Mary and the widow Douglas is all told about in that book, which is mostly a true book, with some stretchers as I said before.

The voice you hear in this passage is that of Huck Finn. The story is therefore told from his point of view. In this case, Mark Twain even used the fictional speaker to poke fun at himself. By carefully reading this passage you begin to understand the kind of person Huck Finn is.

If Mark Twain had chosen to make Huck a little older and more educated, *The Adventures of Huckleberry Finn* might have begun something like this:

Unless you have perused the volume entitled *The Adventures of Tom Sawyer*, you can have little knowledge of me, but that is of small consequence . . .

The meaning is the same in both passages, but the characteristics of the fictional speaker have changed. Huck is a different type of person in the made-up version than he is in the original.

Your experience of literature depends in part upon the author's characterization of the fictional speaker. By paying close attention to this characterization you will be better able to fulfill your role as an oral interpreter. In other words, you are expected to find out as much as you can about the fictional speaker so that you can communicate the story or the poem as if you *were* that speaker.

The text of the literature can help you identify the characteristics of the fictional speaker in two ways: (1) by directly stating facts or details about the speaker; (2) by suggesting details about the speaker.

You will find as you work on your interpretation that in most cases the suggestions far outnumber the facts. Look for a moment at "Stopping by Woods on a Snowy Evening," a poem by Robert Frost.

Whose woods these are I think I know.
His house is in the village though;
He will not see me stopping here
To watch his woods fill up with snow.

My little horse must think it queer
To stop without a farmhouse near
Between the woods and frozen lake
The darkest evening of the year.

He gives his harness bells a shake
To ask if there is some mistake.
The only other sound's the sweep
Of easy wind and downy flake.

The woods are lovely, dark and deep,
But I have promises to keep,
And miles to go before I sleep,
And miles to go before I sleep.

Robert Frost, one of the United States' most famous poets, often gave oral interpretations of his work.

Notice that while the poem tells us a good deal about what the speaker is looking at, it makes almost no direct statement about the speaker. Perhaps only three facts can be stated as certainties:

1. The speaker is familiar with the scene or at least with the probable owner of the woods.

2. The speaker is dutiful and concerned about the fact that there are "promises to keep".

3. The speaker has made promises of some kind.

When you consider suggestions you will find that there are more details to work with. The speaker seems to be alone with the horse since no one else is mentioned. The speaker seems to be sensitive to nature since he or she stops to admire the woods, even though there are many things to do. You can also guess from the manner of talking that the speaker is not a child. But, so far the details still do not give a very clear image of the speaker. Clearly, you must turn to yet another source.

This source is the interpreter's *imagination* while reading the poem. Whenever you interpret a poem, you combine facts and suggestions found in the poem with other details supplied by your own imagination. Perhaps you have never thought about this process, but you use your imagination every time you see anything. Suppose, for instance, you are out for a walk and you stop to admire a particularly beautiful tree. What you actually see is only half the trunk and half the leaves. To see the other half you would have to walk around to the other side of the tree. Yet, as you stand in one place admiring the tree, you assume without thinking that the other side looks roughly the same, that the leaves on the other side are the same color and size as what you can see on this side. If you walked around the tree and discovered that lightning had sliced it neatly in two and there were no bark, limbs, or leaves on the other side, you would be amazed because you had not found what your imagination had told you to be true.

Look at these two drawings:

You will probably have no difficulty recognizing that one is a triangle and the other a heart. Yet you couldn't do this unless your imagination supplied the missing details.

In interpreting literature you have to fill in the missing details just as you did with the heart and the triangle. But, note that any information supplied by your imagination must fit in with what you already know from the selection itself. In other words, none of the three kinds of details—facts, suggestions, or details supplied by your imagination—can contradict or disagree with one another. Your job as an interpreter is to successfully put together all the information you can find about a fictional speaker into a clear understanding of that person.

The most vivid interpretations are those in which the performer has carefully thought out all the necessary details about the fictional speaker. Those details include not just the fictional speaker's physical appearance but his or her state of mind and *motives*—the reasons why the fictional speaker behaves and speaks as he or she does.

Know the imaginary audience

When a fictional speaker relates a story or a poem, he or she "speaks" to an **imaginary audience.** In "Stopping By Woods on a Snowy Evening" the fictional speaker is alone so you know that the speaker is talking to an audience made up only of himself or herself.

Sometimes the imaginary audience is one or more characters within the story or poem. Consider the audience in the following poem by Edward Field.

> At the Coney Island Aquarium:
> "An Ode for Ookie, the Older Walrus Child
> or The Sibling Rival"
>
> Do not worry, sweet little walrus, about the superior cuteness
> Of those two new babies they brought to share your pool.
>
> You keep pushing the twins out of the way
> More concerned about keeping them from getting attention
> Than having your own scrub-brush nose whiskers rubbed
> So that no one gets the chance to give you
> The endless hugs and kisses you deserve.
> It is impossible of course to be more popular than twins
> So finally you sink to the bottom and play dead
> Hoping our hearts break—mine does anyway
> And the Keeper watches anxiously, so you see it works.
> But how long can you sit at the bottom of the water
> When lungs cry for air and the heart for love?
>
> No, Ookie, don't seek indiscriminate love from the many
> As those two simple-minded children do
> Who have not yet met with heartbreak (although they will),
> But leap the railing right into my arms
> And squirm there fishily always, Ookie, mine alone.

In this poem, the fictional speaker is talking to a young walrus. If you were to do an oral interpretation of this poem, you would have to take into account the fact that a walrus is the imaginary audience. In other words, you would have to perform this poem as if speaking to a fictional or real walrus.

The third type of imaginary audience is the most common. Here, the fictional speaker speaks directly to the reader, as in the following passage from *David Copperfield* by Charles Dickens.

Whether I shall turn out to be the hero of my own life, or whether that station will be held by anybody else, these pages must show. To begin my life with the beginning of my life, I record that I was born (as I have been informed and believe) on a Friday, at twelve o'clock at night. It was remarked that the clock began to strike, and I began to cry, simultaneously.

In consideration of the day and hour of my birth, it was declared by the nurse and by some sage women in the neighborhood who had taken a lively interest in me several months before there was any possibility of our becoming personally acquainted, first that I was destined to be unlucky in life; and secondly, that I was privileged to see ghosts and spirits; both these gifts inevitably attaching, as they believed, to all unlucky infants of either gender born towards the small hours on a Friday night.

Your decision about what kind of imaginary audience is involved in a piece of literature will have a direct effect on how you perform the selection. Your performance should also reflect the kind of relationship you believe exists between this audience and the fictional speaker. You know from your own experience that the way people say things is greatly influenced by their relationship with their listeners.

Understand the relationship between the fictional speaker and the imaginary audience

The kind of relationship that exists between the fictional speaker and the imaginary audience is important even when the fictional speaker is talking to himself or herself. Notice, for example, the words used when Lewis Carroll's Alice talks to herself in the following passage from *Alice's Adventures in Wonderland.*

You ought to be ashamed of yourself . . . a great girl like you . . . to go on crying in this way! Stop this moment, I tell you!

Now compare the way Alice talks to herself with the way the fictional speaker in "Stopping by Woods on a Snowy Evening" talks to himself or herself. Though both fictional speakers are giving themselves advice, Alice advises herself rather sharply. Frost's fictional speaker uses a gentler approach. While Alice speaks to herself as a parent might to a naughty child, Frost's fictional speaker talks as if speaking to another adult. Two important kinds of relationships that can exist between fictional speaker and imaginary audience, then, are one in which the fictional speaker is in some way *superior* to the imaginary audience and one in which the fictional speaker is *equal* to the imaginary audience.

A third important relationship is the fictional speaker being in some way *inferior* to the imagined audience. This type of relationship is also found in *Alice's Adventures In Wonderland.* Alice has just fallen down the rabbit hole at the beginning of the story, and as she falls, she talks to herself:

> "I wonder how many miles I've fallen by this time?" she said aloud. "I must be getting somewhere near the centre of the earth. Let me see: that would be four thousand miles down, I think—" (for, you see, Alice had learned several things of this sort in her lessons in the schoolroom, and though this was not a *very* good opportunity for showing off her knowledge, as there was no one to listen to her, still it was good practice to say it over)—"Yes, that's about the right distance—but then I wonder what Latitude or Longitude I've got to?" (Alice had not the slightest idea what Latitude was, or Longitude either, but she thought they were nice grand words to say.)

In the last quotation Alice is showing off her knowledge, trying to impress the listener, much as a child might show off before adults. You could say that the speaker-to-listener relationship is that of a very young child speaking to an adult, or in more general terms, an "inferior" speaking to a "superior."

Following the examples given above, you can capture a major part of the speaker's attitude toward the listener by determining if the speaker's relationship to the listener is superior, equal, or inferior. Keep in mind, however, that relationships can be influenced by many different factors. For example, differences in age and differences in power can greatly influence relationships, sometimes in contradictory ways. Social rank can also have an influence on the relationships between people. The tone of your voice can help make all of these relationships between fictional speaker and imaginary audience clear to your listeners.

Know the setting

If you wish to communicate all of the important elements of a piece of literature to your audience, you must also deal with the **setting**—the place and the time—in which the fictional speaker and imaginary audience are found.

PLACE: THE WHERE OF THE SETTING. To understand how important setting is, return to "Stopping by Woods on a Snowy Evening" on page 338. In the poem most of the details you are given concern the place where the poem occurs. In fact, place seems to be the most important single aspect of the whole situation. Even the title mentions it. In just sixteen lines Frost gives you the following details. The fictional speaker is alone except for the horse, and far from any farmhouses. The speaker is probably in a sleigh, given the mention of the harness. On one side of the speaker is the woods, further described as "lovely, dark and deep" and on the other side is a frozen lake. You also know that the night is very dark (though there must be enough light to see the woods), that it is snowing, and that the wind is blowing gently. As an oral interpreter, you must capture the feeling of this poem by imagining these specifics *vividly* during the performance.

TIME: THE WHEN OF THE SETTING. Now focus your attention on the second element of setting—in Frost's poem the time when the scene takes place. Here you will find fewer details and will need to use your imagination to fill in the spaces. You are given some clues to help you however. You know for instance the season (winter) and the time of day (evening). This isn't just any evening, however. It is described as "the darkest evening of the year." Careful readers of this poem have long been fascinated by this little detail. It is a good example of a writer giving readers part of the information and demanding that they fill in the rest with their imagination. Can this detail really be true? Have you ever tried walking on a truly dark night with no starlight or moonlight to guide you? If so, you probably had difficulty even seeing the path at your feet. Frost's fictional speaker can "watch his woods fill up with snow" and can see deep into the woods as well. Perhaps, as some readers have suggested, the fictional speaker intends the detail about the darkest night to describe his or her personal feeling at the time of the poem rather than the real physical setting. You may not agree with this interpretation. But, as an interpreter, whatever you decide will affect your performance. If you believe that the fictional speaker is going through what another writer has called "the dark night of the soul," the attraction of the speaker for the woods would be far different from the feeling involved if the speaker, in a lighthearted mood, just happens to be attracted by the woods.

Understanding the fictional speaker, the imaginary audience, and the setting of her selection will help this student make her interpretation meaningful for the audience.

DEALING WITH TIME AND PLACE. How do you perform a setting? First, you must see the setting vividly in your imagination and second, you must believe in it throughout the performance. It is one thing to picture in your mind all the necessary elements of the setting and quite another to act as though you really are *in* that setting.

In the Frost poem, for instance, if you are the speaker, where are the woods in relation to you? Where is the frozen lake? From what direction have you come? What direction are you going? Are you standing or sitting? Are you cold, or warmed by lap rugs in a sleigh? Answering these questions can help you see the setting in your imagination.

When you first ask questions about the setting of a selection, you are standing outside the selection looking for clues. What you do when you perform the selection is to stand inside it. You put yourself in the place of the fictional speaker, inside the setting that you have analyzed. When you read a story or poem silently and read it well, that is, when the literature affects you vividly, you are apt to say that you are "absorbed" by it. What is meant is exactly what you must do in oral interpretation—place yourself within the setting of the story.

If you truly believe in the setting that you have imagined as you perform, those who watch you will believe in the setting too. In performing Frost's poem, if you say "whose woods these are I think I know" and look directly at the audience, you are not *in* the poem. You don't believe in the woods and no one watching you perform does either. Instead, you must look at the woods you are imagining and put yourself in the place of the poem's fictional speaker.

Fill in missing details

After you have identified speaker, audience, and setting, there are still likely to be some missing details. Even the most detailed descriptions in literature require a reader to fill in unmentioned details; no description can give a complete picture of the subject described. The reader and the oral interpreter must supply these missing details.

What were the promises mentioned in Frost's poem? They are a missing detail. Why didn't Frost tell the reader what those promises were? Certainly not because they are unimportant. They are the most important motive behind the fictional speaker's decision to move on. One reason for not telling readers what they were could be that Frost wanted each reader to go through what the fictional speaker experienced in this poem. In other words, Frost may have wanted you to identify with the fictional speaker and supply the reasons for not staying yourself. What kind of promises would draw *you* away from the beauty and attractiveness of the woods? Your answer is likely to be different from the answer given by anyone else. This is one reason why you and other people would all perform slightly different interpretations of the poem. But it is also the reason why the poem is able to affect almost everyone personally, whether they are reading, performing, or listening.

Application: Analyzing details

Read the following poem, "May 10th" by Maxine Kumin:

> *I mean*
> *the fiddleheads have forced their babies,*
> *blind topknots first, up from the thinking rhizomes*
> *and the shrew's children, twenty to a teaspoon,*
> *breathe to their own astonishment*
> *in the peephole burrow.*
>
> *I mean*
> *a new bat hangs upside down in the privy;*
> *its eyes are stuck tight, its wrinkled pink mouth twitches*
> *and in the pond, itself an invented puddle,*
> *tadpoles quake from the jello*
> *and come into being.*
>
> *I mean, walk softly.*
> *The maple's little used-up bells are dropping*
> *and the new leaves are now unpacking,*
> *still wearing their dime-store lacquer,*
> *still cramped and wet from the journey.*

Discuss the many different details found and not found in the poem. Is it a narrative or lyric poem? Are there words whose meanings or pronunciations you or your classmates do not know? If so, look them up in a dictionary. Why did the author title the poem "May 10th"? What is the fictional speaker like? The imaginary audience? What is the relationship between them? What is the setting? What feeling do you think the author was trying to express? How can you tell?

Two final steps: Introduction and practice

Your work is not done when you have completed your analysis and interpretation of your selection. You must also prepare an introduction and, perhaps most important, you must practice. As you will see, this practice involves many of the same elements found in practicing for a public speech.

Prepare an introduction for your selection

When you read a piece of literature, your eyes give you certain clues about it. At a glance, you have the title, the name of the author, and perhaps even a number of illustrations. A preface, introduction, or jacket copy may help preview the contents of the work. When you do an

Listeners expect an oral interpreter to supply them with information they may need about the selection in order to understand and enjoy it.

oral interpretation, your listeners cannot see any of these things. They must depend on you for the information they will need to enjoy your selection.

One way to begin an introduction to an oral interpretation is to tell your listeners the kind of literature it is, its title, and something about the author. You will have done some research about the author to increase your own understanding of the selection. Include some of this background information in your introduction. An American author living in the nineteenth century, for example, would have a point of view very different from that of an author who lived in ancient Greece. Your selection will be more meaningful to your listeners if you share this information with them.

The historical background of a story or a poem is also very important and should be included in your introduction to an oral performance. By telling your listeners when the events in your selection take place, and by explaining why the historical period is important to the work, you make it much easier for them to understand and appreciate the author's purpose.

Finally, you should always include an explanation of the piece you are interpreting in your introduction. This is especially important if you are interpreting only part of a selection. It would be very unfair to your audience if you simply began reading from the middle of some piece of literature with no prior explanation. For example, if you are planning to perform a small section of *The Wonderful Wizard of Oz* you should first explain what the story is about, who the major characters are, and what has happened up to the point where the section you will perform begins. Some oral interpreters even go so far as to explain what happens in a story or a poem after the section they orally interpret.

Don't make your introduction too long, however. Your purpose is to insure that your audience will understand and enjoy the piece. You need not give a lecture on either the author or the selection.

Practice your selection

Practice is essential to a good oral performance. Thinking about how you will sound when you perform in front of an audience is not the same as actually doing it. The best way to prepare yourself for a performance is to practice aloud again and again. Don't expect every part of your performance to be perfect the very first time you do it. You must work slowly and carefully on every aspect of your delivery.

Your voice is important in an oral interpretation. Never attempt to vary it artificially. Let the emotion of what you are performing be heard by your audience. If you feel the meaning of what you are saying, your voice will usually take on the characteristics expressed in the words. Your voice should be flexible in pitch, force, and rate so it can respond to various shades of interpretation.

One of the most important aspects of any oral delivery is the use of emphasis. There is no doubt that some words should receive more emphasis than others, but you must be very careful not to disturb the rhythm of the language. This is especially important when dealing with poetry. Poets choose their words carefully to create and maintain a particular rhythm. The words that should be emphasized will be stressed naturally. Skillful speakers use pauses as well as stress for emphasis. Did you ever notice that when a good speaker stops speaking for a moment the last few words seem to take on more significance? Try to use both stress and pauses to emphasize certain words.

Speaking rate is also important in oral interpretation. Speak slowly if the ideas you are expressing are serious or difficult to understand. Light, humorous, or urgent matters can be expressed at more rapid speeds. When dealing with a poem, look closely at its rhythm. Some poems are meant to be read slowly, while others should be spoken quickly. Examples of these different types of rhythm are found in the beginning lines of William Collins' "Ode to Pity" and William Wordsworth's "The Tables Turned."

Ode to Pity

O thou, the friend of man assigned
With balmy hands his wounds to bind,
And charm his frantic woe . . .

The Tables Turned

Up! Up! my Friend, and quit your books;
Or surely you'll grow double:
Up! Up! my Friend, and clear your books;
Why all this toil and trouble?

Dee Knight loves books. "From the time I was a little girl I loved them," she said. "Our family was book-minded. We had a household that was just spilling over with them. When I was in the fifth or sixth grade I started my own lending library." Now Dee Knight is a real librarian who has organized and is running a library in a private school in Tacoma, Washington. The work keeps her close to the books she loves, but it also gives her a chance to do the thing she likes best to do—read out loud. "I think," she said, "that that's the very essence of books, reading out loud."

Dee Knight is an "oral interpreter." Reading out loud, she said, is a way for people, especially families and friends, to share reading experiences they would otherwise have alone. A good reader gives stories special drama and extra meaning, just as color adds meaning and depth to a black and white picture. Young children are taught to listen and to use their imaginations by hearing others read aloud to them. "I think that we have such a visually minded society now that some of us have forgotten the art of listening," Mrs. Knight said. "Children who develop the art of listening often turn out to be more imaginative. When children sit and listen to a story, all those wonderful mental images in their own minds' eye stimulate their imaginations. You can stimulate children to read by reading out loud to them."

Dee Knight reads regularly to the children at her school. Lower-school children meet her in the library, in small groups, once a week for readings. They sit on a large, soft rug around a fire crackling in a free-standing fireplace which Dee Knight has installed to give the library a cozy feeling. Making the children feel comfortable, almost as if they were home, is important, the librarian said. A cozy environment prepares children for relaxed, undistracted listening.

Dee Knight reads slowly, and because she has taken time to become familiar with the books beforehand, she reads fluently, without stumbling. "I like to read stories I'm very familiar with so I don't have to have my eyes constantly glued to the book," she said. This means she can look up and stay in touch with her listeners. She can tell when to explain a difficult word and when to emphasize the story's action with a gesture or a particular voice intonation. Occasionally, Dee Knight pauses to wait for the words and sentences to "sink in." When the story becomes a conversation between characters, she changes her voice to simulate the different voices of the speaking characters. Sometimes she reads loudly, at other times softly, to interpret or shape the sense of the story.

All these reading techniques bring the story to life. In a way, Dee Knight turns herself into a one-woman theater company, taking on several dramatic roles at once and projecting the story's action through the sound of her voice. Watching her audience as she reads, Dee Knight has noticed that some children lean back and close their eyes, as if to concentrate more thoroughly on the pictures the story's narration casts into their minds. Then she knows that to them the sound of her voice has become the story itself, something real and happening, and that listening in its purest form is going on.

The two poems on page 347 begin in very different ways. The words "Up! Up!" show that the second poem, "The Tables Turned," is to be read at a quick pace. On the other hand, the words "O thou, the friend of man . . ." in the first poem, "Ode to Pity," have a solemn ring to them and suggest a much slower reading.

Good articulation and correct pronunciation are both essential in oral interpretation. Don't be afraid to put your tongue, jaw, and lips to their full use in order to say words clearly and correctly. As in public speaking, your audience must be able to hear your words and understand them. In order to remember how you want to say a particular word or phrase, it is a good idea to mark the manuscript. You can develop your own system, which may or may not include underlining words you want stressed or using accent marks to remind you how to pronounce words you may have trouble with.

Above all, you must establish a rapport with your audience. Your listeners must believe that you are speaking directly to them and not to a piece of paper or to the floor. Although it is not recommended for beginners, some oral performers prefer to memorize what they perform. That way, they do not have to worry about losing their place in the manuscript or losing contact with their audience. If you do choose to memorize, be sure to have a copy of the piece you are performing nearby. Nervousness in front of an audience can cause you to forget some or all of a selection you thought you knew well. If you do not memorize the entire selection, you should at least know it well enough that you don't have to read every word from the manuscript. This will leave you free to gauge audience feedback.

Your audience will be influenced by what they see as well as by what they hear. It is important that the nonverbal aspects of your interpretation add to the effect of your performance. As a general rule, your gestures and facial expressions should be natural. If you are genuinely concerned with getting your message across, gesture will come naturally as part of the performance. Remember though that body movement is secondary to the spoken words. Exaggerated or nervous movements can distract your listeners from what you are saying. Gestures should be used to clarify, emphasize, or reinforce what you say. The visual aspects of your performance must be appropriate to your audience, the occasion, and the selection you have chosen. Most important, the visual aspects of your performance should be natural to you.

After you have practiced reading your interpretation aloud and feel comfortable with it, try speaking into a tape recorder so that you can get an idea of how you will sound to others. Then have one or two friends listen and see you perform. In this way you will become used to having an audience in front of you. You will also get a chance to observe and interpret some audience reaction to what you are saying and how you are saying it. By performing first in front of a small audience, you begin to gain the confidence necessary to do the same before a larger group of listeners.

Checklist for preparing a selection for oral interpretation

■ 1. Does my selection have the characteristics of good literature?

■ 2. Am I sure of the meaning and pronunciation of every word in this selection?

■ 3. Have I done research on the background of the author and the selection I have chosen?

■ 4. Do I know and understand the fictional speaker, the imaginary audience, and the relationship between them so I can make them clear to the audience?

■ 5. Have I "seen" the setting in my imagination?

■ 6. Have I prepared an introduction that includes information about the author and the selection for my audience?

■ 7. Have I practiced my performance thoroughly?

Summary

A good speaker can perform literature just as a good musician performs music. Oral interpretation is the process by which a speaker performs literature aloud for an audience.

A BRIEF HISTORY OF ORAL INTERPRETATION. Stories were preserved by being handed down orally from one generation to the next long before they could be preserved by being written. You will probably have many occasions to orally interpret literature including reading stories or reciting poems in school, reading to younger children, or taking part in religious services. People enjoy sharing their reading skills and enjoyment of literature with others. Preparing for oral interpretation can help oral interpreters understand a piece of literature better. Listeners may share the speaker's enthusiasm for a piece of literature, benefit from the speaker's understanding of it, and develop their listening skills.

TYPES OF MATERIAL FOR ORAL INTERPRETATION. Literature says something of lasting value and says it well. Of the two major types of literature, prose is closer to everyday language than poetry is. Prose includes works of fiction, such as novels and short stories, as well as works of nonfiction, such as biographies, autobiographies, and essays.

Poetry is the communication of thought and feeling through the careful arrangement of words for their sound and rhythm as well as their meaning. Narrative poetry tells stories, while lyric poetry is used mainly to express thoughts and feelings.

CHOOSING MATERIAL FOR ORAL INTERPRETATION. Choose literature for oral interpretation that has universal appeal, offers insight, beauty, and technical quality. Be sure to choose a selection that you enjoy as well as one that is suitable for the occasion, your purpose, your audience, and the amount of time you have to interpret it.

INTERPRETING YOUR SELECTION. Although a piece of literature can have many "correct" interpretations, some interpretations are better than others. Be sure you know the meaning and pronunciation of every word in any selection you choose to interpret orally. It may also be helpful to know some background information about the author of the piece and the time or place in which it was written.

Find out as much as you can about the author's fictional speaker. Consider facts and suggested details given in the selection. Use your imagination to fill in other details so that you will have a clear understanding of the fictional speaker including her or his appearance, state of mind, and motives.

The fictional speaker in a piece of literature addresses an imaginary audience. The speaker may talk to himself or herself, one or more other characters within the piece, or directly to the reader. The kind of imaginary audience and the relationship between the fictional speaker and the imaginary audience will affect your performance. The speaker may be superior to, equal to, or inferior to the imagined audience. The tone of your voice can help to make these relationships clear to your listeners.

The setting is the place and time in which your selection takes place. To communicate the importance of the setting to your listeners, you must see it vividly in your imagination as well as believe in it.

After you identify the speaker and setting of your piece, use your imagination to fill in any details that are still missing. Your interpretation of these missing details will probably differ from that of anyone else. This is one reason your performance will be slightly different from the performance given by any other person.

TWO FINAL STEPS: INTRODUCTION AND PRACTICE. An introduction for your selection should include the kind of literature it is, its title, information about its author, and its historical background. If you interpret only part of a selection, be sure to include an explanation of the selection in your introduction.

The best way to prepare yourself for a performance is to work slowly and carefully on every aspect of your delivery. Your voice should be flexible in pitch, force, and rate so it will indicate the emotion of what you are performing.

Good articulation and correct pronunciation are important. Mark your manuscript as a reminder of how you want to say words or phrases. Know your selection well enough so you are free to gauge audience feedback. Be sure your gestures and body movement are natural and enhance your performance. Practice your selection until you feel comfortable. Then rehearse again with a tape recorder and several friends. This will help you gain the confidence necessary for a larger group of listeners.

Vocabulary

oral interpretation

minstrel

bard

literature

prose

fiction

nonfiction

poetry

narrative poetry

lyric poetry

universal appeal

insight

technical quality

fictional speaker

imaginary audience

setting

Review questions

1. What is oral interpretation?

2. What are three occasions that may demand oral interpretation?

3. What is the value of oral interpretation for the speaker?

4. What is the value of oral interpretation for the listener?

5. What types of literature can successfully be used for oral interpretation?

6. What are four characteristics of a literary work to consider when you select a piece for

oral interpretation? Be sure to explain the meaning of each.

7. What are the personal elements to consider when you select a piece for oral interpretation?

8. What elements within a selection must a speaker understand to perform the work effectively?

9. What elements should an introduction to an oral interpretation include?

10. What steps should a speaker take in practicing for oral interpretation?

Discussion questions

1. How does preparation for oral interpretation differ from preparation for delivering an informative or persuasive speech?

2. How does the use of vocal elements—pitch, force, rate—differ in oral interpretation from their use in public speaking?

3. Listen to a recording of Hal Holbrook in *Mark Twain Tonight* or Julie Harris in *Belle of Amherst*. Discuss their performances in light of what you have learned about oral interpretation.

4. Listen to a recording of T. S. Eliot reading his *Four Quartets* or E. B. White reading *Char-*

lotte's Web. Discuss the special elements that the author's oral interpretation of his own work bring to your understanding of the selections you heard.

5. Discuss the complexities of "audience" in oral interpretation of a literary selection. How must the performer allow for both the imaginary audience (of the speaker within a selection) and the real audience (the one in front of the performer)? (You may wish to use your listening to the records mentioned in 3 and 4 above as the basis for your discussion.)

At-home activities

1. Practice choosing materials for oral interpretation. Go to a library and find at least three different books of poetry. Look carefully at each of these books and then compare them to each other. Note particularly (a) the age group the poems are aimed at in each book, (b) the nationality of the poets, (c) whether the poetry was written in the past century, and (d) how the poems have been organized in each book.

2. Go to a library and find at least one story and one poem with universal themes. Identify each of the themes.

3. Read several fairy tales or fables that contain talking animals. Practice the "voices" you would expect these animals to have. Have several of your friends join you in performing some of these stories for a group of children.

4. Choose an amusing poem or story and plan a performance for these types of audiences:
   a. a small group of children
   b. your classmates
   c. a group of parents
Decide how you would change your presentation for each audience.

In-class activities

1. Work with several classmates to prepare and perform a Reader's Theater presentation of a one-act play or a scene from a longer play. Reader's Theater resembles a group oral interpretation. In a Readers' Theater production, actors read their lines from the script and also remain in one place (seated or standing). No scenery or costumes are necessary.

2. Choose a story or a poem that contains two fictional speakers. Orally perform this piece of literature with a classmate. Note that during your preparation of this piece, you must work closely with your classmate to decide who will interpret each part and how it should be interpreted. Work together to produce the best possible interpretation.

3. Choose one of the selections on pages 354 and 355 for oral interpretation. Prepare for your performance using the techniques described in this chapter. When you have prepared an introduction and practiced your piece, perform it for your classmates.

4. Bring in a favorite poem or story and orally interpret it for the rest of the class.

Careers

CHILDREN'S LIBRARIANS make information and books available to children. They plan story hours and read to children to interest them in using the library. High school courses in English and speech are helpful. A master's degree in library science is the educational minimum. Librarians should express themselves well.

NARRATORS read materials that will be reproduced on tape or records. High school courses in English, drama, and speech are helpful. A liberal arts degree is helpful but not required. Training in speech is necessary. Narrators must have clear, pleasant voices and good articulation.

Selections to interpret orally

"Understand." The first word I ever heard out of any of you was that word "understand." Why didn't I "understand" that I must not play with water—cold, black, beautiful flowing water—because I'd spill it on the palace tiles. Or with earth, because earth dirties a little girl's frock. Why didn't I "understand" that nice children don't eat out of every dish at once; or give everything in their pockets to beggars; or run in the wind so fast that they fall down; or ask for a drink when they're perspiring; or want to go swimming when it's either too early or too late, merely because they happen to feel like swimming. Understand! I don't want to understand. There'll be time enough to understand when I'm old. . . . If I ever am old. But not now.

> Jean Anouilh
> from ANTIGONE

WINDOW WASHER

And again the screech of the scaffold
High up there where all our thoughts converge:
Lightheaded, hung
By a leather strap,

Twenty stories up
In the chill of November air,
Wiping the grime
Off the pane, the windows

Which have no way of opening—
Those windows with their brooding interiors,
That figure who lets the light in,
One imponderable stroke at a time.

> Charles Simic

SEA FEVER

I must go down to the seas again, to the lonely sea and the sky,
And all I ask is a tall ship and a star to steer her by,
And the wheel's kick and the wind's song and the white sail's
    shaking,
And a gray mist on the sea's face and a gray dawn breaking.

I must down to the seas again, for the call of the running tide
Is a wild call and a clear call that may not be denied;
And all I ask is a windy day with the white clouds flying,
And the flung spray and the blown spume, and the seagulls
    crying.

I must down to the seas again to the vagrant gypsy life.
To the gull's way and the whale's way where the wind's like
    a whetted knife:
And all I ask is a merry yarn from a laughing fellow rover,
And quiet sleep and a sweet dream when the long trick's over.

> John Masefield

TO JAMES

Do you remember
How you won
That last race . . . ?
How you flung your body
At the start . . .
How your spikes
Ripped the cinders
In the stretch . . .
How you catapulted
Through the tape . . .
Do you remember . . . ?
Don't you think
I lurched with you
Out of those starting holes . . . ?
Don't you think
My sinews tightened
At those first
Few strides . . .
And when you flew into the stretch
Was not all my thrill
Of a thousand races
In your blood . . . ?
At your final drive
Through the finish line
Did not my shout
Tell of the
Triumphant ecstasy
Of victory . . . ?
Live
As I have taught you
To run, Boy—
It's a short dash
Dig your starting holes
Deep and firm
Lurch out of them
Into the straightaway
With all the power
That is in you
Look straight ahead
To the finish line
Think only of the goal
Run straight
Run high
Run hard
Save nothing
And finish
With an ecstatic burst
That carries you
Hurtling
Through the tape
To victory . . .

> Frank Horne

I AM INDELIBLE

Some say the path to spiritual and human awareness
goes by way of humbleness and personal sacrifice
and these words are true
yet
if I am to be aware of my self, my possibilities
and my path in this world
I must recognize the uniqueness of my life and all life.
I am indelible.
From the fingerprint message of my genes
to the exact place where the stars stood at my birth.
From the number of seasons I have survived
to the memory and understanding that I keep of those times.
From all the things I have ever thought or said
to all the little pieces and parts of life I have nurtured and encouraged.
From the time my spirit came and moved in my mother's womb
to the coming time of my completion of my life's cycle . . .
and after,
I am indelible.
I am a part of this world,
whether I draw breath as a physical entity
or if I give my spirit form energy.
I am indelible.
I am my mother's child.

earth lodge woman / minnie two shoes

Tomorrow, and tomorrow, and tomorrow
Creeps in this petty pace from day to day
To the last syllable of recorded time;
And all our yesterdays have lighted fools
The way to dusty death. Out, out, brief candle!
Life's but a walking shadow, a poor player,
That struts and frets his hour upon the stage
And then is heard no more. It is a tale
Told by an idiot, full of sound and fury,
Signifying nothing.

William Shakespeare
from *MACBETH*

(Act 5, Scene 5)

IN HONOR OF DAVID ANDERSON BROOKS,
MY FATHER

July 30, 1883–November 21, 1959

A dryness is upon the house
My father loved and tended.
Beyond his firm and sculptured door
His light and lease have ended.

He walks the valleys, now—replies
To sun and wind forever.
No more the cramping chamber's chill,
No more the hindering fever.

Now out upon the wide clean air
My father's soul revives,
All innocent of self-interest
And the fear that strikes and strives.

He who was Goodness, Gentleness,
And Dignity is free,
Translates to public Love
Old private charity.

Gwendolyn Brooks

15

DRAMA

When you have completed this chapter, you should be able to

Explain the four elements of drama.

Develop understanding of a character by doing background research and by analyzing the script.

Experiment with nonverbal and verbal aspects of character development.

Describe some of the jobs that must be carried out in organizing a theatrical event.

Explain the steps necessary in producing a theatrical event.

Drama is an art form. Like the art forms of painting, sculpture, music, dance and architecture, drama has been a part of people's lives in all parts of the world throughout history. You are surrounded by these art forms every day.

Drama is special, however, because at one time or another it makes use of all the other art forms. Set and costume designers create with wood, plastic, metal, and fabric, putting materials together in colorful, pleasing designs. Musicians provide sound through which mood and thought are communicated. Choreographers devise movement for interpretation of story and emotion, and architects provide adequate stage space. All that is needed are playwrights, directors, actors, and audiences.

The nature of drama

Drama exists to provide people with entertainment, education, and feelings of spiritual uplift and joy. It studies humanity's successes and failures by exploring the relationships of human beings in the past, present, and future.

Drama has four principal elements, all of which are necessary to produce a theatrical event. First, there must be live actors. The major difference between a television show, a film, and the theatrical event of drama is that only in live theater do the actors play and respond to the reactions of a live audience. Second, there must be a plot or story. A stand-up comedy act is not drama because drama presents a story, with a beginning, a middle, and an end. The characters must act and interrelate. Third, there has to be a theatrical area. Drama can occur on a street-corner, in a cafeteria, or in a place specifically designed as a theater; it is essential that some space serve as a stage. Fourth, the presentation must result in a theatrical event. The term **theatrical event** means that there must be both actor and audience. Drama does not truly exist until it is viewed.

A brief history of drama

Throughout history theatrical events have existed because people have felt the need to stand up and act out stories as well as tell them. As you will see, different themes have been favored in different eras, but the four basic elements of drama have always remained.

In **ancient Greece**, rituals were dedicated to Dionysus, the god of wine and fertility. In Athens, each March, Dionysian festivals were held, with choral singing, dancing, and plays. The final two or three days of the festival were reserved for play contests, at the end of which the winning playwright, or dramatist, was crowned with a wreath of ivy. Thespis won the first contest in 534 B.C. Since he is also known as one of

Imagination can transform almost any space into an effective theatrical area.

the first actors, performers are still known as **thespians.** Your own school may have a thespian troupe or club.

Both comedies and tragedies were performed in ancient Greece. Like all good drama, the plays had their basis in human conflict. In **comedy**, the conflict was usually not serious, and the ending was generally happy. In **tragedy**, the conflict was always more serious and generally resulted in the destruction of the hero or heroine.

Greek tragedies were based on ancient myths that were well known to the audience. The philosopher Aristotle (384-322 B.C.) identified certain rules for tragedy in his book *Poetics:*

1. Plays should inspire the audience to reform their lives through **catharsis**, or by releasing their pent-up emotions.

2. The hero or heroine, who must be of a high social standing, must possess a **tragic flaw**, or weakness of character, that leads to his or her destruction.

3. A change of fortune involving **reversal** (in which the character's actions boomerang) or **discovery** (in which the character's attitudes change from ignorance to knowledge) must be included.

4. Dignified, beautiful poetic writing must be used.

Plays of the Greek period are still performed, and some playwrights today still use the rules of Greek tragedy as a basis for their work.

During the **Middle Ages** (about A.D. 500-A.D. 1450), because many people could not read or write, priests presented dramatic representations of Biblical events and parables to their congregations. During this era drama was also performed on street corners by groups of strolling players. These groups are now thought to have been the first professional acting companies. They performed only for the common people.

From A.D. 1350 to 1650 in Europe, during a period called the **Renaissance** (meaning rebirth), there were new developments in all the arts and literature. Drama changed along with everything else. Wealthy nobles and kings and queens became patrons, or sponsors, of the theater and the arts. In Italy splendid buildings were built for **operas**, a new type of musical drama that provided a social gathering place for the wealthy. At the same time, Italy's **commedia dell'arte** provided comedy for the common people in productions performed without a script. Commedia actors worked with outlines called **scenarios,** from which they made up speeches, songs, dances, and pantomimes as they went along. This type of presentation is called **improvisation.** Improvisations also remained popular and are still performed today.

The **Elizabethan era** in England was the climax of the Renaissance. It occurred while Elizabeth I was queen of England (1558-1603). William Shakespeare (1564-1616) was the greatest playwright of that age. Shakespeare wrote thirty-eight plays. They include histories, comedies, and tragedies. Many of the phrases Shakespeare wrote for his characters have become common sayings. The chart on page 360 contains a list of popular ones you may have heard and the plays in which they appear.

The Renaissance came late to **French theater**, which developed in the seventeenth century primarily as drama for the court. Theatrical buildings were grand show-places, like the Italian opera houses. The principal dramatist of this period was Molière (1622-1673). Molière was the first French writer to raise comedy to a point where it could hold its own with tragedy as entertainment for the upper classes. He ridiculed people and ideas. Themes of hypocrisy, medicine and medical fees, and forced marriages recur many times in his thirty-three plays.

After Molière's death the five theatrical companies existing in Paris merged into one group called the **Comédie Française**, the first national theater in the world. Still in existence, this organization is the most important troupe in France today.

In 1660 a new era of drama began in England. Theaters that had been closed during the Commonwealth government led by the strict Puritans were reopened when Charles II became King. During this period known as the **Restoration**, a new style of writing and acting, called the **comedy of manners**, was used to make fun of social customs of the day. Women were allowed for the first time to appear as players, and elaborate stage settings were devised. The free spirit was dampened,

Some common sayings from Shakespeare's plays

Hamlet	"brevity is the soul of wit" "neither a borrower nor a lender be"
Othello	"pomp and circumstance" "wear my heart on my sleeve"
Julius Caesar	"it was Greek to me" "masters of their fates"
Macbeth	"the milk of human kindness"
Henry IV, Part I	"he has eaten me out of house and home"
As You Like It	"too much of a good thing" "all the world's a stage"
The Merry Wives of Windsor	"as luck would have it"
The Merchant of Venice	"it's a wise father that knows his own child"

however, when the Puritans later regained control of the government. Restrictions then limited the number of theaters to three, making all others illegal. Plays had to pass a censoring committee before they could even be performed. Thus, the term **legitimate theater** originated. Eighteenth century English playwrights did, nevertheless, continue to write in the comedy-of-manners style.

During the early nineteenth century, **romanticism** became the most prominent dramatic art style. People tried to escape the problems of reality through imagination and thoughts of adventure and beauty. A reaction to these attitudes took place about mid-century, when a majority of playwrights turned to **realism**. Realism in this period stressed the virtues of directness and truth. **Slice-of-life theater** developed as part of this new movement. Playwrights wrote about everyday, real-life situations, conflicts, and people. Historical works were forgotten for a time. Henrik Ibsen (1828-1906), a Norwegian called "the father of modern drama," August Strindberg in Sweden, and Anton Chekhov in Russia, were important dramatists of realism.

Further changes in theater were brought about in the twentieth century after World War II by the movement that brought the **Theater of the Absurd.** Dramatists in this movement viewed human existence as purposeless, lonely, and out of harmony with its surroundings. They opened the way for the use of very experimental theater techniques. Performances took on a laboratory approach, and experiments were made with attitudes, characters, and ways of using theatrical space.

Today, playwrights make use of all ideas and techniques that have been developed throughout the centuries. They create a great variety of theatrical events that entertain, educate, and uplift today's audiences.

Developing a character

One of the main ways a playwright's work is brought to life is through the characters that are developed in the play. An actor must portray a character in ways that fully represent the author's intent. This section will discuss some specific steps an actor can use to develop a theatrical role. Reading the section, you will receive many ideas about how you yourself might interpret a role in a play.

Just as voice and body are used to get messages across in other communication situations, you as an actor must use your voice and body to portray a character. Facial expressions, posture, gestures, speech, and vocal tone combine to provide the audience with a total overview. Your first responsibility then is to interpret and visualize the playwright's words through the character you are portraying. You must also believably expand the character's personality, actions, emotions, and objectives so that the viewer has a clear understanding of what the playwright had in mind when he or she wrote the play.

Secondly, you as an actor must tell the story. This means that you must develop the storyline for the audience by speaking clearly and effectively and providing insight through vocal variety. For example, if you are creating the role of a strong, domineering employer, you might want to use a loud, aggressive voice to get the character across. On the other hand, a mousy clerk needs a totally different tone. Each of these roles would also require different postures, gestures, and distinctive clothing to further separate them.

Whether you play a lead role, an animal who speaks no lines, or a chorus part, you must believe in yourself, in the other members of the acting company, and in the project as a whole. You must be secure within yourself before you concentrate on portraying others. Obviously, when you are acting, you must block out all of your own problems before you walk onstage. The audience will not tolerate or believe an actor who bounces in and out of a role. Theater creates an imaginary world and the audience must be able to believe in this illusion of reality. The actors must become the characters.

Doing background research

To adequately perform a role, you should begin by researching the history of the play, the playwright, the period in which the play takes place, and the type of work it represents (musical, tragedy, comedy, or

If you were playing a role in Shakespeare's Julius Caesar, *what kind of character research would you need to do? Where would you start?*

other). Begin with the play itself. Frequently, scripts contain an introduction to the play and some background about the playwright and his or her ideas. Study the script carefully. It may suggest additional readings. If the play is a modern one and has been previously produced, read any critical reviews you can find. These can provide different interpretations of the play. Recordings are available in libraries of many plays, operas, and musical comedies. Many of the recordings of Shakespeare's works (and other classics) are performed by famous actors such as Laurence Olivier, Edith Evans, Richard Burton, John Gielgud, Paul Scofield, and Orson Welles. Watch newspaper announcements for film presentations of famous theater works. Attend local college and civic theater productions. Especially if you are a newcomer to acting, immerse yourself in different types of theater literature and performances as much as possible. Watching well-directed and well-performed film and television productions can provide a valuable background of acting techniques.

You should next research the era in which the playwright wrote. The social conditions and political environment of the period may be reflected in his or her writing. For example, Oscar Wilde revealed the shallowness and emptiness of much of English society during his lifetime. His analysis of hypocrisy and society's willingness to close its eyes to unpleasantness have made his plays among the most beloved of English comedies. A knowledge of Victorian society (1837-1901) will therefore help you understand Wilde's works.

Playwrights sometimes write about a period that is different from their own. Shakespeare's *Julius Caesar* was written in 1599, but takes place in Rome during Caesar's time, 100-44 B.C. In this case thorough research of both Shakespeare's time and Caesar's would help you to understand the meaning of the play.

If you are unfamiliar with the different types of theatrical works, study the style of the play you are reading. Become acquainted with the characteristics of Greek tragedy and compare them with Shakespeare's.

Research comedy of ancient Greece, of the Renaissance, the Restoration, and other eras. See if you can find differences in the quality of each type. No matter what the play, the writer intended it to fall within a certain dramatic category. See if you can recognize whether it is a tragedy or comedy or **tragicomedy**, which combines tragic and comic elements.

Analyzing the script

It may take several careful readings to analyze a play. Try to picture in your mind a production of the play as you read it, and be sure you can answer the following questions:

- *What is the theme of the play?*
- *What is the author trying to say?*
- *What is the plot?*
- *Where does each scene and act take place?*
- *What are the thoughts and problems behind the dialogue?*
- *What are each character's reactions to other characters?*
- *What emotional feelings does the play evoke?*
- *What family or friendship relations are presented?*
- *What are the social and cultural backgrounds of the characters?*

If you have trouble with any of these answers, further research is probably in order.

The **structure** of the play, its form, shape, and development, must also be examined. The presentation of who, what, where, and why is called the **exposition.** The first event to take place, from which the plot develops, is called the **initial incident. Rising action** is the series of the events that develop toward the highest point of interest in the play, the **climax.** This point reveals whether the major character will succeed or fail to solve her or his problem. Events following the climax tie the loose ends together and are called **falling action.**

Analyzing character

After you have completed your analysis of the play as a whole, begin to get acquainted with your specific character. Don't waste your time counting the number of lines or entrances you have. It is the quality of your performance, not the quantity that counts! It may help to begin by underlining your lines or highlighting them with a yellow or pink felt transparent marker. This will help you to distinguish your lines from the others on the page more quickly. Some actors also underline their **cue lines,** the previous speaker's last few words.

Information you will want to know about an individual character include these points:

Physical characteristics and age
Personality traits and emotional stability
Intelligence
Social and personal background
Relationship with other characters
Character, motivation, objectives, and state of mind
Strengths, weaknesses, fears, and hopes
Movement, speech, and type of clothing worn

Remember that these elements may change during the course of the action. If the script does not reveal all the answers, you may want to add interpretations of your own that will fit in with the play. A complete understanding of your character is the basis upon which a creative and memorable performance is built.

After you have become familiar with the attitudes and objectives of the character you will portray, you need to begin to study the lines themselves. Study the **dialogue**, or conversation, for emphasis, phrasing, pronunciation, and meaning. Make sure you know the author's intended purpose for every word, sentence, and paragraph. Determine your objectives or motives in each scene. For each scene you should be able to answer the following:

- *Why am I here?*

- *Where did I come from?*

- *Have I been here before?*

- *Do I know the other people in the room?*

- *Why do I leave?*

As you begin to memorize your part, try to think, feel, see, move, and speak with your character in mind.

Once in a while actors have to depart from the script because someone fails to make an entrance, forgets a speech, or part of the set breaks. Actors should be ready for these kinds of mix-ups and be imaginative enough to deal with them. The better you know your character, the better you will be able to cope with performance problems. Obviously, if you are on stage and another actor is supposed to enter and does not, you have a problem! Instead of repeating the cue line loudly several times, try to speak some appropriate lines which fit into the action of the play. If your character would do so, pick up a book and recite a poem, look out a window and comment on the landscape, or simply sit down and wait. Whatever happens, do not panic. Backstage, the stage manager will be finding the tardy actor. If you happen to be that actor, do not suddenly rush out on stage. Listen backstage for a moment and find an appropriate time to enter.

Believability is a word which often is mentioned in connection with the theater. Keep believability in mind as you work on your role. Because the first impressions you make on the audience as your character should be believable, you must get into character long before you walk onstage. Many actors feel that the best time to do this is while applying makeup. Some actors rehearse troublesome scenes in the dressing room before a performance. Some directors require company warmup exercises. In any case, you should not wait to get into character until just before making your first entrance. Only when you are properly prepared ahead of time and are eager to share your knowledge, are you ready to go on stage.

Learning the movements

Your nonverbal communication with your audience is also an important part of the development of your character. Start by becoming aware of how different people move, make gestures, converse, whisper, dress, relax, argue, age, and express themselves. Look around you. Concentrate particularly on facial expressions. Observe the emotions that different parts of the face can convey. Become aware of the ways you can use your own facial expressions by practicing in front of a mirror. See what kinds of expressions you can make using only your mouth. Try to speak holding your mouth in various positions. Then see what feelings you can show using only your eyes and eyebrows.

You might want to try the following exercise some afternoon when you have a couple of hours to spare. In a park or on a downtown street pick a person out of the crowd who interests you. The first time pick a person just a little older than yourself. Later you can experiment studying people even older. Observe carefully, following your subject as he or she proceeds with normal activities. Do not contact this person in any way. Study his or her manner of walking, arm motions, and posture.

Practicing facial expressions in a mirror can help a performer learn to express a variety of emotions effectively.

Concentrate on details. Watch how your subject carriers a purse, a briefcase, a grocery bag, or a baby. After you have observed this person for as long a time as possible, write down a description of what you saw. Begin a diary of observations of different types of people. Refer back to the diary for techniques of movement when preparing for a role.

As you memorize your lines, you should also work on gestures and movements to accompany your dialogue. These details should be written down in the script and memorized along with the words. Some stage movements are naturally required by the plot (Romeo must fight Tybalt, and Juliet must stab herself). Other movements are incidental to the action (Romeo must draw his sword in order to fight). Actions needed to add realism are usually suggested by the plot, stage directions, or dialogue. If a line reads "Please hang up my hat and coat," then one of the actors will have to take the items and hang them up. If the scene calls for a family to sit around a table and eat dinner, then there will have to be food, and it will have to be eaten.

Spending time practicing unusual or difficult movements will help prevent awkward movements during a performance. If you are uncomfortable, the audience will notice it. Be sure that you time movements with the dialogue. Wrapping a package, writing a note, eating a sandwich, or putting on a coat all take longer than you think. Even if you cut out some time-consuming details, you can still suggest realistic movements. A package can already be wrapped, and you can simply add a bow. If the wrapping paper roll is placed alongside the work area, it still appears as though the total wrapping job has taken place.

Stage movements can be used to enhance a thin, empty scene. They can also be used to emphasize a dramatic moment. Think, for example, of a scene in which a young man takes out his handkerchief to wipe the tears from a child's face. Activities are often used to fill a momentary gap in the advancement of the plot—during difficult costume changes, for example. Movement also includes necessary movements across stage, the placement of actors, **choreography** (dance patterns), stage fights, love scenes, and gestures. All must be worked out to fit in with the situations and characters of the play.

Once you are familiar with the type of character you will play, experiment with appropriate body movements outside of rehearsal. If the play is an English Restoration comedy, study the styles of body movement used at the time. Restoration style includes the use of fans, handkerchiefs, and formal deep bows. Tight breeches, heeled shoes, and formal curled wigs for gentlemen and tight corsets and huge skirts placed over padded hip rolls for ladies determined and restricted movements. Elizabethan hoop skirts do not fit in a small armchair. Find out what kind of clothes are called for in your role and be sure to consider the restrictions of your costume. Make sure that you rehearse in shoes and clothing that are similar to those which will be used in performance. An actor walks and moves differently in jeans and sandals than in high heels and formal clothing.

A dancer uses body motion to communicate with the audience.

Application: Experimenting with movement

Experiment with the following walking exercises, concentrating on body posture and expressiveness. The exercises can be practiced in the classroom or at home. Begin your walk across the stage or room suggesting one characterization and change it as you complete the walk:

1. Start walking as a shy person and end as a confident one.
2. Start walking with confidence and end with defeat.
3. Start walking as a short, fat person and end with a tall, thin body.
4. Start walking as though you were bored with life; end as a happy-go-lucky person.
5. Start walking as though you did not want to get to your destination and finish as though you did.
6. Start walking as though your body were as heavy as lead; finish as though it were lighter than a feather.
7. Start walking as a child and finish as an old person.
8. Start walking as a happy person and end as a sad one.

The correct movements will help to define a character for you and for the audience. All of your movements should be written down in the script. They should become as natural to you as what you say.

Developing your character's voice

As you know, clear, expressive speech is a necessary tool for every part of life. In Chapter 2 you read about the physical aspects of proper speech. You may want to review some of the technical aspects at this point.

Actors in particular must become very good vocal technicians. As an actor you must learn:

to stand up straight with good posture so your voice will project better.

to control your breathing.

to change your speaking rate for variation and dramatic emphasis.

to articulate clearly.

to pronounce words correctly.

to project your voice to the last rows of the auditorium.

to have a flexible voice.

to listen to the other characters and respond to them.

Begin your character's voice development by listening to as many voices as you can. Tape record interesting speech patterns. Listen to actors on the stage, in films, or television, and on recordings. Listen to your family and friends. Keep a diary of voices you hear the way you did with peoples' movements. Write down what you like and dislike about each voice in your diary. Does the voice make you want to listen more carefully? Can you distinguish personality, nationality, and age? Is it a monotone? Does it project vitality and energy? Is it boring? Can you recognize if the speaker is sincere in his or her beliefs? Are emotions revealed? Is there variety in pitch, volume, and speaking rate?

As an actor you should become aware of the pitch changes caused by emotional tensions. Low pitch is usually associated with love, sincerity, or sorrow. High pitch is often caused by the emotional stress involved in anger or rage, terror, or excitement.

Three problems related to vocal pitch may arise when you are acting:

1. Your habitual pitch may be too high or too low, limiting the range of pitch changes possible.

2. Lack of variety in pitch may cause uninteresting speech.

3. Your voice may fall into a pitch pattern and thus tend to be repetitive.

An awareness of these potential problems should be very helpful. With practice, you can eventually overcome them.

Another vocal characteristic, volume, is also very important for an actor. Concentration on volume control will allow you to spread a stage whisper across a large auditorium and still maintain the necessary quiet, breathy quality. Ordinarily a director will stand in various parts of the theater during rehearsals to insure that you can be heard at all times.

Like pitch and volume, your rate of speaking can be useful in suggesting changes in emotional states. Anxious or excited characters often speak rapidly. A slower, even sluggish rate might be better for a tragic or awesome passage.

Taking care of your voice, and developing variations in shading, intensity, and mood will be of great help as you begin to develop your character. Look through your diary of voices and pick several types of voices and qualities that might work with your character. Do not be afraid to experiment and overact at first. Use a tape recorder or ask a friend to listen to your ideas. Try the voice out in rehearsal. When you have established a voice that corresponds to your interpretation of the character, return to the script. Note changes of quality, pitch, volume, and speaking rate that should be used for different lines or passages. Continue to rehearse and practice your role until your movements and your voice work well with each other and with the rest of the play.

Exploring character relationships

In order to understand your character's relationships with other characters in the play, you must study each of the other characters as well. Don't take the way they relate to each other for granted. Even if the relationship of one character to another character is a family relationship, it may be one that includes deep-rooted feelings of hatred or distrust. Characters who are not blood relatives might relate to each other in the plot through an emotional situation, a business deal, religious circumstances, or simply friendship. Whatever the relationship, you must discover the underlying feelings the characters have for one another.

Understanding the personalities of and relationships between characters helps identify their function within the plot. Each character ordinarily serves several functions, but one is usually most important. The **protagonist,** or principal character, is the one whose story is being told. The **antagonist** is the chief opponent of the principal character. Other characters revolve around these two major characters.

Recognizing the relationship between the actor and the audience

People go to the theater for a variety of reasons: to be entertained, to lose themselves in the lives of the characters, to be educated, or to see friends perform. Actors have a responsibility to provide a vital, energetic performance. As a beginning actor, you will become aware rather quickly that acting is very demanding work. Plenty of rest, good nutrition, and a full awareness of the play and your role will help prepare you to perform.

The spark between actor and audience is what makes for good theater. You respond to the audience, and they respond to you. Many stories have been published about actors who have felt they "lost" the audience during the first scene of the performance and never got them back. Because live theater is an immediate art form, you can correct your relationship with the audience. By changing your volume or rate of speech, or by speaking more personally, you can work for audience approval.

No two performances of an actor are ever alike. Feelings, outside distractions, and energy level influence performance. In turn, differences in the makeup of each audience—age, culture, or social background—contribute to each audience's awareness of and sympathies toward the play's theme.

Application: Developing characters through improvisation

To help you learn to develop characters, take part in the following improvisations. Choose a partner and improvise short scenes involving the following:

1. principal - student
2. doctor - patient
3. actor - director
4. contractor - brick layer
5. television host - contestant
6. interior decorator - client
7. tennis pro - student
8. astronaut - alien
9. parent - child
10. reporter - bank robber
11. foreign tourist - airline ticket agent

Larger groups can be used to improvise short scenes in the following settings:

1. Bus stop. Suggested characters: old person, student late for school, two shoppers who are friends, librarian reading a book.
2. Talent agency office. Suggested characters: juggler, fire eater, clown, comic, performer with trained bird, office worker.
3. Hotel lobby. Suggested characters: hotel manager, bell hop, taxi driver, politician, famous writer, wealthy person, chauffeur, reporter.
4. Airport waiting area. Suggested characters: pilot, flight attendant, sports personality, sales representative, student, lawyer, old person, fashion model, dentist.

Actors must learn to control the volume of their voices during rehearsals, so they can always be heard by every member of the audience.

Organizing a theatrical event

The **production organization** is the group that works together to choose, finance, cast, direct, design, construct, publicize, and perform a play. Following are some of the roles and functions that are necessary to produce a theatrical event. The Organizational Chart on page 372 shows the relationship between members of such a production organization. As you read the following descriptions of some of these jobs, think of the ones which you would most enjoy doing.

The **producer** heads the organization. This is the person who is responsible for the success or failure of the production and thus the person who has the power to make or overrule all decisions. In the professional theater the producer finances the production or convinces others to do so. Producers make or approve all decisions concerning budget, publicity, hiring, and firing. They often choose the script.

The **director** stages the theatrical production, selecting and controlling everything that happens onstage. After a script is chosen, the director selects the cast and technical designers. The director is also responsible for arranging all movements that take place on stage, teaching dialects (possibly aided by a dialect or vocal coach), developing pace and emphasis, and, perhaps most important of all, establishing an environment of creativity, energy, and trust among all those involved. A director needs to have a thorough knowledge of literature, theatrical periods and styles, as well as scenery, lighting, and costume design. All final technical designs—scenery, costume, lighting, graphics, sound, and properties—are in the director's hands.

The **stage manager** is in charge of daily organization, especially the organization needed to keep rehearsals running smoothly. The stage

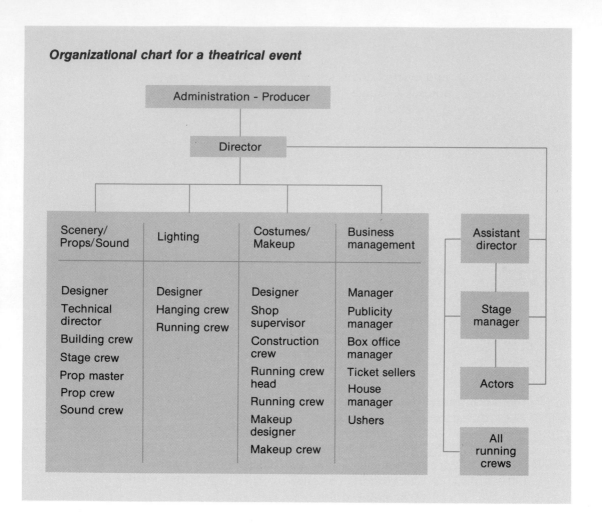

Organizational chart for a theatrical event

Administration - Producer				
Director				
Scenery/Props/Sound	Lighting	Costumes/Makeup	Business management	Assistant director
Designer	Designer	Designer	Manager	Stage manager
Technical director	Hanging crew	Shop supervisor	Publicity manager	Actors
Building crew	Running crew	Construction crew	Box office manager	All running crews
Stage crew		Running crew head	Ticket sellers	
Prop master		Running crew	House manager	
Prop crew		Makeup designer	Ushers	
Sound crew		Makeup crew		

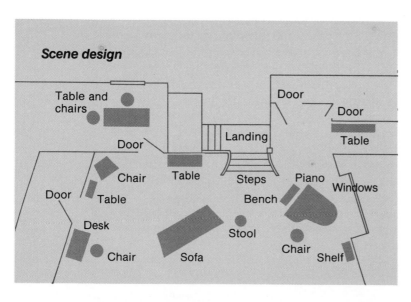

Scene design

Table and chairs — Door — Door — Door — Landing — Table — Door — Table — Steps — Piano — Windows — Chair — Bench — Desk — Stool — Chair — Shelf — Chair — Sofa

Scene designers create drawings that show the position of walls, entrances, and furniture on stage.

manager runs additional rehearsals, posts calls (asks people to attend specific rehearsals), and writes down stage instructions, changes in the script, and actor notes. A stage manager may sometimes act as prompter, reminding actors of forgotten cues or lines. The job includes making sure actors have arrived and are ready to go on stage at the proper time, supervising set-change crews, and taking care of emergencies. When the play goes into technical rehearsals (final rehearsals involving lighting and other technical aspects), the stage manager takes over.

The **scene designer** creates the backgrounds against which a play is performed. Scenery must put the audience in the correct frame of mind for the particular play. The set should, if possible, indicate the type of location, time, and economic and social position of the characters. Effective scenery will suggest a particular emotional atmosphere as well. A comedy might, for example, have scenery that is bright and cheerful. Scenery for a tragedy, on the other hand, might look more somber to reflect the mood of the play.

The time the play takes place and the director's ideas provide the scene designer with a starting place. The designer must then research the script and time period, consult with the director, and devise a **floor plan** which the director must approve. This plan is a drawing of the position of the walls, entrances, and furniture on the stage. It is drawn from above, giving a bird's eye view of the stage. Next sketches of the set from the audience's point of view must be produced and then drawings must be done to scale. **Scale models** of the set are often built to illustrate spatial requirements. They may include miniature furniture, props, and drapes. Directors use models when planning movements and technicians use them when constructing the set, furniture, and props. The designer must create detailed and scaled working drawings for the builders.

The **lighting designer's** chief function is to light both the actors and the set. In small theaters the same person who designs the lighting often hangs it and sometimes even runs the controls during performances.

Many aspects of lighting design are too technical to be discussed here, but the functions of effective lighting should be mentioned. Lighting design should

provide maximum visibility, except where the play requirements suggest otherwise.

assist in suggesting information such as location, time of day, season, weather, or whether or not an offstage room is occupied.

create mood and atmosphere.

contribute to the effectiveness of the entire stage picture.

distribute emphasis from one stage area to another or from one actor to another.

provide theme and style indications.

Sources of light (lamps, fireplaces, windows), direction of light, and changes in intensity can be identified by reading the script. Necessary special events (fireworks, Christmas trees, lightning storms) can be found there, too.

The function of the **costume designer** is to help make the characters more believable visually. Costumes should show at a glance a character's occupation, social background, and age. To do this a costume designer must research the script and period and discuss concepts with the director before developing the designs.

Costume designs are done in color and accompanied by fabric swatches and detailed construction drawings. All design decisions are discussed with and approved by the director before the costumes are made.

A basic understanding of some elements of costuming can be of help to a costume designer. **Proportion** relates to the amount of something balanced against the amount of something else. In costume design this principle is seen in the use of color and design elements. A well-proportioned design utilizes one major color, one minor color, and one accent color.

The amount and location of decorations can also make or break a costume design. Remember that the most important part of an actor is his or her face. So instead of just putting trim or a fabric flower anywhere, the designer must position it so that it will guide the viewer's attention toward the head.

Color can effect mood and atmosphere. Light, warm colors (red, orange, yellow) are better for comedy than dark, cool colors (blue, green, violet). Throughout history, specific colors have come to signify certain occupations or stations in life. Royalty is often dressed in purple and burgundy; young women, or **ingenues,** in baby pink or powder blue; devils in black and red; and angels in white or silver.

Fabric choices also can identify people. Shiny or rich fabrics such as taffeta, satin, velveteen, and velvet can be used for wealthy or flashy characters. Plain or open-weave fabrics can be associated with poor, uneducated, or common characters. The **drape,** or hang, of a fabric should also be considered. Heavy or stiff fabrics do not drape well on the body. Softer fabrics such as chiffon, lightweight cottons, and knits hang loosely. A costume designer must look at the fabric from at least ten feet away to see what it will look like from where the audience sits.

After the costumes are designed, about a week before the first dress rehearsal, a **dress parade** is held. This is the first opportunity for the designer and director to see the costumes all together on stage. It also gives the actors the opportunity to find out if their costumes will withstand stage fights or dance routines. Dress rehearsals allow the actors time to become comfortable in their clothing. An actor who does not work enough in costume will be more likely to look and feel awkward and fidget with stiff collars, lengthy hems, or hooped skirts. The costumer or the crewhead takes care of nightly repairs, washing, and ironing during the run of the show.

Costumes often seem to be last on the list for money. A costume designer must learn to create imaginative and functional costumes with very little money. If you ever work as a costume designer for a school play, you might want to become familiar with the costumes owned by other schools and work out a borrowing arrangement. You might also ask for donations from the PTA and students at your school. Exciting costumes have been made from dyed chenille bedspreads and old curtains, so be creative!

A **publicity manager** provides the public with information concerning the production and its participants. Many weeks prior to the first rehearsal publicity is discussed with and approved by the director and the producer. Poster designs are then created. One good way to find creative graphic designs for a high school production is to hold a poster contest. Contestants should know what the play is about and create their designs so as to include:

name of play (author if necessary)	box office phone
name of organization	permission or royalty information
location	creator's signature
dates	director's name
time	

Characters who wear costumes of rich fabrics identify themselves to the audience as wealthy and important even before they speak.

A well-designed poster catches the eye, can be clearly read, and is interesting and creative. Posters for school performances can be distributed to other schools, area retail stores, churches, and local bulletin boards.

Additional publicity for a school play can take several forms. Advertisements taken out in local newspapers reach a wide range of people. Critical reviews in newspapers are a good way of letting the public know what you are doing. Play announcements might be sent to high school parents or drama teachers at other schools. School window displays can get students excited about the play. Try to present a short scene from the play at an assembly, in the cafeteria, at lunch, for a class, or at a PTA or local club meetings. Publicity stunts are particularly effective. Stage a parade, take costumed players to a local shopping mall, wear buttons or tee-shirts displaying the name of the show, or obtain time on a local television show.

Publicity timing is important. Posters should be distributed no later than two and a half weeks before opening. Newspapers like to receive theater information two to three weeks before publication. Other publicity methods should be employed the week of the opening.

The programs for a show are also part of the publicity manager's responsibility. High school theater departments often sell program advertisements to help offset production costs. Be sure that the program is correct in all its listings of information and names!

Producing a theatrical event

Now that you have some idea of the many people involved in producing a show, you are ready to consider some of the major steps leading up to and including opening night. The play must be cast. Rehearsals must be held. Numerous problems must be solved to insure a successful opening.

Casting

A play's cast is generally chosen through a process of two or three **auditions,** or tryout sessions. Aspiring actors should, if possible, prepare for tryouts by reading the script. Some directors require **prepared readings** from the play or another source of the actor's choice, while other auditions are improvisational in nature. After the initial auditions, most directors post **callbacks,** auditions reserved for actors whom the director wishes to hear again. Although the first consideration of casting is the ability of the actor to interpret the role, most directors are also interested in selecting a hardworking group of actors who work well together.

If you are auditioning for a part in a play, you should wear comfortable clothing, have your hair off your face, wear noiseless shoes, speak in a loud, clear voice, and be alert. If you do not get the part you want you should keep auditioning. There are always many reasons for not being chosen. Experience, physical build, vocal qualities, attitude, and script style all must be considered by the director. You should also not be disappointed by a small role. The old saying, "There are no small parts, only small actors," might well be engraved above every stage.

Rehearsals

During the first rehearsal the director discusses his or her **production concept** with the actors, and the cast reads through the script. This concept, the director's interpretation of the play, helps unify the actions and thoughts of director, actors, and designers. Throughout the rehearsal period the director holds **production meetings** with the staff to give people a chance to air problems and to make sure that every aspect of the production is running smoothly on schedule. Changes in concept, script cuts, additional technical requirements, and budgets are discussed at production meetings.

A schedule of the entire rehearsal period is handed out to everyone involved in the show. The first rehearsal is a good time for designers to discuss their ideas and present color renderings. It is also a good time for making sure that all participants understand the "rules of the game." Some of the most common of these rules have been turned into self-evaluation questions in the checklist on page 381.

When producing a high school play, five to seven weeks of rehearsal, two to three hours per day, five days a week, is ideal. Weekend rehearsal should be reserved for the final weeks. During the week prior to opening, called **tech week,** rehearsals will generally last longer. Depending upon the play, rehearsals are usually divided into scenes, so that not all of the actors have to attend each rehearsal.

During the first few rehearsals, the director gives blocking instructions. **Blocking** is the arrangement of the movements of the actors. It includes how and when actors get onstage and off, as well as how and when they will move about while onstage. Each actor should write blocking instructions down carefully *in pencil,* and then walk through them with the other actors. A normal, full-length play takes about a week to block and set.

The language of stage blocking is not difficult but must be mastered early in the training of all theater people. The diagram on page 378 shows you the terms used for the different areas of a stage. You should also become familiar with the abbreviations used to mark blocking instructions and dialogue interpretation in the script. Some of these symbols are shown in the chart at the bottom of page 378 and in the sample page of marked script on page 379.

The next step for the actors is the memorization of their lines. Both the dialogue and the blocking should be memorized at the same time.

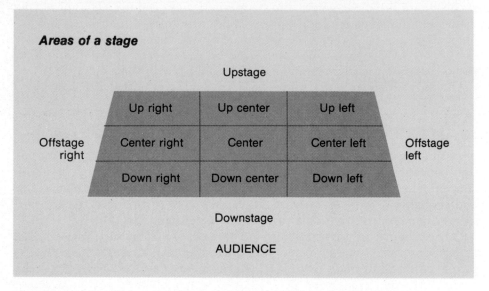

These terms for different areas of a stage are used in directing the movements of actors.

Because it is difficult to handle stage movements with a script in hand, actors should memorize as quickly as possible. If you are acting in a play, remember to memorize your lines exactly as written, including the pauses that have been written in by the playwright. If you have difficulty memorizing, have someone help you by reading the scene with you. Be sure to become familiar with your cue lines. You may also find that writing the lines several times helps establish them in your mind. However you memorize, spend considerable time going over and over the material. After three to five weeks of rehearsals, you should be familiar with all the lines of the play. If you try to capture the spirit of every scene in your mind, you will be better able to handle any problems that arise during performance.

About halfway through the rehearsal period actors are required to be **off book.** This means that they must have all of their dialogue, cues,

Abbreviations for stage directions

X	Cross	¾	Turn ¾ away from facing center front
X)	Cross on curved line	¼L	Turn ¼ away from center front toward stage left
XDR	Cross down right	PSR	Stand in profile towards stage right
↑	Voice up	——	Underline words which are to be emphasized
↓	Voice down	✕	Cut

Scene from Act II of OUR TOWN

by Thornton Wilder

GEORGE. (Hurt) Emily, why are you mad at me?

EMILY. (Defensive) I'm not mad at you.

GEORGE. You've been treating me so funny lately.

EMILY. (Dreading to face the issue) Well, since you ask me, I might as well say it right out, George — (Turns to him, catches sight of TEACHER, who has passed above to their R) Oh, goodbye Miss Corcoran (Faces down again)

GEORGE. (Turning, then back) Goodbye, Miss Corcoran. —Wha-what is it?

EMILY. (Finding it hard to say) I don't like the whole change that's come over you in the last year. (George turns R. a bit, hurt. She glances at him) I'm sorry if that hurts your feelings; but I've just got to — tell the truth and shame the devil.

GEORGE. A change? — Wha-what do you mean?

EMILY. (Facing mostly out, on verge of tears) Well, up to a year ago, I used to like you.

and blocking memorized. They will then be able to run through a rehearsal without too much prompting. Two weeks before opening the company should be ready for **run-throughs**, in which the director will concentrate on polishing details.

Tech week

The first technical rehearsal is held without actors. Often called **paper tech,** this rehearsal involves the director and technical staff. They run through the entire show, writing down specific cues and deciding

Communication is Adrian Hall's business—communication through drama. Hall is director of the Trinity Square Repertory Theater in Providence, Rhode Island, and when he talks about speech delivery, or audience reaction, it is always with a stage in the back of his mind complete with props and costumed actors entering and exiting on cue.

Theater, says Hall, is an art form whose artistry is important not as an end in itself, but as a means of communication. "At its most basic level, theater is a form of one-to-one communication between the performer and each member of the audience," he said. A successful performer is one who can "open the door of the minds and imaginations" of the audience to sway their thoughts. A good public speaker has about the same goal in mind when ascending the podium to speak; so does a debater hoping to persuade a panel of judges to his or her way of thinking, or a salesperson hoping to convince a customer to buy a product.

If theater is different from other forms of communication, it is "the auxiliary things" which make it so, said Hall, a director who has gained national recognition for his unusual staging. Behind a performer delivering lines are numbers of skilled artists and technicians working to enhance the performer's speaking effectiveness. Lights play on a performer's face at strategic moments to lure the audience's attention. Props establish the location and mood of a scene, providing background information for the lines being spoken. Costumes help to flesh out, to make more real, the character which a performer is trying to bring to life. This in turn makes the audience "believe in" the character, and thus more readily believe what the actor is saying.

"Theater is a communal art," continued Hall, whose job as a director is to coordinate the workings of a stage. "Public speaking," he added, "is a singular art." An audience listening to the president of the Board of Education give a speech on, for example, "The Rising Cost of Education," relies heavily for inspiration on the speaker, who almost single-handedly must supply not only information, but shades of meaning, an atmosphere of believability, and an emotional stimulus the audience will respond to. The responsibilities of a public speaker are greater than a performer's because the speaker alone must create a scene which will first attract, then intrigue, and finally communicate the sense of the message.

These differences between theater performance and public speaking explain why the same subject matter treated by each is often so different. A play can afford to show action, as well as to talk about it, to present a story of comings and goings and real happenings, because many performers and technicians are bearing the burden of communication. A public speaker, alone on the stage, first communicates facts, and then can only hope to inspire the audience with carefully chosen phrases to finally act out the drama of the words in their own minds.

Checklist for participating in a theatrical event

☐ 1. Do I get enough sleep before each rehearsal?

☐ 2. Am I on time for all rehearsals?

☐ 3. Do I leave my personal problems outside the theater?

☐ 4. Do I have enough zest and energy for the work to be done?

☐ 5. Do I pay attention at all times?

☐ 6. Do I have a feeling of total commitment to the success of the show?

☐ 7. Have I prepared my characterization and dialogue thoroughly in advance?

☐ 8. Am I willing to trust the director?

☐ 9. Am I making every effort to work together with the other participants to produce an exciting production?

set changes. During other technical rehearsals the lighting designer sets and checks lights, while the actors become familiar with the set, their costumes, and the costume changes. Finally, makeup is added, and production photos taken. During all tech rehearsals, the director and designers take thorough notes and discuss them with the cast and staff after each performance.

Opening night and evaluation

The director's job is not finished on opening night. He or she should continue to watch each performance and take notes. Before each performance, the director talks to the cast and crews, analyzes the

The hard work of the entire production organization is rewarded by the applause of an appreciative audience.

audience's response to the last performance, and encourages a strong, energetic performance. Actors should consider every night "opening night."

When a high school show closes, the actors and staff generally hold an evaluation session. A discussion of strengths and weaknesses, audience reactions, and the benefits gained by the people involved will provide insights useful in future productions.

Summary

Drama is an art form that utilizes all other art forms, such as painting, sculpture, music, dance, and architecture. It has been a part of people's lives in all parts of the world throughout history.

THE NATURE OF DRAMA. Drama as a theatrical event exists only when the following are present: live actors, plot, theatrical space, and an audience. Through these elements drama provides entertainment, education, and spiritual uplift and joy. For the participants, drama offers great challenges, insights into history and human existence, and self-esteem.

A BRIEF HISTORY OF DRAMA. Theater history began with the development of tragedy and comedy in ancient Greece. During the Middle ages, drama was used as an educational tool to present stories of the Bible to the people. During the Renaissance in Italy, comedy was performed for the common people; commedia dell'arte types of improvisations are still done today. The contributions of Elizabethan theater are countless. Shakespeare remains the most read and produced playwright of all times. The French playwright Molière wrote during the seventeenth century. His ability to make fun of society's fashions and rules helped to change society's view of itself. English Restoration dramas also made fun of social customs, while the romantic movement of the early nineteenth century stressed adventure and beauty. Slice-of-life theater developed during the realistic period of the late nineteenth century. Realism presented lifelike details of human suffering, relationships, and conflicts and commented upon contemporary issues and values. The twentieth century has seen many changes in theatrical scripts and styles. The Theater of the Absurd viewed human existence as purposeless and lonely. New playwrights, new actors, new environments, and new concepts continue to stretch the imaginative and creative capabilities of those working in the theater.

DEVELOPING A CHARACTER. Actors spend considerable time learning their craft. They must study the vocal and body presentations of the past and present. Actors conduct background research and analyze the scripts and the specific characters they will play. The characters' voices, movements, and relationships with other characters must be developed carefully. Only then can audiences believe in and relate to the imaginary world created on stage.

ORGANIZING A THEATRICAL EVENT. The chart on page 372 shows some of the major jobs that must be carried out in organizing a theatrical event. Producers bear the basic responsibility for the success or failure of the event. Directors study dramatic literature and theory to help them interpret the playwright's intent. Designers research the decorative styles of bygone eras in order to reproduce them correctly on the stage. Each artist must in turn respect and understand the work of all the others. They must pool their resources toward the realization of a common goal.

PRODUCING A THEATRICAL EVENT. Play production begins with a thorough study of the script. This discloses the playwright's purpose, the style of the play, the physical elements, and the characters. The director establishes a production concept and unifies all theatrical elements. He or she is ultimately responsible for all facets of the production. Every actor and technician must abide by the rules of the game set down by the director. All are expected to work hard, be prepared, act responsibly, keep healthy, pay attention, and believe in the show.

Vocabulary

drama	legitimate theater	scene designer
theatrical event	romanticism	floor plan
ancient Greece	realism	scale model
thespian	slice-of-life theater	lighting designer
comedy	Theater of the Absurd	costume designer
tragedy	tragicomedy	proportion
catharsis	structure	ingenue
tragic flaw	exposition	drape
reversal	initial incident	dress parade
discovery	rising action	publicity manager
Middle Ages	climax	audition
Renaissance	falling action	prepared reading
opera	cue line	callback
commedia dell'arte	dialogue	production concept
scenario	choreography	production meeting
improvisation	protagonist	tech week
Elizabethan era	antagonist	blocking
French theater	production organization	off book
Comédie Française	producer	run-through
Restoration	director	paper tech
comedy of manners	stage manager	

Review questions

1. What are the four elements of drama necessary to produce a theatrical event?

2. What is catharsis?

3. What two characteristics did Aristotle require in a tragic hero?

4. Name two playwrights of the Renaissance period.

5. Who is the playwright known as "the father of modern drama?"

6. What steps must an actor take to develop a character?

7. What are the responsibilities of a director?

8. What are the responsibilities of a stage manager?

9. What elements must a costume designer consider?

10. What are some jobs found on a business staff of a theatrical organization?

Discussion questions

1. Discuss the characteristics of each dramatic form listed. Include a consideration of its purpose and structure.

  Greek tragedy
  commedia dell'arte
  Restoration drama
  slice-of-life drama

2. Discuss the roles of producer and director and the contribution of each to a play's success or failure.

3. Discuss the interaction of performers and audience in a play. How does it differ from the interaction of a persuasive or informative speaker with an audience? How might it be similar?

4. Discuss the functions you think sets, lighting, props, costumes, and makeup have for the actor.

5. Discuss the physical accommodations that must be made by director, designer, and actors when a play is to be presented "in the round" rather than on a conventional stage with the audience seated in front. What advantages might there be in presenting a play "in the round"?

At-home activities

1. Read a Japanese Kabuki play, a Greek tragedy, or one of Shakespeare's history plays. Consider the ways in which characters are developed and be prepared to discuss the similarities and differences among the three with your classmates.

2. Design a poster for your next school production.

3. Write a publicity release for a production of your choice.

4. See a community or professional theater production, and write a critique of the production. Include a discussion of character development, costumes, scenery, and lighting. Mention the reactions of the audience during and after the performance.

In-class activities

1. Prepare a two-minute audition selection from a play of your choice that highlights what you feel are your strongest assets as an actor. Present your selection in class. Ask the class for constructive criticism about your audition.

2. Listen to portions of a recording of a Greek tragedy or one of Shakespeare's plays in class. Discuss with your classmates the reasons you think these plays are still performed for audiences today.

Careers

ACTORS portray roles in dramatic productions. They rehearse under direction to learn lines, cues, and role interpretation through speech, gestures, and body movements. High school courses should include English, speech, drama, music, art, social studies, and psychology. Many actors have college or drama school training. Actors should possess a facility for language, retentive memories, poise, and imagination.

DIRECTORS interpret scripts, direct technicians, and conduct rehearsals to create dramatic presentations. They rehearse casts in individual roles to elicit best performance. Directors suggest voice and movement changes based on script interpretation. They approve scenic and costume designs, sound, special effects, and choreography. High school courses should include English, drama, art, history, speech, and psychology.

STAGE MANAGERS perform duties under the direction of producers or directors. They distribute copies of scripts and arrange for rehearsal quarters. Stage managers lay out acting areas on stage floors. They time scenes and verify that lighting and special effects are ready. High school courses should include English, drama, speech, art, and psychology.

16

RADIO AND TELEVISION

When you have completed this chapter you should be able to

Explain how radio and television are different from other types of communication.

Discuss the development of radio and television and the impact these media have had on people's lives.

Describe types of performers found on radio and television.

Discuss the verbal and nonverbal requirements for radio and television performers.

Describe special communication skills that are necessary for different types of radio and television performers.

Describe some of the jobs that must be done in radio and television production.

Mass communication, whether in the form of newspapers, books, movies, radio, or television, differs from all other types of communication. It is designed to reach large audiences who are not usually physically present and who can "turn off" the senders at will.

The importance of mass communication can be seen in the history of Lincoln's Gettysburg Address. When President Lincoln spoke his Gettysburg Address in 1863, the audience that heard his words was very small compared to the number of people who later read the speech in newspapers, magazines, and books.

Mass communication in these written forms has been available for hundreds of years. Recent technological advancements have not only improved the methods of producing written forms of mass communication but have also made possible the development of electronic forms of mass communication. Through the **electronic media** of radio and television, large audiences can now not only hear and see something happening on the other side of the world, but can also witness it at the moment it occurs. Radio and television have become, by far, the two most effective means of mass communication available.

The nature of radio and television

One reason for radio and television's success is their capacity to continually attract enormously large audiences. It is estimated that many American families own as many as six radios, including those in cars, and that 99 percent of the homes in the United States have at least one television set. Over 80 percent of the population listens to the radio at least once a day, and many people spend several hours each day watching television programs.

Radio and television have also made it possible for countless numbers of people to share a single experience. In 1969, over 600 million people throughout the world heard men speak from the surface of the moon. By 1976, close to a billion people were able to watch the Twenty-first Summer Olympic Games in Montreal.

Another important characteristic of radio and television is their ability to communicate over long distances in very short amounts of time. Think about it. Radio and television have made it possible for someone to hear live music from New York City and to see a football game as it is being played in Dallas, Texas, all without ever leaving the confines of a living room in Boston, Massachusetts. Because radio waves travel at the speed of light or about 186,282 miles (299,792 km.) per second it is even possible for people listening to the sounds of a live concert being broadcast from another state to hear the sounds a split second before the sounds reach the back of the room in which they are being made. Radio and television can bring you into direct and immediate contact with other people and places all over the world.

Through the medium of television, this boy is able to watch events happening in distant places without leaving his home.

Perhaps the most significant aspect of radio and television is the amount of control the audience has over the media. With radio and TV, the listener is not part of a "captive" audience. If you do not like what is being communicated, you can simply flick a switch and change the message. Furthermore, if you do not wish to hear or see any message at all, you are equally free to remove yourself quickly and easily from what is being communicated, or to simply shut the medium off altogether.

The development of electronic media

The electronic media have developed within the last hundred and fifty years. Before the invention of radio and television, long distance communication of sound required the use of wires such as those used in telegraph and telephone service. The gradual development of the "wireless"—as the early radio was called—marked the beginnings of important changes in the way people could communicate. Continual developments in technology have produced rapid changes in the use of electronic media and the effect they have on people's lives.

A brief history of radio

No one person or country can be credited with the invention of the radio. In the late nineteenth and early twentieth centuries many scientists and inventors working in the fields of electricity and magnetism contributed to its development. In 1897 a British patent was obtained for "communication using electro-magnetic waves." In that same year, the first permanent radio installation was established in England.

At first, radio could only transmit coded sounds as the telegraph did. But, by the early twentieth century, radio operators were communicating with each other in words. One of the most important uses of early radio was providing a direct communication link from ship to shore and from ship to ship. In 1912 the survivors of the sunken Titanic were rescued because of their radio distress calls.

In the 1920's, radio began to capture the interest of the American public. By 1923 over five hundred separate radio stations were broadcasting on a regular basis. In the 1930's and 1940's, countless families gathered around household radios to hear voices being transmitted through the air and into their kitchens or living rooms.

Radio became "big business" as well as "show business" when individual companies bought time on radio stations to advertise their products and produced their own live comedy, variety, and musical programs to attract audiences. Soap manufacturers developed continuing drama programs for broadcast during the daytime that have been known ever since as *soap operas*. Situation comedies were also first developed through radio. News and sports programs were broadcast regularly. Joe Louis' championship boxing matches were so popular that movie theater operators would often stop the film in order to broadcast the program for their audiences.

A brief history of television

Almost as soon as people learned how to transmit sound through the air over long distances, experiments to do the same with pictures were begun. As with radio, no one person can take all the credit for the invention of television. Rather, a series of independent discoveries over a relatively short period of about thirty years made television possible. Although experiments with television began as early as 1884, progress was slight until the discoveries made between 1920 and 1950. In 1923 the first television camera suitable for broadcasting was introduced. By 1929 complete television systems were available and by 1939 America was broadcasting television on a regular basis. The American public, however, did not respond very eagerly to this new invention. Few television sets were sold in the late 1930's and early 1940's because of the public's attachment to radio and the expense involved. After World War II ended in 1945, interest in television increased greatly. By 1950, the great television boom was in full swing. It wasn't long before the medium of television had completely overtaken radio in popularity.

One of the reasons television proved to be so popular was the way it was able to incorporate the best of both film and radio. Like a movie, TV was visual. Like a radio broadcast, TV was immediate. With television, people found that they could, for example, not only see an event but could do so almost as quickly as it happened. Taking its cue from radio, television became a commercial business in 1941. By that time most of the successful radio shows and performers had been introduced to television audiences. Milton Berle's "Texaco Star Theater" not only attracted large nationwide audiences, but also helped to establish the comedy routine as a very important part of television entertainment. Variety shows and soap operas continued to be popular after they were adapted for a visual medium. In 1951 Lucille Ball and Desi Arnaz began working on situation comedies for TV. They became extremely popular for their half-hour hit comedy, "I Love Lucy." The longest running television show, "Meet the Press," has been broadcast weekly since 1948.

Early television was almost always broadcast live. Live broadcasting can make programs more interesting, but the possibility of something going wrong always exists. Some people remember the time Betty Furness, while doing a live television commercial, found, to her horror, that the refrigerator she was demonstrating would not open when she pulled on the handle. Later, all TV commercials were put on film even if the rest of the broadcast was live.

The invention and increasing use of **videotape** in the mid-1950's permitted television stations to record not only commercials but also entertainment programs on tape for quick rebroadcast. This led to other recording techniques including instant replay, slow motion, stop action, and split screen. Today, home recording and video-cassette systems have become available for the general public to use.

Even with the many technological advances, some talk shows and sporting events are still broadcast live. Newscasts often use a combination of videotape and live broadcasting. The vast majority of television programs today, however, are completely videotaped.

Another important invention, color, first appeared in television in 1954. Now, over 80 percent of the homes in the United States have at least one color TV set, and almost all programs are produced in color.

The overseas transmission of television through the use of satellites began in 1962. This not only opened up new markets for American broadcasting but also made live television from other countries available to the American public. "What's next?" you may be asking. It is difficult to say exactly what technological changes will be made in television in the future. Most manufacturers promise, at the very least, bigger screens, sharper pictures, and better quality sound.

Radio today

Television's quick rise in popularity had a very negative effect on radio, and at one time even threatened to make it obsolete. Radio's survival has depended upon its ability to adapt. By concentrating on its strengths and making necessary programming changes radio has been able to provide some services that television doesn't.

One advantage radio has is that receivers are often small, lightweight, and inexpensive. Portable radios, run by batteries, have made it

Most radio stations present news broadcasts regularly, while some stations broadcast nothing but news.

possible for people to listen to radio while shopping, sunbathing at the beach, or working outdoors. Most automobiles are equipped with radios. Many people prefer radio because they can listen while they are busy doing other things.

Another factor in radio's favor is the fine quality of sound produced. Stereo broadcasts present sound closer to the quality available at live performances than do most television sets. Some people, in fact, have adopted the habit of listening to concerts on their stereos while they watch them on their television screens.

Radio has also made important changes in its programming in recent years. Gone from most radio stations are the soap operas, situation comedies, and variety shows. In their place radio now offers more news, music, and talk shows. In fact, many radio stations attempt to attract listeners by specializing in specific types of programs. People who are interested, for example, in classical music can easily find radio stations that specialize in presenting classical music. Many radio stations have included more live talk shows in their programming. Studies have indicated that these programs attract large numbers of listeners. Experts speak on foreign affairs, or political or environmental issues. Guest speakers give self-help hints and listeners telephone to discuss their opinions on various subjects.

Television today

Television, too, has adapted itself to changing times by the technological improvements already discussed and also by the types of television service available. Several different kinds of television have emerged in the last thirty years. Each of these has been designed to fulfill specific audience needs.

COMMERCIAL TV. The vast majority of available television programs are transmitted by commercial stations. **Commercial television** is paid for by companies who buy air time to advertise their products. The major criticism of this kind of television is that it has become more of a business than a service. Because producing commercial television programs is expensive, large fees are charged for advertising time. Stations and networks must be able to guarantee large audiences for sponsors paying these large fees. Only those types of programs that will attract the greatest number of people remain on the air. The different commercial stations and networks continually compete against each other for a larger share of the audience.

EDUCATIONAL TV. The Federal Communications Commission has set aside television channels strictly for educational use. By 1979 over 250 stations were being used for exactly that purpose. Many were run by state education departments and universities. Generally, **educational television** broadcasts instructional programs and programs of cultural enrichment such as concerts, operas, and ballets. Educational TV is funded mainly through government grants.

PUBLIC TV. **Public television,** which is funded mainly by company grants and donations from viewers, strives to provide a wide variety of television programs, especially those not provided by commercial stations. Programs include ones that are entertaining, informative, instructional, and culturally enriching. Public television's audiences are usually smaller than those of commercial television, but very dedicated. Programs produced by local public television stations are made available to other public stations throughout the country. Programs are also purchased from other countries and from independent television production companies. Some of public television's most popular shows are its children's programs including "Sesame Street" and "The Electric Company." Because government funds for public television are limited, and it must depend upon company grants and donations from its viewing audience for support, viewers have more direct control over programming than they have over commercial TV.

CABLE TV OR CATV. **Cable TV** began in the 1950's. It was used originally by people who lived in poor television reception areas, such as the mountains or large cities, to improve the quality of reception. These people would pay a monthly fee to a cable TV company to have their television sets connected by a cable to large antennas. Communities decided which cable TV company would be allowed to provide service in their areas. Cable TV also attracted a large number of people who wished to increase the number of television stations they could receive on their sets. Now approximately one in every five households in the United States subscribes to cable television. Some cable systems now produce their own local TV programs as well as televising local sports events.

PAY TV OR TOLL TV. It has taken a long time for **pay TV** to become popular in the United States. Early experiments with this kind of TV failed miserably. The American public has only recently shown a willingness to pay for television viewing. For the most part, pay TV offers its viewers first-run movies and a wide variety of sporting events not available on other stations. Basically, there are two types of pay TV. Closed circuit pay TV uses a cable to transmit its programs within a closed system—from a boxing ring in Las Vegas to a movie theater in New York, for example. In this case, the viewers simply go to the theater and pay the price of admission. Broadcast pay TV uses special receivers that can be connected to regular household TV sets. These receivers are designed to decode signals sent through the air. Some of the receivers record the amount of viewing time so the viewers can be properly billed on a per-program basis later. In other cases the company running the service charges a regular monthly fee and subscribers may watch as often as they like.

Radio's and television's impact on the public

Although both radio and television have changed greatly over the years, both have continued to have a strong impact on the public. Perhaps the best example of the potential impact such media can have is found in an account of a Halloween night radio broadcast in 1938. Orson Welles, then a well known radio broadcaster, gave thousands of people the scare of their lives. In honor of the holiday, Orson Welles broadcast an adaptation of H. G. Wells' *War of the Worlds*—a radio drama made up of fictional news accounts describing a Martian invasion of earth. Many people listening panicked. They besieged police stations with telephone calls; some left their houses in search of safety; still others armed themselves and prepared to do battle with the alien invaders. Although this broadcast had a short-term effect on people, it illustrates the potential radio has to influence the behavior of millions.

Another example of radio's power is illustrated by this quotation from S. I. Hayakawa's *Language in Thought and Action:* "It is only a slight exaggeration to say that Hitler conquered Austria by radio."

President Franklin D. Roosevelt in the 1930's and early 1940's was one of the first American public figures to understand the political potential of electronical mass communication. By using radio to broadcast his "Fireside Chats," Roosevelt was able to sway public opinion in support of his social reforms. Since then, radio and television have greatly affected political campaigns in America. Because candidates are now able to reach millions of people at a time, the public has become more politically aware. This has affected the outcome of many local and national elections. The televised debates between John F. Kennedy and Richard Nixon for the 1960 presidential election are believed by many to have been an important factor in Kennedy's election.

Some people are very concerned about the long-term effects television has upon the public. TV has raised the hopes of many people for a higher standard of living, but it has also been a source of deep frustration for others who perceive a big difference between the way they have to live and the ideal world television sometimes seems to portray.

Many parents worry about the effect of TV violence on their children. It is estimated that most American children 14 years old have seen the violent deaths of over ten thousand people on television. Many people believe seeing so much violence is harmful to children.

Television has also affected people's social lives. For the past twenty years television has dominated all leisure-time activity in America. In fact, next to sleeping and working, Americans spend the most time watching television.

A recent public survey asked people to name what item in their home was most important to them. Revealingly, 32 percent said, "My TV." Television has long been referred to as the "electronic babysitter." But now many parents are not sure that they approve of the amount of time their children are spending in front of "the tube." Studies show that children (or adults for that matter) who are always "tuned in" to television are often "tuned out" to other, equally or more important activities such as reading, participating in sports, or homework. Some parents have begun to take positive action. They have installed devices that prevent children from turning on the television set. Parents who have used these devices have reported positive changes in the behavior and habits of their children. Others try to guide their children toward what they consider the most worthwhile television programs.

The purposes of radio and television

Radio and television have three major purposes: to entertain you, to inform or educate you, and to sell you something.

For entertainment

The number of ways radio and television have entertained their audiences in the past sixty years is practically limitless. Comedy has always been one of the most popular forms of radio and television entertainment. Individual comedians like Bob Hope, George Burns, Carol Burnett, and Bill Cosby have become famous for telling jokes and funny stories. The TV comedy series, pioneered by people such as Lucille Ball, Jack Benny, and Red Skelton, have used everything from "one liners" to slapstick in order to make people laugh. Probably the most important development in mass comic entertainment has been the situation comedy. With its beginnings in radio, this type of comedy has come to dominate modern television programming.

Drama is another important form of radio and television entertainment. Westerns, police stories, science fiction, and soap operas are only a few of the kinds of drama that have been used by both radio and television at one time or another.

A third form of entertainment that has always been available is music. Whether played or sung—rock, jazz, classical, country western, or easy listening—music has been an important part of radio's and television's past and present.

The type of entertainment that has attained the largest single radio and television audiences is the live broadcast of sporting events. Audiences have always enjoyed listening to and viewing events such as the Olympic Games and championship matches between professional sports teams.

For information

One of radio's and television's most useful functions is to inform and educate the public. Many broadcasts over the past sixty years have been very successful in accomplishing this. The most common way to inform the public has been through frequent news broadcasts. Almost every radio station provides its listeners with some local and world news every hour. And all of the major TV networks schedule several one-half hour and hour-long newscasts every day.

What kind of music do you like? Chances are, whenever you turn a radio dial, you will be able to hear your favorite kind of music being played by one disc jockey or another.

"I hate the way these commercials exploit us kids and subtly implant desires in us for nonessential material goods."

The television **news magazine** is another way people have kept informed. Programs such as "60 Minutes" and "20-20" are news programs that encourage reporting in greater depth.

The **documentary** is another important source of information. Both radio and television present documentary programs. They provide the public with in-depth reports on one important subject.

Finally, educational television and radio also play their part in transmitting important information. Because these special fields of broadcasting tend to deal mostly with academic subjects, the messages they send are more concerned with educational facts than with contemporary up-to-the-minute news.

For profit

The third major purpose of radio and television broadcasting is to make a profit. Commercial radio and TV stations sell time to advertisers. In this business, time is money. If the stations are able to take in more money from their advertisers than they spend on programming, they make a profit. In turn, individual advertisers make money by using commercials to sell a product or a service. The problem with this system is that the public is caught in the middle. The money that first goes to the advertisers and later to the commercial radio and TV stations comes from the public. Yet, because the public doesn't directly pay for any broadcast time, it has very little control over the quality of programs and commercials.

Someone once said that the trouble with commercials is that they first give you a headache, and then try to sell you something to get rid of it. While this isn't an entirely accurate statement, it does illustrate a common advertising strategy.

But commercials can also fulfill all three major purposes of radio and television by being entertaining, as well as informing the American public about the existence of new products and enabling people to compare the advantages and disadvantages of competing ones. Finally, how much would you be willing to pay for television if advertisers were no longer willing to pay the money necessary to get most programs produced?

Application: Exploring the influence of radio and television

Discuss with your classmates the benefits you feel you have received from radio and television. Which form of electronic media do you depend on most? For what purposes? How have radio and television affected your interests, attitudes, and behavior? Have you experienced any disadvantages by having radio and television readily available to you at all times?

Performing on radio and television

Radio and television performers are all people who have learned important and valuable verbal and nonverbal communication skills. In addition, different types of performers have developed special skills in order to be successful at this type of work. This section will look at various types of performers and then at the particular communication skills they must develop.

Types of radio and TV performers

Many people immediately connect the word *performer* with the word *actor*. But actors are only one type of performer that appears on radio and television. In fact, on radio today, actors rarely perform.

While actors do perform in television drama, actors and other entertainers often appear not as characters but as personalities on television programs called "specials". One of the most popular types of entertainer is the comedian. Other types of entertainers, including singers, dancers, and musicians, usually communicate by demonstrating a particular talent. These performers spend long hours practicing their skills in preparing for their appearances on television.

Another type of radio and television performer is the talk show host. This job, common on both radio and TV, is very difficult. Above all else, the talk show host must be able to communicate with all types of people.

A large number of television and radio performers can be grouped under the category of announcer. One type of announcer is the radio disc jockey. It is the disc jockey's responsibility to establish a warm, close, friendly, relationship with the listening audience. Disc jockeys must be good speakers and have the talent to ad-lib between records and commercials.

Another type of announcer is the newscaster. Radio and television newscasters are sometimes responsible for writing and editing news stories as well as for reading them accurately. Newscasters have become very specialized in recent years. Several newscasters appear on the same program, each reporting on a particular specialty. What the audience hears and/or sees is different performers handling different news topics, including world news, local news, sports, weather, the arts, and special reports.

Another type of announcer is the news commentator. Most news commentators have had many years of newscasting experience. Now, their job is to analyze the news and give their own, informed opinion about important news stories.

The final group of radio and television performers can be called specialists. Some are specialists in the field of children's programming. "Mr. Rogers" and "Captain Kangeroo" are television specialists in children's programs. Another famous specialist performer is Julia Child, who presents cooking lessons on television. There are almost as many different types of specialists as there are interests held by listeners and viewers.

Some news announcers specialize in presenting weather forecasts. Here a TV weather reporter prepares a map for use on an evening news program.

Special skills needed for different types of performances

All performers on radio and television must develop their skills as communicators. Special skills are also needed for different types of performers.

If you plan to portray roles in dramatic productions on television as an actor, you must develop your abilities to analyze and develop characters, memorize lines, and relate to audiences. Chapter 15 presents a discussion of these aspects of acting. In addition, television performances require other skills. Viewers of television drama are usually watching and listening alone or in small groups. This makes it necessary for actors to adapt their voices and gestures to a small audience rather than to a larger one. Microphones and cameras are controlled by others, and the timing of performances must be carefully monitored. These aspects of television acting must be considered during rehearsals as well as during performances.

If you are interested in becoming a comedian, you should develop all of the skills required of other radio and television performers. Your words must not only be understood by the audience but your voice should have a quality that catches and holds people's attention. Remember, it isn't only the joke that makes someone sound funny. It's also the way the joke is told. TV comedians must also have good nonverbal communication skills. Their facial expressions and the way they move communicate something to their audiences. This can be a positive feeling or a negative one, depending on how good the performer is. Comedians must be able to think quickly on their feet, gauge audience reaction, and make slight adjustments in their performances. If a studio audience is present, these tasks are somewhat easier than if a comedian must judge only the effect the performance is having on people in their homes. Timing lines so that audiences have time to laugh without missing what the comedian says next is most important. This can be a difficult task for comedians when no studio audience is present. Being a successful comedian takes a great deal of practice and experience.

If you plan to perform as a singer, dancer, or musician on radio or television, concentrate on developing your skill in communicating your particular talent. Be sure to take advantage of every opportunity to perform in public.

A talk show host on radio or television should have a wide range of interests, be well informed about current events, and be genuinely concerned about people and their problems. Good interviewing techniques (see Chapter 4) and listening skills (see Chapter 3) are essential. You may wish to review Chapter 4 for one-to-one communication skills used by hosts.

If you want to be an announcer, take as many speech classes as you can while you are still in school. Debate, drama, foreign languages, journalism, and English can also be helpful. Announcers must be able to communicate exceptionally well verbally. Their whole line of work centers around what and how they speak.

In studying to be an announcer, you should also develop your ability to read from a script. Make sure you don't rattle it while you read because it will sound to your listeners as if the furniture is being moved. This is because the microphone is designed to pick up the smallest bit of sound and amplify it. Practice using a microphone correctly. Review that section in Chapter 10 that discusses using a microphone. Have someone watch you to see if you have the habit of moving your head back and forth. Moving your head back and forth will do strange things to the volume and pitch of your voice as it is broadcast over the air. If you are interested in television announcing, practice reading from a script or cue cards while looking at an imaginary camera. Develop any special interests you have that could improve your skills in announcing in that field. Scientific subjects, sports, music, and political affairs are only a few of the specialties from which you might wish to choose.

You should be aware that even radio performers are in the public eye. They have a responsibility to be neat, clean, and well dressed when in public or at least to remember that they are creating an image, however unusual or exotic they may choose to be. Radio and television performers must also be dependable people. They always have to show up for work on time. Performers must also be willing to work odd hours of the day and night.

Checklist for performing on radio or television

1. Have I learned to use a microphone properly?

2. Have I practiced enough to become familiar with my script?

3. Have I considered the fact that most of the audience will be listening and/or watching alone or in small groups? Will I adapt my voice and movements accordingly?

4. Does the timing of my performance allow listeners or viewers time to react to what I say without missing what comes next?

5. Am I dependable?

Producing for radio and television

The production of a radio or television broadcast requires the work of many people you never hear on the air or see on camera. These "behind the scenes" people need a wide variety of creative and technical skills to bring radio and television programs to the audience. Many of these skills are similar to those found in producing theatrical events. It should

If you perform on television, remember to look directly into the camera to give members of the home audience the impression that you are speaking to each of them personally.

be mentioned that most of the jobs in production today are found in television. Radio programs require small production staffs. In fact, radio performers often do most of the production work themselves. Disc jockeys or newscasters will frequently ad-lib to fill extra seconds between recorded music or commercials. On television, every second of time is carefully planned, and each taped segment of a show or commercial must fit into its time slot exactly. This kind of programming requires professional production people.

Before any production work is started on a television program, a programming committee meets to decide on the kind of program needed. This committee develops what is called a **program concept** and then hires a producer to fulfill this concept. The producer is the executive in charge of all aspects of the production. He or she is responsible for both the budget and the actual activities of the production staff.

A producer's first step in transforming the program concept into a performance is to hire a director and a script writer. The script writer develops a detailed outline and script for the broadcast. Scripts can vary in size from an outline of topics an interviewer will cover with a guest, to a fully developed dramatic dialogue including stage directions. The script is usually revised in rehearsals as the director and performers help to develop their interpretations of it. What finally develops is called the working script.

In cooperation with the director, the producer must then audition and hire any performers needed for the programs. Production specialists, such as a costumer, a set designer, a stage manager, and a composer, must also be hired.

Working very closely with the producer, the director is the one who must imagine the scenes and guide the performers into a unified

When the red light flashes on in the television camera set up a few feet away, Bud Collins knows he is on the air. He can see his face on the small television monitor in front of him. He can watch himself talk, even as, at that moment, he opens his mouth to introduce himself to his audience. He can't see the audience but he knows they are there, thousands of people watching him and listening.

Collins is a television sports commentator. His specialty is interpreting tennis matches, as they are being played, for television viewers across the country. He also emcees boxing matches and such events as the Boston Marathon or the Olympic's barrel jump. Last year he covered 55 events. Sometimes he works with a partner, called a "color commentator," who is responsible for filling the audience in on the players' backgrounds, their personalities, and won-lost records, during the lulls in the game. Sometimes he works alone describing the play-by-play action ("Tracy Austin is on the court now speaking to an official") and talking about the players' backgrounds by himself. Either way, Collins is on television, except for brief advertising breaks, for several hours at a stretch. During that time he is required to communicate constantly.

Speaking on television is different from platform speaking (a speaker addressing a room full of people), Collins said. In the first place, the audience being spoken to is invisible so that audience reaction, the means by

which other speakers gauge the impact of their speeches, is not available. In a vacuum, so to speak, the television commentator establishes eye contact with the viewers, discusses and analyzes subject matter, and makes a joke to lighten the atmosphere. "One of the hardest things to learn is that you really have to look at the camera as if you were looking at a friend," Collins said.

For feedback on how his remarks sound to viewers "out there," and for on-the-air instructions, Collins relies almost exclusively on a television director. But the director is invisible to Collins too, occupying a special broadcasting headquarters off stage. Instead, Collins receives information through a small, telephonic receiver plugged into his ear. "It's difficult," he said, "because often I have to listen to instructions in my ear while I am talking. The director may say, 'You have a minute and a half to close,' and I'll know that I have 90 seconds before a commercial, or a break, to wind things up. But things may change and suddenly the director will say, 'There's been a change. You must close in 15 seconds,' or 'in five seconds,' or 'You must now plug a feature for tomorrow's show.' "

Time is a primary consideration for the television speaker, Collins said. Commentators learn quickly to tailor their remarks to fit scheduled time slots, and they learn to adjust the length of the speeches, often on a split second's notice. Occasionally Collins finds himself with unexpected amounts of time on his hands. If rain forces the tennis players off the court, it is up to the commentator to "fill in," to tide the broadcast over until play resumes.

"You just keep talking," said Collins, adding that he doesn't prepare ahead of time for such gaps except for the intensive research he ordinarily does on players before a game. "We've filled in for hours at a time. Sometimes we fill in with interviews with the players, sometimes with topics my partner and I discuss between ourselves." It is a measure of a commentator's professional skill to be able to continue speaking intelligently when the time limit is uncertain.

Television directors must be sure that camera operators understand the special camera shots and angles needed for each program.

presentation. A director runs rehearsals. Rehearsals include coordinating all movement on the stage and working with the performers to help them understand the role each one plays in the program. The director may also guide the composer in writing music suitable to the program's theme.

The technical side of directing involves careful planning of camera shots, angles, and special photographic techniques needed for a particular program. Most performances are run with the assistance of many technical specialists under the supervision of a stage manager. Technicians and engineers who have special training and licenses are needed to mix the sounds and to combine background music with the show. Other technicians do the lighting changes, operate the microphones, and run the cameras. Program assistants and stage hands work with a stage manager to help the director. Making copies of the script, distributing them, notifying performers of rehearsal times, taking notes, getting copyright clearance for music, and typing script revisions may be included in a program assistant's tasks. Stage hands move furniture, sets, and props. They also handle cue cards or operate a teleprompter which is used to help the performers remember their lines.

Application: Creating a commercial

With your classmates, prepare and perform a radio or television commercial advertising your school. Choose performers to record the commercial on tape or videotape, if possible. Try to fulfill the entertainment and informative purposes of electronic media in your commercial. You may want to consider using one of the following familiar techniques: hidden camera, celebrity endorsement, case study, dramatic scenario, or comparison with a competing product (school).

Summary

Mass communication involves large audiences who are usually not physically present and who can "turn off" the sender at will. The electronic media of radio and television are available every day to almost every member of this society.

THE NATURE OF RADIO AND TELEVISION. Radio and television continually attract enormously large audiences. They can reach people over long distances very quickly and bring people into immediate contact with the rest of the world and even with outer space. With radio and television, the audience has a great deal of control. If you do not like the message being communicated you can easily and quickly switch to another message, leave the area, or turn the radio or television off.

THE DEVELOPMENT OF ELECTRONIC MEDIA. Many scientists and inventors working in the fields of electricity and magnetism between 1880 and 1920 contributed to the development of radio. The American public became fascinated with radio in the mid 1920's. Radio advertising helped radio become big business. Comedy, variety, and musical programs were very popular between 1930 and 1950. A series of independent discoveries by a large number of people from all over the world aided the development of television. The public became very interested in television after World War II. In the 1950's television overtook radio in popularity. Most of the successful radio personalities and programs were quickly adapted for television. Variety shows, soap operas, and situation comedies made very successful transitions from radio to television. Early television was almost always live. Now, most television shows are videotaped. Many new developments, including color and video-cassette systems, have also become available for public use.

At first, television threatened radio's very existence. In order to survive, radio has had to adapt. The size and cost of modern radios have helped. In addition to technological advances, many program changes have been made in radio broadcasting. Now, radio stations concentrate on music, news, and talk shows. Television programming has also changed with the times. There are five basic kinds of television. Commercial TV exists by selling broadcast time to companies who use it to advertise their products. Commercial programs are designed to reach the largest possible audiences. Educational TV mainly broadcasts programs that either teach or are culturally enriching. It is funded mainly by government grants. Public TV, which is funded mainly by company grants and public donations, provides a wide variety of programs. Cable TV offers people a greater number of available television stations through the use of community antennas. Subscribers to Cable TV are charged on a monthly basis. Pay TV broadcasts mainly first-run movies and sporting events. Viewers pay for this kind of service on a per-program or monthly subscription basis.

Radio and television are powerful media that affect the behavior of millions of people. Radio and television have greatly affected recent politics by making candidates more prominent. Many parents are worried about the effect on their children of television violence and the amount of time spent watching it.

THE PURPOSES OF RADIO AND TELEVISION. The three main purposes of radio and television are to entertain, to inform or educate, and to sell products and services. The types of programs broadcast for entertainment include comedy, music, and sporting events. Newscasts, news magazine programs, and documentaries all inform audiences. Educational radio and television often provide the public with information in more depth. Commercial radio and television stations make a profit by selling broadcast time to advertisers. In turn, individual advertisers make their profit from increased sales of the products or services they advertise.

PERFORMING ON RADIO AND TELEVISION. Radio and television performers are professionals who have learned important and valuable verbal and nonverbal communication skills. The major types of television and radio performers include actors, entertainers (comedians, singers, dancers, musicians), talk show hosts, announcers (disc jockeys, newscasters, news commentators), and specialists. Each type of performer must develop special skills, as well as those general skills necessary for all effective speakers.

PRODUCING FOR RADIO AND TELEVISION. The production of a radio or television broadcast requires the work of many people who have a wide variety of creative and technical skills. The producer is the executive in charge of all aspects of the production. The director helps to hire the performers and musicians, runs rehearsals, directs the movement and action of the performers, and guides composers in writing suitable music. The scriptwriter develops an outline and later writes a script. There are also many production specialists involved, including technicians, engineers, program assistants, and stage hands, under the supervision of a stage manager.

Vocabulary

mass communication

electronic media

videotape

commercial television

educational television

public television

cable TV

pay TV

news magazine

documentary

program concept

Review questions

1. What is mass communication?

2. What are electronic media?

3. How has the use of satellites affected television programming?

4. What are several advantages that radio has to offer when compared with television?

5. How has radio programming changed since the development of television?

6. Name five types of television service available today.

7. What are the three purposes of radio and television?

8. What types of performers are presented by radio and television?

9. What are some of the special communication skills required for each type of radio and television performer you mentioned in your answer to Question 8?

10. Name at least five jobs that must be performed in television production.

Discussion questions

1. Discuss the differences that exist in the relationships between speaker and audience in mass media situations and other public speaking situations.

2. Explain how some commercials can fulfill all three purposes of radio and television.

3. Compare the weekly offerings of your local public television station with those of the commercial networks. Discuss what types of material appear on each. How do you think the need to produce profits affects the material offered by commercial networks?

4. Discuss the impact of radio and television on political campaigns. What types of radio and television broadcasts might influence your opinions about the candidates?

5. Compare a front-page story in your evening newspaper with radio and television coverage of the same story. Discuss ways in which the treatments differ.

At-home activities

1. Interview someone who remembers radio of the 1930's and 1940's and the beginning of television. Ask for comparisons of the two, the person's preference, and the reasons for that preference.

2. Obtain photographs of film footage of a local sports event. Prepare and present a sports summary or an in-depth sports report for both radio and television broadcast. Note the difference in style and copy for the two media.

3. As a new radio disc jockey, you must plan a 30-minute taped program for a prospective employer. Decide on the format, the time of day, and the intended audience. Select your records and write your script. Be sure to include commercials that would be appropriate for your show. After you tape your program, submit it to your classmates who will evaluate the quality of music, the script, and the commercials, as well as your presentation.

In-class activities

1. Bring a newspaper to class. Work with your classmates to choose the stories you would present if you were producing a fifteen-minute news program for television. Be sure you and your classmates consider the importance of each of the news items as well as the visual possibilities they present.

2. Work with your classmates to prepare a 30-minute documentary program for television about your speech class. Write a script that includes performances of the various types of speech-communication situations you took part in during your speech course. If your school has videotape equipment, tape the program.

Careers

SPORTS ANNOUNCERS broadcast sports news over radio or television. They learn scripts, read, or ad-lib. High school courses in social studies, English, journalism, and speech, as well as a variety of sports experiences are helpful. Two- and four-year colleges offer appropriate degree programs.

DISK JOCKEYS announce radio programs of musical selections. They select recordings to be played. Disc jockeys comment on music and other matters of interest to audiences. High school courses should include English, drama, speech, foreign languages, and electronics. A college degree in broadcasting is helpful.

ICH BIN EIN BERLINER

John F. Kennedy, June 26, 1963

I am proud to come to this city as the guest of your distinguished Mayor, who has symbolized throughout the world the fighting spirit of West Berlin. And I am proud to visit the Federal Republic with your distinguished Chancellor who for so many years has committed Germany to democracy and freedom and progress, and to come here in the company of my fellow American, General Clay, who has been in this city during its great moments of crisis and will come again if ever needed.

Two thousand years ago the proudest boast was *"civis Romanus sum."* Today, in the world of freedom, the proudest boast is *"Ich bin ein Berliner."*

I appreciate my interpreter translating my German!

There are many people in the world who really don't understand, or say they don't, what is the great issue between the free world and the Communist world. Let them come to Berlin. There are some who say that communism is the wave of the future. Let them come to Berlin. And there are some who say in Europe and elsewhere we can work with the Communists. Let them come to Berlin. And there are even a few who say that it is true that communism is an evil system, but it permits us to make economic progress. *Lass' sie nach Berlin kommen.* Let them come to Berlin.

Freedom has many difficulties and democracy is not perfect, but we have never had to put a wall up to keep our people in, to prevent them from leaving us. I want to say, on behalf of my countrymen, who live many miles away on the other side of the Atlantic, who are far distant from you, that they take the greatest pride that they have been able to share with you, even from a distance, the story of the last 18 years. I know of no town, no city, that has been besieged for 18 years that still lives with the vitality and the force, and the hope and the determination of the city of West Berlin. While the wall is the most obvious and vivid demonstration of the failures of the Communist system, for all the world to see, we take no satisfaction in it, for it is, as your Mayor has said, an offense not only against history but an offense against humanity, separating families, dividing husbands and wives and brothers and sisters, and dividing a people who wish to be joined together.

What is true of this city is true of Germany—real, lasting peace in Europe can never be assured as long as one German out of four is denied the elementary right of free men, and that is to make a free choice. In 18 years of peace and good faith, this generation of Germans has earned the right to be free, including the right to unite their families and their nation in lasting peace, with good will to all people. You live in a defended island of freedom, but your life is part of the main. So let me ask you, as I close, to lift your eyes beyond the dangers of today, to the hopes of tomorrow, beyond the freedom merely of this city of Berlin, or your country of Germany, to the advance of freedom everywhere, beyond the wall to the day of peace with justice, beyond yourselves and ourselves to all mankind.

Freedom is indivisible, and when one man is enslaved, all are not free. When all are free, then we can look forward to that day when this city will be joined as one and this country and this great Continent of Europe in a peaceful and hopeful globe. When that day finally comes, as it will, the people of West Berlin can take sober satisfaction in the fact that they were in the front lines for almost two decades.

All free men, wherever they may live, are citizens of Berlin, and, therefore, as a free man, I take pride in the words *"Ich bin ein Berliner."*

IT'S HARD TO BE HUMAN

Beth Simmons' speech won third place in a national high school speech competition.

545-19-3939
G007193709
N4282238
Number 8 Speaker
Red Dress
Brown Hair
5'6", 115, 35-24-36

After sixteen years of striving to be unique, it's ironic that my humanness boils down to convenient symbols and immediate impressions. Like an incompleted jigsaw puzzle, I'm seen only in fragmented pieces. I'm not just organized numbers, or speaker number eight, and even though the college board may find this upsetting, I'm even more than a convenient SAT ranking.

In a world of three billion, a country of 200 million, even in a speech tournament, the rate of people flowing into and out of our lives is so great that creating a personal style is nearly impossible. In a mass society, differences are sacrificed for similarities, individuality for conformity, humanness for Social Security.

Humanness, or in other words, our unique qualities, good and bad, seems to be lost in a society which caters to the mass-produced man. It is easier to live in houses in which the only differing characteristic is the address, so that nobody criticizes the design. In the same way, it is easier to enter an oratory contest nameless, and schoolless so that if I expose my humanness nothing is lost, nothing is gained.

From early America's melting pot to today's claim that "Everybody Needs Milk," our differences have been homogenized to produce an era of paper people. Now you take a society, fold it into convenient sizes, cut carefully, unfold, and PRESTO! Nameless, faceless, expressionless silhouettes meaninglessly holding hands.

Whoever you are, today's horoscope will apply; the message in any fortune cookie is universally didactic. Dial a prayer, dial an inspiration, or, if you need a friend, phone dial-a-smile to hear continuous laughing for three minutes, only interrupted by a voice reminding you that it is just a recording. It's easy to become satisfied with having things done for us by our computers, tape recorders, and HP 45's. And, just as easy, is to slip into the efficiency of automatic communication.

Automatic communication simply means to "plug in" to a memorized set of responses at appropriate times. It has been estimated that six out of every ten people at some point in their conversation discuss the weather. T.S. Eliot in his play *The Cocktail Party* remarked on our memorized, pedantic phrases: "It no longer seems worthwhile to speak to anyone anymore; they make noises and think they are talking to each other. They make faces and think they understand each other." The process of communication becomes a convenient shortcut.

No time to visit someone, so I'll just make a quick phone call. I don't have time to apologize, so I'll just send flowers. I'll let Snoopy say it for me in a Hallmark card. How simple! We've become the Hallmark Generation. We choose to communicate in an artificial manner. Technology allows us to say almost any personal message in an impersonal way. Snoopy represents what is "cute" and "acceptable;" an honestly written letter reflects our humanness more accurately, but there's a risk involved in baring ourselves in letter writing; it may reveal human weakness. But who can find fault with Snoopy?

The Hallmark Generation's actions are based on more than conformity; they rely on inner security: security in similarity. We are secure to know that our personality is so similar to everyone else's that no one could find any element of personal style: a bit of childishness, perhaps an unusual sense of humor, maybe even a tear.

Perhaps the epitome of our woes is a show called *The Waltons*. Every Thursday night John and Olivia Walton cordially invite fifty million viewers to spend an hour with America's most sentimentalized family. Even though John Boy may lose five of his most prized manuscripts in a fire, and Olivia may come close to dying of polio, and Grandma traumatically figures out she's getting old all in one hour, you can bet at the end of the show, the soft lights in the windows will be glowing as Pa calls goodnight.

The Waltons have become an appropriate symbol for today's packaged humanness; they have created the one dimensional person. At the end of the hour, the wrapping of the package will always be the same, all the episode's conflicts neatly resolved. After all, if you miss a few programs, the Waltons have to be the same for summer re-runs.

It becomes very easy to want to meet people in a one dimensional manner. Subconsciously, we put the same restrictions on our acquaintances as we place on the Waltons: Don't make too many mistakes; don't be too different; don't change too much. Perfection is the only alternative. In short, it's hard to be human. See, we'd rather deemphasize our rough edges and poor judgments. Unfortunately, that's what humanness is all about.

In his play *Our Town*, Thornton Wilder describes Emily Gibbs, who returns to life only to notice that we don't take the time to look at each other and accept each other, flaws and all. As she turns to her mother, Mrs. Gibbs turns away, having matters of consequence on her mind, and her father?—too busy reading the newspaper. Trying one last time, she stands in the center of the stage and asks: "Won't somebody please look at me? I've almost forgotten how hard it is to be human."

The tragedy of *Our Town* is its realism and its long run. It's replayed night after night, in countless front rooms as parents exchange children's pesky enthusiasm ironically for *All in the Family* serials. It's replayed at the dinner table where functional conversation replaces personal interaction. It was replayed just a short time ago in a note found in a home in the Haight-Ashbury District of San Francisco: "I'm going to the Golden Gate Bridge and I'm going to jump off because I'm alone; nobody sees me. But if just one person smiles at me on the way, no one's ever going to have to read this suicide note." What a small inconvenience—fifty facial muscles, to draw the line between life and death.

Our response—to build higher fences on bridges to prevent the jump, rather than building bridges between people. You know, to build human bridges takes time. There's no convenient shortcut to understanding.

The answer is not simply to burn all Hallmark cards, and it doesn't lie in unplugging the television set every time the Waltons come on. Rather the answer, as philosopher Rollo May implies, is the realization of our capacity to experience and have faith in ourselves as worthy beings, without like or equal. Everyone has the need to feel and be told their humanness is special. Man has the sensitivities and consciousness to develop a quality which sets him apart from all others of the species. W.C. Fields called it, "Style, the surest outward sign of substance of a special and original inward view." It is in our differences that our humanness shows through, and it's through our humanness that we learn what life is all about.

Can't you visualize a world where barriers will be broken and men will be able to cry? Can't you envision a world where prepackaged personalities will be replaced by acceptance of each other's flaws? Can't you see a world where you will really be able to look and smile at me? All it takes is to be human.

Number eight would like to thank you for a unique part of your day.

DEUS EX MACHINA

Bart Wojciehowski's speech won fifth place in a national high school speech competition.

Deus ex machina, the ancient Greeks called it. God, from a machine. Those of you familiar with Greek drama may recall that this was a theatrical contrivance which descended from the stage heavens and extricated the hero, or other central characters, when the playwright was unable to solve the existing dramatic conflicts. With the heroes whisked away to the gods, the audiences promptly forgot that any dilemma existed.

It is hard to believe that the concept of *deus ex machina* still exists some two thousand years later—not in the theater where one might find it a welcome reprieve, but in the twentieth century bastion of technology ... the hospital. Unlike its early prototype, today's *deus ex machina* does not carry its hero off to Olympus. It pumps blood, breathes, feeds, and removes his poisonous fluids. It performs amazing feats—replaces organs, the doctor, the family—for its dying prey. It does all of this and more. What its genius does not allow, however, is the simple act of dying.

This past year held two unique events for me. The first involved my oldest friend, an elderly man forewarned of his impending death of malignant cancer. At that time, with the Socratian wisdom of someone who had fought the good fight for eight decades, my friend requested of his wife and family, that he be allowed to die as comfortably as possible in the security of his own home. Family members rallied to provide the attending support and health care for his last few remaining months. Little did they realize that Americans don't have the right to die naturally without the machine.

Preposterous, you say? Not at all. How many accounts have you read, this past year, of comatose patients who were not allowed to be disengaged from their life maintaining machinery. For every Karen Quinlan who made news headlines, thousands of other families suffered silently without the recourse or the emotional stamina to assert their rights via the legal system. Many were already too economically devastated and emotionally exhausted. It is almost unbelievable that a nation with the highest standard of living, should have a standard of dying that even the most primitive cultures would find inhumane. How can this be?

The truth of the matter is that Americans are most reluctant to consider death. In a recent editorial in *Newsweek*, George Will suggested that because of lengthened life spans, smaller families, and geographic dispersion, death is too "remote to be readily conceivable." Unlike the rural past, death is not woven into the fabric of contemporary American life, but remains a specter who touches everyone's life—but our own. Death has been a fearful thing always, but it was accepted. Today's dying person is often abandoned by his friends, and not infrequently, his doctors. In the days before advanced medical technology, doctors gave of themselves to the dying patient, but today

more often than not, the patient is abandoned at the most critical stage of his illness, and assigned to *deus ex machina*. He is carried off to the isolated hospital room, away from the compassion of those who love him. He then faces the sterile, stainless steel environment, and is left with no gentle hands or caresses as the machines take over. We are left, like the Greek audiences, to forget that a problem exists. It is only when the machine finally envelops us that we face the horror of its reality.

And yet, it would be foolish to attribute evil to the machine itself. The machines of our time have evolved for the purpose of good. It is only our abdication of responsibility and love that has made them a negative force. We must shake our abhorrence of death. We must accept it as truthfully as birth, as in the submission of vivid autumn leaves drifting from the tree's limbs. As in nature, we must admit death. Hold it gently.

My dear friend became critically ill on Thanksgiving. The doctor of five years made a single house call and insisted that the patient be placed in a hospital and attached to life maintaining machinery. Death at home, he advised, could not include his prescription for Demerol, the drug now necessary for the old man to bear the agony of the cancer's final destruction. There was no freedom of choice despite the availability of round-the-clock professional nurses. But a promise made was a promise fulfilled. The family obtained the drug. The old man died peacefully, his hands held by his wife and children as he left life as gently as a falling leaf. The doctor refused to come to the home at the time of death. And the death certificate bore the final reprimand for those who defied *deus ex machina*—"Inanition: death by starvation" was the final indictment for the gently passing of my grandad.

The second unique event, prior to my first encounter with death, involved a visit to my home by Dr. Cecily Saunders—nurse, social worker, Cambridge Doctor of Medicine, and founder of St. Christopher's Hospice in London, a center for the terminally ill and their families. Dr. Saunders is a pioneer in the field of care for the dying. Her hospice advocates the alleviation of pain, both for the patient and the family. There is no *deus ex machina* at St. Christopher's. The hospice offers efficient loving care, appropriate drugs, and treatment for all aspects of pain—physical, social, emotional, and spiritual. Dr. Saunders told of a visit by the chairman of the Euthanasia Society of Great Britain. After completing his rounds, he said, "If all patients could have the opportunity to die like this, we could disband the society." Dr. Saunders' hospice is not a dream for the terminally ill, it is a reality. It is based on a single woman's determination, skill, love, hope, and firm belief in life after death. She has given England, as well as the rest of the world, a beautiful alternative to *deus ex machina*.

Death awaits each of us. Pondered by the finest philosophical minds since the onset of time—envisaged in a million ways by muses and poets; yet none is more appropriate for my granddad's final departure than William Cullen Bryant's all encompassing verse.

"Thou go not like a quarry slave at night, scourged to his dungeon; but sustained and soothed by an unfaltering trust, approach thy grave like one who wraps the drapery of his couch around him, and lies down to pleasant dreams."

Glossary

abstract words: words that cannot be perceived directly through the senses; opposite of concrete words.

adjourn: a privileged motion that legally concludes a meeting.

affirmative: the side in a debate upholding the proposition being debated; the side in a debate that has the task of attacking the *status quo* and arguing for a specific change.

agenda: list of the items to be discussed at a meeting.

agreed goal: a purpose or outcome on which both the affirmative and negative sides of a debate agree.

amend: to change a pending motion.

analogy: an extended comparison, proving the truth of something by showing its similarity to something else.

ancient Greece: the area in which the dramatic forms of tragedy and comedy were first developed.

antagonist: in a play, the chief opponent of the principal character.

appeal: an incidental motion that allows a member who disagrees with a ruling by the chair to put that ruling to a vote.

appointed leader: a person designated before the discussion begins to perform all the leadership duties.

articulation: the way in which the tongue, teeth, lower jaw, and soft palate are used to produce speech sounds; the process of forming sounds into words.

articulators: the tongue, teeth, lower jaw, and soft palate, which are used to form sounds into recognizable words.

attention device: a technique used to gain or maintain the attention of the audience.

audience analysis: learning everything you can about the background, attitudes, and interests of the people who will listen to you.

audition: a tryout session, as for a play.

bandwagon technique: the logical fallacy that asks people to become part of the supposedly overwhelming group in favor of some person, product, or idea.

bard: a professional storyteller who traveled from village to village with both news and entertaining stories in ancient times. (See *minstrel*.)

begging the question: the logical fallacy that states that an idea is true without providing proof.

blocking: arranging the movements on stage of actors in a play.

brainstorming: rapidly suggesting ideas without taking time to evaluate each one.

brief: a complete outline of a debate case, written in complete sentences.

burden of proof: the obligation of the affirmative side in a debate to prove what is asserted by the proposition.

cable TV: a television system that allows people to improve reception by connecting their sets to a large antenna for a fee.

callback: an additional audition for an actor whom the director wishes to see and hear again.

card stacking: presenting only evidence that supports the point being made.

cartoon: a visual aid consisting of a funny or satirical drawing used to make a point.

case: in debate, a team's argument on any given proposition.

catharsis: a purifying of the emotions or relieving of emotional tensions, especially through drama.

cause to effect: reasoning from what began something to its result.

central idea: a main point.

chair: a name given to the person presiding over a meeting.

chart: a visual aid that is a drawing showing the relationships among the parts of a whole (often relies on words rather than simply on lines).

choreography: dance patterns; the arrangement of the movements of a dance.

chronological pattern: an organizational arrangement of a speech that proceeds from past to present to future.

cliché: an overused expression that has become almost meaningless.

climax: in a play, the turning point which reveals whether the major character will succeed or fail in solving the problem; the highest point of interest.

climax ordering: stating items in a series and moving from less significant to more significant, ending with the most important item.

closed-group discussion: communication only among members to solve a common problem, arrive at a decision, or answer a question of mutal interest.

close-minded: refusing to consider ideas that are different from your own.

code: a symbol system.

cohesiveness: a uniting or sticking together; group spirit; morale.

Comédie Française: first national theater in the world. This organization still exists in France today.

comedy: a drama or narrative with conflict that is not usually serious and a happy ending.

comedy of manners: style of writing and acting used to make fun of social customs of the day (developed during the reign of Charles II of England).

commedia dell'arte: a type of Italian comedy developed in the 16th century and employing a stereotyped plot, improvised dialogue, and stock characters.

commercial television: television broadcasting financed by companies who buy air time to advertise their products.

committee: a small subgroup of a larger organization, which has been given a specific task or set of tasks to perform.

common ground technique: a means of gaining listener attention by identifying mutual interests or things the speaker shares in common with the audience.

communication: the process of sending and receiving messages to achieve understanding.

comparative advantages case: in a debate, an affirmative case that uses the Agreed Goals → Plan → Comparative Advantages form of argument.

comparison: the presentation of similarities and differences.

competence: the condition of being well qualified; capableness.

compromise: a settlement in which each member or group of members agrees to give up part of the solution or decision they want, retaining some other part of the solution they favor.

concrete words: words that enable the listener to perceive the idea by means of the senses.

confidence: a belief in one's own abilities.

connotation: a meaning attached to a word that goes beyond the dictionary meaning.

consensus: the agreement of all the members about a solution or decision.

constructive speech: in a debate, a speech used to present and develop the major points of a team's case.

contrast: a language device used to point up differences.

controlled stage fright: the realization that a feeling of tension is natural and can actually sharpen thinking, so that nervousness can be regulated.

conversation: interpersonal communication about matters of common interest to the people involved.

costume designer: a person who designs clothes worn by actors in a play.

critical listener: one who analyzes and interprets messages carefully.

cross-examine: to question the opposing side about their arguments.

cross-examination format: in a debate, the format that provides for questioning (cross-examination) by a member of the opposing team following each constructive speech.

cue line: the previous speaker's last few words.

cutaway: a visual aid consisting of a model with a section of the outer covering removed to show the interior parts.

debate: a reasoned argument between two parties.

decision-making group: a type of discussion in which members meet with the specific purpose of reaching a judgment or conclusion.

decode: to translate incoming information or messages into understandable concepts.

deduction: reasoning from general principles to specific cases.

denotation: the basic meaning of a word.

diagram: a visual aid used to show the relationship of parts to a whole (relies mainly on lines rather than on words).

dialogue: a conversation; passages of talk in a play.

diaphragm: a thick muscle at the base of the rib cage.

director: a person who stages the theatrical production, selecting and controlling everything that happens onstage.

discovery: in drama, a change in the character's attitudes from ignorance to knowledge.

disinterested audience: an audience that knows about the topic but is unconcerned.

distraction: anything that draws the mind or attention away in another direction.

division of assembly: an incidental motion requesting that a close voice vote be retaken by a show of hands or by having members rise.

division of question: an incidental motion that requests the division of a motion having two or more parts into separate motions for purposes of separate debate and voting.

documentary: an in-depth report on one important subject.

drama: public communication which uses both language and actions to tell a story of human conflict.

drape: in costuming, the hang of a fabric.

dress parade: the first stage viewing of all the costumes by the designer and the director, usually a week before the first dress reheasal.

economy of language: the use of as few words as necessary to state ideas clearly.

educational television: television that is broadcast on stations set aside for instructional and culturally enriching programs.

effect to cause: reasoning from a result back to what started it.

electronic media: radio, television, records, and movies.

Elizabethan era: the time of the reign of Elizabeth I of England (1558-1603).

emergent leadership: a form of leadership in which one or another of the group members will handle each function of leadership as the need arises.

encode: to put a message into symbols.

enlightenment group: a type of discussion in which members meet to share information.

ethos: the speaker's character in the minds of the audience (including competence, sincerity, and goodwill).

euphemism: a gentle expression for a harsh or unpleasant reality.

evidence: raw material with which you prove or support statements.

example: a specific instance or occurrence.

exposition: in a play, the presentation of who, what, where, and why.

extemporaneous method: a type of speech delivery in which speakers prepare ideas for their speeches but do not memorize exact words.

fact: an event or a truth that is known to exist or has been observed.

falling action: the events following the climax of a play, which tie the loose ends together.

false consensus: several group members keeping serious disagreement to themselves, allowing the outcome to be the reverse of what they desire, and leading others to believe all are in agreement.

feedback: the reactions of the receiver to the message of the sender, consisting of words or nonverbal symbols.

fiction: material created in the imagination.

fictional speaker: the voice you hear telling a story or poem when you read silently.

figure of speech: phrases and sentences that make a point by stating something that is not to be taken literally.

filibustering: the extension of debate for the sole purpose of delaying or preventing a vote.

floor plan: a drawing showing the position of the walls, entrances, and furniture on the stage.

flow sheet: a summary outline of how the arguments on each issue have progressed during a debate.

formal debate: a type of reasoned argument between parties, which is used in school contests.

French theater: drama in France, which in the seventeenth century presented the comedies of Molière for the royal court.

germane: logically or directly connected with the subject.

glittering generality: a fine sounding term, so vague that the exact meaning is unclear.

good will: the showing of interest in or "good feeling" toward a person or audience.

graph: a visual aid that gives large amounts of information (usually quantitative or numerical) at a single glance.

group discussion: interpersonal communication involving three or more people with a common purpose; the meeting of three or more people to solve a common problem, arrive at a decision, or answer a question of mutual interest.

handout: a visual aid given to each member of an audience.

hasty generalization: a type of faulty reasoning occurring when the speaker does not have adequate evidence to support the broad conclusion drawn.

hearing: the reception of sound.

humor: an attention device utilizing something funny.

hyperbole: a figure of speech that consists of intentional exaggeration to emphasize a point.

imaginary audience: the audience to whom the fictional speaker relates a story or poem.

impromptu method: a type of speech delivery in which the speaker talks "off the cuff," with no chance for preparation.

improvisation: a composing and performing on the spur of the moment, without any preparation.

incidental motion: a type of formal proposal that relates to procedures having to do with the conduct of parliamentary business.

induction: reasoning from specific facts or cases to general principles.

informative speech: a public communication in which a speaker imparts new knowledge or more in-depth information on a specific topic to an audience.

ingénue: an innocent, inexperienced, unworldly young woman.

initial incident: in a play, the first event to take place, from which the plot develops.

insight: a clear understanding of the inner nature of some specific thing.

interpersonal communication: the transmission of messages between two or more people.

interview: a formal kind of interpersonal communication often involving two persons with a particular or definite goal in mind.

interviewee: the person being interviewed or questioned.

intrapersonal communication: an inward talking to oneself.

irony: a figure of speech in which the literal meaning expressed is the opposite of the meaning intended.

issue: a major point of disagreement in a debate.

kinesics: the study of the use of body motion to communicate.

lack of confidence: a feeling often experienced when the symptoms of stage fright are uncontrolled.

larynx: the voice box.

lavalier microphone: an amplification device (microphone) which hangs around the neck.

lectern: a speaker's stand.

legitimate theater: in the Restoration period, the name given to theaters whose plays had passed a censoring committee before being performed.

lighting designer: a person who designs the lighting for both actors and set, sometimes running the controls during performances.

limit or extend debate: a subsidiary motion that either restricts the time to be devoted to discussion on a pending motion or removes any time restrictions already in force.

listening: understanding and interpreting sound in a meaningful way.

literature: prose or poetry considered to have permanent value and excellence of form.

logical fallacies: methods of false reasoning.

lyric poetry: "song-like" poetry expressing emotions.

main heads: the major division of an outline.

main motion: a formal proposal which deals directly with an item of business.

majority vote: a decision by over half the members.

manuscript method: a type of speech delivery in which the speech is read to the audience.

map: a visual aid showing information of a geographical nature.

mass communication: one or several senders using printed or electronic media to communicate with a large number of people who are not necessarily present; one or more senders communicating with large groups of people who may be separated from each other and from the sender by great distances.

mass media: ways of sending messages to huge groups of people.

memorization method: a type of speech delivery in which the manuscript is learned and delivered word-for-word without the use of manuscript.

memory: the brain's storage bin; the power, act, or process of recalling to mind facts previously learned or past experiences.

metaphor: a figure of speech containing a direct comparison omitting the words *like* or *as*.

Middle Ages: the period of European history between ancient and modern times; the period from about A.D. 500 to about A.D. 1450.

minority: less than half of the members who voted.

minstrel: a professional storyteller of ancient times who traveled from village to village bringing news and stories or entertainment. (See *bard*.)

model: a visual aid consisting of a scaled-down version of an object.

monotone: speaking successive syllables or words without change of pitch.

Monroe's Motivated Sequence: a speech pattern consisting of five steps—attention, need, satisfaction, visualization, and action.

motion: a formal proposal made by a member for consideration and action by a group.

name calling: faulty reasoning that gives a person or idea a bad label without providing evidence to support it.

narrative: supporting material in the form of a story, either real or imaginary.

narrative poetry: a poem that tells a story.

nasal cavities: the passages in the nose which act as resonators.

need-plan wedge case: an argument in which the negative does not attack the affirmative's need or plan directly but attacks the logical link between the two.

needs case: a form of affirmative argument based on Need → Plan → Advantages approach.

negative: the side in a debate that supports the status quo or denies or attacks the affirmative position.

neutral audience: an audience that is neither for nor against a topic and needs more information in order to form an opinion.

news magazine: a publication or television program that presents informative coverage of several important subjects in some depth.

nominal technique: a form of decision making sometimes substituted for group discussion that involves listing, discussing, voting, and ranking of possible solutions.

nonfiction: material based entirely on truth as the author understands it.

non sequitur: "It does not follow." (Latin) A remark that does not follow from what has just been said.

nonverbal: communicating without the use of words.

nonverbal symbols: any means used to encode ideas without words including gestures, facial expressions, and movements.

notice: an announcement sent when an organization plans to hold a meeting.

object: a visual aid that is the actual item being referred to.

object of consideration: an incidental motion that allows an assembly to avoid debate and a decision on a pending motion.

off book: without a script, having memorized dialogue, cues, and blocking.

one-to-one communication: interpersonal communication between just two persons; speaking with only one other person.

open-minded: listening to all aspects of a question before making a decision.

opera: a musical drama.

opposed audience: an audience which disagrees with the speaker's stand on a topic.

oral interpretation: the process by which a speaker performs literature aloud for an audience.

order of business: the sequence in which various items on the agenda will be taken up during a meeting.

order of precedence: a ranking system that lists the order in which motions may be made and acted upon in parliamentary procedure.

overconfidence: having confidence without adequate reason or preparation.

panel: a group that discusses a topic in front of an audience.

panel-forum: a group discussion that is opened to questions or comments from the audience.

paper tech: the first technical rehearsal, held without actors, involving only the director and technical staff.

paralanguage: the ways in which you say words, including volume, pitch, speaking rate, and voice quality, as well as sounds that are not words.

parallelism: the beginning or ending of several nearby sentences with the same single word or short phrase.

parliamentarian: an expert on rules governing meetings who serves as an advisor to a chair.

parliamentary inquiry: an incidental motion that requests information on the parliamentary procedure dealing with a motion under consideration at that time.

parliamentary procedure: a set of rules used to conduct a meeting in an orderly manner; the established rules of order for conducting group meetings.

pattern of ideas: the flow of the main points of the speech.

pay TV: closed-circuit television broadcasts that people pay an admission fee to see in a theater or television broadcasts received in homes with special equipment that is paid for by viewers on a per-program or a monthly-fee basis.

pending motion: a formal proposal that is under consideration.

personification: a figure of speech that gives human qualities to inanimate objects, ideas, or non-human creatures.

persuasion: a means by which one person can cause another to want to believe, think, or do something.

pharynx: the back part of the throat; the muscular and membraneous cavity of the alimentary canal leading from the mouth and nasal passages to the larynx and esophagus.

picture: a visual aid in the form of a drawing, photograph, slide, filmstrip, or film.

pitch: the highness or lowness of sounds.

platform movement: the movement of the entire body while speaking.

poetry: the communication of thought and feeling through the careful arrangement of words for their sound, rhythm, and meaning.

point of order: an incidental motion requesting the attention of the chair and the assembly to an error that has just been made.

positive audience: an audience that already agrees with your basic persuasive purpose.

poster: a visual aid consisting of print or lettering.

postpone definitely: a subsidiary motion putting off consideration of a motion with the intention of reconsidering the motion at a specific time.

postpone indefinitely: a subsidiary motion preventing further discussion or voting on a pending main motion.

postpone temporarily: a subsidiary motion setting aside consideration of a pending matter until some time later in the same meeting; lay on the table.

prepared reading: an audition reading which has been read or rehearsed beforehand.

prestige: the power to impress or influence which comes from one's character or position.

prima facie case: in a debate, the first responsibility of the affirmative side to present a logical argument that would convince a neutral judge who had not heard the response of the other side.

privileged motion: a type of formal proposal considered to be of an urgent nature which may be considered ahead of any other class of motion; question of privilege, recess, or adjourn.

problem-solution pattern: a type of speech organization in which the first part of the speech describes the problem and the second part develops solutions.

process of association: the connecting of new information with something you already know in order to remember.

producer: a person who heads the organization of the play production and is responsible for the success or failure of the production.

production concept: the director's interpretation of the play.

production meeting: a group session that meets frequently during the rehearsal period to discuss changes and/or problems in production.

production organization: the group that works together to choose, finance, cast, direct, design, construct, publicize, and perform a play.

program concept: an overall plan for a television broadcast.

pronunciation: the producing of the correct sounds and the proper syllable stresses when speaking.

proportion: the balancing of one thing against another.

proposition: in formal debate, a statement to be debated, which can be answered by yes and no and generally demands that some specific action be taken or not taken.

prose: the ordinary form of written or spoken language, without rhyme or meter.

protagonist: in a play, the principal character.

proxemics: the study of spatial communication.

public communication: interpersonal communication in which one or more people communicate with an audience.

public discussion: group communication involving members of the group as well as listeners outside the discussion group.

publicity manager: a person who provides the public with information concerning a dramatic production and its participants.

public speaking: communicating ideas verbally to an audience.

public television: television broadcasting financed mainly by company grants and donations by viewers.

purpose sentence: a sentence stating the specific intent of a speech.

question of fact: a discussion question dealing with whether a situation exists, under what circumstances it exists, or how it may be defined.

question of policy: a discussion question directed toward some course of physical or mental action often including the word *should*.

question of privilege: a privileged motion that requests immediate action on an urgent matter related to the comfort, convenience, rights, or privileges of the assembly or one of its members.

question of value: a discussion question revolving around the worth of an object, person, or situation.

quorum: the number of members that *must* be present before any meeting can be held or any official business conducted.

realism: a dramatic art style which stresses the virtues of directness and truth.

reasoning: the ability to think, form judgments, and draw conclusions; the process of putting evidence together into a logical argument.

rebuttal: in a debate, an opposing argument whose main purpose is to refute the opposition's major arguments.

reception: the process of receiving and decoding a message from a sender.

recess: a privileged motion that calls a temporary halt to the meeting in progress.

recognizing: acknowledging the right of a member of an assembly to speak.

refer to committee: a subsidiary motion to submit a matter to a sub-group for further deliberation.

refute: in a debate, to prove an argument or statement to be false or wrong.

Renaissance: the period from about A.D. 1350 to about A.D. 1650 in Europe; a period of "rebirth" in all the arts and literature; a revival of learning.

repetition: the stating of an idea several times using the same words.

resonators: the pharynx, nasal cavities, and mouth, which act as amplifiers to increase the sound of a voice.

restatement: saying again in a different way; stating the same idea several times using different words.

Restoration: the period during the reign of Charles II of England when the theaters were reopened.

reversal: in drama, a change of fortune in which the character's actions do a complete turnaround.

rhetorical question: questions that are not meant to be answered aloud.

rising action: the series of events that develop toward the climax of a play.

romanticism: a dramatic art style seeking to escape the problems of the day through imagination and thoughts of adventure and beauty.

round-table discussion: a closed-group session in which information sharing or enlightenment of those taking part is usually the object.

runaway stage fright: feelings of anxiety that are so intense that one loses control; the loss of control of the feelings of anxiety experienced before or during a speech or performance.

running-refutation negative case: in a debate, an argument in which the negative side attacks all parts of the affirmative case.

run-through: a rehearsal, as of a dramatic or musical work or section, straight through from beginning to end.

scale model: a visual aid consisting of a smaller version of an object; a miniature set design built to illustrate spatial requirements of the stage.

scenario: in drama, an outline or synopsis of a play, opera, or the like, indicating scenes, characters, and so forth.

scene designer: a person who creates the backgrounds against which a play is performed.

second: an indication that one other member of the assembly wishes to see the motion debated and acted upon.

setting: the time, place, environment, and surrounding circumstances of an event, story, or play.

shock technique: an attention device used to demand instantaneous attention from the audience by using a hard-to-believe or upsetting statement.

simile: a figure of speech that presents a brief comparison of two basically unlike items using the words *like* or *as*.

simple majority: at least one more than half the people who voted.

sincerity: truthfulness; genuineness; straightforwardness; honesty.

slang: informal language that is outside of conventional or standard usage, which often comes in and goes out of style very rapidly.

slice-of-life theater: a realistic dramatic art style in which playwrights write about everyday, real-life situations, conflicts, and people.

spatial pattern: in a speech, an organizational pattern by space arrangement.

speaking rate: the speed at which one talks.

specific words: words that refer to a limited class of objects.

speech communication: the transmission of ideas by words using voices.

stage fright: the nervousness felt when appearing as a speaker or performer before an audience.

stage manager: in a dramatic production organization, the person who is in charge of daily organization, especially that organization needed to keep rehearsals running smoothly.

standard format: the debate format in which each of the speakers gives both a constructive speech and a rebuttal.

statistic: a fact stated in numerical terms.

status quo: "the state in which" (Latin); the existing state of affairs at a particular time.

stereotyping: assigning qualities to people or objects because they are part of a general group without considering individual differences.

stress: the amount of emphasis placed on different syllables in a word or words in a sentence.

string-of-beads pattern: a type of speech organization consisting of a series of items strung together like beads on a string and tied loosely to a central theme, used mainly for entertaining.

structure: the form, shape, and development of a play.

subheads: the subdivision of the main heads in an outline.

subsidiary motion: a type of motion that allows members to change the nature of a main motion or to alter the way in which it is debated or voted upon.

summary: the presentation of the basic message again in very brief form.

support: evidence (facts, statistics, testimony, narrative, examples, and comparisons) used in speeches to prove the accuracy of statements.

suspend the rules: an incidental motion that allows members to set aside some procedural rule so that members can do something not ordinarily allowed by that rule.

suspense: an attention device developed by withholding specific information from the audience.

symbol: anything that stands for an idea and is used to communicate.

symposium: a series of short, uninterrupted public speeches often given by a panel of experts.

symposium-forum: a symposium that is opened to questions or comments from the audience.

syntality: the personality of a group as a whole.

technical quality: the way a piece of literature is put together.

tech week: usually the week prior to the play opening in which technical problems are resolved.

tension: mental or nervous strain; apprehension.

testimonial: the opinion of a well-known person on a particular issue.

testimony: the quoting or restating of opinions of others to support a point.

Theater of the Absurd: a dramatic art movement in which dramatists viewed human existence as purposeless, lonely, and out of harmony with its surroundings.

theatrical event: live actors performing a plot or story in a space serving as a stage before a live audience.

thespian: an actor.

thinking: the ability of humans to put two or more ideas together and produce a new idea.

timeliness: the quality of being current, up-to-date.

topical pattern: a type of speech organization in which the subject is broken down into its natural parts.

trachea: the windpipe.

tragedy: a play that presents serious conflict dealing with the problems of a central character and that has an unhappy or disastrous ending.

tragic flaw: a weakness of character that leads to a major character's destruction.

tragicomedy: a dramatic category that combines both tragic and comic elements.

transition: a word, phrase, sentence, or group of sentences that relates a preceding topic to a succeeding one.

understatement: a figure of speech highlighting the significant by making it seem insignificant; the opposite of hyperbole.

universal appeal: common, recognizable experiences or problems with which everyone can identify.

unsupported assertion: a statement made without giving any evidence to support it.

verbal: of or by means of words.

verbal symbols: spoken or written language symbols or words.

videotape: a magnetic tape on which the electronic impulses of the picture and sound portions of a television program can be recorded for later broadcast.

vocal cords: the two folds of membrane, located in the larynx, which vibrate to produce sound.

vocalized pause: the habit of filling in time between words or sentences with "uh," "er," "like," "you-know" or similar non-meaningful sounds.

voice quality: the uniqueness of vocal sound, which enables people to recognize others by their voices alone.

volume: the loudness or softness of sound.

vote immediately: a subsidiary motion to cut off debate on a pending motion and bring it to a vote at once.

withdraw a motion: an incidental motion that enables a member who has made a motion to remove it from consideration before a vote is taken.

Index

Photo Credits

Front cover: Michal Heron, bottom left; Magnum/Glinn, bottom right; McConnell McNamara & Co., center left, top right; Monkmeyer/Forsyth, center right; Shostal/W. Hamilton, top left.
Back cover: Black Star/Dennis Brack, second from bottom; Jill Peterson, bottom; McConnell McNamara & Co., top-and center; Monkmeyer/James Theologos, second from top.

Text: Black Star/Dennis Brack **274-275**; Culver **103, 130, 163, 171, 191**; DeWys **62, 141, 362**; DeWys/Englebert **222**; DeWys/Fishman **91**; DeWys/Levine **231**; DeWys/Linden **128**; De-Wys/Sidney **102, 105, 388**; DeWys/Weldon **119**; DPI/Gordon **80, 279**; DPI/Griffiths **5, 35**; DPI/Kohli **97**; DPI/Langley **367**; DPI/Lettau **78**; DPI/Sokoloff **331**; DPI/Wilson **69**; EPA/Joshua Tree **155**; EPA/Vadnai **41** top; Focus on Sports **86**; John Lidington/Focus on Sports **190**; Granger **293, 303, 328**; H. A. Roberts **19** bottom; Jill Peterson **8, 20, 324-325, 358, 375**; Magnum/Glinn **338**; Magnum/Godfrey **185**; Magnum/Stock **356**; McConnell McNamara & Co. **2-3, 6** bottom, **12-13, 14, 39, 54, 85, 106, 126-127, 134, 138, 139, 200, 203, 228, 259, 276, 302, 326, 343, 365, 371, 403**; Monkmeyer/Anderson **207**; Monkmeyer/Deller **224**; Monkmeyer/Forsyth **7, 19** top, **117, 158, 310, 317, 318, 391**; Monkmeyer/Leinwand **57**, Monkmeyer/Rogers **337**; Monkmeyer/Shackman **6** top, **111**; Monkmeyer/Strickler **401**; Monkmeyer/Sydney **36**; Monkmeyer/Theologos **76-77**; Nancy Palmer/Hinton **114, 334**; Nancy Palmer/Hopkins **346**; Nancy Palmer/Sherman **217**; New Yorker cartoon/William Miller (Oct. 22, 1979) **64**; New Yorker cartoon/Joe Mirachi (Sept. 3, 1979) **314**; New Yorker cartoon/Saxon (Oct. 29, 1979) **94**; New Yorker cartoon/Weber (Oct. 8, 1979) **239**; Peter Arnold/Chih **386**; Retna/Stephen Morley **208**; Shostal/G.S. Bernard **395**; Shostal/D. Ellessen **25** right; Shostal/A. Felix **247**; Shostal/D. Forbert **84**; Shostal/P. Grace **309**; Shostal/P. Guntner **23**; Shostal/A. Hart **304**; Shostal/M. Helfer **178**; Shostal/R. Moore **149**; Shostal/T. Morton **41**; Shostal/D. Patterson **83**; Shostal/A. Upitis **212**; Shostal/E. Wade **269**; Shostal/G. Zabriskie **32**; Sidney Harris cartoons **27, 34, 396**; Taurus/Kroll **254**; Taurus/McKay **131**; Taurus/Menschenfreund **146**; Taurus/Rhodes **180**; Taurus/Rose **21**; Taurus/Wicks **18, 60, 150, 183**; Woodfin Camp/Eagan **280**; Woodfin Camp/Hubbell **285**; Woodfin Camp/McElhinney **266**; Woodfin Camp/McNamee **15**; Woodfin Camp/Marmaras **92**; Woodfin Camp/Seitz **398**; UPI **25** left, **152, 202, 234**

Text Acknowledgments

Unit one: Page 28, written by Janet Taylor; 42, adapted from Edward T. Hall, *The Silent Language,* Fawcett Publications, Inc., Greenwich, CT, 1959, pp. 136–7; 48, 70, written by Janet Taylor.
Unit two: Pages 96, 120, written by Janet Taylor.
Unit three: Page 129, George Jessel quotation in *Reader's Digest Treasury of Wit and Humor,* The Reader's Digest Association, Pleasantville, NY, 1958, p. 257; 132, Mark Twain, *The Adventures of Tom Sawyer,* Harper-Row, Publisher, New York; 142,

written by Janet Taylor; **155,** Helen Keller, *The Story of My Life,* Doubleday & Co., Inc., Garden City, NY, © 1905 by Helen Keller, p. 100; **156,** "Edward Kennedy Says Good-bye to a 'Good and Decent Man,' " *Courier Journal,* Louisville, KY, June 9, 1968, p. A–4; **156,** *Vital Speeches of the Day,* vol. 35 no. 14, May 1, 1969, Keith M. Flake (speaker), City News Publishing Co., Southold, NY, p. 441; Carl Hall, "A Heap of Trouble," a speech given at Interstate Oratorical Association at Peoria, IL, May 2–3, 1975; **160,** Ella V. Aldrich, *Using Books and Libraries,* 5th ed., Prentice-Hall, Inc., Englewood Cliffs, NJ, © 1967, pp. 25, 26, and 28; **164,** Alan H. Monroe and Douglas Ehninger, *Principles and Types of Speech Communication,* 7th ed., Scott, Foresman & Company, Glenview, IL, 1974, pp. 353–78; **172,** written by Janet Taylor; **181,** "Those Happy Days," a speech by Debra Morris, Eisenhower High School, Lawton, OK; **183,** "We Must Fight for Our Liberties" by Frank Knox in Lewis Copeland and Lawrence Lamm, eds., *The World's Great Speeches,* 2nd rev. ed., Dover Publications, Inc., New York, 1958, pp. 571–3; **186,** Arthur M. Schlesinger, Jr., *A Thousand Days: John F. Kennedy in the White House,* Fawcett Publications, Inc., Greenwich, CT, 1967, pp. 331–2; **187,** Martin Luther King, Jr., "I've Been to the Mountaintop," *A Martin Luther King Treasury,* Educational Heritage, Yonkers, NY, 1964; **188,** Elsie M. Gould, *American Woman Today,* Prentice-Hall, Inc., Englewood Cliffs, NJ, 1972, p. 9; **188,** Earnest Brandenburg and Waldo W. Braden, "Franklin Delano Roosevelt," *A History and Criticism of American Public Address,* vol. 3, Marie Kathryn Hochmuth, ed., Russell and Russell, Inc., New York, 1965, pp. 511–12; **188–9,** General Douglas MacArthur, "Farewell to the Cadets," in *Contemporary American Speeches: A Source Book of Speech Forms and Principles,* 3rd ed., Will A Linkugel, R. R. Allan, and Richard L. Johannesen, eds., Wadsworth Publishing Co., Belmont, CA, 1972; **190,** "The Abstruse Leech," a speech by Hubert Farbes, Northeast High School, Oklahoma City, OK; **191,** Earnest Brandenburg and Waldo W. Braden, "Franklin Delano Roosevelt," *A History and Criticism of American Public Address,* vol. 3, Marie Kathryn Hochmuth, ed., Russell and Russell, Inc., New York, 1965, p. 514; **192,** Ralph Zimmerman, "Mingled Blood," in *Contemporary American Speeches: A Source Book of Speech Forms and Principles,* 3rd ed., Will A. Linkugel, R. R. Allan, and Richard L. Johannesen, eds., Wadsworth Publishing Co., Belmont, CA, 1972; **193,** Robert G. Ingersoll, "The Liberty of Man, Woman, and Child," Wayland Mayfield Parrish and Marie Hochmuth, eds., *American Speeches,* Longmans, Green and Company, New York, 1954, pp. 429, 433–4, Courtesy of David McKay Company, Inc.; **194,** written by Janet Taylor; **198,** John Henry Cardinal Newman, *The Idea of a University,* Image Books, Doubleday & Co., Garden City, NY, 1962, pp. 181–2; **211,** J. Jeffery Auer, *Brigance's Speech Communication,* Appleton-Century-Crofts, New York, 1967, pp. 142–3; **216,** written by Janet Taylor; **225,** "Runaways," a speech by Belinda Moyers, Smith's Grove, KY; **226,** Thom Mayer, "The Population Bomb," a speech given at Interstate Oratorical Contest, May 1971, Omaha, NB; **227,** Marie Ransley, "The Life and Death of Our Lakes," in *Contemporary American Speeches: A Source Book of Speech Forms and Principles,* 3rd ed., Will A. Linkugel, R. R. Allan, and Richard L. Johannesen, eds., Wadsworth Publishing Co., Belmont, CA, 1972; **229,** Caroline Bird, "What Do Women Want?" *Vital Speeches of the Day,* City News Publishing Co., Southold, NY, 1977, p. 598; **230,** Louis Housman, "Older Americans: A Natural Resource," *Vital Speeches of the Day,* City News Publishing Co., Southold, NY, 1976, p. 189; **234,** Arthur M. Schlesinger, Jr., *A Thousand Days: John F. Kennedy in the White House,* Fawcett Publications, Inc., Greenwich, CT, 1967; **235,** Joseph Palmer, "Africa: Continent of Change," in *Contemporary American Speeches: A Source Book of Speech Forms and Principles,* 3rd ed., Will A. Linkugel, R. R. Allan, and Richard L. Johannesen, eds., Wadsworth Publishing Co., Belmont, CA, 1972; **235,** Marie Ransley, "The Life and Death of Our Lakes," in *Contemporary American Speeches: A Source Book of Speech Forms and Principles,* 3rd ed., Will A. Linkugel, R. R. Allan, and Richard L. Johannesen, eds., Wadsworth Publishing Co., Belmont, CA, 1972; **238,** R. L. Birdwhistell, *Introduction to Kinesics,* University of Kentucky Press, Louisville, KY, 1956; **240,** adapted from David R. Berman, *State and Local Politics,* 2nd ed., Copyright © 1978 by Holbrook Press, Inc., Subsidiary of Allyn and Bacon, Inc., Boston, MA. Adapted with permission; **243,** adapted from Nila Banton Smith, *Be A Better Reader, Level I,* Prentice-Hall, Inc., Englewood Cliffs, NJ, 1979, p. 195; **244,** adapted from Harry M. Lindquist, *China: Focus on Revolution,* Prentice-Hall, Inc., Englewood Cliffs, NJ, 1975; **248,** written by Janet Taylor; **258–9,** "It's Hard to Be Human," a speech by Beth Simmons, Monta Vista High School, Cupertino, CA; **259,** President Carter, "Nuclear Arms Reduction," *Vital Speeches of the Day,* vol. 44, Oct. 1978, City News Publishing Co., Southold, NY, p. 2; **266,** "Deus Ex Machina," a speech by Bart Wojciehowski, Brophy Preparatory School, Phoenix, AZ; **270,** written by Janet Taylor.

Unit four: Pages **288–9,** Terry Barnes; **296,** written by Janet Taylor; **319,** adapted from Alice Sturgis, *Sturgis Standard Code of Parliamentary Procedure,* 2nd ed., McGraw-Hill Book Company, New York. Copyright © 1966 by Alice Sturgis; **320,** written by Janet Taylor.

Unit five: Page **332,** "I'm Nobody! Who Are You?" by Emily Dickinson. Reprinted by permission of the publishers and the Trustees of Amherst College from *The Poems of Emily Dickinson,* Thomas H. Johnson, ed., The Belknap Press of Harvard University Press, Cambridge, MA. Copyright © 1951, 1955 by the President and Fellows of Harvard College; **332–3,** Frederick Morgan, *The Tarot of Cornelius Agrippa,* Sagarin Press, Sand Lake, NY, © 1978 by Frederick Morgan; **333,** Henry David Thoreau, *Walden,* Macmillan, Inc., New York, 1966; **334,** Sarah Orne Jewett, "A White Heron," in *Adventures in American Literature,* Harcourt Brace Jovanovich, Inc., New York, Copyright © 1963; **337,** Mark Twain, *The Adventures of Huckleberry Finn,* Harper-Row, Publishers, New York; **338,** "Stopping by Woods on a Snowy Evening," by Robert Frost in *You Come Too.* Copyright © 1951 by Robert Frost. Reprinted by permission of Holt, Rinehart and Winston, Inc., New York; **340,** "An Ode for Ookie, the Older Walrus Child," in *Stand Up, Friend, With Me* by Edward Field, Grove Press, New York, 1962; **341,** Charles Dickens, *David Copperfield,* Macmillan, Inc., New York, 1962; **341, 342,** Lewis Carroll, *Alice's Adventures in Wonderland,* Macmillan, Inc., New York, 1966; **345,** Maxine Kumin, "May 10th," in *Up Country,* Harper & Row, Publishers, Inc., New York, © 1972 by Maxine Kumin; **347,** William Collins, "Ode to Pity," in *Poems of Gray & Collins,* 4th rev. ed., A. L. Poole and Christopher Stone, eds., Oxford University Press, New York, 1941; **347,** William Wordsworth, "The Tables Turned," in *Complete Poetical Works,* A. J. George, ed., Houghton Mifflin Co., Boston, 1932; **348,** written by Janet Taylor; **354,** from *Antigone* in *Anouilh: Five Plays,* vol. 1, by Jean Anouilh, Hill & Wang, Inc., Div. of Farrar, Straus & Giroux, Inc., New York, 1958; **354,** Charles Simic, "Window Washer," in *The Virginia Quarterly Review,* Charlottesville, VA, Fall 1977; **354,** John Masefield, "Sea Fever," in *Poems,* rev. ed., Macmillan, Inc., New York, 1953; **354,** Frank Horne, "To James," in *Literature III,* Albert R. Kitzhaber, Gen. ed., Stoddard Malarkey and Donald MacRae, Holt, Rinehart and Winston, Inc., New York, 1969; **355,** "I Am Indelible," by Earth Lodge Woman/Minnie Two Shoes, Box 111, Kodak, TN; **355,** William Shakespeare, *Macbeth,* in *Complete Works of William Shakespeare,* Doubleday & Company, Inc., Garden City, NY, 1946; **355,** Gwendolyn Brooks, "In Honor of David Anderson Brooks, My Father," in *Selected Poems,* Harper & Row, Publishers, Inc., New York, Copyright © 1963 by Gwendolyn Brooks Blakely; **379,** *Our Town,* Acting ed., Coward McCann, Inc., New York; **380,** written by Janet Taylor; **393,** S. I. Hayakawa, *Language in Thought and Action,* 2nd ed., Harcourt Brace Jovanovich, New York, 1964.